D0175070

The Case against Education

The Case against Education

WHY THE EDUCATION SYSTEM
IS A WASTE OF TIME AND MONEY

Bryan Caplan

PRINCETON UNIVERSITY PRESS

PRINCETON AND OXFORD

Copyright © 2018 by Princeton University Press

Published by Princeton University Press,
41 William Street, Princeton, New Jersey 08540

In the United Kingdom: Princeton University Press,
6 Oxford Street, Woodstock, Oxfordshire OX20 1TR

press.princeton.edu

All Rights Reserved

ISBN 978-0-691-17465-5

British Library Cataloging-in-Publication Data is available

This book has been composed in Minion Pro

Printed on acid-free paper. ∞

Printed in the United States of America

10 9 8 7 6 5 4 3 2

To my homeschoolers,
Aidan and Tristan.
You are the case *for* education, my sons.

Contents

Illustrations

Tables

Preface

When I started writing this book, I knew I'd need to read piles of research but failed to foresee the enormity of the piles. Education isn't just a major industry; it inspires researchers' curiosity because it's *their* industry. No one discipline owns the topic: departments of education, psychology, sociology, and economics all contain armies of education researchers. While I personally hail from the economist tribe, I've tried to read broadly and deeply in all four fields. My synthesis is contrarian, but my evidence is not. My strategy is to collect standard findings in education, psychology, sociology, and economics, then snap them all together.

Given the mass of the evidence, it would be easy to handpick a grossly biased basket. Readers must judge how well I've countered this ever-present temptation, but I offer one upfront disclosure: I consciously place extra weight on basic statistics over high-tech alternatives. When relevant experimental evidence is thin or nonexistent (as it usually is), I put my trust in Ordinary Least Squares with control variables. When the results seem questionable, I just seek richer data. This approach isn't perfect, but it's easy to understand, easy to compare, and hard to manipulate. High-tech statistics can improve on basic methods, but the cost is high: to fix the flaws you understand, you usually have to introduce new flaws you don't understand.

Socially speaking, this book argues that our education system is a big waste of time and money. Selfishly speaking, however, the six years I've spent writing this book at George Mason University have truly been well spent. In any other industry, a whistle-blower would be an outcast. My industry, in contrast, appears to welcome whistle-blowers with open arms—or at least bemusement. While some of my colleagues reject my thesis, our dispute has been great fun. When I've reached out to researchers in other schools and fields, they've been reliably curious and generous. I almost want to thank the Ivory Tower itself, but credit belongs to all the researchers, students, and autodidacts who have lent me their insight, especially John Alcorn, Joseph Altonji, Omar Al-Ubaydli, Chris Andrew, Kartik Athreya, Michael Bailey, David Balan, Patrick Bayer, Jere

Behrman, Truman Bewley, David Bills, Pete Boettke, Don Boudreaux, Jason Brennan, Aidan Caplan, Corina Caplan, Larry Caplan, Tristan Caplan, Art Carden, Steve Ceci, David Cesarini, Damon Clark, Greg Clark, Angel de la Fuente, Douglas Detterman, Rachel Dunifon, James Gambrell, Andrew Gelman, Zac Gochenour, Eric Hanushek, David Henderson, Dan Houser, Mike Huemer, Chad Jones, Garett Jones, Tim Kane, Dan Klein, Arnold Kling, Mark Koyama, Alan Krueger, Kevin Lang, Jacob Levy, David Livingstone, Adriana Lleras-Muney, Phil Maguire, Greg Mankiw, Kevin McCabe, Jonathan Meer, Stephen Moret, Charles Murray, Vipul Naik, David Neumark, John Nye, Philip Oreopoulos, Steve Pearlstein, Lant Pritchett, Paul Ralley, Russ Roberts, Fabio Rojas, Steve Rose, Bruce Sacerdote, Jim Schneider, Joel Schneider, Jeffrey Smith, Thomas Stratmann, Sergio Urzua, Richard Vedder, Amy Wax, Bart Wilson, Sam Wilson, Ludger Woessmann, and seminar participants at the Federal Trade Commission and George Mason University. The Center for Study of Public Choice and the Mercatus Center provided generous financial support, and Nathaniel Bechhofer provided invaluable graphics assistance. Further thanks to my editor Peter Dougherty, anonymous referees for Princeton University Press, research assistants Caleb Fuller, Zac Gochenour, Colin Harris, and Julia Norgaard, and my loyal corps of volunteer spreadsheet checkers: Matthew Baker, David Balan, Nathaniel Bechhofer, Zac Gochenour, Garett Jones, Jim Pagels, and Fabio Rojas. My apologies to anyone I've forgotten.

My deepest gratitude, though, goes to Nathaniel Bechhofer, Tyler Cowen, Robin Hanson, and Alex Tabarrok for sharing my intellectual journey, day by day. Whatever they think about education as it really is, these dear friends exemplify education as it ought to be.

The Case against Education

Introduction

> Why, anybody can have a brain. That's a very mediocre commodity. Every pusillanimous creature that crawls on the Earth or slinks through slimy seas has a brain. Back where I come from, we have universities, seats of great learning, where men go to become great thinkers. And when they come out, they think deep thoughts and with no more brains than you have. But they have one thing you haven't got: a diploma.
>
> —*The Wizard of Oz*

I have been in school continuously for over forty years.[1] First preschool, kindergarten, elementary, junior high, and high school. Then a four-year bachelor's degree at UC Berkeley, followed by a four-year Ph.D. at Princeton. The next step was what you could call my first "real job"—as a professor of economics at George Mason University. Twenty years later, I'm still here. In the fall, I'll be starting forty-first grade.

The system has been good to me. Very good. I have a dream job for life. I'm expected to teach five hours of class, thirty weeks per year. Unlike many professors, I love teaching; but even if I hated it, 150 hours a year is a light burden. The rest of the time, I think, read, and write about whatever interests me. That's called "research." My salary doesn't make me wealthy, but I wouldn't trade places with Bill Gates. His billions can't buy me anything I crave I don't already have. And I bet that even in retirement, Gates lacks my peace of mind.

Personally, then, I have no reason to lash out at the education system. Quite the contrary. Yet a lifetime of experience, plus a quarter century of reading and reflection, convince me that our education system is a big waste of time and money. Almost every politician vows to spend more on education. As an insider, I can't help gasping, "Why? You want us to waste even more?"

Most critics of our education system complain we aren't spending our money in the right way, or that preachers in teachers' clothing are leading our nation's children down dark paths.[2] While I semisympathize, these critics miss what I see as our educational system's supreme defect: *there's way too much education.* Typical students burn thousands of hours studying material that neither raises their productivity nor enriches their lives. And of course, students can't waste time without experts to show them how.

Schools obviously teach some broadly useful skills—especially literacy and numeracy. High schools often include a few vocational electives—auto shop, computer programming, woodworking. Most colleges offer some career-oriented majors—engineering, computer science, premed. But what about all the other courses? All the other majors?

Think about all the classes you ever took. How many failed to teach you *any* useful skills? The lessons you'll never need to know after graduation start in kindergarten. Elementary schools teach more than reading, writing, and arithmetic. They also require history, social studies, music, art, and physical education. Middle and high schools add higher mathematics, classic literature, and foreign languages—vital for a handful of budding scientists, authors, and translators, irrelevant for everyone else. Most college majors don't even pretend to teach job skills. If you apply your knowledge of Roman history, Shakespeare, real analysis, or philosophy of mind on the job, you have an odd job.

You might defend this allegedly "useless" education on humanistic grounds. Teachers habitually claim to enrich students' lives or broaden their horizons. As a professor, I don't just sympathize with these arguments; I've lived them. The great ideas have enriched me, and I try to pay it forward. To effectively defend education, however, you need to do more than appeal to humanistic ideals. You need to ask: How often do academics *successfully* broaden students' horizons? Empirically, the answer is bleak: while great teachers can turn students into Shakespeare fans, Civil War buffs, avant-garde artists, and devoted violinists, such transformations are rare. Despite teachers' best efforts, most youths find high culture boring—and few change their minds in adulthood.

Learning doesn't have to be useful. Learning doesn't have to be inspirational. When learning is neither useful nor inspirational, though, how can we call it anything but wasteful?

Signaling: Why the Market Pays You to Kill Time

Posing this question to our sacred educational system sparks a chorus of objections. The most vexing objections, however, are my fellow economists'. How can anyone call education *wasteful* in an age when its financial payoff has hit a record high? The earnings premium for college grads has rocketed to over 70%. Even high school graduation pays a hefty 30% premium relative to dropping out.[3] If education really fails to raise worker productivity, why do employers bid so lavishly for educated labor?

Later, I will explain why these premiums are gross overestimates. For now, though, let the numbers stand. How could such a lucrative investment be wasteful? The answer is a single word I seek to burn into your mind: *signaling*. Even if what a student learned in school is utterly useless, employers will happily pay extra if their scholastic achievement provides *information about their productivity*. Suppose your law firm wants a summer associate. A law student with a Ph.D. in philosophy from Stanford applies. What do you infer? The applicant is probably brilliant, diligent, and willing to tolerate serious boredom. If you're looking for that kind of worker—and what employer isn't?—you'll make a generous offer. You could readily do so knowing full well that *nothing* the philosopher learned at Stanford applies on the job.

We're quick to draw inferences from educational history—and with good reason. Your educational record reveals much about your ability and character. When you hear someone finished a B.A. at MIT in three years, you think "genius." When you hear someone has been one class short of a bachelor's degree for the last decade, you think "slacker." When you hear someone flunked out of high school, you think "not too bright." When you hear someone flunked out of high school, then immediately aced the GED, you think "pretty bright, but really lazy" or "pretty bright, but deeply troubled."

Lesson: even if a degree did raise your pay by 70%, that would hardly prove your education "made you what you are today." Perhaps you *already were* what you are today the first time you entered the classroom. Look at your transcript, and check it against what you've actually done with your life. You could have missed a ton of coursework with no loss of on-the-job competence. Unfortunately, if you tried to skip school and leap straight to your first job, insisting, "I have the right stuff to graduate, I just choose not to," employers wouldn't believe you. Anyone can say "I have the right stuff to graduate, I just choose not to"—and firms don't give a 70% wage premium to just anyone.

Lest I be misinterpreted, I emphatically affirm that *some* education teaches useful skills, or, as economists put it, "builds human capital." People learn literacy and numeracy in school. Most modern jobs require these skills. I learned statistics in graduate school. I use statistics in my job. When this book criticizes human capital stories, it does not reject the view that schools build *some* human capital. It rejects "human capital purism"—the view that (a) virtually *all* education teaches useful job skills and (b) these job skills are virtually the *sole* reason why education pays off in the labor market.

When this book defends the signaling theory of education, similarly, it does not claim *all* education is signaling. It claims a *significant fraction* of education is signaling. What precisely does "significant fraction" mean? First: at least one-third of students' time in school is signaling. Second: at least one-third of the financial reward students enjoy is signaling.

Personally, I think the true fraction exceeds 50%. Probably more like 80%. My rhetoric reflects this judgment. As *The Case against Education* unfolds, however, we shall see that even if the share of signaling in our education system is as low as one-third, our education system wastes a mountain of time and money. And when you reflect on your firsthand experience with school and work, one-third signaling is the lowest share you can plausibly maintain.

To be fair, people rarely self-identify as "human capital purists." Human capital purism is a default position, a path of least resistance. We see human capital purism whenever politicians or pundits call education funding "investment in people" without hinting that education might be anything else. We see human capital purism whenever social scientists measure the effect of education on *earnings*, then call it "the effect of education on *skill*." We see human capital purism whenever teachers or parents end an educational sermon with, "Schools teach kids what they need to know when they grow up."

At this point, one could object, "Though education teaches few practical skills, that hardly makes it wasteful. By your own admission, education serves a vital function: certifying the quality of labor. That's useful, isn't it?" Indeed. However, this is a dangerous admission for the champion of education. If education merely certifies labor quality, society would be better off if we all got less. Think about it like this: A college degree now puts you in the top third of the education distribution, so employers who seek a top-third worker require this credential.[4] Now imagine everyone with *one fewer degree*. In this world, employers in need of a top-third worker would require only a high school diploma. The quality of labor would be certified about as accurately as now—at a cost savings of four years of school per person.

Education: Private Profit, Social Waste

Does this book advise you to cut your education short, because you won't learn much of value anyway? Absolutely not. In the signaling model, studying irrelevancies still raises income by impressing employers. To unilaterally curtail your education is to voluntarily leap into a lower-quality pool of workers. The labor market brands you accordingly.

For a single individual, education pays. On this point, the standard "education as skill creation" and the "education as signaling" theories agree. The theories make different predictions, however, about what happens if *average* education levels decline. If education is all skill creation, a fall in average education saps our skills, impoverishing the world. If education is all signaling, however, a fall in average education leaves our skills—and the wealth of the world—unchanged. In fact, cut-backs *enrich* the world by conserving valuable time and resources.

Suppose you agree society would benefit if average education declined. Is this achievable? Verily. Government heavily subsidizes education. In 2011, U.S. federal, state, and local governments spent almost a trillion dollars on it.[5] The simplest way to get less education, then, is to cut the subsidies. This would not eliminate wasteful signaling, but at least government would pour less gasoline on the fire.

The thought of education cuts horrifies most people because "we all benefit from education." I maintain their horror rests on what logicians call a *fallacy of composition*—the belief that what is true for a part must also be true for the whole. The classic example: You want a better view at a concert. What can you do? Stand up. Individually, standing works. What happens, though, if everyone copies you? Can *everyone* see better by standing? No way.

Popular support for education subsidies rests on the same fallacy. The person who gets more education, gets a better job. It works; you see it plainly. Yet it does not follow that if everyone gets more education, everyone gets a better job. In the signaling model, subsidizing everyone's schooling to improve our jobs is like urging everyone to stand up at a concert to improve our views. Both are "smart for one, dumb for all."[6]

To be maximally blunt, we would be better off if education were *less affordable*. If subsidies for education were drastically reduced, many could no longer afford the education they now plan to get. If I am correct, however, this is no cause for alarm. It is precisely because education is so affordable that the labor market expects us to possess so much. Without the subsidies, you would no longer *need* the education you can no longer afford.

Ultimately, I believe the best education policy is no education policy at all: the separation of school and state. However, you can buy the substance of my argument without embracing my crazy extremism. You can grant the importance of signaling in education, and still favor substantial government assistance for the industry. If you conclude education is only one-third signaling, your preferred level of government assistance will noticeably fall, but not to zero. At the same time, I do not downplay potentially radical implications. If, like me, you deem education 80% signaling, ending taxpayer support is crazy like a fox. This is especially clear if, as I ultimately argue, the humanistic benefits of education are mostly wishful thinking.

Anyone reading this book has almost certainly spent over a decade in school. You have *vast* firsthand knowledge of the education industry. The unfolding argument takes full advantage of your decade-plus of personal experience. Please test all claims about the true nature of education against your own abundant educational experience.

This does not mean my contrarian thesis is obvious; far from it. Yet for the most part, the book does not try to change your mind about brute facts. It tries to change your mind about the best way to *interpret* facts you've known for ages. Once you calmly review your experience through my lens, I bet you'll admit I've got a point.

Education is a strange industry, but familiarity masks the strangeness. I want to revive your sense of wonder. Consider the typical high school curriculum. English is the international language of business, but American high school students spend years studying Spanish, or even French. Few jobs require knowledge of higher mathematics, but over

80% of high school grads suffer through geometry.[7] Students study history for years, but history teachers are almost the only people alive who use history on the job. Required coursework is so ill suited to students' needs you have to wonder if your eyes are playing tricks on you.

In part, we accept this strange curriculum as "normal" because we're used to it. On a deeper level, though, we accept our education system because it "works." If you get more school and better grades, employers reward you.[8] What more must you know?

If you're only looking out for number one, nothing. Go to school, get good grades, make more money—the recipe is sound. But if you want to know whether your education system is a good deal for society, or if you're a curious person, the strange stuff students study is a vital clue. So is the fact that employers *pay* students extra for studying strange stuff. Faced with these clues, the orthodox view that students go to school to acquire job skills only shrugs. The signaling model of education uses these clues to detect—and solve—a great neglected social mystery.

CHAPTER 1

The Magic of Education

> Don't tell fish stories where the people know you; but particularly,
> don't tell them where they know the fish.
>
> —Mark Twain

For an economics professor I have broad interests.[1] Economics aside, I read widely in philosophy, political science, history, psychology, and education. But what do I really know how to *do*?

In all honesty, not much. In junior high and high school, I worked a few hours a week manually collating sections of the *Los Angeles Times*. In 1990, I had a summer data-entry job with a homebuilder. I haven't had a real job since. People pay me to lecture, write, and think my thoughts. These are virtually my *only* marketable skills. I'm hardly unique. The stereotype of the head-in-the-clouds Ivory Tower academic is funny because it's true.

The Ivory Tower routinely ignores the real world. Strangely, though, the disinterest is not mutual. Employers care deeply about professors' opinions. Not, of course, our opinions about epistemology or immigration. But employers throughout the economy defer to teachers' opinions when they decide whom to interview, whom to hire, and how much to pay them. Students with straight As from top schools write their own tickets. A single F in a required course prevents graduation—closing the door to most well-paid jobs.

Every now and then, foolhardy critics of the education industry flatly deny the financial benefits. Since all statistics are against them, they turn to anecdotes. "I know a girl who finished her B.A. four years ago, but still works at Starbucks." "My son has a Ph.D. in philosophy—and he drives a cab." "I can't get a job with my M.F.A. in puppetry." While such things do happen, the world is vast. The key question is whether anecdotes about failed investments in education are the exception or the rule.

Statistics give a clear answer: as a rule, education pays. High school graduates earn more than dropouts, college grads earn more than high school grads, and holders of advanced degrees do better still.[2] Enduring another year of school will, on average, get you a raise for the rest of your career. What kind of raise? A standard figure is about 10%. Better-educated workers also enjoy higher noncash benefits, better quality of life, and lower unemployment.[3] Apparent rewards shrink after various statistical corrections; we'll see how later on. Still, no matter what corrections you make, schooling pays in the labor market.

Otherworldly Education

> Most actual job skills are acquired informally through on-the-job training after a worker finds an entry job and a position on the associated promotional ladder.
>
> —Lester Thurow, "Education and Economic Equality"[4]

The key question isn't *whether* employers care a lot about grades and diplomas, but *why*. The simple, popular answer is that schools teach their students useful job skills. Low grades, no diploma, few skills. This simple, popular answer is not utterly wrong. Literacy and numeracy are crucial in most occupations. Yet the education-as-skills story—better known to social scientists as "human capital theory"—dodges puzzling questions.

First and foremost: from kindergarten on, students spend thousands of hours studying subjects irrelevant to the modern labor market. How can this be? Why do English classes focus on literature and poetry instead of business and technical writing? Why do advanced math classes bother with proofs almost no student can follow? When will the typical student use history? Trigonometry? Art? Music? Physics? "Physical Education"? Spanish? French? Latin! (High schools still teach it, believe it or not.)[5] The class clown who snarks, "What does this have to do with real life?," is on to something.

The disconnect between curriculum and job market has a banal explanation: educators teach what they know—and most have as little firsthand knowledge of the modern workplace as I do. Yet this merely amplifies the puzzle. If schools boost students' income by teaching useful job skills, why do they entrust students' education to people so detached from the real world? How are educators supposed to foster our students' ability to do the countless jobs we can't do ourselves?

Anyone who thinks I exaggerate the gap between the skills students learn and the skills workers use can look at the current graduation requirements for my alma mater, Granada Hills High School (now Granada Hills Charter High School).[6] Students need four years of English, two years of algebra, two years of the same foreign language, two years of physical education, and a year in each of the following: geometry, biology, physical science, world history, American history, economics/government, and a visual or performing art. Students also have to complete ten to fourteen elective classes. If you fail more than two classes, you do not graduate.[7]

Passing all this coursework serves one practical function: college entry. Granada's high school graduation requirements almost perfectly match admission requirements for the University of California and California State University systems.[8] But what *additional* practical function do these requirements serve? For college-bound students, the honest answer is "not much"; few college graduates use higher mathematics, foreign languages, history, or the arts on the job.[9] For students who aren't college bound, the honest answer is "virtually none." If you don't go to college, your job almost certainly won't require knowledge of geometry, French, world history, or drama.

Graduation requirements for the University of California, Berkeley, where I earned my bachelor's degree, are similarly otherworldly. Suppose you're in the College of Letters and Science. To graduate, you need a total of 120 credits—roughly four courses a semester for four years. You have to pass your "Breadth Requirements"—one course in each of the following: Arts and Literature, Biological Science, Historical Studies, International Studies, Philosophy and Values, Physical Science, and Social and Behavioral Sciences.[10] You also have to complete your major requirements. Suppose you major in economics, widely seen as a "practical," "realistic" subject. Graduates need introductory economics, statistics, intermediate microeconomics, intermediate macroeconomics, econometrics, five upper-division courses, and a year of calculus.[11] While this coursework is decent preparation for econ graduate school, students are likely to use only *two*—statistics and econometrics—in a nonacademic job. Even that shouldn't be overstated: statistics and econometrics courses at elite colleges emphasize mathematical proofs, not hands-on statistical training.[12]

Permanent residents of the Ivory Tower often congratulate themselves for broadening students' horizons. For the most part, however, "broaden" means "expose students to yet another subject they'll never use in real life." Put yourself in the shoes of a Martian sociologist. Your mission: given our curriculum, make an educated guess about what our economy looks like. The Martian would plausibly work backward from the premise that the curriculum prepares students to be productive adults. Since students study reading, writing, and math, you would correctly infer that the modern economy requires literacy and numeracy. So far, so good.

From then on, however, the Martian would leap from one erroneous inference to another. Students spend years studying foreign languages, so there must be lots of translators. Teachers emphasize classic literature and poetry. A thriving market in literary criticism is the logical explanation. Every student has to take algebra and geometry. The Martian sociologist will conclude the typical worker occasionally solves quadratic equations and checks triangles for congruence. While we can picture an economy that fits our curriculum like a glove, that economy is out of this world.

If education boosts income by improving students' skills, we shouldn't be puzzled merely by the impractical subjects students have to study. We should be equally puzzled by the eminently practical subjects they *don't* have to study. Why don't educators familiarize students with compensation and job satisfaction in common occupations? Strategies for breaking into various industries? Sectors with rapidly changing employment? Why don't schools make students spend a full year learning how to write a resume or affect a can-do attitude? Dire sins of omission.

The puzzle isn't merely the weak tie between curriculum and labor market. The puzzle is the weak tie between curriculum and labor market *combined with the strong tie between educational success and professional success*. The way our education system transforms students into paid workers seems like magic. Governments delegate vast power to a caste of Ivory Tower academics. The caste wields its power as expected: Every child has to study teachers' pet subjects. Educators then rank students on their mastery of the material. Students rapidly forget most of what they learn because "they'll never need to know it again." Employers are free to discount or disregard the Ivory Tower's verdicts. Yet they use academic track records to decide whom to hire and how much to pay.

The process seems even more magical when you're one of the wizards. I go to class and talk to students about my exotic interests: everything from the market for marriage, to the economics of the Mafia, to the self-interested voter hypothesis. At the end of the semester, I test their knowledge. As far as I can tell, the only marketable skill I teach is "how to be an economics professor." Yet employers seemingly disagree.

Anyone who's not dumbstruck should be. Do students *need* to understand the market for marriage, the economics of the Mafia, or the self-interested voter hypothesis to be a competent manager, banker, or salesman? No. But because I decide these topics are worth teaching, employers decide students who fail my class aren't worth interviewing. Abracadabra.

Unlike many magic tricks, this is not a case of "the hand is quicker than the eye." The mystery doesn't go away when you review the process in slow motion:

Step 1: I talk about topics I find thought-provoking.
Step 2: Students learn something about the topics I cover.
Step 3: Magic?
Step 4: My students' prospects in management, banking, sales, etc. slightly improve.

When I train Ph.D. students to become economics professors, there's no magic. They want to do my job; I show them how it's done. But the vast majority of my students won't be professors of economics. They won't be professors of anything. How then do my classes make my students more employable? I can't teach what I don't know, and I don't know how to do the jobs most of my students are going to have. Few professors do.

Making Magic Pay

Magic isn't real. There *has* to be a logical explanation for the effect of Ivory Tower achievement on Real World success. And here it is: despite the chasm between what students learn and what workers do, academic success is a strong *signal* of worker productivity. The labor market doesn't pay you for the useless subjects you master; it pays you for the preexisting traits you reveal by mastering them.

Certifying preexisting skills is so easy that, despite my life-long sequestration in the Ivory Tower, I know how to do it. How? By acting like a typical professor. I lecture about my nerdy obsessions. I make my students do some homework and take some tests. When the semester ends, I grade them based on their mastery of the material. Absent a miracle, my students will never apply the economics of the Mafia on the job. No matter. As long as the right stuff to succeed in my class overlaps with the right stuff to succeed on the job, employers are wise to prefer my A students to my F students.

I naturally have to share influence with my fellow educators. I can tip my students' Grade Point Average by only a decimal point. Still, mild influence adds up; I've taught thousands of students over the years. And my condemnation is devastating. A single F can derail graduation—and prompt employers to trash your resume. Students who value worldly success therefore strive to impress educators with their brilliance and industry—or at least avoid appalling us with their stupidity and sloth. Practical relevance makes little difference: you won't use Shakespeare on the job, but without the right credentials, the job you crave will forever elude you.

Basics of Signaling

Signaling is no fringe idea. Michael Spence, Kenneth Arrow, Joseph Stiglitz, Thomas Schelling, and Edmund Phelps—all Nobel laureates in economics—made seminal contributions.[13] The Nobel committee hailed Michael Spence's work on signaling as his prize-winning discovery and added:

> An important example is education as a signal of high individual productivity in the labor market. It is not necessary for education to have intrinsic value. Costly investment in education as such signals high ability.[14]

Signaling models have three basic elements. First, there must be different types of people. Types could differ in intelligence, conscientiousness, conformity, whatever. Second, an individual's type must be nonobvious. You can't discover a person's true work ethic with a glance. You certainly can't ask, "How good is your work ethic?" and expect candor. Third, types must visibly differ *on average*; in technical terms, "send a different signal." Deviations from average are okay. A signal doesn't have to be definitive, just better than nothing.[15]

Given these three basic elements, employers' honest answer to "Who's *truly* the best worker for the job?" will always be, "I'm stumped." The question's unanswerable with available information. Fortunately, employers can bypass their ignorance by answering an easier question: "Which worker sends the best signals?"[16] There's no cheap way to directly measure conformity. But perhaps people with crew cuts are, on average, more conformist than people with mohawks. If so, prudent employers treat hairstyle as a signal of conformity. As long as short-haired rebels and compliant hippies are exceptions that prove the rule, hiring by hair beats hiring by coin flip.

Once employers reward mere signals of productivity, would-be workers have a clear incentive to modify the signal they send—to tailor their behavior to make a good impression. To what end? Getting favorable treatment. If suspected conformists make more money, and conformists are more likely to have crew cuts, crew cuts pay. They pay even if you're a rebel at heart: the rebellious worker with a crew cut *impersonates* a conformist.

You might jump to the conclusion that signaling sows the seeds of its own destruction. If a crew cut creates a favorable impression and elicits favorable treatment, why wouldn't every worker head straight to the barber? The signaling model contains a simple answer: viable signals must be *less costly* for types in higher demand. This cost could be measured in money or time. Or it could be purely emotional: if rebels detest "square" haircuts, and conformists don't, hairstyle is an excellent signal of conformity. Once every worker has a crew cut, you can "top-up" your conformity signal with a gray flannel suit. The rat race stabilizes when impersonating a conformist is, on average, such a chore that rebels stop pretending to be something they're not.

The "on average" qualifier is crucial. Suppose 10% of good workers can't afford a suit. If employers can't figure out *why* you're underdressed for your interview, a good worker who doesn't have a suit to wear will be treated the same as a bad worker who can't bear to wear one. As the fraction of good workers who can't afford a suit rises, however, the less your attire shows about you—and the less employers care about what you wear. Clear signals carry a strong stigma, fuzzy signals a weak stigma.

Critics often paint the signaling model of education as weird or implausible. But the model is just a special case of what economists call "statistical discrimination": using true-on-average stereotypes to save time and money.[17] Statistical discrimination is everywhere. The elderly pay higher life insurance premiums because the elderly *tend* to die sooner. Cab drivers are more willing to pick up a young man in a suit than a young man in gang colors because the latter is *more* likely to rob him. Statistical discrimination may be unfair and ugly, but it's hardly weird or implausible. Why is it any more weird or implausible to claim employers statistically discriminate on the basis of educational credentials?

What Does Education Signal?

> From the standpoint of most teachers, right up to and including
> the level of teachers of college undergraduates, the ideal student is
> well behaved, unaggressive, docile, patient, meticulous, and em-
> pathetic in the sense of intuiting the response to the teacher that is
> most likely to please the teacher.
>
> —Richard Posner, "The New Gender Gap in Education"[18]

Like many great ideas, signaling is obvious once you think about it. Yet almost no economist denies that Spence, Arrow, Stiglitz, Schelling, and Phelps were brilliant pioneers. They *made* signaling obvious. Still, for all the homage they pay these Nobelists, economists have kept the model in a ghetto. Theorists play with the idea at the highest level. But when empiricists study the real world, signaling is lucky to get a footnote. This book's goal is to emancipate the signaling model from its ghetto—then use the theory to explain the mismatched marriage between school and work.

When you're hunting for a job, you send an array of signals: haircut, clothes, punctuality, polite laughter at interviewers' jokes. Yet in modern labor markets, one signal overshadows the rest: your education. Many employers won't deign to read your application unless you possess the right educational credentials—even when it's common knowledge your book learning won't come up on the job.

Why is educational signaling so central? An initially tempting answer: good jobs are intellectually demanding, and education is just a signal of intelligence. This intelligence-alone story looks solid on the surface. Our information age has unleashed the revenge of the nerds. Education really is a strong signal of intelligence—and reality TV stars notwithstanding, today's lucrative occupations reliably require high cognitive ability.[19] If you put pressure on the intelligence-alone story, however, it cracks. Consider this vignette:

> Mark and Steve both got perfect scores on their SATs when they were sixteen years old. Twenty years later, Mark has a Ph.D. from MIT, but Steve has only a high school degree.

If the *only* thing you knew about Mark and Steve were their educational credentials, you would jump to the conclusion that Mark is a lot smarter. Given their SAT scores, though, you almost automatically shift to the view that Mark is a harder worker. Indeed, once you know Steve's test scores, you swiftly infer he's pathologically lazy—or perhaps a "free spirit." In an interview, Steve would pose as a diligent worker bee. He'd make excuses or change the subject to his strengths. But given his educational history, the typical employer would be nervous.

What then does education signal besides intelligence? As Socrates would say, you already know the answer. Mark and Steve's vignette shows that education signals not just intelligence, but conscientiousness—the student's discipline, work ethic, commitment to quality, and so forth.

Is that everything? No, we're still overlooking a crucial trait. Consider another vignette:

> Jenn and Karen scored higher on their SATs than three out of four students. After high school graduation, both took full-time jobs. However, they spent their evenings differently. Jenn spent twenty hours a week earning her college degree part time. Karen, in contrast, spent twenty hours a week creating the world's biggest ball of yarn. Five years after high school graduation, Jenn has her degree, and Karen her record-breaking ball of yarn.

Jenn and Karen don't just seem equally smart; they seem equally conscientious. Both had the stick-to-itiveness to complete a challenging project in their spare time. Yet Jenn sounds more employable because she toiled in the service of socially approved goals. Karen, in contrast, pursued her eccentric vanity project. Jenn's degree signals her deference to social expectations; she's a team player. When the boss says, "Jump," she'll ask, "How high?" Karen's ball of yarn sends a mixed signal at best. She works hard when she puts her mind to something. But will she work hard to please her boss? The vignette's lesson: education also signals conformity—the worker's grasp of and submission to social expectations.

Actually, that's an understatement. In our society, educational achievement *is* a social expectation. Model workers are supposed to pursue and obtain traditional credentials: a high school diploma for virtually any job, a bachelor's degree for a good job. If you violate these expectations, you're moderately nonconformist. If you defy these expectations, you're extremely nonconformist. When you lack credentials, the best back-up signal of conformity isn't to denounce credentialism, but to humbly hold your tongue.

To be clear, employers aren't looking for workers who conform in some abstract sense. As anthropologists emphasize, almost everyone conforms to *something*. Hippies strive to look, talk, and act like fellow hippies.[20] This doesn't make unkempt hair and tie-dye shirts any less repugnant to employers. Employers are looking for people who conform to the folkways of today's workplace—people who look, talk, and act like modern model workers.

What are modern model workers like? They're team players. They're deferential to superiors, but not slavish. They're congenial toward coworkers but put business first. They dress and groom conservatively. They say nothing remotely racist or sexist, and they stay a mile away from anything construable as sexual harassment. Perhaps most importantly, they know and do what's expected, even when articulating social norms is difficult or embarrassing. Employers don't have to *tell* a modern model worker what's socially acceptable case by case.

Now we're up to three broad traits that education signals: intelligence, conscientiousness, and conformity. We could easily extend this list: education also signals a prosperous family, cosmopolitan attitudes, and fondness for foreign films.[21] For a profit-maximizing employer, however, the extensions are a distraction. The road to academic success is paved with the trinity of intelligence, conscientiousness, and conformity.[22] The stronger your academic record, the greater employers' confidence you have the whole package.

Why do employers seek this package? Because the road to academic success and the road to job success are paved with the same materials. An intelligent worker learns quickly and deeply. A conscientious worker labors until the job's done right. A conformist worker obeys superiors and cooperates with teammates. If you lack the right stuff to succeed in school, you probably lack the right stuff to succeed in the labor market.

Exceptions exist, of course. Fantastic workers might have weak educational credentials because their family is poor. They might have weak educational credentials because they're averse to student debt. They might have weak educational credentials because they couldn't wait to start "doing things in the real world"—or fail to grasp the signaling model. As long as the exceptions remain exceptions, signaling works.

Employers are running businesses, not logic classes. Hiring decisions, like all business decisions, are about prudence, not proof.

Locked-In Syndrome

Education is clearly *one* good way to show employers you've got the right stuff to succeed on the job. For many jobs, however, education is practically the *only* route to success. Peculiar. After all, there are endless signals of intelligence, conscientiousness, and conformity. You could signal intelligence by blogging about science fiction. You could signal conscientiousness by copying the dictionary by hand. You could signal conformity by keeping kosher, even though you aren't Jewish. When you seek a job, however, such signals are worthless. Why do employers find educational credentials so much more enticing?

Education signals a *package* of socially desirable strengths. People at the top of their class usually have the trifecta: intelligent, conscientious, and conformist. Humbler students send a weaker but still lucrative signal: they're sufficiently intelligent, conscientious, and conformist to earn a degree. This doesn't mean they're above average in all three. As long as you manage to graduate, though, you're probably strong in at least one, and woefully deficient in none.

Heterodox signals of your strengths, in contrast, automatically suggest *offsetting weaknesses*. Suppose you scored well on the SAT but never went to college. Employers will readily believe you're smart. But if you're so smart, why didn't you go to college? As long as your conscientiousness and conformity were in the normal range, finishing college would have been a snap. Once employers see your SATs, they naturally infer you're *below* average in conscientiousness and conformity. The higher your scores, the more suspicious your missing diploma becomes.[23]

This is even clearer if you try to signal your braininess by, say, blogging about science fiction. If you have the brains to master Isaac Asimov, you should also excel in school—unless, of course, your "issues" keep getting in the way.

The logic of offsetting weakness holds for signals of conscientiousness, too. If you have the work ethic to copy the dictionary by hand, completing college should be a cakewalk—unless you're slow-witted or play poorly with others. So when you offer odd displays of conscientiousness instead of conventional diplomas, employers are doubly suspicious. If you're such a workhorse, why strive to bypass four years of academic drudgery? Maybe you're so deficient in smarts and social skills that your undivided effort isn't enough to get through college.

Unconventional signals of conformity suffer from a deeper flaw—an outright catch-22: "alternative" signals of conformity signal *non*conformity. Once a conventional bachelor's degree is the standard signal of conformity, "outside the box" substitutes are suspicious at best. Telling employers, "I'm self-taught" or "I graduated from a brand-new Internet university" makes you sound weird. The further outside the box your substitute signal of conformity, the more it backfires. Try telling employers, "I'm not Jewish, but I keep kosher to prove I can conform to intricate rules." They'll take you for a freak. It's no surprise, then, that graduation years are *much* more lucrative than ordinary years. Students are *supposed* to graduate; if they don't, employers fear they're deeply defective.[24]

The catch-22 of conformity signaling is so binding that people occasionally withhold *good* signals to avoid looking socially unaware. Consider norms against bragging. You aren't supposed to trumpet your strengths, even if you can prove every word you say. Braggarts therefore send mixed signals at best: even if they're as smart and accomplished as they say, they're boors.

A striking illustration from the job market: while employers rarely *request* applicants' standardized test scores, applicants remain free to *provide* these scores on their resumes. Few do. What do applicants have to lose? The word on the street: putting high scores on your resume suggests you're smart but socially inept.[25] You're doing something that's "simply not done." As I once heard a professor berate a graduate student: "Putting your GRE scores on your resume make you look like a student. Departments want to hire promising assistant professors, not brilliant pupils."

What's most special about education, though, is that almost everyone in our society *believes* education is special. In modern America, kids with the right stuff to succeed in real life ask, "How can I excel in school?" not "Isn't there some other signal I could send instead?" The connection between educational success and career success is naturally strong because both challenges call for similar strengths. Social norms take this naturally strong connection and make it unnaturally strong. The process is self-reinforcing:

Step 1: Employers notice the link between success at school and success at work, so they use education as a gatekeeper of the labor market. If good uncredentialed workers are sufficiently rare, employers ignore their very existence.

Step 2: Talented, motivated people notice education's gatekeeping role, so they devote themselves to educational success in order to fulfill their career ambitions.

Step 3: The frequency of talented, motivated people without a strong academic record falls, tightening the link between success at school and success at work.

Step 4: Return to Step 1.

Plenty of alternatives to traditional education already exist, but—unaccompanied by standard credentials—these alternatives send employers the wrong message. The problem: the people most eager to abandon traditional education in favor of "alternatives" tend to be subpar workers. Employers judge you by the company you keep. If you have the right stuff to earn traditional credentials, you face a stark choice: do what's socially expected, or take your chances with the outcasts. This father-daughter talk from 2009's *An Education* is a telling dramatization:

JENNY: Can I stop going to the youth orchestra, then?
DAD: No. No, no. The youth orchestra is a good thing. That shows you're a joiner-inner.
JENNY: Ah. Yes. But I've already joined in. So now I can stop.
DAD: No. No. Well, that just shows the opposite, don't you see? No, that shows you're a rebel. They don't want that at Oxford.
JENNY: No. They don't want people who think for themselves.
DAD: No, of course they don't.[26]

In short, education suffers from what I call "locked-in syndrome." If you want the labor market to recognize your strengths, and most of the people who share your strengths hold a credential, you'd better earn one too. Otherwise employers won't take you seriously enough to give you a chance. Eventually, we end up where we are: an economy where hard-headed employers say, "Education über alles," curricular relevance notwithstanding.

Signaling "Simply Doesn't Make Sense"

The leading objections to the signaling model of education are not that it contradicts experience. Virtually everyone has spent years *experiencing* the irrelevant education the labor market demands. Rather, the leading objections insist experience is deceiving. Paying workers to study useless subjects year after year "just doesn't make sense." Appearances notwithstanding, the signaling model *can't* be right.

All such complaints suffer a shared flaw: critics assume a simplistic version of signaling, then beat it to a pulp. In the end, happily, their complaints are constructive. Simplistic objections to signaling help us craft a subtle, true-to-life version of the model.

Signaling=100% signaling. The most egregious straw man treats signaling as all-or-nothing. Critics then "refute" signaling by pointing out that schools teach reading, writing, and arithmetic. What a devastating objection . . . to a version of the signaling model no one holds. Nobel Prize winner Kenneth Arrow anticipated and disavowed "100% signaling" way back in 1973:

> Perhaps I should make clear that I personally do not believe that higher education performs only a screening purpose. Clearly professional schools impart real skills valued in the market and so do undergraduate courses in the sciences. The case is considerably less clear with regard to the bulk of liberal arts courses.[27]

To the best of my knowledge, no proponent of the signaling model ever challenged Arrow on this point. The curriculum clearly contains useful subjects; the labor market predictably rewards you for learning them. The point of the signaling model of education isn't to deny the obvious, but to explain the mysterious: How come so many subjects in the curriculum *don't* seem useful—and why does the labor market nevertheless reward you for learning them?

Signaling="Signaling intelligence alone." Other critics equate signaling with the view that education signals nothing but intelligence. Then they demolish it. Sure, a diploma signals intelligence. But so does an IQ test.[28] Why should employers insist on a four-year degree if a three-hour exam is equally revealing?[29] Firms that refused to test would pointlessly cull qualified applicants.

The right lesson to draw is not that the signaling model is wrong, but that education signals more than intelligence. Most of the model's friends learned this lesson long ago. Kenneth Arrow, as usual, knew it from the start. "Higher Education as a Filter" calls education a signal of *ability*, and explicitly states that ability depends on "socialization" as well as intelligence.[30] Or as Peter Wiles succinctly said one year later, "What employers need is *intelligent conformism,* or great independence and originality within a narrow range."[31]

Signaling shouldn't take years. Another top antisignaling talking point: education drags on for years, which "doesn't make sense." Why can't hardworking team players signal their worthiness with, say, one year in school, then instantly get a good job in the real world? If education were largely signaling, employers would have discovered a cheaper, quicker way to evaluate worker quality ages ago.

The critics again take a simplistic version of the model for granted. They picture a signal as definitive proof of a worker's quality; once you send the signal, the truth shines forth for all to see. For many traits, however, there are no definitive "show-stopping" signs. You can always enhance employers' confidence. When the competition sends better signals and you don't, employers unsurprisingly think less of you. Consider this vignette:

> Fred and Dana seem equally smart in their interviews. Both insist they're "hardworking team players." But Fred dropped out of college after his first year. Dana, in contrast, has her degree in hand.

The labor market will clearly favor Dana. Employers may get a good read on Fred and Dana's intelligence during their interviews. Their conscientiousness and conformity, however, are fakeable. An employer can't ask Fred, "Are you a hardworking team player?" and hire him when he says "Yes." An employer can't just watch Fred work for a few hours. With a job at stake, even a slacker will work like a dog. The same holds when Fred finishes one year of college. A lazy rebel will toil and conform for two semesters if the wage is right. To signal you're the real deal, a hardworking team player must *outlast* the posers and wannabes. As my colleague Tyler Cowen, ordinarily a signaling skeptic, once admitted:

> It does not suffice to give everyone a test and hire people with the highest scores.... Doing well on a test is no guarantee of perseverance. The signal must be costly and grueling, otherwise it fails to sort out the best job candidates.[32]

Contrary to critics, then, the sheer duration of education doesn't refute signaling. Since easy-to-fake traits like conscientiousness and conformity are valuable, education *has* to take years. Signaling is a war of attrition. Giving up early is surrender. The longer you endure, the stronger you look. The victors—the people who get the best jobs—are the last students standing.

"You can't fool the market for long." Is signaling superfluous? Some critics maintain employers discern their employees' true productivity in a matter of months. After this brief trial period, the market no longer pays big bucks for mere credentials. Nobel laureate Gary Becker speculates that the signaling model

> declined because economists began to realize that companies rather quickly discover the productivity of employees who went to college, whether a Harvard or a University of Phoenix. Before long, their pay corrects to their productivity rather than to their education credentials.[33]

When researchers explicitly gauge the speed of employer learning, the process seems to take years or decades, not months—especially for the sizable majority that doesn't finish college. We'll explore this evidence later on.[34] For now, suppose Becker's right: in three months, employers see beyond credentials to reality. This hardly makes signaling futile. Instead, it suggests the main reason to signal is to get your foot in the door—to secure your first good job. By definition, this happens only once in a lifetime, yet it is no small affair. Until your foot is in the door, your talent and character go to waste. "You can't fool the market for long" doesn't imply "The market won't overlook you forever."

Becker hails employers' ability to spot phonies—to discover workers whose diplomas overstate their performance. Even if he's right, he overlooks the flip side of the problem: employers' ability to spot "diamonds in the rough"—to discover workers whose diplomas *under*state their performance.[35] To do so is exorbitantly costly: employers can't afford to give every applicant an interview, much less a job.[36]

What's a diamond in the rough to do? Get the credentials you need for your "big break." Three months later, when your new boss finally sees "the real you," your credentials don't suddenly become a mistake. Without those credentials, your career would never have gotten off the ground in the first place.

Signaling and hirer's remorse. Becker's critique also naively assumes that employers automatically dismiss any worker who falls short of expectations. Labor regulations and lawsuits aside, firms are not run by robots.[37] When humans work side by side, they develop fraternal feelings for one another. As long as their business is not in jeopardy, many employers retain moderately subpar employees indefinitely. And even if the boss is bereft of empathy, most of their employees won't be. Disgruntled workers are less productive workers. Any boss who "deprives someone of their livelihood" has to fear the blow to remaining workers' morale.

Give people a chance, observe how they do, fire them if they don't measure up: a "Hire, Look, Flush" personnel policy sounds both profitable and fair. Yet group identity and pity get in the way. After a firm hires you, you're part of the team. If you don't measure up, firing you isn't like returning a blender to Walmart. Your teammates either have to live with your poor performance, or feel sorry to see you go.

Employers do have one guilt-free way to reverse a bad hiring decision. Human resources calls it "dehiring."[38] Instead of firing the unwanted worker, help them jump ship. Privately urge them to find new opportunities. When firms call for a reference, shade the truth—or lie. Labor law punishes firms that reveal negative information about their personnel.[39] Yet the law merely reinforces social psychology. As soon as the unwanted worker leaves for their new job, their coworkers and boss can stop feeling sorry for the departed—and start feeling happy for themselves. Everyone wins—except the next firm.[40]

The more firms fear to fire, the more educational signaling matters. Once employers get hirer's remorse, they're stuck in an awkward position. Relying on credentials is a good way to avoid getting stuck in the first place. A strong academic record tells employers, "I'm not going to make you choose between feeling like a sucker and feeling like a heel."

Employers who ignore the uncredentialed may seem narrow-minded, but they hire with peace of mind.

The lesson: strong educational signals durably help your career, employer learning notwithstanding. In the real world, Harvard degrees pay off handsomely because Harvard grads are great workers. Imagine, however, that you have the world's only perfectly forged Harvard diploma. With any luck, you'll ride the Harvard gravy train for years. Your fake diploma lands you a sweet job. By the time your boss sees your flaws, some of your coworkers will be your friends. Maybe the boss retains you out of pity, or to avoid a blow to morale. If and when the boss's patience runs out, they probably won't blatantly fire you. Instead, they'll nudge you to "find a better match." When potential employers check up on you, your current employer has every reason to cover for you—allowing you to reboot your saga of deception and disappointment.

Riddle Me This

> Higher education is the only product where the consumer tries to get as little out of it as possible.
>
> —Arnold Kling, "College Customers vs. Suppliers"[41]

Critics of the signaling model are quick to insist that signaling "simply doesn't make sense." The truth is the opposite: human capital purism is what "simply doesn't make sense." Some big blatant facts are inexplicable *without* the signaling model.

The best education in the world is already free. All complaints about elite colleges' impossible admissions and insane tuition are flatly mistaken. Fact: *anyone* can study at Princeton for *free*. While tuition is over $45,000 a year,[42] anyone can show up and start attending classes. No one will stop you. No one will challenge you. No one will make you feel unwelcome. Gorge yourself at Princeton's all-you-can-eat buffet of the mind. Colleges do not card. I have seen this with my own eyes at schools around the country.

If you keep your learn-for-free scheme to yourself, professors will assume you're missing from their roster owing to a bureaucratic snafu. If you ask permission to sit in, most professors will be flattered. What a rare pleasure to teach someone who wants to learn! After four years of "guerrilla education," there's only one thing you'll lack: a diploma. Since you're not in the system, your performance will be invisible to employers. Not too enticing, is it?

Imagine this stark dilemma: you can have either a Princeton education without a diploma, or a Princeton diploma without an education. Which gets you further on the job market? For a human capital purist, the answer is obvious: four years of training are vastly preferable to a page of paper. But try saying that with a straight face. Sensible versions of the signaling model don't imply the diploma is *clearly* preferable; after all, Princeton teaches *some* useful skills. But you need signaling to explain why choosing between an education and a diploma is a head-scratcher rather than a no-brainer.

You could demur, "There's far more to a Princeton education than the coursework." But if you're already attending Princeton's classes, why couldn't you also join its study groups, intellectual discussions, and social life? You won't live in the dorm, but as long as you make the extra effort, rich peer interaction is within your grasp. In any case, to the best of my knowledge, there's no evidence that residing in dormitories has *any* extra payoff in the labor market. Students usually see off-campus living as a luxury, not a threat to their career success.

The main objection to the "guerilla education" argument, though, is simply, "Almost no one takes advantage of it." That's precisely my point: the fact that almost no one grabs a free elite education shows human capital purism is false. For the signaling model, in contrast, the freebie is mere illusion. Universities don't card because they don't need to. Unofficial education is vanishingly rare because it sends employers an invisible signal—also known as no signal at all.

Failing versus forgetting. You've studied many subjects you barely remember. You might have motivated yourself with, "After the final exam, I'll never have to think about this stupid subject again." Question: How would your career have been different if you flunked all the classes you've forgotten?

If employers rewarded well-educated workers for skills alone, failing a class and forgetting a class would have identical career consequences. They plainly don't. Take me. After three years of Spanish homework, Spanish exams, and Spanish presentations, I remember nearly nada. Yet if I had failed high school Spanish, I couldn't have gone to a good college, wouldn't have gotten into Princeton's Ph.D. program, and probably wouldn't be a professor. Luckily, I learned enough to get As on my report card. As a result, I'm living my dream—linguistic amnesia notwithstanding.

Human capital purists have one way to cope with these facts: claim studying a subject improves you in subtle ways long after you forget all your explicit lessons. Educational psychologists have spent a century measuring such subtle learning; we'll hear them out next chapter. For now, this story simply strains credulity. My Spanish teachers' official goal was to teach me Spanish. It was their native language. They failed. Are we really supposed to believe my Spanish teachers successfully taught me something that *wasn't* on their agenda? Something that's actually useful on the job? If my Spanish teachers couldn't achieve their official goal despite their expertise, you'd have to be awfully gullible to believe they covertly taught me "how to work." Yet they were no worse than most of my teachers—and, in all likelihood, no worse than most of yours.

Unlike human capital purism, signaling can explain these facts without torturing them first. Failing to learn course material sends a lousy signal: you were lacking in intelligence, conscientiousness, and/or conformity—and probably still are. Forgetting course material on the other hand, merely signals you lack the superpower of photographic memory. Since failing students send a far more negative signal than forgetful students, employers favor the forgetful. Since failing students suffer far more in the job market than forgetful students, students cram for the final exam, then move on with their lives.

Easy As. Students struggle to win admission to elite schools. Once they arrive, however, they hunt for professors with low expectations. A professor who wants to fill a lecture hall hands out lots of As and little homework.[43] On the popular Rate My Professors website, students grade their professors' "easiness," "helpfulness," "clarity," and "hotness," not "marketable skills taught" or "real-world relevance."[44] If human capital purists are right, why do students struggle to get into the best schools, then struggle to *avoid* acquiring skills once they arrive?

Signaling to the rescue. Schools have national, even global reputations. Students and employers know the difference between Princeton and Podunk State. Most professors, in contrast, have only local reputations. George Mason students know I'm not an easy A; their future employers don't. Anyone who likes money and dislikes studying has an obvious two-part strategy: choose the best school that admits you so you get a good job after graduation, and choose the easiest professors on campus so you have a good time before graduation.

Cheating. According to human capital purists, the labor market rewards only job skills, not academic credentials. Taken literally, this implies academic cheating is futile.[45] Sure, a failing student can raise their grade by copying an A+ exam or plagiarizing a term paper from the Internet. Unless copying and plagiarizing make people more productive *for their employer*, however, the human capital model implies zero financial payoff for the worker. Cheaters proverbially "only cheat themselves."

The human capital model doesn't just imply all cheaters are wasting their time. It also implies all educators who try to *prevent* cheating are wasting their time. All exams might as well be take-home. No one needs to proctor tests or call time. No one needs to punish plagiarism—or Google random sentences to detect it. Learners get job skills and financial rewards. Fakers get poetic justice.

Signaling, in contrast, explains why cheating pays—and why schools are wise to combat it. In the signaling model, employers reward workers for the skills they *think* those workers possess. Cheating tricks employers into thinking you're a better worker than you really are. The trick pays because *unless everyone cheats all the time*, students with better records are, on average, better workers.

Why discourage cheating? Because detecting and punishing cheaters preserve the signaling value of your school's diploma. When more of your students cheat their way to graduation, firms that hire your students are less likely to get the smart, hardworking team players they're paying for. Every time your school expels a cheater, you protect the good name of your graduates—past, present, and future. Even habitual cheaters abhor a diploma mill: you're free to slack, but on graduation day, the master of ceremonies hands you a worthless sheet of paper.

Why do students rejoice when the teacher cancels class? Teachers have a foolproof way to make their students cheer: cancel class. If human capital purists are right, such jubilation is bizarre. Since you go to school to acquire job skills, a teacher who cancels class rips you off. You learn less, you're less employable, yet your school doesn't refund a dime of tuition. In construction, contractors don't jump for joy if their roofers skip shingling to go gambling. In school, however, students jump for joy if their teachers cancel class to attend a conference in Vegas.

When students celebrate the absence of education, it's tempting to blame their myopia on immaturity. Tempting, but wrongheaded. Once they're in college, myopic, immature students can unilaterally skip class whenever they like. Why wait for the teacher's green light? For most students, there's an obvious answer: When you skip class, your relative performance suffers. When your teacher cancels class, *everyone* learns less, leaving your relative performance unimpaired.

Human capital purists must reject this "obvious answer." Employers reward you for your skills, not your skills compared to your classmates'. Signaling, in contrast, takes the "obvious answer" over the finish line. Why do students cheer when a teacher cancels class? Because they've escaped an hour of drudgery without hurting their GPA. Why don't students unilaterally skip class? Because if they skip class and their classmates don't, their grades suffer. Why do students focus on grades rather than learning? Because they follow the money.

Lead into Gold

If you single-mindedly focus on graduates' paychecks, education turns lead into gold. Waiters walk in; economic consultants walk out. For teachers, it's so tempting to take credit—to gaze on our former students in their mortarboards and gloat, "I amaze even myself." If teachers were honest with ourselves, we would be slower to self-congratulate. Do we really *transform* waiters into economic consultants—or merely *evaluate* whether waiters have the right stuff to be economic consultants?

By analogy, both sculptors and appraisers have the power to raise the market value of a piece of stone. The sculptor raises the market value of a piece of stone by *shaping it*. The appraiser raises the market value of a piece of stone by *judging it*. Teachers need to ask ourselves, "How much of what we do is sculpting, and how much is appraising?" And if we won't ask ourselves, our alumni need to ask for us.

CHAPTER 2

The Puzzle Is Real

The Ubiquity of Useless Education

> He rambled on about how Rembrandt captured the "soul state" of
> each of his figures, and then he made an analogy to Beethoven's
> music. He extended the analogy for several minutes not realizing
> that nobody in the class knew anything about Beethoven. Three
> weeks into summer vacation most students won't remember any-
> thing about Rembrandt.
>
> —James Schneider, "Flight into L.A."

Highlighting the stark contrast between what students have to learn and
what workers need to know throws us off balance.[1] Many accept the
signaling explanation and move on. Yet others recover their footing and
start asking troubling questions. Could education be more useful than it
seems on the surface? Less lucrative than it seems on the surface?

The signaling model solves a puzzle: Why does the labor market reward useless education? Yet perhaps we're getting ahead of ourselves.
Before we solve this alleged puzzle, we must scrutinize precisely what
students learn and what employers reward. Perhaps the magic of education can be dispelled.

There are several common approaches. Educators' favorite: insisting
that no matter what they study, students are learning "how to learn"
or "how to think." Laymen prefer stories about blood, sweat, and tears:
suffering in school "teaches discipline" or "builds character." Self-made
curmudgeons occasionally harrumph that anyone smart and disci-
plined enough to succeed in school could have done as well by skipping
college and starting their own business. My father, a Ph.D. in electrical
engineering, routinely denied that "soft" majors pay. When I was growing up, he gave me the impression there were only two education/career
tracks. Some students study engineering to become engineers; the rest
study liberal arts to become taxi drivers.

Do any attempts to dispel the magic of education pass muster? If so, how successful are they? For clarity, I split the evidence into two chapters. The chapter at hand focuses on learning; the chapter to follow, on earning. Can we reconcile the skills students acquire before graduation with the payoffs workers enjoy after graduation? After good hard looks at learning and earning, we'll know the true size of the puzzle.

The Content of the Curriculum

> You obviously learn some valuable skills in school (engineering, computer science, signaling models).
> —David Autor, "Lecture Note 18"[2]

Every school teaches a mix of useful skills and filler, of "wheat" and "chaff." The crucial question is: What's today's mix? 90% wheat and 10% chaff? 50/50? 20/80? While we'll never perfectly measure the breakdown, the basic facts are a good place to start.

High school. What do students actually study in grades 9–12? The *Digest of Education Statistics* shows high school grads' completed coursework by subject. It's all "useful" in the trivial sense that it improves students' odds of high school graduation and college admission. But what about "useful" in the stronger sense that students eventually *apply* their lessons on the job? After breaking down the curriculum by subjects, I sort them into three categories of usefulness: "High," "Medium," and "Low" (see Figure 2.1).

"High" usefulness means knowledge of the subject improves job performance in a wide range of occupations; most students in a class will eventually use what they learn. "Medium" usefulness means knowledge of the subject improves job performance in some common occupations; a few students in a class will eventually use what they learn. "Low" usefulness means knowledge of the subject at best improves job performance in rare occupations; students are likely to apply what they learn only if they become teachers of the subject.

These ratings are my personal judgment drawing on forty years in school. Fortunately, though, every reader has enough firsthand educational experience to make an independent expert judgment. If you

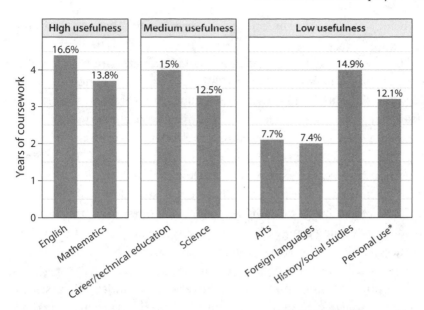

Figure 2.1: Average Years of Coursework Passed by High School Graduates (2005)
Source: Snyder and Dillow 2011, pp. 228–30, 642. "Years of coursework" is measured in Carnegie units. One Carnegie unit is 120 hours of class time over the course of a year. To get credit for a class, students need at least a D.
* Includes general skills, personal health and physical education, religion, military sciences, special education, and other courses not included in other subject fields.

question my rankings, please substitute your own. The basis for my breakdown:

High usefulness: In a modern economy, literacy and numeracy are the only skills that almost all jobs require, so English and math make the cut. Why not science? The subject is highly useful for our *society*. However, only a handful of specialists apply their knowledge of science on the job. The rest of us merely follow their recipes.

Medium usefulness: Career/technical classes are potentially useful stepping-stones for students who plan to enter a short list of trades like cooking, sewing, metalworking, woodworking, drafting, or computer programming. By themselves, though, high school–level classes do not open career doors. Students who take a class in cooking, then stop, are not yet employable as cooks. High school science classes, similarly, are only stepping-stones for the tiny share of students who pursue careers in science or engineering. How tiny? About one-third of high school graduates have a bachelor's degree; only 14% of students who earn a bachelor's degree major in science or engineering. That multiplies out to roughly 5%.[3]

Low usefulness: To belabor the obvious, the arts are rarely useful. We don't speak of "starving artists" for nothing. The staunchest fans of painting, sculpture, and music know pursuing a career in the arts is a "Hail Mary" pass. Foreign languages, similarly, are all but useless in the American economy. Thanks to immigration, employers have a built-in pool of native speakers of almost every living language.[4] The average American high school student nevertheless spends *two full years* sitting in Spanish, French, German, Italian, or even Latin. Physical education, the most recognizable form of "Personal use" coursework, trains only a handful of budding professional athletes and the next generation of gym teachers.[5] Finally, almost no one pursues a *career* in history or social studies—except teachers of history and social studies.

An optimist might emphasize that over half of students' courses are useful to some degree, and nearly one-third are highly useful. The optimist should keep in mind that I grade usefulness on a curve. Even "highly useful" subjects are more academic and less practical than they sound. Take math. Almost every modern occupation uses *some* math. Yet high schools teach and often require math rarely used outside a classroom. Figure 2.2 shows the fraction of high school grads who passed various high school math courses—and rates the courses' usefulness.

Geometry is the most common of all math courses: over four-fifths complete it in high school. Yet the subject, featuring countless proofs of triangles' congruence, is notoriously irrelevant. Geometry rarely pops up after the final exam, even in other math classes. Algebra I, which teaches students graphing and one- and two-variable equations, has many practical applications. Most students, however, continue on to Algebra II, which largely exists to prepare students for calculus.[6] Calculus, in turn, gets you into college. Once college begins, however, you'll probably never differentiate another equation unless you pursue a degree in math, science, or engineering.[7] Knowledge of statistics, in contrast, is useful whether or not you go to college. Nobel Prize winner Daniel Kahneman shows that statistical illiteracy underpins many foolish real-world choices.[8] Yet only 7.7% of high school students pass a stats class.

The point isn't that the current curricula of the American high school is silly by historic or world standards. The status quo is more practical

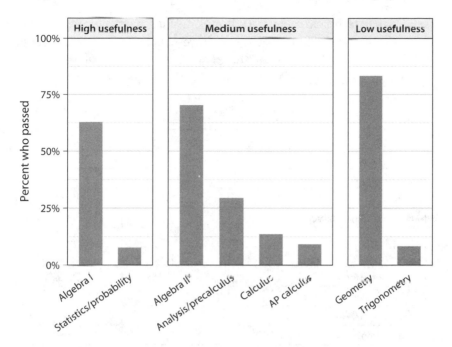

Figure 2.2: Math Coursework Passed by High School Graduates (2005)
Source: Snyder and Dillow 2011, p. 234.
* Includes Algebra/Trigonometry and Algebra/Geometry.

than a "classical education" in Latin and Greek.[9] The point, rather, is that American high school is far from the skill factory we often imagine it to be. Being more relevant than Oxford in 1750 is nothing to brag about.

College. We can ballpark the practicality of higher education by looking at the distribution of majors. Table 2.1 breaks down all bachelor's degrees conferred in 2008–9 by field of study—and rates their usefulness.

High usefulness: Defenders of the real-world relevance of education love to invoke engineering. Engineering students learn how to make stuff work; employers hire them to make stuff work. Engineering has well-defined subbranches, each with straightforward applications: electrical, mechanical, civil, nuclear. Before we get carried away, we should accept a key fact: Engineering is a challenging, hence unpopular, major. Psychologists outnumber engineers. Artists outnumber engineers. Social scientists plus historians outnumber engineers almost two to one.

What other majors deserve to be in engineering's august company? Let's grade leniently. As long as a major explicitly prepares students for well-defined technical careers, it's "highly useful." By this forgiving standard, "health professions" and agriculture majors end up in the same boat as engineers—and the fraction of graduates who earn highly useful degrees remains under 25%.

Table 2.1: Bachelor's Degrees by Field of Study (2008–9)

Field of Study	# Graduates	%
High Usefulness		
Agriculture and natural resources	24,988	1.6%
Architecture	10,119	0.6%
Biological/biomedical sciences	80,756	5.0%
Computer/information sciences	37,994	2.4%
Engineering	84,636	5.3%
Health professions	120,488	7.5%
Legal professions	3,822	0.2%
Other*	162	0.0%
Physical sciences/science technology	22,466	1.4%
Statistics/applied mathematics	1,913	0.1%
Subtotal	384,431	24.1%
Medium Usefulness		
Business	347,985	21.7%
Education	101,708	6.4%
Mathematics	13,583	0.8%
Parks/recreation/leisure/fitness studies	31,667	2.0%
Public administration	23,851	1.5%
Security/protective services	41,800	2.6%
Transportation	5,189	0.3%
Subtotal	567,696	35.3%
Low Usefulness		
Area/ethnic/cultural/gender studies	8,772	0.5%
Communications	83,109	5.2%
English	55,462	3.5%
Family/consumer sciences	21,905	1.4%
Foreign languages	21,158	1.3%
Liberal arts	47,096	2.9%

Multi/interdisciplinary studies	37,444	2.3%
Philosophy/religious studies	12,444	0.8%
Psychology	94,271	5.9%
Social sciences/history	168,500	10.5%
Theology	8,940	0.6%
Visual/performing arts	89,140	5.6%
Subtotal	648,242	40.5%
Total	1,601,368	100%

Source: Snyder and Dillow 2011, p. 412.
* Library science, military technologies, and precision production.

Medium usefulness: Majors like business, education, and public administration sound vaguely vocational and funnel students toward predictable occupations after graduation. At the same time, they teach few technical skills, and nonmajors readily compete for the same jobs. While you could dismiss these majors as Low in usefulness, let's give them the benefit of the doubt. You don't need a business degree to work in business, but perhaps your coursework gives you an edge. You don't need an education degree to land a teaching job, but explicitly studying education could enhance your teaching down the road. You don't need a degree in public administration to be a bureaucrat, but maybe such coursework builds a better bureaucrat. By this standard, about 35% of majors end up in the Medium category.

Why put math majors in the same box as students of education or "parks and recreation"? In a sense, no one acquires more technical skills than mathematicians. However, graduates in pure mathematics have no clear occupational track. Many employers hire them for their general quantitative ability. Outside of academia, however, no one pays you to prove theorems.

Low usefulness: The status of most of the majors in this bin—fine arts, philosophy, women's studies, theology, and such—should be un-controversial. Liberal arts programs uphold the ideal of "knowledge for knowledge's sake." Few even pretend to prepare students for the job market. You could argue I underrate the usefulness of communications and psychology. Don't they prepare students to work in journalism and psychology? Yet this objection is almost as naive as, "Don't history programs prepare students to work as historians?" Psychology, communications, and history's usefulness is Low because they prepare their students for fields where paying jobs are almost impossible to get. In 2008–9, over 94,000 students earned their bachelor's in psychology, but there are only 174,000 practicing psychologists in the country.[10] In the same year, over 83,000 students earned their bachelor's degree in communications. *Total* jobs for reporters, correspondents, and broadcast news analysts number 54,000.[11] Historians, unsurprisingly, have the bleakest prospects of all. There were over 34,000 newly minted history graduates—and only 3,500 working historians in the entire country.[12] The vast majority of students who earn these degrees find employment outside their field. There's no other way to balance the books.

The staunchest defenders of education reject the idea of sorting subjects and majors by "usefulness." How do you know Latin, trigonometry, or Emily Dickinson *won't* serve you on the job? A man told me his French once helped him understand an airport announcement in Paris. Without high school French, he would have missed his flight. Invest years now and one day you might save hours at an airport. See, studying French pays!

These claims remind me of *Hoarders*, a reality show about people whose mad acquisitiveness has ruined their lives. Some hoarders collect herds of cats, others old refrigerators, others their own garbage. Why not throw away some of their useless possessions? Stock answer: "I might need it one day." They "might need" a hundred empty milk cartons.

Taken literally, the hoarders are right: there is a chance they'll need their trash. The commonsense reply is that packing your house with trash is *almost* always a bad idea. You must weigh the storage cost against the likely benefits.

The same goes for knowledge. Yes, you "might need" Latin one day. Maybe a time machine will strand you in ancient Rome. Still, does it make sense to study a dead language for years to prepare for a scenario you almost certainly won't face? You cannot retreat to agnosticism. "No one knows if this trash will come in handy" is a crazy argument for hoarding trash. "No one knows if this knowledge will come in handy" is a crazy argument for hoarding knowledge.

Measured Learning

For human capital purists, education pays only because students learn. Sitting in class year after year is not sufficient; students must actually acquire knowledge. Given the size of the education premium, human capital purists ought to believe students acquire *a lot* of knowledge in school. That's not all. Human capital purists also ought to believe workers *retain* a lot of the knowledge they acquire in school. The labor market pays you for what you know now—not what you knew on graduation day. For human capital purists, the coexistence of a high education premium and low learning/retention would be a puzzle. The less students know and remember, the greater the puzzle.

For the signaling model, in contrast, the coexistence of a high education premium and low learning/retention raises no eyebrows. While students could signal their intelligence, conscientiousness, and conformity by acquiring and retaining a vast stock of knowledge, they don't have to. Students can win employers' favor by learning *enough* to get a good grade—then forgetting every lesson.

How much do schools teach students—and how much do students retain? Measurement is tricky. Using students' standardized test scores implicitly assumes students learn everything they know in school. What about *changes* in students' standardized test scores? A little better, but the basic problem remains: the fact that students improve from grade to grade does not show schooling caused their improvement. Maybe they're maturing, or learning in their spare time.[13] Given these doubts, most researchers strongly prefer controlled experiments: randomly give some kids extra education, then measure their surplus knowledge.[14]

Unfortunately, all these approaches—controlled experiments included—neglect retention. Even if schooling indisputably raises students' scores, the gain could be fleeting. Teachers often lament "summer learning loss": students know less at the end of summer than they did at the beginning.[15] But summer learning loss is only a special case of the problem of *fadeout*: human beings poorly retain knowledge they rarely use.[16] Researchers are especially prone to neglect postgraduation fadeout: they measure how quickly fourth-graders forget third grade, but not how quickly high school graduates forget twelfth grade.

A rare—and discouraging—exception: One major study tested roughly a thousand people's knowledge of algebra and geometry.[17] Some participants were still in high school; the rest were adults between 19 and 84 years old. The researchers had data on subjects' full mathematical education. Main finding: Most people who take high school algebra and geometry forget about half of what they learn within five years and forget almost everything within twenty-five years. Only people who continue on to calculus retain most of their algebra and geometry.

Is long-term retention really this weak? Despite the shortage of long-term retention studies, we can fall back on a compelling shortcut. Instead of measuring the enduring effect of education on adult knowledge, we can place an *upper bound* on that effect. It's a two-step process. Step one: measure adult knowledge about various school subjects. Step two: note that schools can't be responsible for *more than 100%* of what adults know about these subjects. What people now know is therefore an upper bound on the school learning they retain.

My shortcut is easy to implement. Surveys of adults' knowledge of reading, math, history, civics, science, and foreign languages are already on the shelf. The results are stark: Basic literacy and numeracy are virtually the *only* book learning most American adults possess. While the average American spends years and years studying other subjects, they recall next to nothing about them. If schools teach us everything we know about history, civics, science, and foreign languages, their achievement is pitiful.

Literacy and numeracy. In 2003, the United States Department of Education gave about 18,000 randomly selected Americans the National Assessment of Adult Literacy (NAAL).[18] The NAAL tested prose literacy ("knowledge and skills needed to search, comprehend, and use information from continuous texts"), document literacy ("knowledge and skills needed to search, comprehend, and use information from noncontinuous texts"), and quantitative literacy ("knowledge and skills needed to identify and perform computations using numbers that are embedded in printed materials").[19]

For each of these three subtests, the NAAL charitably grades respondents' knowledge as "Below Basic," "Basic," "Intermediate," or "Proficient." Take a look at official examples of Below Basic, Basic, Intermediate, and Proficient Tasks (see Table 2.2). Summing two prices and finding a table in an almanac are Basic (*not* Below Basic) tasks.

Table 2.2: Sample NAAL Tasks, by Level

	Below Basic	Basic	Intermediate	Proficient
Prose	Identify what it is permissible to drink before a medical test, based on a short set of instructions.	Find information in a pamphlet for prospective jurors that explains how citizens were selected for the jury pool.	Summarize the work experience required for a specific job, based on information in a newspaper job advertisement.	Compare viewpoints in two editorials with contrasting interpretations of scientific and economic evidence.
Document	Circle the date of a medical appointment on a hospital appointment slip.	Find a table in an almanac with information on a specified topic.	Find the time a television program ends, using a newspaper television schedule that lists similar programs showing at different times on different channels.	Contrast financial information presented in a table regarding the differences between various types of credit cards.
Quantitative	Add two numbers to complete an ATM deposit slip.	Calculate the cost of a sandwich and salad, using prices from a menu.	Calculate the total cost of ordering office supplies, using a page from an office supplies catalog and an order form.	Calculate an employee's share of health insurance costs for a year, using a table that shows how the employee's monthly cost varies with income and family size.

Source: Kutner et al. 2007, pp. 5–7.

Given these low standards, you might think that virtually all Americans would score at the Intermediate or Proficient level in every subject. Not even close (see Figure 2.3).

The ignorance revealed by the NAAL is numbing. Only modest majorities are Intermediate or Proficient on the prose and document tests. Under half are Intermediate or Proficient on the quantitative test. Reviewing spe-

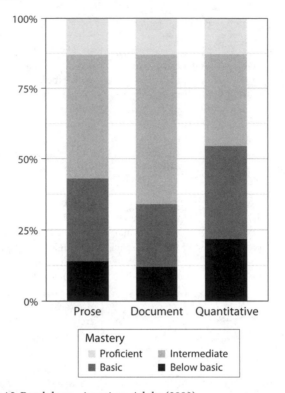

Figure 2.3: NAAL Breakdown: American Adults (2003)
Source: Kutner et al. 2007, p. 13.

cific questions underscores the severity of the ignorance. Barely half know that saving $.05 per gallon on 140 gallons of oil equals $7.00. Thirty-five percent of Americans can't correctly enter a name and address on a Certified Mail form—with no points off for misspelling![20] Schools do far less to cure illiteracy and innumeracy than we'd like to think.

Still, "Illiterate and innumerate compared to what?" is a fair response. Conceivably, in the absence of English and math courses, *all* Americans would be "Below Basic" in *all* three categories. From this perspective, the NAAL puts a fairly high upper bound on schools' total effect on Americans literacy and numeracy. Eighty-six percent of Americans exceed "Below Basic" for prose; 88% exceed "Below Basic" for documents; 78% exceed "Below Basic" for quantitative. For each of the three categories, 13% are actually "Proficient." While these results are meager given the typical American student's years in English and math, they're way better than nothing from employers' point of view.

How do the NAAL results look if you break them down by education? If you mentally picture "high school graduates," you probably see them as Intermediate or Proficient in literacy and numeracy. If you mentally picture "college students," you probably see them as Proficient in literacy and numeracy. Such mental pictures do not fit the facts. Figure 2.4 shows composite scores for high school dropouts, high school graduates with no college, and college graduates.[21]

While today's dropouts almost always spend at least nine years in school,[22] over half remain functionally illiterate and innumerate. Over half of high school grads have less than the minimum skills one would naively expect them to possess. Though college grads spend at least seventeen years in school, under a third have the level of literacy and numeracy we assume of every college freshman.

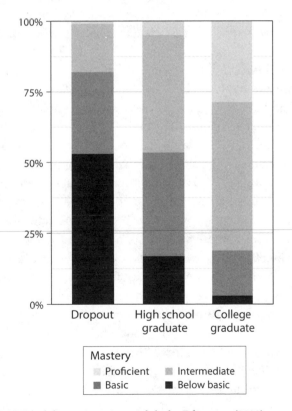

Figure 2.4: NAAL Breakdown: American Adults by Education (2003)
Source: Kutner et al. 2007, pp. 38–39.

History and civics. What does the average American learn in school *besides* basic literacy and numeracy? Precisely how much of our knowledge of history, civics, science, and foreign languages do we owe to education? Once again, we can use surveys of adult knowledge to put a ceiling on the answer.

Starting with history and civics, all national surveys find *severe* ignorance. The American Revolution Center tested 1,001 adult Americans' knowledge of the American Revolution.[23] Eighty-three percent earned failing grades. The Intercollegiate Studies Institute tested over 2,500 adult Americans' knowledge of American government and American history.[24] Seventy-one percent earned failing grades. *Newsweek* magazine gave 1,000 Americans the U.S. Citizenship Test.[25] Thirty-eight percent scored too low to become citizens of their own country. On the 2000 American National Election Study, the typical person got 48% of the factual questions right; you would expect 28% by guessing.[26] These results are consistent with a vast academic literature on Americans' (lack of) political knowledge.[27]

You could blame low scores on the difficulty of the tests rather than the ignorance of the test takers. When you read them, however, you'll notice the public struggles with easy multiple choice questions. How many American adults know the Bill of Rights is part of the Constitution? The American Revolution Center reports a dismal 57%, but the truth is far worse. Since there were only four response options, you would expect roughly 25% of the ignorant to guess the right answer by chance. And this is no isolated blind spot. Table 2.3 shows some other basic history and civics questions, with scores corrected for guessing.[28]

One could look at these facts and conclude the public's historical and civic knowledge is no worse than its literacy. Yet such optimism overlooks a key point: knowing half a subject's *basic* facts does not make you "halfway proficient." If you know only half the letters in the alphabet, you are illiterate. Why? Because you lack knowledge of basic facts on which all reading depends. The same holds for the ABCs of history and civics. Not knowing the three branches of government isn't like not knowing *Hamlet*; it's like not knowing the letter "h." If you don't know that the Civil War came after the Declaration of Independence, you don't understand American history. If you don't know which parties control the House and the Senate, you don't understand American politics.

Table 2.3: Adult History/Civics Knowledge: Some Telling Questions

Question	Response Options	% Who Answer Correctly	% Who Really Know
From the American Revolution: Who Cares? Survey			
Which of the following rights is not protected by the Bill of Rights?	Freedom of speech Trial by jury The right to bear arms *Right to vote*	39%	21%
The U.S. Constitution establishes which of the following forms of government in the United States?	A direct democracy *A Republic* A Confederacy An Oligarchy	42%	24%
Which of the following events came BEFORE the Declaration of Independence?	*Foundation of Jamestown, VA* The Civil War The Emancipation Proclamation The War of 1812	49%	26%
When did the American Revolution begin? Was it in the . . .	*1770s* 1640s 1490s 1800s	65%	55%
From *Our Fading Heritage* (Cribb 2008, p. 18)			
What are the three branches of government?	[Free response]	50%	50%
The Bill of Rights explicitly prohibits . . .	Prayer in public school Discrimination based on race, sex, or religion The ownership of guns by private individuals *Establishing an official religion for the United States* The president from vetoing a line item in a spending bill	26%	8%
What part of the government has the power to declare war?	*Congress* The president The Supreme Court The Joint Chiefs of Staff	54%	39%

If taxes equal government spending, then:	Government debt is zero Printing money no longer causes inflation Government is not helping anybody *Tax per person equals government spending per person* Tax loopholes and special-interest spending are absent	28%	10%
From the 2000 American National Election Study			
Would you say that compared to 1992, the federal budget deficit is now smaller, larger, or about the same?	Larger About the Same *Smaller*	58%	41%
Is Al Gore more liberal than George Bush, more conservative, or about the same?	*More* About the Same Less	57%	44%
Do you happen to know which party had the most members in the House of Representatives in Washington BEFORE the election (this/last) month?	Democrats *Republicans*	55%	22%
Do you happen to know which party had the most members in the U.S. Senate BEFORE the election (this/last) month?	Democrats *Republicans*	50%	21%
Correct responses in italics.			

The average American high school graduate completes four years of history/social studies coursework. Four years: ample time to learn the ABCs of history and civics by heart, to acquire the knowledge base to discuss America's past, present, and future. Yet few adults possess this knowledge. If we owe everything we know about history and civics to history and civics classes, we owe next to nothing.

Science. Few American adults know the ABCs of science. The General Social Survey provides the best evidence of their ignorance. In recent years, this survey has tested the public's knowledge of twelve elementary scientific facts (see Table 2.4).[29] Adults correctly answer 60%. While this may seem low, it is a gross overstatement. These are true/false questions, so people should get 50% only guessing!

Table 2.4: Adult Science Knowledge: Some Telling Questions

Question	Response Options	% Who Answer Correctly	% Who Really Know
From the General Social Survey 2006–10			
The center of the Earth is very hot.	*TRUE* FALSE	81%	76%
The continents on which we live have been moving their locations for millions of years and will continue to move in the future.	*TRUE* FALSE	78%	68%
Does the Earth go around the Sun, or does the Sun go around the Earth?	*Earth goes around the Sun* Sun goes around the Earth	73%	54%
All radioactivity is man-made.	TRUE *FALSE*	68%	50%
Electrons are smaller than atoms.	*TRUE* FALSE	52%	32%
Lasers work by focusing sound waves.	TRUE *FALSE*	46%	25%
The universe began with a huge explosion.	*TRUE* FALSE	33%	−3%
The cloning of living things produces genetically identical copies.	*TRUE* FALSE	80%	71%
It is the father's gene that decides whether the baby is a boy or a girl.	*TRUE* FALSE	62%	39%
Ordinary tomatoes do not contain genes, while genetically modified tomatoes do.	TRUE *FALSE*	47%	29%

Antibiotics kill viruses as well as bacteria.	TRUE *FALSE*	53%	14%
Human beings, as we know them today, developed from earlier species of animals.	*TRUE* FALSE	44%	2%

Accounting for guessing, the public's scientific illiteracy is astonishing. Barely half of American adults know the Earth goes around the sun. Only 32% know atoms are bigger than electrons. Just 14% know that antibiotics don't kill viruses. Knowledge of evolution barely exceeds zero. Knowledge of the Big Bang is actually *less* than zero; respondents would have done better flipping a coin. Guess-corrected, the average respondent knows 4.6 answers. If adults learned everything they know about these twelve juvenile questions in high school science, they learned 1.4 answers per *year*.[30]

Educators can arguably blame the majority's disbelief in the Big Bang and evolution on Christian fundamentalism. Yet ignorance of the ABCs of science is nondenominational. Only 7% of adult Americans who *deny* the Bible's literal truth answered all twelve questions correctly.[31] Given the ease of the questions, we shouldn't conclude Americans' knowledge of science is mediocre. We should conclude Americans' knowledge of science is virtually nonexistent.

Foreign languages. High school graduates average two years of foreign language coursework. What do adults have to show for it? The General Social Survey allows rather precise estimates. It asks respondents, "Can you speak a language other than English?," "How well do you speak that language?," and "Is that a language you first learned as a child at home, in school, or is it one that you learned elsewhere?"[32]

The results could scarcely be worse. Schools make virtually *no one* fluent in a foreign language (see Figure 2.5). Only .7% claim to have learned a foreign language "very well" in school; another 1.7% claim to have learned a foreign language "well" in school. Since these are self-reports, true linguistic competence must be even worse. The hard truth: if you didn't acquire fluency in the home, you almost certainly don't have it.

Classroom sitting is easily measured and plainly massive. In our society, virtually everyone sits in school for over a decade. Yet this hardly shows students' *learning* or *retention* is massive. Adult knowledge is a superior measure: while people obviously learn outside of school, their total knowledge puts a ceiling on what they learned inside of school. The results are disheartening. Most Americans possess basic literacy and numeracy, but only 13% are proficient. For history, civics, science, and foreign language, few Americans grasp the ABCs. The claim that schools "teach these subjects" is an overstatement. Schools only "teach *of* these subjects." After *years* of exposure, American adults know history, civics, science, and foreign languages exist. That's about it.

Americans' staggering ignorance may not be a death blow for human capital purism, but it is an awkward fact. If we learn so little in school, why do employers so heavily reward education? The simplest response is that employers, like teachers, grade on a curve. Intermediate literacy and numeracy horrify intellectuals. From an employer's point of view, however, intermediate is way better than basic—or below basic.

The main weakness with this response: even adults who did *well* in school usually lack basic knowledge of history, civics, science, and foreign language. Yet employers still hold failing grades in these subjects against you. If you fail Spanish, you don't finish high school, you can't go

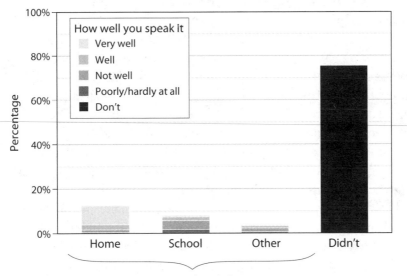

Figure 2.5: The Level and Origin of Foreign Language Competence in the General Social Survey

to college, and the labor market punishes you—even though most B.A.s are equally monolingual. How can human capital purists explain that?

The Relevance of Relevance

Youths spend years studying subjects adults rarely use on the job. Adults are amazingly ignorant about subjects they studied since childhood. Is there any way to square these facts with the popular assumption that employers value your education solely because they value your learning?

There is. Maybe course catalogs and standardized tests fail to capture most of what students learn. When students challenge the relevance of their lessons, teachers often reply, "I teach you how to think—not what to think." Teachers could dismiss adult ignorance in roughly the same way: "They learned how to think—not what to think." So what if most students won't use European history or the periodic table on the job? "Relevance" is irrelevant. As long as students learn *something*, they tacitly acquire marketable skills en passant.

If these teachers are right, defenders of education can draw a line in the sand: the prevalence of "useless" subjects and scarcity of "measured learning" is an illusion. The fact that you neither use nor remember your coursework in history and science does not make your coursework a waste of time. A history class can teach critical thinking; a science class can teach logic. Thinking—*all* thinking—builds mental muscles. The bigger students' mental muscles, the better they'll be at whatever job they eventually land.

Comforting claims. They sooth teachers' consciences and quiet our self-doubt. But are they true—or merely wishful thinking? Can believers in the power of learning how to think back up teachers' boasts with hard evidence? For the most part, no. Educational psychologists who specialize in "transfer of learning" have measured the hidden intellectual benefits of education for over a century.[33] Their chief discovery: education is narrow. As a rule, students learn only the material you specifically teach them . . . if you're lucky. In the words of educational psychologists Perkins and Salomon, "Besides just plain forgetting, people commonly fail to marshal what they know effectively in situations outside the classroom or in other classes in different disciplines. The bridge from school to beyond or from this subject to that other is a bridge too far."[34]

Many experiments study transfer of learning under seemingly ideal conditions. Researchers teach subjects how to answer Question A. Then they immediately ask their subjects Question B, which can be handily solved using the same approach as Question A. Unless A and B look alike on the surface, or subjects get a heavy-handed hint to apply the same approach, learning how to solve Question A rarely helps subjects answer Question B.[35]

One classic experiment teaches subjects how to solve a military puzzle, then tests whether subjects apply what they learned to solve a medical puzzle. The military puzzle:

A general wishes to capture a fortress located in the center of a country. There are many roads radiating outward from the fortress. All have been mined so that while small groups of men can pass over the roads safely, any large force will detonate the mines. A full-scale direct attack is therefore impossible. The general's solution is to divide his army into small groups, send each group to the head of a different road, and have the groups converge simultaneously on the fortress.

The medical puzzle:

Suppose you are a doctor faced with a patient who has a malignant tumor in his stomach. It is impossible to operate on the patient, but unless the tumor is destroyed the patient will die. There is a kind of ray that can be used to destroy the tumor. If the rays reach the tumor all at once at a sufficiently high intensity, the tumor will be destroyed. Unfortunately, at this intensity the healthy tissue that the rays pass through on the way to the tumor will also be destroyed. At lower intensities the rays are harmless to healthy tissue, but they will not affect the tumor either. What type of procedure might be used to destroy the tumor with the rays, and at the same time avoid destroying the healthy tissue?

The connection:

There is an analogous "convergence" solution to the radiation problem. The doctor could direct multiple low-intensity rays toward the tumor simultaneously from different directions, so that the healthy tissue will be left unharmed, but the effects of the low-intensity rays will summate and destroy the tumor.[36]

Since subjects hear these two stories back to back, you might think almost everyone would leap to the convergence solution for the medical problem. They don't. A typical success rate is 30%. Since about 10% of subjects who *don't* hear the military problem offer the convergence solution, only one in five subjects transferred what they learned. To reach a high (roughly 75%) success rate, you need to teach subjects the first story, then bluntly *tell* them to use the first story to solve the second.[37]

To repeat, such experiments measure how humans "learn how to think" under *ideal* conditions: teach A, immediately ask B, then see if subjects use A to solve B. Researchers are leading the witness. As psychologist Douglas Detterman remarks:

> Teaching the principle in close association with testing transfer is not very different from telling subjects that they should use the principle just taught. Telling subjects to use a principle is not transfer. It is following instructions.[38]

Under less promising conditions, transfer is predictably even worse. Making the surface features of A and B less similar impedes transfer.[39] Adding a time delay between teaching A and testing B impedes transfer.[40] Teaching A, then teaching an irrelevant distracter problem, then testing B, impedes transfer.[41] Teaching A in a classroom, then testing B in the real world impedes transfer.[42] Having one person teach A and another person test B impedes transfer.[43]

To apply schoolwork in the real world, you must normally overcome *each and every one* of these hurdles. You must see through surface features to underlying structure. You must select the few relevant lessons, and ignore the rest. You must remember relevant lessons years or decades after encountering them. You must apply what you learned in a nonacademic location, without your original teacher (or any teacher!) to hold your hand. No wonder even transfer optimists like Robert Haskell lament:

> Despite the importance of transfer of learning, research findings over the past nine decades clearly show that as individuals, and as educational institutions, we have failed to achieve transfer of learning on any significant level.[44]

You might protest that transfer experiments are too artificial or superficial to show much about real-world education. If each lesson microscopically hones your thinking skills, the total effect of education on general thinking skills could still be large. Researchers generally find, for example, that college attendance boosts scores on tests of critical thinking.[45] But this is a hollow victory: researchers also generally find that education fails to *durably* improve critical thinking *outside the classroom*.[46]

The most impressive study of the effect of education on thinking skills collected a sample of first-year high school students, fourth-year high school students, first-year college students, fourth-year college students, first-year graduate students, and fourth-year graduate students.[47] The researcher then orally tested their *informal* reasoning on issues like, "Does violence on television significantly increase the likelihood of violence in real life?" and "Would a proposed law in Massachusetts requiring a five-cent deposit on bottles and cans significantly reduce litter?" By design, there were no right or wrong answers; the point of the test was to measure the *quality* of subjects' reasoning on issues that "permitted elaborate arguments on both sides of the case, led to divided opinions, proved accessible even to the first-year high school group, and did not depend for their analysis on background knowledge that varied greatly across the subject population."[48] Judges listened to recordings of the original responses, counting (a) number of sentences, (b) number of lines of argument, (c) number of objections considered, and (d) how many times the experimenter had to remind the subject to stay on topic. The experimenter also asked subjects to *explain* the connection between one of their arguments and their conclusion. Judges graded the quality of these explanations, as well as overall quality of reasoning.

The measured effect of education on informal reasoning, though positive, was tiny. Fourth-year high school students were slightly better than first-year high school students. Fourth-year college students were no better than first-year college students. Fourth-year graduate students were barely better than first-year graduate students. Table 2.5 shows the average overall quality of their reasoning on a 1–5 scale (5 being highest).

Table 2.5: Average Overall Reasoning Score (1–5 scale, 5 being highest)

	1st Year	4th Year
High School	1.6	2.1
College	2.8	2.8
Graduate School	3.1	3.3
Source: Perkins 1985, p. 566.		

Respondents with more educational credentials definitely get higher scores. The point is that students barely improve *between* their first and fourth years of study.[49] While people with better reasoning skills do complete more education, their reasoning skills are *better at the outset*. If education seriously showed students "how to think," three additional years of study would sharply amplify their initial advantage. Yet students' scores barely budge.

Other evidence is equally disappointing. One researcher tested several hundred Arizona State University students' ability to "apply statistical and methodological concepts to reasoning about everyday-life events."[50] How, for example, would subjects assess the claim that students should eat more nutritiously because "the majority of students needing psychological counseling had poor dietary habits"? Would subjects realize psychological problems might *cause* poor dietary habits, rather than the other way around? Would they feel the need for experimental evidence? No. In the author's words:

> The results were shocking: Of the several hundred students tested, many of whom had taken more than six years of laboratory science in high school and college and advanced mathematics through calculus, almost none demonstrated even a semblance of acceptable methodological reasoning about everyday-life events described in ordinary newspaper and magazine articles. The overwhelming majority of responses received a score of 0. Fewer than 1% obtained the score of 2 that corresponded to a "good scientific response." Totally ignoring the need for comparison groups and control of third variables, subjects responded to the "diet" example with statements such as "It can't hurt to eat well."[51]

The point is not merely that college students are bad at reasoning about everyday events. The point is that college students are bad at reasoning about everyday events despite *years* of coursework in science and math. Believers in "learning how to learn" should expect students who study science to absorb the scientific method, then habitually use that fruitful method to analyze the world. This scarcely occurs. By and large, college science teaches students *what* to think about topics on the syllabus, not *how* to think about the world.

Counterexamples do exist, but compared to teachers' high hopes, effects are modest, narrow, and often only in one direction. One experiment randomly taught one of two structurally equivalent topics: (a) the algebra of arithmetic progression, or (b) the physics of constant acceleration.[52] Researchers then asked algebra students to solve the physics problems, and physics students to solve the algebra problems. Only 10% of the physics students used what they learned to solve the algebra problems. But a remarkable 72% of the algebra students used what they learned to solve the physics problems. Applying abstract math to concrete physics comes much more naturally than generalizing from concrete physics to abstract math.

More impressively, studying statistics enhances statistical reasoning on real-life questions outside the classroom. One research team phoned 193 male introductory statistics students from the University of Michigan in their homes. Interviewers withheld the fact that they were targeting statistics students. Half the subjects were interviewed in the semester's first week; the rest were interviewed in the semester's last week.[53] The "official" purpose of the phone call was to solicit students' opinions about sports. The true purpose was to see if statistics students would spontaneously apply their lessons to a novel topic (sports) in a nonacademic setting (their homes).[54] Researchers recorded the conversations, measuring the presence and quality of statistical reasoning.

A semester of statistics mattered, but the effect was uneven. Students substantially improved on two out of four statistically relevant questions. Why does the Rookie of the Year usually perform worse in his second year? At the beginning of the semester, only 16% gave a statistical answer; at the end of the semester, 37% did so. Why are top batting averages higher after two weeks of play than at the end of the season? At the beginning of the semester, 50% gave a statistical answer; at the end, 70% did so. The *quality* of statistical reasoning on these two questions improved as well. On the other two statistically relevant questions, however, the experimenters were surprised to find no gain.[55]

Compared to most experiments, the sports/statistics study found impressive transfer of learning. Compared to teachers' aspirations, however, the results are a let-down. The experimenters deliberately wrote easy questions, and the participants were students at one of the most elite universities in the country.[56] Yet statistical reasoning improved on only half the questions, and most students did not improve. Furthermore, the researchers measured statistical learning at its peak: the final week of the class. How much of their modest edge would intro stats students retain months or years after the final exam?

College majors also measurably hone *specific* kinds of reasoning. One ambitious study tested undergraduates at the University of Michigan during the first term of their first year, then retested the same students during the second term of their fourth year.[57] The test covered verbal reasoning, statistical reasoning, and conditional reasoning. Researchers included four kinds of majors: natural sciences, humanities, social sciences, and psychology.

Each major sharply improved on precisely one subtest. Social science and psychology majors became much better at statistical reasoning—the ability to apply "the law of large numbers and the regression or base rate principles" to both "scientific and everyday-life contexts." Natural science and humanities majors became much better at conditional reasoning—the ability to correctly analyze "if . . . then" and "if and only if" problems.

On remaining subtests, however, gains after three and half years of college were modest or nonexistent. Social scientists' verbal and conditional reasoning scores slightly fell. Psychologists' verbal scores slightly rose, but their conditional reasoning failed to improve. Natural science and humanities majors gained slightly in verbal reasoning, and modestly in statistical reasoning.

With zero transfer, psychologists could only statistically analyze psychological issues, and natural scientists could only conditionally reason about their scientific specialty. Matters are not quite so dire. As the researchers conclude, their results show "different undergraduate disciplines teach different kinds of reasoning to different degrees."[58] Yet their results also undermine the view that students gain general reasoning skills. Students primarily improve in the very tasks they study and practice. Even this isn't guaranteed; humanities majors' verbal reasoning barely budged.

The same researchers also measured the effect of two years of graduate training on verbal, statistical, and conditional reasoning.[59] The subjects were law students, medical students, and graduate students in psychology and chemistry at the University of Michigan. No one, not even law students, improved much in verbal reasoning. Chemists' scores on all three subtests stayed about the same. But medical and especially psychology students improved in statistical reasoning, and law, medical, and psychology students all improved in conditional reasoning.

Takeaway: if all goes well, students learn what they study and practice. Psychology and medical students heavily use statistics, so they improve in statistics; law and chemistry students rarely encounter statistics, so they don't improve in statistics. Why don't chemistry students improve in conditional reasoning? Because unlike psychology, medical, and law students, chemists have "little need to differentiate among the various types of causal relations because chemistry deals primarily with necessary-and-sufficient causes."[60] What chemistry students learn is . . . chemistry.

Actually, that's optimistic. Educational psychologists have also discovered that much of our knowledge is "inert." Students who excel on exams frequently fail to apply their knowledge to the real world.

Take physics. A student once joked, "Objects in motion remain in motion in the classroom, but come to rest on the playground," but the pedagogical problem is serious.[61] Renowned psychologist Howard Gardner explains:

> Researchers at Johns Hopkins, M.I.T., and other well-regarded universities have documented that students who receive honor grades in college-level physics courses are frequently unable to solve basic problems and questions encountered in a form slightly different from that on which they have been formally instructed and tested.[62]

If you throw a coin straight up, how many forces act on it midair? The textbook answer is "one": after it leaves your hand, the *only* force on the coin is gravity.[63] The popular answer, however, is "two": the force of the throw keeps sending it up, and the force of gravity keeps dragging it down. Popular with whom? Virtually everyone—physics students included.[64] At the beginning of the semester, only 12% of college students in introductory mechanics get the coin problem right. At the end of the semester, 72% still get it wrong. After students learn how to handle complex homework and exam problems, few apply their lessons to simple real-world cases.

The same goes for students in biology, mathematics, statistics, and, I'm embarrassed to say, economics.[65] I strive to teach my students how to "think like economists," to connect lectures to the real world and daily life. When teaching educational signaling in labor economics, I tell students:

> Do you think you're going to get a job that uses your knowledge of educational signaling? Probably not. Yet if you don't learn the material, employers hold it against you. That's the puzzle.

My exams are designed to measure comprehension, not memorization. They're completely open book. Yet students' performance reliably disappoints me. Half the answers repeat semirelevant passages from the notes and hope for mercy. In a good class, four exams out of forty demonstrate true economic understanding. Howard Gardner captures my experience perfectly:

> Nearly every teacher I know would claim to teach for understanding; certainly I would make that claim myself. But if pressed to demonstrate that our students understand . . . we soon realize how slender is the reed of our confidence.[66]

Transfer researchers usually begin their careers as idealists. Before studying educational psychology, they take their power to "teach students how to think" for granted. When they discover the professional consensus against transfer, they think they can overturn it. Eventually, though, young researchers grow sadder and wiser. The scientific evidence wears them down—and their firsthand experience as educators finishes the job. Hear the pedagogical odyssey of psychologist Douglas Detterman:

> When I began teaching, I thought it was important to make things as hard as possible for students so they would discover the principles for themselves. I thought the discovery of principles was a fundamental skill that students needed to learn and transfer to new situations. Now I view education, even graduate education, as the learning of information. I try to make it as easy for students as possible. Where before I was ambiguous about what a good paper was, I now provide examples of the best papers from past classes. Before, I expected students to infer the general conclusion from specific examples. Now I provide the general conclusion and support it with specific examples. In general, I subscribe to the principle that you should teach people exactly what you want them to learn in a situation as close as possible to the one in which the learning will be applied. I don't count on transfer and I don't try to promote it except by explicitly pointing out where taught skills may be applied.[67]

Detterman is admittedly fatalistic even for an educational psychologist. Many of his peers struggle to learn from the rare examples of successful transfer.[68] A few earnestly claim to have discovered novel teaching techniques that *do* reliably lead to transfer.[69] For our purposes, however, this debate is a red herring. Though some educational psychologists deny that education *must* yield minimal transfer, almost all admit that actually existing education *does* yield minimal transfer. The upshot: human capital purists can't credibly dismiss the disconnect between what we learn in school and what we do on the job. Relevance is highly relevant. If what you learn in school lacks obvious real-world applications, you'll probably never apply it. When a rare opportunity to use trigonometry knocks, it knocks too faintly to hear.

The clash between teachers' grand claims about "learning how to learn" and a century of careful research is jarring. Yet commonsense skepticism is a shortcut to the expert consensus. Teachers' plea that "we're mediocre at teaching what we measure, but great at teaching what we don't measure" is comically convenient. When someone insists their product has big, hard-to-see benefits, you should be dubious by default—especially when the easy-to-see benefits are small.

In the classroom, educators strive to achieve tangible, self-contained goals—like teaching key Civil War facts. Should we believe educators are *better* at intangible, open-ended goals like teaching students "how to think"? When we hand teachers an explicit goal and measure their success, it's disappointing. Should we believe teachers are *better* at achieving unmeasured afterthoughts? Students quickly forget most of the material we deliberately try to teach them. Should we believe that students retain *more* of the skills we idly hope they'll acquire?

You could object common sense cuts both ways. The strongest reason to believe in "learning how to learn" is also a commonsense claim:

Since physical exercise builds physical muscles, we should expect mental exercise to build mental muscles.

But on reflection, this is another reason to *dis*believe in "learning how to learn." You don't exercise your legs to improve your bench press. You don't even exercise your right leg to strengthen your left leg. Instead, you exercise the muscles you seek to build. Why would "mental muscles" be any less specific? Furthermore, when you stop going to the gym, your physical muscles soon atrophy.[70] Why would "mental muscles" be any slower to wither? If exercise analogies prove anything, they prove our education system rests on educators' conceit—the self-serving line that when we teach students whatever interests us, they durably acquire whatever skills they need to succeed in life.

Making You Smarter

While educators often promise to teach students how to think, they rarely vow to raise students' intelligence. Trying to "make your pupils smarter" smacks of hubris. However, when you look at data on IQ—psychologists' standard measure of intelligence—education matters. Summer vacation, intermittent attendance, delayed school entry, and dropping out all measurably depress IQ.[71] Some experimental early childhood programs have increased IQ by over 30 points—moving kids' performance from roughly the 2nd percentile to the 50th percentile of their age group.[72] Extra years of education usually seem to boost IQ.[73] Studies that carefully measure students' time show IQ rises more on school days than non–school days.[74] Isn't this conclusive evidence that education makes us smarter?

Not really. While the facts are secure, the interpretation is shaky. The first major worry: *people can sharply improve on virtually any test by practicing*—and a little practice goes a long way. A major review pulled together fifty relevant studies of practice on cognitive tests. On average, "a candidate who scored at the 50th percentile on the first test could be expected to score at the 60th percentile on the second test and at the 71st percentile on the third test."[75] Explicit coaching—"teaching to the test"—works even better.[76]

A cockeyed optimist might rejoice that mankind is only a few hours of practice away from massive intelligence gains. This optimism, however, leads to absurdity: Can you transform average students into geniuses by handing them the answer key before their IQ test? Most researchers draw the sobering conclusion that test preparation yields only "hollow gains."[77] Preparation inflates *measured* intelligence without raising *genuine* intelligence.[78]

The fact that test preparation yields large but hollow gains hardly shows that *all* large gains are hollow. Still, the power of preparation should make us suspicious. Maybe education raises IQ because education is a diluted form of IQ test preparation. As psychologist Stephen Ceci explains:

> It is through direct forms of instruction . . . that children learn the answers to many of the questions that appear on a popular IQ (and other aptitude) tests. For example, within a given grade level there is a correlation between the

total number of hours of schooling a child receives and scores on verbal and mathematical aptitude tests. Similarly, there are negative correlations between the total number of teacher or student absences and scores on such tests. Also, quantitative and language-related scores are strongly correlated with the length of the school day and with the actual amount of time on task, beginning in first grade. So it makes intuitive sense that much of the knowledge that aptitude tests, including IQ, tap is accumulated through direct encounters with the educational system. Answers to questions on the WISC-R, such as "In what continent is Egypt?"; "Who wrote Hamlet?"; "What is the boiling point of water?"; and "How many miles is New York from L.A.?" are probably learned through direct teaching methods. Teachers may not be aware that they are teaching answers to questions on IQ tests, but this is precisely what they are doing in their history, reading, literature, geography, and math classes.[79]

Ceci also notes that schools teach students to offer the *kinds* of answers IQ tests favor. How are an apple and an orange alike? IQ tests award only partial credit for such factually correct answers as, "They're both round," "They're both edible," or "They both have seeds." For full credit, you have to say, "They're both fruits." School also trains students to sit still and pay attention. These help test scores but aren't "intelligence" in any normal sense of the word.[80]

If education truly raised intelligence, education would enhance performance on all sorts of cognitive challenges—in and out of the classroom. In reality, the gains are spotty. Probably the best study of the effect of education on IQ looks at the scores of over one hundred thousand 18-year-old Swedish men.[81] The researchers knew each student's exact age and test date, yielding a precise measure of their time in school. Major finding: school days noticeably raise scores on synonym and technical comprehension subtests *without* raising scores on spatial and logic subtests. The authors infer that education raises "crystallized intelligence" but not "fluid intelligence." A better interpretation, though, is that education improves some specific skills without increasing intelligence *at all*. Given how little students usually learn, Swedish schools' measured effect on the synonym and technical comprehension subtests is impressive. Still, to equate subject-specific gains with higher intelligence smacks of double-counting.

Worries about "hollow IQ gains" are admittedly a tad philosophical. The other major worry about the effect of education on IQ, however, is completely pragmatic. Suppose for the sake of argument that

IQ perfectly captures genuine intelligence. When IQ goes up, genuine intelligence automatically rises in sync. Even in this scenario, a large effect of education on IQ would be impressive only if it were *lasting*. In the short story "Flowers for Algernon," a mentally retarded man named Charlie Gordon receives an experimental treatment to cure his disability.[82] Charlie's intelligence eventually rises to the level of genius, but the transformation is tragically short-lived. By the end of the story, all of Charlie's intellectual progress evaporates. In one sense, the experiment worked. In a deeper sense, it failed.

"Flowers for Algernon" is science fiction, but life mirrors art. Making IQ higher is easy. *Keeping* IQ higher is hard. Researchers call this "fadeout." Fadeout for early childhood education is especially well documented. After six years in the famous Milwaukee Project, experimental subjects' IQs were 32 points higher than controls'. By age fourteen, this advantage had declined to 10 points.[83] In the Perry Preschool program, experimental subjects gained 13 points of IQ, but all this vanished by age 8.[84] Head Start raises preschoolers' IQs by a few points, but gains disappear by the end of kindergarten.[85]

You could object that preschoolers are unusually prone to forget what they learn, but the pattern extends all through high school. Extensive research on "summer learning loss" compares students' scores at the end of one school year to their scores at the beginning of the next school year. The average student intellectually regresses roughly one full month during a three-month summer vacation.[86] The older the students, the *steeper* their decline. For reading, to take the clearest case, first- and second-graders actually slightly improve over the summer. By the time students are in middle school, however, one summer vacation wipes out over three months of reading proficiency.[87]

Reformers tend to see summer learning loss as an argument for year-round school. If summer makes students stupid, let's abolish summer. The flaw in their thinking: everyone graduates *eventually*. Once you graduate, you're no longer in school—and learning loss kicks in. To quote "Tiger Mother" Amy Chua, "Every day you don't practice is a day that you're getting worse."[88]

Does education have *any* effect on genuine intelligence? Despite decades of research, we really don't know. What we do know is that education has far less effect than meets the eye. The effect of education on intelligence may not be *entirely* hollow, but it is largely hollow. The effect of education on intelligence may not be *entirely* temporary, but it is largely temporary.

In any case, suppose each year of school permanently made you a whopping 3 IQ points smarter. According to standard estimates, this would raise your earnings by about 3%, leaving a supermajority of the education premium unexplained.[89]

How People Get Good at Their Jobs

If schools teach few job skills, transfer of learning is mostly wishful thinking, and the effect of education on intelligence is largely hollow, how on earth do human beings get good at their jobs? The same way you get to Carnegie Hall: *practice*. People learn by doing specific tasks over and over. To get better at piloting, you fly planes; to get better at obstetrics, you deliver babies; to get better at carpentry, you build houses.[90]

For the unskilled, progress is easy. Given commonsense conditions, it's almost guaranteed. In the words of K. Anders Ericsson, the world's leading expert on expertise, novices improve as long as they are, "1) given a task with a well-defined goal, 2) motivated to improve, 3) provided with feedback, and 4) provided with ample opportunities for repetition and gradual refinements of their performance."[91] Before long, though, the benefit of mere practice plateaus. To really get good at their jobs, people must advance to *deliberate* practice. They must exit their comfort zone—raise the bar, struggle to surmount it, repeat. As Ericsson and coauthors explain:

> You need a particular kind of practice—*deliberate practice*—to develop expertise. When most people practice, they focus on the things they already know how to do. Deliberate practice is different. It entails considerable, specific, and sustained efforts to do something you *can't* do well—or even at all.[92]

Attaining world-class expertise in chess, music, math, tennis, swimming, long-distance running, writing, and science requires many years of deliberate practice.[93] Fortunately, the labor market offers plenty of subpinnacle opportunities. A few thousand hours of deliberate practice rarely makes you a superstar, but is ample time to get good in most occupations.[94] People don't become skilled workers by dabbling in a dozen different school subjects. They become skilled workers by devoting years to their chosen vocation—by doing their job and striving to do it better.[95]

Discipline and Socialization

"I doubt very seriously whether anyone will hire me."
"What do you mean, babe? You a fine boy with a good education."
"Employers sense in me a denial of their values."

—John Kennedy Toole, *A Confederacy of Dunces*[96]

Educators boast that they teach their students how to think. Laymen tend to favor a colder, more credible story about what kids learn in school: discipline and socialization. Life isn't a picnic—or a game of solitaire. Schools build discipline by making students show up on time, sit still, keep their mouths shut, follow orders, and stay awake. Schools build social skills by making students cooperate, manage conflict, work as a team, dress nicely, and speak properly. The typical worker spends the day doing boring work in a hierarchical organization. Perhaps education acclimates children to their future role.

These are all plausible claims, especially when you ponder the many thousands of hours of drudgery and mingling students endure. Yet discipline-and-socialization stories overlook a vital question: *If students weren't in school, what would they be doing instead?* Young adults who spent their teens sitting home alone playing video games might be feral. But what if young adults spent their teens working? Work teaches discipline. Work teaches social skills. Why would education be any better at readying us for the world of work than the world of work itself?

What school inculcates is not so much the work ethic as the *school* ethic. The two ethics do not perfectly coincide. Both school and work teach you to follow orders and cooperate with others. Yet they define and measure success differently. School elevates abstract understanding over practical results, passing exams over passing the market test, and fairness over dollars and cents. Andrew Carnegie caustically captures this tension:

Men have sent their sons to colleges to waste their energies upon obtaining a knowledge of such languages as Greek and Latin, which are of no more practical use to them than Choctaw. . . . They have been crammed with the details of petty and insignificant skirmishes between savages, and taught to exalt a band of ruffians into heroes; and we have called them "educated." They have been "educated" as if they were destined for life upon some other planet than this. . . . What they have obtained has served to imbue them with false ideas and to give them a distaste for practical life. . . . Had they gone into active work during the years spent at college they would have been better educated men in every true sense of that term. The fire and energy have been stamped out of them, and how to so manage as to live a life of idleness and not a life of usefulness has become the chief question with them.[97]

Educators who dismiss Carnegie as a Neanderthal or philistine prove my point: school inculcates many attitudes that, regardless of their moral worth, impede on-the-job success. If you're preparing kids for their adult roles, a year of work experience instills more suitable discipline and socialization than a year of school.

The imperfect overlap between the school ethic and the work ethic is especially blatant in modern American colleges. Fifty years ago, college was a full-time job. The typical student spent 40 hours a week in class or studying.[98] Since the early 1960s, effort collapsed across the board. "Full-time" college students average 27 hours of academic work per week—and only 14 hours of studying. As the leading researchers on this topic explain:

No group appears to have bucked the trend. . . . Study times fell for all choices of major, overall and within both subperiods. Students at liberal arts colleges studied more than other students, but study times fell at all types of colleges. . . . Finally, data on SAT scores and school size . . . show declines in study time for students of all ability levels and at universities of all sizes and levels of selectivity.[99]

What are students doing with their extra free time? Having fun. Instead of being socialized for lives of boring work in hierarchical organizations, they're being socialized for lives of play and self-expression. As Richard Arum and Josipa Roksa frostily remark in their *Academically Adrift*:

If we presume that students are sleeping eight hours a night, which is a generous assumption given their tardiness and at times disheveled appearance in early morning classes, that leaves 85 hours a week for other activities. . . . What is this additional time spent on? It seems to be spent mostly on socializing and recreation.[100]

A week in modern college is a great way to teach students that life *is* a picnic:

> A recent study of University of California undergraduates reported that while students spent thirteen hours a week studying, they also spent twelve hours socializing with friends, eleven hours using computers for fun, six hours watching television, six hours exercising, five hours on hobbies, and three hours on other forms of entertainment.[101]

Grade inflation completes the idyllic package by shielding students from negative feedback. The average GPA is now 3.2.[102] Instead of making students conform and submit, college showers students with acceptance. This doesn't merely fail to prepare students for their future roles; it actively *un*prepares them. College raises students' expectations to unrealistic heights, leaving future employers the chore of dragging graduates back down to earth.

Yes, there's always the "college molds character compared to sitting alone in your basement playing video games" fallback. The relevant alternative, though, is a full-time job—and compared to that, college is a joke. As long as you avoid rare, demanding paths like engineering and premed in college, you bask in the warmth of a four-year vacation. If that's "socialization," it's dysfunctional socialization.

In any case, imagine school and work really were equally effective ways to shape kids' souls to suit the workplace. How effective would that be? Labor economists have spent decades measuring the reward for work experience. A year of experience typically raises income by 2–3%.[103] Some of this payoff has to reflect task-specific learning as opposed to discipline and socialization. Say it's half. Then a year's worth of character building is worth a 1–1.5% raise. Most estimates say a year of education is *many* times more lucrative. Even on generous assumptions, then, discipline and socialization explain a tiny sliver of the education premium.

Who You Know

About half of all workers used contacts—relatives, friends, acquaintances—to land their current job.[104] You could argue that education pays despite "low measured learning" because we're inappropriately measuring *what* you know instead of *who* you know. Perhaps studying is overrated.

Instead, the upwardly mobile student wins friends and influences people. The better your school, the better your connections after graduation.

This story has a kernel of truth and is occasionally dead right. Overall, though, it's weak. The modern economy is vast and diverse. Few of the students you meet will end up in your line of work—even if they share your major. As a result, they'll probably never be in a position to help you. If you're looking for a good job, you don't want generic contacts. You want *relevant* contacts.[105]

Friends in your narrowly defined occupation are quite lucrative.[106] So are older male relatives (father, uncle, grandfather) who know the boss or vouch for you.[107] When researchers estimate the *average* benefit of "contacts" or "social networks," though, some find a positive effect on employment and wages, some no effect, and others a negative effect.[108] If this seems implausible, bear in mind: even if your cousin or college roommate plainly "got you your job," you might have swiftly found as good or better a job on your own.

Who *does* meet useful contacts in school? If you want a job in education, school is the ideal place to network. Once I resolved to become an economics professor, I strove to meet other economics professors. One, Tyler Cowen, got me my job. (I also met many philosophy, history, and law professors. Career payoff so far: zero.) If you're earning a professional degree in law or medicine, or majoring in more vocational subjects like engineering, you and your classmates will plausibly trade career favors down the line. Stanford's computer science program could be your passport to Silicon Valley. At some elite schools, fraternities funnel brothers into finance and consulting.[109] Hell Week could land you on Wall Street. Normally, however, lucrative networking begins *after* students graduate and find a niche in the sprawling modern economy.

The False Promises of Education

> We asked the young people whether they remember having learned something important at school. It seemed to be a difficult question for most. Often the question was followed by long silences and embarrassed laughs.
>
> —Elina Lahelma, "School Is for Meeting Friends"[110]

Education seems to pay. Human capital purism advances a single explanation: education pays because education teaches lots of useful job skills. A tempting story . . . until you stare at what schools teach, what students learn, and what adults know. Then human capital purism looks not just overstated, but Orwellian. *Most* of what schools teach has no value in the labor market. Students fail to learn *most* of what they're taught. Adults forget *most* of what they learn. When you mention these awkward facts, educators speak to you of miracles: studying anything makes you better at everything. Never mind educational psychologists' century of research exposing these so-called miracles as soothing myths.

An optimist could admittedly reframe my summary of the facts. If most of what schools teach has no value in the labor market, then *some* of what schools teach has value. If students fail to learn most of what they're taught, then students learn *some* of what they're taught. If adults forget most of what they learn, then adults remember *some* of what they learn.

Fair enough. Yet the question remains: Can the modest job skills we learn in school explain the extra pay we earn after graduation? The answer hinges on the size of the premium. At least on the surface, modern education seems highly lucrative. Does modest learning genuinely lead to immodest earning? Or are the apparently ample rewards of education a statistical illusion?

CHAPTER 3

The Puzzle Is Real

The Handsome Rewards of Useless Education

The world is full of unemployable experts. If you master all there is to know about the Civil War or *Star Trek*, employers will still scoff that you can't "do anything" with your esoteric knowledge. A tempting inference is that all the useless coursework students endure pays as poorly as any other geeky hobby. Daily life feeds temptation: every unemployed college grad and cashier with a Ph.D. seem like further proof that conventional academic curricula fail the market test.

When you peruse income statistics, however, you behold a starkly different picture. As individuals' schooling rises, so does their pay. The earnings gap is enormous. In 2011, holders of advanced degrees made almost *three* times as much as high school dropouts. Each step up the educational ladder seems to count. A high school diploma may sound unworthy of mention in our Information Age, but high school graduates out-earn dropouts by 30%.[1] The numbers come straight from the Census Bureau. Check out Table 3.1 to see the pattern for full-time, year-round adult workers.

Table 3.1: Average Earnings by Educational Attainment (2011)

	Some High School	High School Graduate	Bachelor's Degree	Master's Degree
Average $ Earnings	31,201	40,634	70,459	90,265
Premium over H.S.	−23%	+0%	+73%	+122%
Source: United States Census Bureau 2012a.				

These stats are solid, but what do they mean? Mainstream defenders of education tend to take the numbers at face value. Since college grads earn 73% more than high school grads, expect a 73% raise when you finish college. Contrarian detractors of education tend to take the numbers at *no* value. For all we know, college grads would have made 73%

extra even if they never set foot on a college campus. Each side snubs the other. Defenders of education say, "Education must provide lots of job skills, because it pays so handsomely"; detractors of education say, "Education can't pay handsomely, because it provides so few job skills."

Last chapter sided with detractors: education as we know it fails to transform students into skilled workers. This chapter, however, sides with defenders: education as we know it successfully transforms students into *rich* workers. After tempering defenders' optimism about learning, it's time to temper detractors' pessimism about earning.

Affirming the financial rewards of education often confuses critics of the signaling model. Isn't it contradictory to claim the market rewards irrelevant education? No; a thousand times no. The signaling model's whole purpose is to explain why education raises income more than job skills. Unless education has a larger effect on income than on job skills, there's nothing for the model to explain. The case for the signaling model is *strongest* if students learn zero in school—and employers treat graduates like kings.

My task would be simple—and the chapter short—if optimism about earning were bulletproof. Alas, matters are more complex. The raw numbers in Table 3.1 almost certainly exaggerate education's financial reward. Most of the statistical complaints you've heard—and several you haven't—hold water. Yet once we fix every major flaw with the raw numbers, a hefty effect of education on earnings persists.

Credit Where Credit Is Due: The Specter of Ability Bias

Human capital and signaling models both take the effect of education on income for granted. Should they be more skeptical? Key doubt: The labor market pays for the *combined* effect of two traits that go hand in hand: schooling and preexisting ability. As Nobelist James Heckman puts it, "Ability and education are distinct, and both have economic rewards."[2] To properly measure the effect of education on earnings, to avoid what economists call "ability bias," you must compare workers with equal ability but *un*equal education.[3]

Consider Bill Gates, Harvard's most famous dropout. He plainly had the raw talent to finish his studies. Gates was already a prize-winning programmer by his sophomore year.[4] It's unsurprising, then, that he out-earned run-of-the-mill college dropouts. To scan Table 3.1, then announce, "Gates would have earned 73% more if he'd finished college," is obtuse.

The same holds for everyone besides Bill Gates. The typical high school dropout was a below-average high school student. Dropouts who wonder how much they would have earned if they'd stayed in school should not, therefore, compare themselves to average high school graduates. They should compare themselves to *below-average* high school graduates. The typical college grad, similarly, was an above-average high school student. B.A.s who wonder what they owe to their college diploma should not compare themselves to average high school graduates. They should compare themselves to *above-average* high school graduates.

The effect of education on income is like the effect of athletic practice on athletic prowess. People who practice more play better. Professional athletes practice the most and play the best. This doesn't mean I can be a professional football player if I practice enough. Why? Because professionals have *two* separate advantages over me: practice *and* preexisting athletic ability—strength, size, agility, aggressiveness, youth, pain tolerance, and so on. To properly measure the benefit of football practice, to avoid ability bias, you shouldn't compare me to pros who practice a lot. You should compare me to 165-pound 46-year-old nerds with bad knees who practice a lot.

So far this book has raced the human capital model against the signaling model. Ability bias challenges *both* models. Human capital, signaling, and ability bias are three separate, competing stories about education, skill, and income. These stories are easiest to grasp in their pure forms—and each takes a stand on three distinct issues (see Table 3.2).

Table 3.2: Human Capital, Signaling, and Ability Bias

Story	Visibility of Skill	Education's Effect on Skill	Education's Effect on Income
Pure Human Capital	Perfect	WYSIWYG	WYSIWYG
Pure Signaling	Zero	Zero	WYSIWYG
Pure Ability Bias	Perfect	Zero	Zero
⅓ Human Capital, ⅓ Signaling, ⅓ Ability Bias	2/3	1/3*WYSIWYG	2/3* WYSIWYG
WYSIWYG = "What You See Is What You Get."			

Issue #1: *Visibility of skill.* In the pure human capital and pure ability bias stories, skill is obvious. Employers effortlessly, instantly, and infallibly know what workers can and cannot do. In the pure signaling story, in contrast, skill is invisible. Employers must *infer* your skill from your resume.

Issue #2: *Education's effect on skill.* In the pure human capital story, schooling enhances skill. Indeed, schooling is the sole reason why more-educated workers are more skilled than less-educated workers: What You See Is What You Get. In the pure signaling and pure ability bias models, in contrast, schooling has zero effect on skill. If students learn anything useful, they forget it all before joining the workforce.

Issue #3: *Education's effect on income.* The pure human capital story says schooling raises your income by enhancing your skill. The pure signaling story says schooling raises your income by *certifying* your skill. Their bottom lines match: schooling raises your income. Indeed, schooling is the sole reason why more-educated workers out-earn less-educated workers: What You See Is What You Get. In the pure ability bias story, though, schooling has zero effect on income. Since skill is obvious to employers, and schooling fails to enhance skill, schooling does not pay.

Given a clear explanation, most people readily grasp the conflict between human capital and its rivals. Yet even experts occasionally confuse signaling with ability bias. Both stories agree that employers value workers' skill; both deny that schooling enhances workers' skill. The two stories diverge on the question of *visibility*. In a pure signaling story, employers never see your skill. So if your skills mismatch your credentials, the labor market rewards your credentials, not your skills. In a pure ability bias story, in contrast, employers see your skill plain as day. So if your skills mismatch your credentials, the labor market rewards your skills, not your credentials.

Although human capital, signaling, and ability bias are best grasped in their pure forms, the truth is almost surely a mixture of the three. Suppose the mixture is one-third human capital, one-third signaling, one-third ability bias. In this scenario, employers gradually and fallibly detect the right stuff, so the labor market rewards *both* skills and credentials. If you're good, you can rise without diplomas. Still, unless you're a Bill Gates superstar, you'll rise faster and higher with the right diplomas to aid your ascent.

Correcting for Ability Bias: What You See Is More Than
What You Get

How big is ability bias? The most compelling answers (a) measure ability, then (b) compare the incomes of people with different educations but identical ability. Statistically speaking, you want to estimate the effect of education on earnings, correcting for ability. A solid answer required solid measures of *all* abilities that matter.

In practice, education economists who worry about ability bias focus heavily on cognitive ability, especially general intelligence as measured by IQ. Imperfect though they are, IQ tests are a good-faith effort to measure how smart people are, and predict success inside and outside the classroom.[5] Many researchers have recalculated the education premium after correcting for IQ and other measures of cognitive ability. Almost all the research has two conclusions in common.

First, IQ pays. Holding education constant, an extra point of IQ raises earnings by about 1%.[6]

Second, holding IQ constant, the education premium shrinks but never vanishes. In 1999, a comprehensive review of earlier studies found that correcting for IQ reduces the education premium by an average of 18%.[7] When researchers correct for scores on the Armed Forces Qualification Test (AFQT), an especially high-quality IQ test, the education premium typically declines by 20–30%.[8] Correcting for mathematical ability may tilt the scales even more; the most prominent researchers to do so report a 40–50% decline in the education premium for men and a 30–40% decline for women.[9] Internationally, correcting for cognitive skill cuts the payoff for years of education by 20%, leaving clear rewards of mere years of schooling in all 23 countries studied.[10] The highest serious estimate finds the education premium falls 50% after correcting for students' twelfth-grade math, reading, and vocabulary scores, self-perception, perceived teacher ranking, family background, and location.[11]

A thinner body of research weighs the importance of so-called noncognitive abilities such as conscientiousness and conformity.[12] The results parallel those for IQ: noncognitive ability pays, and correcting for noncognitive ability reduces the education premium. Correcting for

AFQT, self-esteem, and fatalism (belief about the importance of luck versus effort) reduces the education premium by a total of 30%.[13] The sole study correcting for detailed personality tests finds the education premium falls 13%.[14] The highest serious estimate says that once you correct for intelligence and background, correcting for attitudes (such as fear of failure, personal efficacy, and trust) and personal behavior (such as church attendance, television viewing, and cleanliness) further cuts the education premium by 37%.[15]

There are admittedly two big reasons to mistrust these basic results: reverse causation and missing abilities. The former could systematically overstate the severity of ability bias. The latter could systematically understate the severity of ability bias. Need we fret over either flaw?

Reverse causation. When you estimate the education premium correcting for ability X, you implicitly assume education does not enhance X. If this assumption is false, correcting for X leads to misleadingly low estimates of the effect of education on earnings. The best remedy for this "reverse causation" problem is to measure ability, then estimate the effect of *subsequent* education on earnings.

Research on cognitive ability bias routinely applies this remedy—and uncovers little evidence of reverse causation. The comprehensive review article mentioned earlier separated studies into two categories: those that measured IQ *before* school completion and those that measured IQ *after* school completion. If reverse causation were at work, studies that relied on IQ after completion would report more ability bias than studies that relied on IQ before completion. In fact, both categories yield similar estimates of cognitive ability bias.[16] Researchers who rely on the AFQT and related tests reach a similar result: When you correct for cognitive ability in 1980, the payoff for posttest education falls at least as much as the payoff for pretest education.[17] Correcting for mathematical ability in the senior year of high school shaves 25–32% off the male college premium and 4–20% off the female college premium.[18]

What about reverse causation from education to *non*cognitive ability? Truth be told, relevant research is sparse. A few papers grapple with the issue, with mixed results.[19] Most research, however, either measures noncognitive ability and education at the same point in time, or fails to distinguish between the effect of pre- and posttest education. The shortage of evidence hardly shows reverse causation is a serious problem, but caution is in order.

Missing abilities. Correcting for ability doesn't fully eliminate ability bias unless you measure *all* relevant abilities. Are there any important abilities we've overlooked?

Family background—via nature or nurture—is a plausible contender. Perhaps wealthy families use their money to help their kids get good educations and good jobs. Maybe college is a four-year vacation for rich kids—and a status symbol for their parents. Perhaps children from large families get less educational and professional assistance from their parents. Maybe well-educated workers come from high-achieving families—and would have been high achievers even without their schooling. The mechanism is hard to nail down, but most researchers find correcting for family background reduces the education premium by 0–15%.[20]

On reflection, though, correcting for family background probably "double-counts." Both cognitive and noncognitive ability are moderately to highly hereditary, so you should correct for individual ability before you conclude family background overstates school's payoff.[21] This caveat matters. Rare studies that correct for intelligence *and* family background find that correcting for intelligence alone suffices.[22] Armed with good measures of cognitive *and* noncognitive ability, we can probably safely ignore family background.[23]

The most troubling evidentiary gap: researchers usually settle for mediocre measures of noncognitive ability. Most studies that correct for noncognitive ability rely on one or two hastily measured traits and find only mild ability bias.[24] Yet when asked, employers hail the importance of workers' attitude and motivation—and the study with the best measures of noncognitive ability finds large ability bias.[25] Until better measures come along, we should picture existing results as a lower bound on noncognitive ability bias rather than a solid estimate.

So how severe is ability bias, all things considered? For cognitive ability bias, 20% is a cautious estimate, and 30% is reasonable. For noncognitive ability bias, 5% is cautious, and 15% is reasonable. Figure 3.1 shows education premiums correcting for both abilities, assuming equal bias for all education levels.

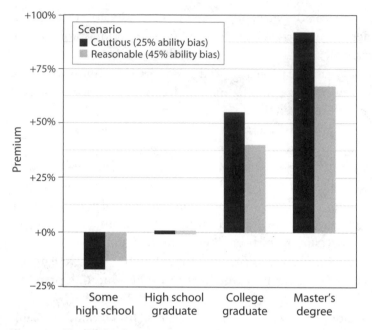

Figure 3.1: Two Ability Bias Scenarios
Source: Table 3.1 and text.

Correcting for ability gives the education premium quite a haircut—but not a shaved head. Education has a large payoff in every scenario, but the payoff you think you see is bigger than the payoff you really get. On the reasonable assumption of 30% cognitive plus 15% noncognitive ability bias, dropping out of high school cuts income by almost 15%, a college degree boosts income by 40%, and a master's degree boosts income by almost 70%. When fans of education trumpet the raw education premium, skeptics are right to protest, "College graduates and high school graduates differ in *many* ways besides the time they sat in classrooms." Yet after correcting for all the differences we see or suspect, education still pays.

Labor Economists versus Ability Bias

Labor economists aren't merely attuned to the possibility of ability bias. They've long felt a professional responsibility to measure it. But over the last quarter century, labor economists have surprisingly moved to the view that there's not much bias to measure. A famous review of the evidence by eminent economist David Card concludes ability bias is small, nonexistent, or even negative.[26] I call this verdict the Card Consensus. Many, perhaps most, elite labor economists not only embrace it but rely on it for practical guidance. We see the Card Consensus in top scholarly venues like the *Journal of Economic Literature*.

> The return to an additional year of education obtained for reasons like compulsory schooling or school-building projects is more likely to be greater, than lower, than the conventionally estimated return to schooling.[27]

We see the Card Consensus in top policy initiatives like the Brookings Institution's Hamilton Project:

> It's possible (and even likely) that individual college graduates have different aptitudes and ambitions, and might even have access to different levels of family resources. All of these factors can impact earnings. However, the evidence suggests that these factors don't drive the impressive return to college; instead the increased earning power of college graduates appears to be caused by their educational investments.[28]

Even analysts who don't cite the Card Consensus enjoy its protection. Well-publicized calculations of the "value of college" typically ignore ability bias altogether.[29] The Card Consensus neuters criticism of this omission. How can you attack a tacit "0% ability bias" assumption as a fatal flaw when plenty of experts stand ready to defend it as a harmless simplification?

This is a disorienting intellectual situation. Statistically naive laymen infer causation from correlation: since college grads earn 73% more than high school grads, college causes a 73% raise. Economists who *don't* specialize in labor smirk at the laymen's naïveté; they take sizable ability bias for granted. But economists who *do* specialize in labor now largely stand with *laymen*. While ability bias is intuitively plausible, the Card Consensus tells us, "Move along, nothing to see here."

What about abundant research from last section that detects hefty ability bias? The Card Consensus barely acknowledges it.[30] Why not? Labor economists' most common rationale is that no one can measure *all* the abilities that cause both academic and career success. True enough; but that just means ability bias is *worse* than it looks. Supporters of the Card Consensus also occasionally muse that high-ability students might leave school sooner:

> Some people cut their schooling short so as to pursue more immediately lucrative activities. Sir Mick Jagger abandoned his pursuit of a degree at the London School of Economics in 1963 to play with an outfit known as the Rolling Stones. . . . No less impressive, Swedish épée fencer Johan Harmenberg left MIT after 2 years of study in 1979, winning a gold medal in the 1980 Moscow Olympics, instead of earning an MIT diploma. Harmenberg went on to become a biotech executive and successful researcher. These examples illustrate how people with high ability—musical, athletic, entrepreneurial, or otherwise—may be economically successful without the benefit of an education. This suggests that . . . ability bias, can be negative as easily as positive.[31]

Straightforward rebuttal: name *any* ability the well-educated tend to lack. Outliers have ye always. But the well-educated are, on average, abler across the board. No one hears about someone quitting high school or college and says, "Wow, what a talented kid."

At best, then, the Card Consensus casually throws away a large body of contrary evidence to get off the ground. But it's worse than that. The Card Consensus casually throws away the *best* evidence. Worried you're improperly giving school credit for preexisting ability? There's a clear statistical cure: measure preexisting ability to allow an apples-to-apples comparison of people with equal ability but unequal schooling. The cures the Card Consensus prizes, in contrast, are anything but clear. Instead of sending researchers in search of better ability measures, it sends them in search of "quasi-experiments"—naturally occurring situations that *mimic* experiments.

As a result, labor economists have collected a zoo of alleged educational quasi-experiments. Some study twins. As long as identical twins have equal ability but unequal educations, education's true payoff equals their earnings gap divided by their education gap.[32] Other scholars study the effect of season of birth, on the theory that kids who are young for their grade are less legally eligible to drop out of high school.[33] Since 2000, researchers have been most transfixed by changes in compulsory attendance laws. If government forces students who would have dropped out to stay in school, what happens to their income after graduation?[34] While technically impressive, all these papers raise more questions than they answer. To treat changes in compulsory attendance laws as a quasi-experiment, for example, we must assume states change these laws at random—or at least for reasons unrelated to the labor market.

Once a quasi-experimental approach picks up steam, moreover, critics usually uncover deep flaws. Identical twins with different educations *don't* have identical ability; the more educated twin is usually the smarter twin.[35] Season of birth is not random; it correlates with health, region, and possibly income.[36] On closer look, the supposed fruits of U.S. compulsory attendance laws mask unrelated regional trends, especially in the South.[37] None of this means quasi-experimental studies of the education premium are worthless, or their critics invariably on target.[38] But compared to directly measuring preexisting ability, such studies are speculative and unconvincing. Since the cleanest approach reveals hefty ability bias, and the messy alternatives yield mixed results, we should reject the Card Consensus in favor of the commonsense view that ability bias is all too real.

Wheat versus Chaff?

How can education be so irrelevant yet so lucrative? There exists one clean explanation—call it the wheat/chaff theory—that *doesn't* appeal to signaling. In this story, education is a mixture of high-paid wheat (literacy, numeracy, critical thinking, technical training) and unpaid chaff (history, Latin, gym, French poetry). Schooling is lucrative because official statistics take "real" classes and "real" majors and lump them together with "Mickey Mouse" classes and "Mickey Mouse" majors.

The wheat/chaff theory is no ringing endorsement of the status quo. "The curriculum is a mixed bag of invaluable preparation and irrelevant filler," leaves ample room for improvement. You might even say wheat/chaff damns the education system with faint praise. Still, if this story is correct, the education system—for all its faults—genuinely transforms student lead into worker gold.

Looking at the evidence, however, the wheat/chaff story is exaggerated at best. Wheat arguably pays *more* than chaff, but chaff definitely pays too. Since most academic programs *require* ample chaff for admission and/or graduation, the financial rewards of accrued chaff should not surprise you.

Wheat, chaff, and coursework. Several research teams use people's high school transcripts to predict their adult earnings.[39] One of the earliest and most influential papers found that, ignoring preexisting ability, extra classes in math, foreign language, and industrial arts modestly increase earnings—but extra classes in English, social studies, and fine arts modestly *reduce* earnings. Correcting for ability, however, the bonus for extra math steeply declines. An extra year of foreign language has a higher payoff than the combined effect of an extra year of math *and* an extra year of science.[40]

Later researchers usually detect a bigger payoff for math—but not science. One pair of researchers finds that extra high school math raises pay for female college graduates. For males and less-educated women, however, the payoff for extra math is unclear.[41] Another research team reports that, correcting for ability, the following courses increase adult earnings: algebra/geometry (+1.9% higher income), average English (+1.5%), English literature (+1.5%), above-level English (+2.5%), and foreign language (+1.6%).[42] In Britain, high school students who attain the A-level in math earn almost 10% extra six years after graduation. However, natural science is no more lucrative than humanities or social science.[43] The most optimistic estimate of the benefit of high school math finds that Danish students who were nudged into advanced math eventually earned 21% more. The reason: students who take advanced math are more likely to go to college. Danes who took advanced math without upping their educational ambitions reaped little or no gain.[44]

Overall, these are *not* the patterns a devotee of the wheat/chaff theory should expect. Yes, math classes probably pay extra. But natural science classes probably don't. Yes, English courses sometimes seem lucrative. But foreign language courses *consistently* seem lucrative. A stubborn fan of the wheat/chaff theory could declare that physics is a "Mickey Mouse" subject and French is a "real" subject. The natural explanation, though, is that the wheat/chaff theory is overblown. Since employers value diplomas, and diplomas require chaff, chaff pays.

Wheat, chaff, and major. Wheat/chaff theory is right about one thing: major matters. Engineering majors are near the top of the financial pecking order. Business majors are roughly average. Education majors are near the bottom. The massive American Community Survey measures earnings for every college major you've heard of, and many you haven't.

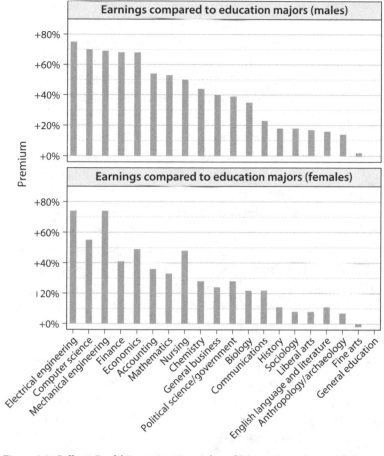

Figure 3.2: College Grads' Earnings: How Selected Majors Compare to Education Majors
Source: Altonji et al. 2012a, p. 216, selected majors, correcting for highest level of education attained. Observations included if the individual has at least a bachelor's degree, works >34 hours per week and >40 weeks per year, and is 23–59 years old. Original results converted from log dollars to percentages.

Fortunately for education majors, the *average* college premium is high (see Figure 3.2). In the American Community Survey, college grads earn 78% more than high school grads.[45] Business, the most common major, is roughly average. So while a pessimist could report, "Business majors earn 40% more than education majors," an optimist could with equal accuracy insist, "Education majors earn 27% more than high school graduates."[46]

As usual, don't take these numbers at face value. The major premium, like the college premium, steeply falls after correcting for ability. Strong students tend to major in high-earning subjects. Natural science majors, for example, outshine social science and humanities majors on the math *and* verbal sections of the SAT.[47] To measure the true effect of majoring in engineering rather than education, you need to correct for standardized test scores, high school grades, math background, and so on. When researchers make these vital corrections, the college major payoff falls by about half.[48]

Take engineering. On a naive reading, Figure 3.2 says the average education major would make 75% more money by switching to engineering. But the average education major's SAT scores, high school GPA, and math preparation say otherwise. How much extra would the average education major who switched really earn? Estimates from ten separate papers range from +25% to +60%, with an average of +44%. These corrected figures are actually optimistic, because they take the education major's ability to complete the engineering curriculum for granted. In practice, even eager engineering students frequently flee to easier majors.[49] When I was an undergrad at UC Berkeley, a popular T-shirt read, "As the limit of GPA approaches 0, go to poli sci." Ex–engineering students failed to see the humor.

In any case, a proper test of the wheat/chaff theory shouldn't compare high-earning college majors to low-earning college majors. Since the wheat/chaff theory claims that chaff is *worthless* in the job market, a proper test should compare low-earning college majors to high school grads. Figure 3.3 shows how various majors fare, correcting both the college premium and the major premium for preexisting ability.

The wheat/chaff theory is believable if you focus on the best-paid majors. To test wheat/chaff, though, you should scroll to *worst*-paid majors. Result: the least lucrative majors in the student handbook command an earnings premium of roughly 20%. Many widely ridiculed majors— anthropology, archaeology, English, liberal arts, sociology, history, communications—boost earnings by around 30%. Political scientists earn about as much as business students—and both slightly out-earn biologists.

For an economics professor, the most vivid strike against the wheat/ chaff theory is that econ majors earn almost as much as engineers.[50] I assure you that my profession makes near-zero effort to train our undergrads for the job market. We're easy on our students, even at elite

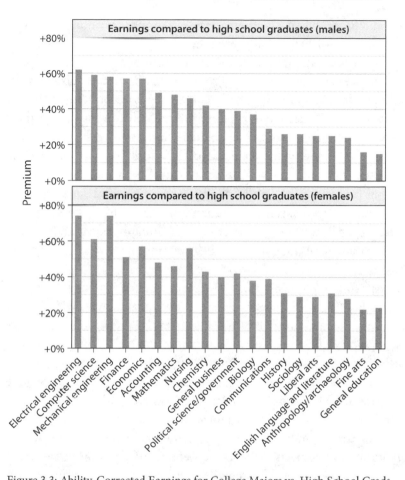

Figure 3.3: Ability-Corrected Earnings for College Majors vs. High School Grads
Source: Figure 3.2 and text, assuming:
(a) 45% ability bias for both the college and major premiums.
(b) Male business majors earn the average return for men; female business majors earn the average return to women.
Original results converted from log dollars to percentages.

schools like Berkeley and Princeton. Frankly, most econ professors practice a variant of the old Soviet adage, "We pretend to teach, they pretend to learn." During four years of study, our better students acquire only two marketable skills: elementary statistics, and ability to calculate a present discounted value.

How then do economists fill eight semesters of coursework? With watered-down versions of topics that fascinate the faculty: supply-

and-demand problems, mathematical economics, economic growth, and a long list of fields that are far less "applied" than they sound—macroeconomics, industrial organization, labor economics, regulation, public choice, economic history. From the standpoint of job skills, an economics degree is almost entirely chaff (except for budding economics professors). Yet despite our failure to prepare econ majors for their careers, the job market treats our graduates like engineers.

To be fair to the wheat/chaff theory, economics is an outlier. The most lucrative majors *tend* to be vocational. Engineers and computer scientists rule the roost—and finance, accounting, and nursing aren't far behind. Yet the fact remains: students can major in underwater basket weaving, enjoy a four-year party, and reasonably expect to out-earn peers who said "I'm not going to college because it's a waste of time" by 25%.

Wheat, chaff, and mismatch. How closely related is your job to your major? About 55% of college graduates say "closely related," 25% say "somewhat related," and 20% say "not related." Ego presumably skews these answers; who wants to confess their job and their major are "not related"? Yet the responses are meaningful. People who admit to mismatch earn 10–12% less than the typical person in their major. The more vocational the major, the lower the mismatch risk.[51]

While all these facts are consistent with the wheat/chaff theory, there's one telling discrepancy: the market penalty for mismatch is greater for *more* vocational subjects. Mismatched engineers and computer scientists earn over 20% less; mismatched health professions majors earn almost 30% less. For less vocational majors, in contrast, the mismatch penalty is roughly zero. Mismatched English and foreign language majors earn about 1% less. Mismatched philosophy and religion majors earn 20% extra![52] To capture the full benefit of a "real major," you need a job that uses your training. To capture the full benefit of a "Mickey Mouse major," in contrast, you need only a job that requires a degree. And contrary to the wheat/chaff theory, the full benefit of Mickey Mouse majors is nothing to laugh at.

Comedian Jay Leno is probably the most famous promoter of the wheat/chaff theory: "In college, philosophy majors study if the glass is half full or is the glass half empty. See, this prepares them for careers later as waiters."[53] Leno's not entirely wrong: philosophy is a low-paid major, and *some* philosophy majors do indeed wait tables. Statistically, though, Leno overstates. The average philosophy B.A. earns almost 30% more than an equally able worker who never went to college.[54] The degree may not help you do a better job but still helps you get a better job. And there's nothing special about philosophy. Studying *anything* pays more than studying nothing.

Is Credentialism a Creature of the State?

Why do employers reward useless education? The signaling model assumes they do so of their own free will: firms filter on credentials because credentials are the most cost-effective way to tell good workers from bad. Some argue, however, that government is ultimately to blame. Maybe useless education pays because good government jobs require credentials. Maybe useless education pays because good jobs require occupational licenses—and government limits such licenses to people with credentials. Maybe useless education pays because government persecutes IQ testing, forcing employers to rely on credentials instead. How do such stories fare against the facts?

Government credentialism. Some Third World governments employ the vast majority of their country's educated workers. In the 1960s, Egypt notoriously guaranteed every college graduate a government job. By 1988, two-thirds of Egypt's male college graduates and 80% of its female college graduates worked in the public sector.[55] Throughout the world, public-sector workers tend to be more educated than private-sector workers.[56] In the United States, 52% of government employees have a bachelor's degree or more, versus 34% for private employees.[57] Government positions for high school dropouts have all but vanished; between 1960 and 2000, the fraction of American public sector workers who hadn't finished high school dropped from 34% to 3%.[58]

If government credentialism really explained the payoff for useless education, we would expect the education premium to be *higher* in the public than the private sector. When government pays the educated more than they're worth, private employers need not follow suit. Business could instead scoff, "If government wants credentialed workers so badly, it can have them." Indeed, if government credentialism artificially inflates the education premium, refusing to match inflated government salaries is the profit-maximizing response.

In the real world, however, the private sector values education *more* than the public sector. Researchers consistently find that government pay scales are "compressed": governments overpay the least-educated workers and underpay the most-educated workers.[59] The U.S. federal government is a case in point (see Table 3.3).

Table 3.3: U.S. Education Premium, Public vs. Private Sector

	Federal Government			Private Sector		
	Average Total Compensation ($/hour)	Raise	Education Premium over H.S./ Less	Average Total Compensation ($/hour)	Raise	Education Premium over H.S./ Less
High School Diploma or Less	$39.10	–	–	$28.70	–	–
Some College	$45.70	$6.60	+17%	$34.70	$6.00	+21%
Bachelor's Degree	$57.20	$11.50	+46%	$49.70	$15.00	+73%
Master's Degree	$65.30	$8.10	+77%	$60.50	$10.80	+111%
Professional Degree or Doctorate	$73.20	$7.90	+87%	$89.60	$29.10	+212%

Source: Falk 2012, p. 11.
Estimates correct for occupation, experience, demographics, location, and size of employer.

Public debate focuses primarily on the issue: "Do we overpay federal workers?" On average, the answer is clearly Yes. But "Do we overpay federal workers *for credentials*?" is a distinct question—and the answer is No. The least-educated federal workers hit the jackpot. Yet once they're on the federal payroll, the *extra* rewards for credentials are modest. In the federal government, the average college grad makes $18.10 per hour more than the average worker who never went to college—a 46% premium. In the private sector, the average college graduate makes $21.00 per hour more than the average worker who never went to college—a 73% premium. In the federal government, a professional degree/doctorate gets you $16.00 per hour more than a bachelor's degree—a 28% pay bump. In the private sector, a professional degree/doctorate gets you $39.90 per hour more than a bachelor's degree—an 80% pay bump. Researchers find similar patterns for U.S. state and local government and abroad.[60] The rise of government unions seems a key factor.[61] Whatever its origin, the fact remains: if the private sector adopted the civil service pay scale, education would pay less, not more.

In any case, government jobs aren't numerous enough to explain why useless education pays. Yes, government is a major employer. Almost a quarter of college graduates works for federal, state, or local government.[62] But as we saw last chapter, over three-quarters of college degrees aren't vocational. By basic arithmetic, most people with such degrees end up in the private sector. If the private sector ignored nonvocational degrees, they would be far less lucrative.

Licensing. Occupational licensing is now more prevalent than union membership at its peak in the 1950s. Almost 30% of U.S. workers need a government license to legally do their jobs.[63] The most obvious effect of licensing is to raise wages by restricting competition. While payoffs vary from job to job, the average license raises income by 10–15%.[64]

Why bring this up? Because education and licensing often pair up. Only 12% of high school dropouts need a license to do their jobs—versus 44% with advanced degrees.[65] In some occupations, licenses *require* educational credentials. Given these facts, you could say, "Who needs the signaling model? Employers reward useless education because government forces them."

Yet this story has a fatal flaw: the education premium dwarfs the licensing premium. Suppose licensing boosts income by 15%. Since advanced degree holders are 32 percentage points more likely to need licenses than high school dropouts, licensing should, on average, boost advanced degree holder's earnings by 5%.[66] Even correcting for ability, however, master's degree holders earn *92%* more than dropouts.[67]

Licensing has large effects on the overall labor market. The topic deserves more attention from researchers, policy makers, and voters. The case for deregulation is strong; do we really need government to protect us from bad barbers, florists, or decorators? Yet if occupational licensing were abolished today, the market's rewards for useless education would barely budge.

IQ "laundering." Human capital purists often protest, "Why on earth do workers signal ability with a four-year degree instead of a three-hour IQ test?" My response: employers reasonably fear high-IQ, low-education applicants' low conscientiousness and conformity. Other critics of the education industry, however, have a more streamlined response: American employers rely on educational credentials rather than IQ tests because IQ tests are effectively illegal.

Thanks to the landmark 1971 *Griggs vs. Duke Power* case, later codified in the 1991 Civil Rights Act, anyone who hires by IQ risks pricey lawsuits. Why? Because IQ tests have a "disparate impact" on black and Hispanic applicants. To escape liability, employers must prove IQ testing is a "business necessity."[68] Since this legal hurdle is nigh insurmountable, employers turn to higher education to "launder" their workers' IQ scores. As Jonathan Last succinctly states:

> In *Griggs*, the Court held that employers could not rely on IQ-type tests if minorities performed relatively poorly on them. . . .
>
> So what employers do is this: They launder their request for test scores through the college system, because colleges *are* allowed to use such considerations. The universities get rich, students and their parents go into hock, and everyone pretends that Acme Widgets is hiring Madison because they value her B.A. in sociology from Haverford, and not because her *admission* to Haverford proved that she is bright—a fact which a three-hour written test could have demonstrated just as well. If *Griggs* were rolled back, it would upend the college system at a stroke.[69]

The IQ laundering story has a kernel of truth. Taken literally, the "business necessity" standard for IQ-based hiring is almost impossible to meet.[70] Yet this argument proves too much. Taken literally, relying on diplomas to "launder" IQ is equally illegal. The original *Griggs* case explicitly ruled that *both* IQ tests and educational credentials have a disparate impact, so *neither* is permissible unless employers prove their business necessity.[71] Yet in the real world, employers require educational credentials without bothering to prove a thing.

How do employers get away with it? Because the legal system normally ignores the letter of the law.[72] For all its bluster, *Griggs* "bans" nothing; it's more like a tax on out-of-favor hiring methods. Defenders of the IQ laundering story can't make their case by reciting the law. They have to show the tax on IQ-based hiring is steep enough to convince employers to hire educated workers for inflated prices instead of smart workers for bargain prices.

At the outset, the IQ laundering story faces an awkward fact: 10–30% of large employers *admit* they use cognitive ability tests.[73] The obvious retort is that without the "test tax," cognitive ability tests would be much more common. How can we measure the burden of the test tax? By studying enforcement: number of lawsuits, size of awards and settlements, legal costs, and plaintiffs' chance of winning. No one has comprehensive data, but existing research yields a ballpark figure.

The total number of employment discrimination cases filed in federal court peaked at about 23,000 in 1998, then gradually declined to about 14,000 in 2007.[74] The average cash award if you win a trial is large— about $1.1 million for 1990–2000.[75] But only 2% of plaintiffs actually go to trial and win, so annual awards sum to less than $600 million.[76] Most plaintiffs—58%—manage to get an out-of-court settlement.[77] Settlements are usually confidential, but the average settlement is about 5% as large as the average trial award.[78] Annual settlements therefore sum to less than $800 million.[79] If plaintiffs' lawyers work for a 40% contingency fee, and defense outspends them by a factor of three, employers' legal costs still sum to less than $1.7 billion. Updating these mid-1990s figures for inflation, employers' total legal burden sums to under $5 billion per year.

Compared to total labor costs, $5 billion is trivial. Now remember that $5 billion is a high estimate of the cost of *all* employment discrimination cases. The tax on IQ testing is far smaller. Only 4% of federal discrimination cases brought between 1987 and 2003 alleged disparate impact.[80] That amounts to under a thousand annual cases against *any* form of employment testing. If disparate impact cases cost the usual amount, employers' total test tax is under $200 million a year.[81]

Compared to the total upcharge a nation of employers pays for college graduates, this is a pittance. If IQ testing really let employers hire college-quality workers for high school wages, prudent employers would freely test IQ and treat the occasional lawsuit as a minor cost of doing business. Remember: correcting for ability, college grads earn 40% more than high school grads. If IQ laundering were a central function of higher education, courts could raise the test tax a hundredfold—and IQ testing would remain profitable.[82]

To the best of my knowledge, proponents of the IQ laundering story have never grappled with this arithmetic. Their main evidence is timing: The education premium started its meteoric ascent suspiciously soon after the 1971 *Griggs* decision. Yet on closer look, their own data show the college premium stayed flat for almost a decade.[83] Why would it take years for the slightest hint of IQ laundering to surface?

In long-run historical perspective, IQ laundering is even less credible. Employers amply rewarded college diplomas decades before discrimination laws were on the books. Between 1914 and 2005, the U.S. college premium was roughly U-shaped: high for the three decades before World War II, moderate for the three decades after World War II, then high again.[84] By prewar standards, today's college premium is normal. Instead of viewing the rise in the college premium as a belated response to discrimination law, why not view it as a rebound from an historic low?

Proponents of the IQ laundering story should also be troubled by the labor market's lackadaisical hunt for loopholes. The world is full of covert IQ tests. Employers could replace IQ tests with tests of "job knowledge," "skill," or "problem solving." Don't want to leave a paper trail? Measure IQ with intellectually challenging interviews. If employers' hands are tied, ambitious applicants will gladly help them bend the rules by stapling their SATs to their applications. In every other area of the economy, costly regulations inspire creative evasion. Why not here?

The most blatant flaw of all: the IQ laundering story implies the labor market will reward not college diplomas, but college *admission letters*.[85] Instead of paying a college $100,000 to launder your test scores, you'd pay a $100 application fee. If you object, "An admission letter signals good IQ, but skipping college signals bad character," you're back to my story: the root cause of educational signaling is the timeless problem of imperfect information, not a lawsuit from 1971.

Disparate impact laws are like speed limits. Taken literally, almost every driver breaks the law. Why? Because speed limits, like disparate impact laws, are highly inconvenient and laxly enforced. If employers really wanted to test applicants' IQs, IQ-based hiring would be as common as driving 60 when the "maximum" is 55.

We shouldn't totally dismiss IQ laundering. If disparate impact law were suddenly abolished, IQ testing might *slightly* expand, leading to a slightly lower education premium. Employers arguably overestimate the size of the test tax; clear-cut legalization would calm their fears.[86] Testing job seekers' intelligence is somewhat more common outside of the United States.[87] Furthermore, while the average test tax is low, plenty of firms aren't average. Copyright violation is rampant, but copyright litigation still bankrupted Napster. If Walmart loudly embraced IQ testing, it might meet Napster's fate.[88] Overall, though, IQ laundering is an extreme tail-wagging-the-dog story. The idea that employers pay hundreds of *billions* in extra labor costs to avoid hundreds of *millions* in extra legal costs is not credible.

Underrating the Benefits of Education?

Does the labor market really reward useless education? Skeptics have a long list of doubts. After careful review, many turn out to be partly valid. Yet after amply correcting for each and every doubt, education still pays. Even fine arts degrees.

To fairly measure the payoff of a fine arts degree, however, you can't just review the main reasons to think the degree is *less* lucrative than it seems on the surface. You must also review the main reasons to think the degree is *more* lucrative than it seems on the surface. We'll ponder intangible benefits later in the book. For now, let's stick to crude materialism.

Unemployment. Educated workers are, as a rule, less likely to face unemployment. Between 1972 and 2000, the average unemployment rate was almost 8% for high school dropouts, slightly under 4% for high school graduates, and about 2% for college graduates.[89] Since the Great Recession, the media has been full of stories about college-educated workers losing their jobs—and recent college graduates who can't find jobs in the first place.[90] Yet the rule that educated workers are *less* jobless is as true as ever—and recent graduates are no exception (see Figure 3.4).

The real question, as usual, is not *whether* educated workers have lower unemployment rates, but *why*. Ability bias takes many forms. Perhaps the well-educated were better at finding and keeping jobs before they set foot on campus.

The best way to handle ability bias, once again, is to measure ability, then correct for it. Such research is sadly sparse, but one high-quality study measures the effect of Americans' education on unemployment, correcting for a host of abilities.[91] Twenty-nine percent of the effect of education on unemployment vanishes once you correct for IQ. Correcting for IQ, fatalism, self-esteem, and antisocial behavior, less than half the apparent effect of education on unemployment remains.

Fringe benefits. Health insurance, pensions, and other employee benefits are now almost a third of total private sector pay, and over a third of total public sector pay.[92] Better-educated workers get better benefits.[93] In the 2010 wave of the National Longitudinal Survey of Youth, educated Americans are more likely to have all the following employee benefits: medical insurance, life insurance, dental insurance, parental leave, a supplemental retirement plan, flexible hours, training, and child care.[94]

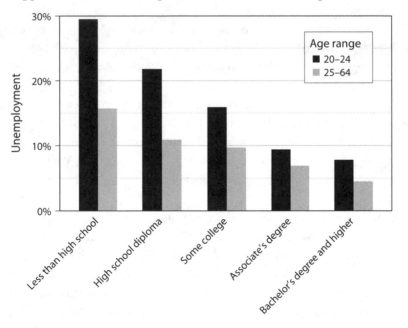

Figure 3.4: Unemployment Rates by Education (2011)
Source: Snyder and Dillow 2013, pp. 620, 622.

Correcting for intelligence shears education's impact but normally leaves it well above zero.[95]

Mismeasurement. How do researchers measure people's education? The ultimate source, in most cases, is asking them, "How many years of education do you have?" or "What's the highest degree you completed?" Since people err and lie, all real-world education data is flawed.

Education skeptics could use these undeniable flaws to dismiss everything we think we know about the payoff of education. Yet the correct statistical inference is almost the opposite. The less reliably you measure X, counterintuitively, the *greater* X's true effect.[96] Ignoring mismeasurement lets competing factors "steal" credit from education, leading us to underestimate how valuable education really is.

Imagine a world where five workers have high school diplomas, and five have college degrees. Workers with high school degrees earn $50,000 a year. Workers with college degrees earn twice as much. Yet neither high school nor college teaches students to carefully complete surveys. When the census inquires about their education, one of each group checks the wrong box.

What happens? The data *over*state earnings for high school grads and *under*state earnings for college grads. Measured earnings are $60,000 for high school grads (because one alleged high school grad went to college), and $90,000 for college grads (because one alleged college grad didn't go to college). The true difference in earnings is $50,000; the true college premium is +100%. Yet thanks to human error, the measured difference is only $30,000, and the measured premium is only +50%. This example illustrates a general principle: mismeasurement of education shrinks the perceived education premium. Labor economists frequently correct for this distortion and conclude the true effect of education on income is about 10% larger than it looks on the surface.[97]

On closer look, however, their approach stacks the deck in education's favor. While labor economists often correct for mismeasurement of education, to prevent competing variables from "stealing" credit for the effect of education, they rarely correct for mismeasurement of intelligence, to prevent education from "stealing" credit for the effect of intelligence.[98] They rarely correct for mismeasurement of personality, to prevent education from "stealing" credit for the effect of personality.[99] Indeed, they rarely correct for mismeasurement of *anything* other than education. As a result, labor economists bypass the crucial question: Is education, on net, a victim or a thief?[100] Do intelligence, personality, and so on steal more credit from education than education steals from them? The rare papers that face this challenge find measurement error is a red herring.[101] The true effect of education on income is no bigger than it looks.

The Real Rewards of Education

The link between practical skill and worldly success is subtler than either mainstream defenders or contrarian detractors of modern education imagine. The skillful *do* a good job. The successful *have* a good job. Despite its weak effect on skill, education remains the modern economy's surest stairway to prosperity. If you personally know many wealthy dropouts and indigent college grads, you personally know many atypical people.

Challenge the data all you like. Correct for brains, motivation, family background, choice of major, and beyond. The education premium will shrink before your eyes. Yet the shrinking stops long before the education premium disappears. Vocational majors are especially lucrative, but even archaeology degrees boost your income by 25%.

Why would shrewd, money-grubbing employers pay such exorbitant rates for archaeologists? Education's contrarian detractors typically blame the government, but their stories fall flat. Government sinecures? The private sector pays *more* for education than the public sector. Regulation? The education premium in licensed and unlicensed jobs is roughly the same. Lawsuits? Legal doctrine notwithstanding, the IQ "test tax" is a pittance.

Contrarian detractors should stop avoiding the cleanest explanation: signaling. Going to school to *certify* skill can be as lucrative as going to school to *enhance* skill. If archaeology B.A.s are better workers than high school grads, employers needn't waste time wondering, "What useful skills do archaeology programs really teach?" Instead, they'll skip to the bottom line: "When I pay 25% extra for an archaeologist, I get my money's worth. End of story."

Education's contrarian detractors and mainstream defenders have one illusion in common: Both think they can kill two birds with one stone. The detractors find little effect of education on job skills, so they ignore the evidence that education mightily enhances worldly success. The defenders find a large effect of education on worldly success, so they ignore the evidence that education barely enhances job skills. Both sides make strong cases as long as they stick to the evidence they know.

The wise approach is to take *all* the evidence seriously. To understand education, we have to look at skill and success, learning and earning. Irrelevant education really is financially rewarding. Human capital purism can respond only with denial and dismay. The signaling model, thankfully, is ready, willing, and able to pick up the slack.

CHAPTER 4

The Signs of Signaling

In Case You're Still Not Convinced

> In short, whoever you may be,
> To this conclusion you'll agree,
> When every one is somebodee,
> Then no one's anybody!
>
> —W. S. Gilbert and Arthur Sullivan, *The Gondoliers*

In the modern world, your first quarter century of life is deeply weird.[1] You spend your earliest years learning incredibly useful skills: How to walk. How to talk. How to get along with others. Everything's going so well . . . until your parents decide you're old enough to start school. School teaches you a few more incredibly useful skills: reading, writing, math. Most of the day, though, you just kill time. Parents, teachers, and other adults guarantee that formal education is vital preparation for adult life. Thirteen years later, your elders grant you the option to quit school but urge you to finish at least four more years. The link between what you have to study in school and what you'll do on the job is an ongoing mystery. Yet when you finally graduate, the wisdom of your elders is undeniable. The better your transcript, the richer your opportunities in the labor market.

When you have a weird experience, you doubt yourself. What's really weird: the World, or you? The answer for education, as we've seen, is the World. Learning few useful skills in school—and laughing all the way to the bank—is normal. The signaling model of education elegantly rationalizes the weirdness. Signaling doesn't just reconcile the psychology of learning with the economics of earning. Once signaling clicks, your first quarter century of life finally makes sense. It fits our firsthand experience—and it's hard to imagine any other way to reconcile the facts about learning with the facts about earning.

But does the evidence we've covered really justify this triumphalism? Many smart people remain skeptical—especially if they put little stock in firsthand experience. Indirect evidence about learning and earning isn't good enough for them. They want social science that directly confirms the power of educational signaling.

This chapter serves these skeptics the social science they seek. Four major research literatures spanning economics, psychology, and sociology explicitly or implicitly try to detect and measure educational signaling. Let's unpack of the logic behind these four approaches, and scrutinize what each reveals.

The Sheepskin Effect

Suppose you're one class away from a B.A. You're biking to the final exam, secure in your mastery of the coursework. Suddenly, a car smacks into you. Though your injuries are minor, you miss your test. The professor denies you a makeup, so you flunk the class and fail to graduate. Once your outrage cools, you weigh your options. Should you enroll for one more semester to complete your diploma, or give up and get on with your life?

The pure human capital model urges you to quit school. While your accident deprived you of a diploma, you still possess all the skills required to earn that diploma. Hiring you for a "college graduate's job" is usually perfectly legal. Since employers value skills, not diplomas, retaking your missing class would waste your time and money.

The signaling model, in contrast, advises you to finish what you started. In our society, graduation is a sacred milestone. Graduation tells employers, "I take social norms seriously—and have the brains and work ethic to comply." Quitting tells employers, "I scorn social norms—or lack the brains and work ethic to comply." If you graduate, the signaling model says the market will lump you with the winners and pay you a special diploma bonus—often called a "sheepskin effect" because diplomas used to be printed on sheepskin. If you quit, the signaling model says the market will lump you with the losers and withhold the sheepskin's reward. After all, employers won't know *why* you failed to finish your degree. They'll only know you failed.

Labor economists normally neglect sheepskin effects. By default, they assume all years of education are created equal, then estimate "the" effect of a year of education on earnings.[2] Yet economists who trouble to look almost always find pay spikes for diplomas.[3] High school graduation has a big spike: twelfth grade pays more than grades 9, 10, and 11 combined. In percentage terms, the average study finds graduation year is worth 3.4 regular years. College graduation has a huge spike: senior year of college pays over *twice* as much as freshman, sophomore, and junior years combined.[4] In percentage terms, the average study finds graduation year is worth 6.7 regular years. Results are similar for advanced degrees; in several studies, their payoff is nothing *but* a sheepskin effect.[5]

When pay spikes, so does education itself. "Finish your degree, then rest on your laurels" is the classic student strategy. One-third of the U.S. population spends 12 years in school, gets a high school diploma, then stops. Only 2% quit high school right after eleventh grade. One-seventh spends 16 years in school, gets a bachelor's degree, then stops. Only 2% quit college right after their junior year.[6]

Signaling has an instant explanation for all the spikes. Why does pay spike for degree years? Because finishing sends employers a much better signal than quitting. Why does education spike for degree years? Because students run, walk, or crawl to grab the handsome cash prize they see just over the finish line.

To get a better feel for the sheepskin effect, let's put workers in the General Social Survey (GSS) under the microscope. This massive survey of the U.S. public, begun in 1972, is still under way. The GSS is ideal for isolating sheepskin effects: 99.5% of participants declare both their years of education and their highest completed degree. Ignoring degrees, the GSS features a large education premium: take another year of school, get a 10.9% raise (see Table 4.1). Correcting for degrees, however, this annual payoff plummets to 4.5%.[7] Over 60% of the education premium turns out to be a sheepskin effect. High school and four-year college diplomas are especially lucrative: crossing each of these thresholds boosts income by almost a third. As expected, the most lucrative years are also the most popular. Thirty percent have a high school diploma with exactly 12 years of schooling; only 5% finish 11 years but not 12. Eleven percent have a bachelor's degree with exactly 16 years of school; only 3% finish their junior year but not their senior year.

Table 4.1: Sheepskin Effects in the General Social Survey (1972–2012)

Education	Effect on Earnings	
	If Only Years of Education Matter	If Diplomas Matter Too
Years of Education	+10.9%	+4.5%
High School Diploma	–	+31.7%
Junior College Diploma	–	+16.6%
Bachelor's Degree	–	+31.4%
Graduate Degree	–	+18.2%
All results correct for age, age squared, race, and sex; are limited to labor force participants; and are converted from log dollars to percentages.		

In the good old days, when the reality of the sheepskin effect was still in doubt, economists took the sheepskin-signaling connection for granted. Every paper that found sheepskin effects scored a point for signaling; every paper that failed to find sheepskin effects scored a point for human capital. But now that the sheepskin effect is undeniable, some economists reinterpret the evidence to deny signaling a victory.

How could sheepskin effects *not* reflect signaling? The simplest story is that schools save the best for last: graduation years pay extra because that's when schools suddenly focus on marketable skills. As far as I know, no one defends this idea. Graduation year is "goof-off" year, not "finally-learn-some-job-skills" year.

Most skeptics try to undermine the sheepskin-signaling connection from a totally different angle: ability bias.[8] Sure, graduation *looks* lucrative. Yet the reason, supposedly, is that graduates had far better career prospects than dropouts all along. If ability bias fully explains the sheepskin effect, an untimely bike accident that derails your graduation will leave your career unscathed.

As usual, the best way to test for ability bias is to measure and correct for ability. Multiple papers on the sheepskin effect carry out such tests. None concludes that sheepskin effects vanish after correcting for ability.[9] Instead, correcting for ability usually modestly cuts the effect of both years of education and diplomas—holding the *relative* payoff for diplomas steady.[10]

Results from the General Social Survey are typical. Table 4.2 shows what happens to Table 4.1 after correcting for cognitive ability. Standout result: the sheepskin effect for junior college falls by about a third.

Otherwise, there's not much to see. Absolute payoffs for high school diplomas, bachelor's degrees, and graduate degrees barely budge—and their relative payoffs actually rise.[11]

Table 4.2: Sheepskin Effects and Ability Bias in the General Social Survey (1972–2012)

Education	Effect on Earnings	
	Only Years of Education Matter	Diplomas Matter Too
Years of Education	+10.3%	+4.2%
High School Diploma	–	+32.0%
Junior College Diploma	–	+10.4%
Bachelor's Degree	–	+29.8%
Graduate Degree	–	+17.8%
All results adjust for age, age squared, race, sex, and cognitive ability; are limited to labor force participants; and are converted from log dollars to percentages.		

Ability bias explanations for sheepskin effects aren't just hard to square with the statistical evidence; they're hard to square with the glaring fact that education spikes in degree years. If the labor market ignores credentials, why do so many high school grads opt for *zero* college—and so many college grads opt for *zero* graduate education? Are we supposed to believe one-third of the population has exactly the right ability to finish high school, but not advance to college?[12] One-seventh of the population has exactly the right ability to finish college, but not advance to grad school? You could say, "College is far harder than high school, so many decent high school students reasonably expect to fail in college." Yet nowadays, high school and college curricula plainly overlap: about 40% of traditional undergraduates take at least one remedial course.[13]

True believers can always protest, "The sheepskin effect shall vanish once we get better ability measures." Such forecasts, to be blunt, are empty promises. Sheepskin effects look massive. To debunk them, researchers would have to pinpoint fantastically potent yet neglected abilities. But that's not all. To debunk sheepskin effects, correcting for these neglected abilities would have to drastically cut the payoff for degrees but *not* the payoff for years of schooling. What abilities would even conceivably qualify?

After digesting all the evidence on the sheepskin effect, you may feel ready to channel King Solomon. Human capital and signaling come before you as litigants. They ask you to split the education premium between them.[14] A ruling with a great ring to it: "Human capital gets credit for the payoff for years of education; signaling gets credit for the payoff for degrees." This implies a human capital/signaling split of roughly 60/40 for high school, and 40/60 for college.

Yet on reflection, this Solomonic ruling treats human capital too generously. The sheepskin effect doesn't measure signaling. Instead, the sheepskin effect sets a *lower bound* on signaling. King Solomon should award signaling all the payoff for diplomas, plus some of the payoff for years of education—and hand human capital whatever's left.

To see why, picture a world that lacks the notion of "graduation." Can we safely declare educational signaling would vanish in such a world?[15] Of course not. In the absence of diplomas, education continues to signal intelligence, conscientiousness, and conformity. The main difference between this imaginary world and our own: its signals are smooth. If you get slightly more education, you look slightly more employable.

In the real world, we know what graduation is—and view graduates and dropouts as separate species. This doesn't mean, however, that we *ignore* unfinished education. In our society, credentials define you in broad strokes, but years of education add valuable details. Consider this vignette:

> Jane got her high school degree and never went to college. Doris got her high school degree, finished a year of college, then quit school for good. Who do you hire?

Suppose Doris learned no job skills in college. You would still expect her to be a better worker than Jane. Why? Because Jane met minimal social expectations, while Doris surpassed them. If you want a worker who goes the extra mile, Doris is the better bet. We should not be surprised, then, that some sheepskin studies find solid rewards for the *first* year of college.[16] In the eyes of the labor market, 'tis better to try and fail than never to have tried at all.

If you live outside the Ivory Tower, research on the sheepskin effect may seem redundant. Normal people don't need research to know the labor market amply rewards graduation. They experience credentialism firsthand. If you live inside the Ivory Tower, research on the sheepskin effect may seem even more redundant. Professors dwell in one of the most credentialist habitats on the planet. They *never* hire people without "suitable" degrees. How can they wonder if diplomas really pay?

Still, sheepskin scholarship has paid off. Modern life tells us the sheepskin effect is big, but only scholarship can tell us how big. It also inoculates us against the seductive view that diplomas no longer matter in the age of billionaire dropouts. Perhaps most importantly, sheepskin scholarship shows common sense and social science converge. You can scorn firsthand experience—and still reach the obvious conclusion.

Malemployment and Credential Inflation

Many workers have more education than they actually use. Laymen call them "overqualified"—their education is too good for their jobs. Researchers often call them "malemployed"—their jobs aren't good enough for their education.[17] Yet the two ideas are the same: if your waiter has a Ph.D. in astronomy, something somewhere has gone terribly awry.

Researchers have three main measures of malemployment.[18] There is the "atypical education" method: see if your education is abnormally high given your occupation.[19] This method usually yields a 10–20% malemployment rate.[20] The atypical education approach's main drawback: it rules out the possibility that the *typical* worker in an occupation is overeducated. If every bartender has a Ph.D., the "atypical education" approach reports 0% malemployment for bartenders.

Then there is the "self-report" method: researchers ask workers if they have too much, too little, or just enough education for their jobs. This method usually yields a 20–35% malemployment rate.[21] The self-report approach's main drawback: calling yourself "overqualified" is a bitter admission of failure, so true rates are likely higher.

Finally, there is the "job analysis" method: after dissecting occupations one by one, researchers judge how much education the occupation "really requires"—then check whether workers' education exceeds this requirement.[22] This method also usually yields a 20–35% malemployment rate.[23] The job analysis approach's main drawback: skill requirements both rise and fall over time. Some innovations simplify once-complex jobs; other innovations complicate once-simple jobs.

Regardless of your preferred measure, all three approaches reveal abundant malemployment. This is a rare topic where economists and sociologists have a meeting of the minds. The only way to deny the ubiquity of malemployment is to dogmatically insist, "The education workers have is *by definition* the education workers need."[24] Try telling that to a waiter with a Ph.D. in astronomy.

Most researchers agree malemployment is on the rise. One leading team found U.S. college grads' malemployment rate rose from 25.2% in 2000 to 28.2% in 2010. During the depths of the Great Recession, malemployment for the youngest college grads neared 40%.[25] Another research team focused on the long-run evolution of education in 500 occupational categories. From the early 1970s to the mid-1990s, workers' average education rose by 1.5 years. About 20% of this increase—.3 years—reflected the switch to higher-skill occupations. The remainder stemmed from credential inflation: average education *within* individual occupations rose 1.2 years.[26] A longer-run study for 1972–2002 gets nearly the same ratio: average education rose by 1.75 years, but growth of higher-skilled jobs drove only 19% of the increase.[27] Credential inflation has even ravaged academia itself: today's professors are *much* more likely to have Ph.D.s than they were in the 1960s.[28] Despite clichés about the Information Age, workers are changing much more rapidly than their work.[29]

By itself, malemployment is compatible with the human capital model. How? Graduates could be "malemployed" because they failed to acquire marketable job skills in school. This might mean malemployed graduates failed to learn and retain the curriculum; recall that on the National Assessment of Adult Literacy, over 50% of high school grads and almost 20% of college grads have less than Intermediate literacy and numeracy. Or it might mean malemployed graduates learn an irrelevant curriculum; recall that over 40% of high school coursework and over 40% of college majors score Low in usefulness. When a B.A. bartender asks, "Why oh why can't I get a better job?" human capital bluntly answers, "Because despite your credentials, you didn't learn how to *do* a better job."

Signaling weaves a contrary tale—one where malemployment reflects workers' never-ending struggle to outshine each other. Picture the labor market as an arms race. Rising education automatically sparks credential inflation; as credentials proliferate, you must study harder and longer to convince employers to hire you. In an everyone-has-a-B.A. dystopia, an aspiring janitor might need a master's in Janitorial Studies to land a job scrubbing toilets.[30] When a B.A. bartender asks, "Why oh why can't I get a better job?" signaling ruefully answers, "Because too many competing workers have even more impressive credentials than you do." As two noted sociologists explain:

> In an over-qualified labor market, employers will fill the "highest" jobs with those who have the "highest" credentials. Since over-schooling means there are too many workers who are highly educated, some of these workers are necessarily allocated to "mid-level" jobs. This process is repeated for those with mid-level qualifications, where, since there are not enough mid-level jobs, many are forced to compete for low-level jobs.[31]

If both human capital and signaling allow for malemployment, why raise the issue? Because the two stories diverge on one crucial point: Does the labor market reward workers for education *they do not use*? Human capital says no; signaling says yes. Take bartenders with B.A.s. Plausibly assuming college does not transform students into better bartenders, the human capital model predicts B.A.s will fail to raise bartenders' income. The signaling model predicts the opposite: bartenders with B.A.s will out-earn bartenders without B.A.s. Why? Because bars, like all businesses, seek intelligent, conscientious, conformist workers—and a B.A. signals these very traits. Given a choice, then, bars favor applicants with B.A.s despite the on-the-job irrelevance of the academic curriculum.

How well does the labor market pay workers for education they do not use? The best data on this question, ironically, comes from enthusiastic promoters of college expansion. Researchers at Georgetown University's Center on Education and the Workforce use the 2007–9 American Community Survey to tabulate earnings by education level for over a quarter million workers in 500 occupational categories.[32] Their data strongly confirm two patterns:

First, high school grads out-earn high school dropouts in almost all occupations. Out of their 500 occupations, 214 include at least ten high school dropouts and at least ten high school grads. High school grads out-earn dropouts in 93% of these occupations, with a median earnings premium of +37%.

Second, college grads out-earn high school grads in almost all occupations. Out of the same 500 occupations, 270 include at least ten high school grads and at least ten college grads. College grads out-earn high school grads in 90% of these occupations, with a median earnings premium of +28%.

To weigh the power of human capital versus signaling, however, we must zero in on occupations with little or no plausible connection to traditional academic curricula. Despite many debatable cases, there are common jobs that workers clearly *don't* learn in school. Almost no one goes to high school to become a bartender, cashier, cook, janitor, security guard, or waiter. No one goes to a four-year college to prepare for such jobs. Yet as Figure 4.1 shows, the labor market pays bartenders, cashiers, cooks, janitors, security guards, and waiters for high school diplomas and college degrees.

None of these occupations are weird outliers. True, most bartenders, cashiers, cooks, janitors, security guards, and waiters lack college degrees.

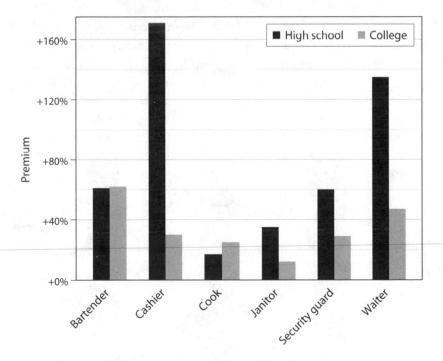

Figure 4.1: Education Premiums in Selected Nonacademic Occupations
Source: Supplementary data for Carnevale et al. 2011, supplied by coauthor Stephen Rose.
High school premium = [(median earnings for high school graduates)/(median earnings for high school dropouts)] −1.
College premium = [(median earnings for college graduates)/(median earnings for high school graduates)] −1.

Yet in the modern economy, all are common jobs for college grads. More work as cashiers (48th most common job for college grads) or waiters (50th) than mechanical engineers (51st). More work as security guards (67th) or janitors (72nd) than network and computer systems administrators (75th). More work as cooks (94th) and bartenders (99th) than librarians (104th). I selected Figure 4.1's occupations to minimize controversy. Human capital purists could insist college provides useful training for electricians, real estate agents, or secretaries. But even the staunchest fans of human capital theory struggle to state, "College prepares the next generation of cashiers and janitors for their careers," without smirking.[33]

Now let's cast a wider net. Roughly one-third of occupations in the American Community Survey have at least ten workers in each of the main education categories (high school dropouts, high school graduates, four-year college graduates). About one-third of these occupations at least arguably build on traditional academic coursework.[34] The remaining occupations' tie to the academic curriculum is tenuous at best. Figure 4.2 compares median educational premiums for "arguably academic" and "nonacademic" occupations.

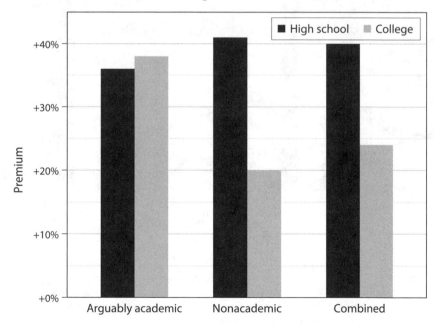

Figure 4.2: Median Education Premiums by Occupational Category
Source: Supplementary data for Carnevale et al. 2011, supplied by coauthor Stephen Rose.

Human capital theorists can draw comfort from the fact the college premium is almost twice as high for arguably academic occupations. But not too much comfort: the high school premium is slightly higher for *non*academic occupations. When high school dropouts and college graduates are in the same line of work, college graduates typically earn 70–90% more—even in occupations high schools and colleges studiously ignore.

What would King Solomon conclude about the human capital/signaling split? The combined premium plainly reflects both human capital and signaling. The nonacademic premium, in contrast, presumably reflects something close to pure signaling. What is signaling's share? The Solomonic verdict just divides the nonacademic premium by the combined premium. This works out to nearly 100% signaling for high school, and 80% for college.

Why are academic credentials so lucrative, even in decidedly nonacademic lines of work? The Georgetown researchers who compiled this data propose two conspicuously implausible options: (a) employers are fools, or (b) schooling greatly boosts productivity in virtually any line of work:

> Unless we concede that employers are paying more to some than to others for the same skill sets—an irrational economic action—it becomes clear that workers with a Bachelor's degree are able to translate their added skills into higher pay. Further, jobs that were once held by workers without college degrees decades ago have been transformed to require many more skills, as evidenced by a wage premium in those positions.[35]

Signaling is the obvious alternative.[36] School *certifies* employability. Yes, waiting tables for four hours teaches you more about being a waiter than taking classes for four years. But the chasm between the academic curriculum and the food service industry is beside the point. From the employer's point of view, only one thing matters: hiring good students is a shortcut to better waiters. From the waiter's point of view, similarly, only one thing matters: being a good student is a shortcut to better restaurants.

Is there any way to escape signaling's grip? Skeptics could appeal to ability bias: high-paid waiters with college degrees would have been every bit as successful if they skipped school. But there's no reason to believe this extreme story; controlling for ability shrinks but never eradicates the education premium.[37] In any case, the overall education premium and the nonacademic premium are almost the same. This parity would make sense only if workers with above-average ability were *less* likely to use their book learning on the job. The opposite holds.[38] Critics of signaling could also affirm that education "builds character," so it's not absurd to claim school transforms students into better bartenders, cashiers, cooks, janitors, security guards, and waiters. The chief flaw in this story, as we've seen, is that *both* work experience and education "build character"—and it would be amazing if a year of school better instilled the work ethic than a year of work.

Malemployment is not mere "man bites dog" hype designed to terrify English majors' parents. The amount of education you need to *get* a job really has risen more than the amount of education you need to *do* a job. Bartender, cashier, cook, janitor, security guard, and waiter are now common jobs for college grads. Education helps workers advance in almost any line of work—whether or not they tap their education on the job. Technology has made many mentally undemanding jobs like cashiering simpler than ever, but the market still pays educated cashiers a hefty premium.

Signaling is the only theory that explains the totality of these otherwise baffling facts. In our society, education is a seal of approval. Employers know it. Workers know it. As seals proliferate, workers need extra seals to upstage the competition. You'll never apply most of what you study, but so what? Academic success opens doors. A dysfunctional game, but if you refuse to play, the labor market brands you a loser.

The Speed of Employer Learning

The signaling theory of education is a special case of what economists call "statistical discrimination": using true-on-average stereotypes to save time and money. Safe young male drivers pay exorbitant insurance premiums because hiring private detectives to rate riskiness person by person is not cost-effective. Prudence makes insurers play the averages.

While many take offense at the very idea of statistical discrimination, we're all guilty of it. You statistically discriminate every time you delete a "make money fast" e-mail unread, or cross the street to avoid a muscular tattooed man. The e-mail could be a legitimate business opportunity; the muscular tattooed man could be a friendly circus performer in need of directions. But idealists who reserve judgment until they closely study the facts pay a high price for their integrity.

The idealist does get a consolation prize: gradually phasing out statistical discrimination is profitable. Entering a relationship unleashes a flow of cheap information. Every time you deal with your partner, you discover a little more. As time goes by, discrepancies between true-on-average and true-in-fact come into focus. Prudence urges you to revise your behavior in light of such discrepancies. When a young male driver has a clean record for five years, a shrewd insurer cuts his rates to retain a great customer.

These truisms extend to educational signaling. Credentials are undeniably important at the hiring stage. Yet once you're hired, your employer comes to know you as an individual. If your education understates your skill, the boss will fear to lose you. Expect good raises, or even a promotion. If your education overstates your skill, your employer might *hope* to lose you. Expect meager raises, or even a pink slip. As time goes by, then, employers should lose interest in mere credentials.

This logic is impeccable but dodges crucial questions. Employers eventually get to know the Real You. But how long is "eventually"? In the end, employers pay you what you're Really Worth. But when is "the end"? Economists have spent twenty years searching for answers, measuring what they call "the speed of employer learning."

When they attack this problem, economists never measure employer learning directly. Instead, they infer what employers *know* from what employers *pay*. As workers gain experience, does the payoff for education go down and the payoff for cognitive ability go up? Then researchers infer learning: as employers get to know workers, they pay less and less for superficial credentials, and more and more for underlying merits. When payoffs for education and cognitive ability plateau, researchers often conclude employers have reached the truth.

What does this approach reveal? For most workers, employer learning takes years or even decades, not months. Two seminal studies of employer learning found that during your first decade in the workforce, the ability premium sharply rises, while the education premium falls

25–30%.[39] A subsequent prize-winning article found the education and ability premiums plateau after roughly ten years of experience; the education premium stops falling, and the ability premium stops rising.[40]

Employers seem to see through college graduates much more quickly than less-educated workers. One early researcher confirmed academic ability is a strong predictor of job *performance* in both blue- and white-collar jobs. Unlike college graduates, however, high school graduates capture little or no job *reward* for academic ability during their first eight years in the labor force.[41] A recent high-profile study claims employers see college graduates' ability "nearly perfectly" as soon as they join the labor market.[42] Yet the same piece finds less-educated workers wait over a decade to get full credit for their talent.[43] The logic of employer learning also suggests sheepskin effects matter less and less as careers progress.[44] The only paper to test this prediction finds sheepskin effects take about two decades to disappear.[45]

In light of all the evidence, I'd call employer learning slow. Yes, a few studies hail employer's "perfect" or "almost perfect" knowledge. When closely read, however, they paint a sluggish picture. Take the study that provocatively claims employers see college graduates' ability "nearly perfectly." The same piece reports high school dropouts, high school graduates, and college dropouts enjoy virtually *zero* payoff for their ability when they first join the labor force. Full catch-up takes over ten years.[46] In other words: to win your rightful place in the world, you must either enter the labor force and work for a decade-plus, or graduate from a four-year college. Somber news for "diamonds in the rough" whose skills surpass their credentials.

You can use employer learning studies to ballpark signaling's importance. Before you do, however, there are three crucial caveats—caveats leading researchers never deny but casual readers rarely grasp.

Employer learning research neglects noncognitive ability. When researchers say, "After seven years, employers have full information about workers' ability," they almost always mean, "After seven years, employers have full information about workers' intelligence." They gloss over *everything* else that could come out in the wash.[47] If researchers measured extra abilities like conscientiousness and conformity, estimates of the speed of employer learning could—and probably would—plummet. After all, high intelligence is hard to fake, yet almost anyone can temporarily feign high conscientiousness and conformity. "The boss is coming, look busy!" is sound advice. "The boss is coming, look smart!" is not.

Learning plateaus do not imply perfect knowledge. Casual readers often equate learning plateaus with perfect knowledge, but stagnation and omniscience are not the same. Perfect knowledge is one plateau. Abject ignorance is another. My knowledge of Swahili has been stuck at zero for my whole life, and I never expect to improve. And of course, you can plateau anywhere in between.

The same goes for employers: their knowledge can plateau anywhere. The boss who learns more about you has a reason to adjust your pay. But when your boss *stops* tinkering with your pay, you shouldn't imagine the Real You has finally shone through. When the education premium hits a floor, there's no reason to declare employers omniscient or signaling dead. In most European countries studied, the education premium does *not* decline over time; should we really conclude European employers instantly see through their workers?[48]

Suppose during workers' first decade in the workforce, the yearly education premium falls from 10% to 5%, then plateaus. This could mean that after you spend ten years on the job, employers learn all there is to know about you. In this story, the human capital/signaling premium starts at 5% for human capital and 5% for signaling, and stabilizes at 5% for human capital and 0% for signaling. The split goes from 50/50 to 100/0. A less fanciful interpretation, though, is that after you spend ten years on the job, employers learn all they can *conveniently* know about you. In this story, the human capital/signaling premium breakdown could start at 1% for human capital and 9% for signaling, and stabilize at 1% for human capital and 4% for signaling. The split goes from 10/90 to 20/80.

If you have trouble believing in persistent employer ignorance, consider marriage. The fact you've stopped learning new things about your spouse hardly shows you know your spouse perfectly. How many bewildered souls have cried, "After twenty years of marriage, she suddenly demanded a divorce"? The same applies with greater force in the labor market. If a husband can "never really know" his own wife, how can we expect an employer to "ever really know" each and every long-term employee?

Signals can affect pay even after employers know the truth. Employer learning researchers speak as if the payoff for signaling ends as soon as employers know a worker's true worth. They should be more circumspect. For starters, firms often give new workers valuable on-the-job training. As a result, signaling can indirectly boost your productivity. Step 1: Signal in school. Step 2: Land a good job. Step 3: Learn useful job skills on the job. Step 4: Persistently profit. If your signal modestly overstates your skill, your employer may soon wish they'd hired someone else. By the time they spot their mistake, however, your new marketable skills permanently justify higher pay.[49]

The more fundamental reason why signals durably affect pay, though, is employers underreact to what they learn. Why? Because they want to match pay and perceived productivity *without seeming unfair.*[50] When employers spot poor performance, they could swiftly respond with wage cuts, demotions, or terminations. The catch: such "unfair" measures are bad for morale—and make employers feel guilty.[51]

Stingy raises are less odious, but stingy raises year after year create "inequitably" large pay spreads for workers with the same job description. Most firms avoid such inequities with formal pay scales: every job has a pay grade, and every pay grade has a salary range.[52] Unless they change jobs, good workers eventually max out, and bad workers eventually min out. This process is slower than it sounds because few firms base raises on merit alone. Instead, firms tend to give across-the-board raises to all their workers, then tack on merit raises for high achievers.[53] In the long run, employers who strive for fairness must underreact to bad news about their workers.

Fallout: A subpar worker can profit from their fancy degree long after their employer sees their true colors. The degree lands them a good job. As truth unfolds, the typical employer responds with stingy raises, not outright pay cuts or demotion. This slowly erodes the value of the signal, but squeamish firms show mercy long before they sync pay with performance. If and when the employer vows to eject the underperformer, both prudence and pity tell them to informally "dehire" rather than blatantly fire. As long as the subpar worker lands another position suitable for their paper persona, the cycle of disappointment, mercy, and deception is reborn.

Armed with the research on employer learning, we are once again ready to play King Solomon. What human capital/signaling split best fits the evidence? Two key papers face it head-on. The first finds that if the initial human capital/signaling split is 50/50, a plausible lifetime split is somewhere between 60/40 and 70/30.[54] The second estimates a lifetime split anywhere from roughly 50/50 to 100/0, but the author's favorite estimate is 86% human capital, 14% signaling.[55] While the two papers' conclusions differ, neither is near the 20/80 split I've been pushing.[56] My response is twofold. First, both papers concede their results are fragile; alternate assumptions imply a much bigger signaling share.[57] Second, both papers sidestep a glaring hole in their approach: though they claim to estimate *the* speed of learning, they measure learning speed only for easy-to-see cognitive ability, ignoring hard-to-see noncognitive ability.

Employer learning research begins promisingly: prudent employers gradually phase out statistical discrimination. Contrary to casual readers, though, research building on this truism never shows the signaling model is dead on arrival. When scholars declare employer learning "fast" or "perfect," you have to read the fine print. To discredit the signaling model, they must make a series of unreasonable assumptions. Drop these assumptions, and signaling holds its own.

The Education Premium: Personal versus National

According to the pure human capital model, education lifts income by making you more productive. A worker gets more education; their productivity and income go up. A nation gets more education; its productivity and income go up. If human capital is the truth, the whole truth, and nothing but the truth, education is a path to individual *and* national prosperity: education makes the pie bigger, so every worker can enjoy a bigger slice.

According to the pure signaling model, education raises income by making you *look* more productive. A worker gets more education; their productivity stays the same, but their income goes up. A nation gets more education; its productivity *and* income stay the same. The personal and national effects diverge because signaling is a rat race. Only one worker can look like the Best Worker in the Country, and only 25% can look like the Best 25%. If signaling is the truth, the whole truth, and nothing but the truth, education is a path to individual prosperity and national *stagnation*: education fails to make the pie bigger, so bigger slices for some means smaller slices for others.[58]

Actual education lies between these extremes. Yet the polar cases of pure human capital and pure signaling highlight another strategy to nail down the human capital/signaling split. Step 1: Estimate the effect of a year of *personal* education on *personal* income. Step 2: Estimate the effect of a year of *national* education on *national* income. Step 3: Compare. Human capital's share of the truth equals the *national effect divided by the personal effect*.[59] The rest is signaling.

Suppose a year of personal education raises personal income by 10%. Then once you know the effect of a year of national education on *national* income, you are ready to deduce the human capital/signaling split. A 10% effect on national income? The split is 100/0. Six percent effect? 60/40. Zero percent effect? 0/100. Alas, such comparisons are easier said than done. Let's walk through the steps and see where we end up.

Step 1: Estimate the effect of a year of personal education on personal income. We already spent a full chapter examining the effect of education on personal income. Punch line: education is lucrative, but less lucrative than it looks. In the modern United States, a year of education raises earnings by 5–10%. When making international comparisons, though, we can't assume the U.S. is typical. Fortunately, several research teams have studied the education premium country by country, learning two big facts.

First big fact: for a rich country, the U.S. education premium is unusually high, especially in recent decades. The United States has the largest high school premium and close to the highest college premium in the OECD (Organization for Economic Cooperation and Development).[60] Two research teams confirm the U.S. has one of the highest—if not *the* highest—college premiums in the developed world.[61] Another study estimated the education premium in 27 developed countries, plus the Philippines. In the average country, a year of education raised male earnings by 4.8% and female earnings by 5.7%. The U.S. premiums were at least 50% higher.[62]

Second big fact: the education premium is lower in richer countries. A comprehensive study of 50 countries finds an average annual education premium of 7.4% in high-income countries, 10.7% in middle-income countries, 10.9% in low-income countries, and 9.7% for the world as a whole.[63] Correcting for ability bias, the world education premium roughly matches the U.S. education premium.[64]

Step 2: Estimate the effect of a year of national education on national income. The effect of personal education on personal income is undeniable. Every economy on earth works the same way: the more school you take, the more money you make. Yes, some of the data are crummy, and clever wonks can lie with statistics. Yet if you mercilessly torture the best data in the world, it never recants its original story: selfishly speaking, education has its rewards—at least on average.

When we move to the national level, these clean results vanish.[65] Some prominent economists find that boosting national education slightly *impoverishes* countries rather than enriching them.[66] Others report small positive effects; one typical estimate is that an extra year of national education boosts national income by 1.3%–1.7%.[67] Remaining papers find moderate positive effects; the effect of national education on national income roughly equals the effect of personal education on personal income.[68] No matter what they find, researchers usually confess their answers are highly uncertain.[69]

You could blame the decidedly mixed results on Third World statistics. When you analyze data from Niger, Bolivia, or Azerbaijan, you have to recall the old programming adage "Garbage in, garbage out." But answers remain messy in the developed world. One unusually thorough study examines 21 OECD countries using eight different measures of education from five separate research teams.[70] The estimated effect of national education on national income ranges from slightly negative to modestly positive (see Figure 4.3). Averaging over all eight sets of results yields a puny +1.3% effect.

Do better measures lead to bigger estimates? It depends on who you ask. Researchers predictably rate their own data highly. The creators of the last three measures eagerly market them as new and improved.[71] Neutral observers are less sanguine. After comparing top contestants in the "best education data" contest, a major review article concludes, "we are not convinced that any one of the available data series is clearly preferable to the alternatives."[72]

Most economists are less than thrilled by these results: they're "puzzling," or even "discouraging."[73] While some lament their lack of a

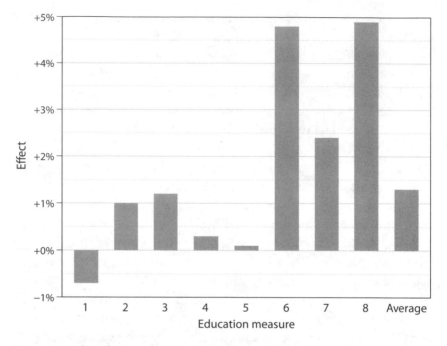

Figure 4.3: Effect of a Year of National Education on National Income
Source: de la Fuente and Doménech 2006b, appendix, p. 52, table A.1.f.

definite answer, many crave a clear proeducation verdict.[74] They *know* education is vital for development. How can the data be so agnostic?[75]

The leading fallback is to point out that country-level education data are riddled with measurement error. Several research teams deploy arcane statistical techniques to fix this flaw.[76] The most prominent reports a big payoff. When you fix the data, the effect of a year of education on national income leaps from +1.3% to +6.7%. Yet the answer's uncertainty goes from bad to worse: the team reports a 95% chance that the true effect lies somewhere between *negative* 26% and *positive* 40%.[77] Deeper worry: the arcane statistical fixes assume everything *except* education is perfectly measured.[78] This crazy assumption automatically magnifies the apparent effect of education, regardless of its true efficacy.[79]

Economists are so eager to argue education is underrated they neglect a strong reason to think education is *overrated*: reverse causation. Instead of "When countries invest more in schooling, they get richer," the real story could be, "When countries get richer, they consume more schooling." Almost everyone buys reverse causation at the personal level. Why do the rich spend more money on fancy prep schools and bloated college tuition? Because the rich have more money to spend.

On reflection, this reverse causation should be *stronger* at the national level. After all, governments, not individuals, pay most of the education tab. Consider K–12. Since the vast majority of American kids go to public school, private spending per student in 2008 averaged about $900.[80] Government spending, in contrast, was roughly $11,000 per student. Picture what would happen if the United States suddenly became 10% richer, prompting both private and public sectors to spend 10% extra on education. Private spending would go up by a measly $90 per student—trivial reverse causation. Government spending would jump by $1,100 per person—serious reverse causation.

Intuitively, the idea that national prosperity causes schooling is hard to escape. What real-world country *wouldn't* spend more on education when its tax coffers overflow? Yet serious research on reverse causation is sadly thin.[81] The leading paper on this theme strongly supports my suspicions, finding only one-third of the alleged "effect of education on national income" is genuine.[82] To be honest, though, this research rests on too many debatable assumptions to convince me.[83]

A less rickety approach compares short-run and long-run estimates, on the theory that newfound riches take years to "trickle down" to education budgets, and bigger budgets take years to noticeably elevate the average worker's years of schooling. This theory seems to fit the facts: when a country's workforce's education rises, the apparent effect on national income is small over five years, moderate over ten years, and large over twenty years.[84] One way to suppress the taint of reverse causation, then, is to rely on the short-run results.

Step 3: Compare. At the global level, a typical year of personal education seems to raise personal income by 8–12%. A typical year of national education, in contrast, seems to raise national income by only 1–3%. While these ranges are compatible with a wide range of human capital signaling splits, signaling consistently overshadows human capital. If King Solomon had to announce a precise human capital/signaling split, 20/80 again sounds about right.[85]

Critics of the signaling model often appeal to international evidence to discredit the signaling model. "If signaling is so important, why does extra education have such a big effect on countries' economic growth?" Their question is ill conceived. Macroeconomists, to their dismay, find no clear effect of education on growth. Answers range widely from study to study, but the *average* answer matches signaling's prediction.

Critics could decry the quality of the macro evidence. They should. When researchers vary measures of education, answers change. When they vary statistical strategies, answers change. When they vary the countries or eras they study, answers change.[86] Yet none of this salvages the confident platitude that education is the path to prosperity. "The evidence reveals a tiny effect of education, so I concede a dominant role for signaling" is one reasonable reaction to the research. "The evidence reveals inconsistent effects of education, so I stick with common sense" is another. The reasonable take-away, though, lies in the middle: "The evidence, such as it is, suggests a tiny effect of education. Advantage, signaling."

What is *the* decisive argument for signaling? There isn't one. "Why education pays" is a thorny real-world issue, not a calculus problem. And to repeat, this book claims that "education is mostly signaling," never "education is all signaling." Its verdict rests on a package of arguments, all of which suggest education as we know it is *closer* to pure signaling than to pure human capital. Table 4.3 pulls all the main arguments together.

Table 4.3: Signaling in Sum

Issue	What Pure Human Capital Says	What Pure Signaling Says	Advantage?
Learning-Earning Connection	Only job-relevant learning pays.	Irrelevant learning pays too, as long as it's correlated with productivity.	Signaling
Collegiate Exclusion	Colleges prevent unofficial attendance so students actually pay tuition.	Colleges ignore unofficial attendance because the market doesn't reward it anyway.	Signaling
Failing vs. Forgetting	Employers reward workers only for coursework they still know.	Employers also reward workers for coursework they used to know.	Signaling

Easy As, Cancelled Classes, and Cheating	Students care about only marketable skills, not graduation requirements or grades.	Students care about only graduation requirements and grades, not marketable skills.	Signaling
Sheepskin Effect	Graduation years won't be especially lucrative.	Graduation years may be especially lucrative.	Signaling
Malemployment	Degrees required to *get* a job depend solely on skills required to *do* a job.	Degrees required to get a job rise when those degrees become more common.	Signaling
Employer Learning	Employers instantly discover and reward true worker productivity.	Employers never discover or reward true worker productivity.	Signaling
Personal vs. National Returns	Education equally enriches individuals and nations.	Education enriches individuals but not nations.	Signaling

What about Test Scores?

Social scientists usually measure education the lazy way: years of completed schooling. Over the past decade, however, leading researchers have upped their game. Instead of tallying how much time students put *into* school, why not measure how much knowledge students take *away* from school? Better yet, why not pinpoint the knowledge that predicts adult success and national prosperity?

The fruits of this toil are intriguing. The *Los Angeles Times* keeps tabs on L.A. teachers' "value-added"—how much each educator's students' test scores improve over a year. Value-added varies widely: Los Angeles teachers in the "most effective" category raise their classes' math scores by more than 11 percentiles in math and 6 percentiles in English.[87] Academic gains largely fade out in a few years, but researchers detect lasting effects on adult success. The "kindergarten study" by acclaimed economist Raj Chetty and coauthors finds that kids in high-scoring K–3 classrooms grow up to have higher college attendance and earnings.[88] Chetty and other coauthors report the same effects for high value-added teachers in grades 3–8.[89] The average effect of a good teacher is only a few hundred dollars per student per a year. But multiplied by thirty students over their working lives, measured benefits come to hundreds of thousands of dollars.

Many observers see a grave tension between value-added research and signaling. But where's the tension? The fact that some teachers cause higher earnings is no more informative than the fact that some high school courses and college majors cause higher earnings. The optimistic story is that better teachers give their students a little extra human capital. Since test gains are fleeting, perhaps good teachers inspire slightly higher conscientiousness and conformity. The pessimistic story is that better teachers give their students a slight edge in the ongoing signaling tournament. A good teacher convinces students that school is vital for success, so they study harder and stay in school longer, which eventually impresses employers. Neither story conflicts with my conclusion that education is *mostly* signaling.

Other researchers, most notably Eric Hanushek and coauthors, document that national test scores strongly predict national prosperity.[90] Unlike years of education, test scores are *more* crucial for national prosperity than personal prosperity.[91] Hanushek and company maintain that higher national test scores sharply lift the *rate* of economic growth: in time, modest academic gains would enrich the United States by tens of *trillions* of dollars.[92] They argue these astronomical figures are legitimately causal, especially for math and science scores.[93]

Ultimately, I'm unconvinced, largely because the vast majority of modern jobs use little math and virtually no science.[94] Why then do test scores look so potent? Probably because they reflect a deeper—and far less malleable—ability that promotes success in virtually every line of work: intelligence.[95] But even if Hanushek is completely right about what education *could* do, the signaling model correctly describes most of what education currently *does*. Hanushek himself finds little effect of educational resources on test scores—even though employers around the world amply reward mere time in school.[96] Signaling neatly explains both patterns.

Labor Economists versus Signaling

Signaling has been one of economists' more successful intellectual exports. After Spence and Arrow developed the signaling model of education in the 1970s, the idea soon spread to sociology, psychology, and education research.[97] While few experts are staunch converts, most grant the idea is plausible and the evidence suggestive. Yet strangely, one body of experts sees little or no merit in the signaling model: labor economists, particularly education specialists.[98]

In applied labor economics, human capital theory now reigns supreme. Most scholars see signaling as an irrelevant distraction. Very few would endorse anything approaching a 20/80 split in signaling's favor. A high-profile chapter in the *Handbook of the Economics of Education* fairly represents labor economists' consensus: "Our review of the available empirical evidence on Job Market Signaling leads us to conclude that there is little in the data that supports Job Market Signaling as an explanation for the observed returns to education."[99]

This is a disquieting intellectual development. Economists have plenty of blind spots, but they spend *years* studying economic theory. You would expect labor economists to have a crisp grasp of the signaling model. Yet after forty years of research, the most qualified experts turn out to be the least persuaded. If I denied I was disturbed by labor economists' disdain, I'd be lying. If they're right, I'm wrong.

Where precisely do I part company from mainstream labor economics? For the most part, I accept their empirical evidence—especially when they rely on standard, transparent statistical methods. My complaint is that mainstream labor economists have an interpretive double standard. When their evidence supports the human capital model, they take the evidence at face value. When their evidence supports the signaling model, they wrack their brains to deny signaling an iota of credit.

Consider the sheepskin effect. Almost everyone senses that big payoffs for graduation support signaling and undermine human capital. As long as the rewards for degree completion were in doubt, labor economists took the sheepskin-signaling link for granted.[100] Once evidence of large sheepskin effects became undeniable, however, labor economists moved the goal posts. Theoretically, the sheepskin effect *could* stem purely from selection; maybe students who finish their degrees would have been equally well paid if they'd dropped out a day before graduation. Sure, the sheepskin effect survives standard ability corrections unscathed. But human capital purists can demur, "You didn't correct for not-yet-measured abilities."[101] If labor economists scrupulously enforced this unmeetable burden of proof, their field would vanish.

Or take the cross-national evidence. Signaling predicts education will be more lucrative for individuals than for countries. This is precisely what researchers typically find. Yet few labor economists even grudgingly admit, "Signaling wins this round." Instead, they rush to figure out how they've erred. Maybe better data or fancier statistical methods would help. No? Then the question's beyond us. Move along, nothing to see here. My point is not that cross-national evidence is strong enough to settle the human capital/signaling debate. But if the evidence supported human capital purism, labor economists would have danced on signaling's grave instead of second-guessing their work.

Labor economists don't merely misinterpret their own evidence. They also ignore *everyone else's* evidence. Psychology, education, and sociology all have useful insights for the human capital/signaling debate, but judging from citations, labor economists rarely read their research—or admit its existence—classic Not Invented Here Syndrome.

Case in point: human capital says education raises income by imparting useful skills; signaling says education raises income without imparting useful skills. To weigh the two theories, then, you *must* investigate what students learn and retain. Psychologists and education researchers are the go-to experts on these matters. Yet labor economists almost never go to these go-to experts. If they did, they would hear lurid tales of a yawning chasm between learning and earning—precisely as signaling predicts.

Labor economists' root problem: They fall in love with education years before they study the evidence. When they meet human capital theory, they're instant converts. Two things they love—education and prosperity—go hand in hand. When budding labor economists discover signaling, they rush to reject it. Most latch on to one of the flimsy "signaling doesn't make sense" arguments from Chapter 1—"Employers would just do IQ tests instead," "You can't fool employers for long," "There's got to be a cheaper way." By the time they explore the scholarly research, labor economists can't give signaling a fair shake.

Personal experience would admittedly cloud labor economists' judgment even if love of education did not. Why? Because the link between what academics learn in school and what academics do on the job is eerily close. I call it "intellectual inbreeding." We sit in class, learn some material, then get jobs teaching the very material we studied. Professors can "acquire human capital" by recycling our old professors' lecture notes. The upshot: when we academics reflect on our own lives, school almost automatically seems "relevant." To see the labor market clearly, professors would have to contemplate the alien career paths of the vast majority of students who never enter academia.

When I argue with mainstream labor economists, they grow frustrated. "Is *everything* signaling? I have trouble believing workers can't find a cheaper way to certify their quality," they say. I'm tempted to snap, "Is *everything* human capital? I have trouble believing studying Latin makes you a better banker." My constructive answer, however, is: Of course everything isn't signaling. Students definitely learn useful job skills. School lasts over a decade. It would be amazing if students didn't learn *something* useful before they left. My claim is that education is *mostly* signaling. Given all the evidence, a 20/80 human capital/signaling split seems reasonable. I'm happy to debate the exact figure. Until labor economists renounce human capital purism, though, I cannot take their approach seriously—and neither should anyone else.

CHAPTER 5

Who Cares If It's Signaling?

The Selfish Return to Education

Human capital says education increases the size of the pie; signaling says education redistributes the pie. But what difference does it make? Who cares if the human capital/signaling split is 50/50, 20/80, or 0/100? The answer hinges on whether you analyze education from a selfish or social point of view.

Selfishly speaking, the human capital/signaling breakdown is a distraction. Bigger pie? Bigger slice? Whatever. The burning question for a selfish student is, "Will my education pay?" not "*Why* will my education pay?" True, knowing why is sporadically helpful. Human capital recommends hard-grading good teachers over easy-grading bad teachers; signaling does the reverse. Yet for most purposes, the ambitious can safely scorn theory and follow the money.

Socially speaking, however, the human capital/signaling split is all important. The closer we get to human capital purism, the more education benefits mankind. As signaling's share rises, education's social benefits fade. When we near the pure signaling pole, education becomes an incinerator that burns society's money, time, and brains in a futile attempt to make everyone look special.

When individuals weigh how to spend their own resources, most take a selfish point of view. I'm no different. When I enrolled in UC Berkeley, I didn't ponder the consequences for mankind; I was looking out for number one. When individuals weigh how to spend taxpayer resources, in contrast, most try to make the world a better place.[1] Citizens arguing about funding for public schools rarely announce, "I'm childless, so we should slash funding for public schools," or "I'm a teacher, so we should raise property taxes to double teachers' salaries." Instead, political arguments center on policies' *social* consequences: What's best overall?

Self-help gurus tend to take the selfish point of view for granted. Policy wonks tend to take the social point of view for granted. Which viewpoint—selfish or social—is "correct"? Tough question. Instead of taking sides, the next two chapters sift through the evidence from *both* perspectives—and let the reader pick the right balance between looking out for number one and making the world a better place.

The chapter in progress asks: When you invest in your own education, how well does your investment pay off for you? The question is surprisingly involved. You have to consider income, fringe benefits, unemployment risk, job satisfaction, health, and beyond—not to mention the fact that, motivational speakers notwithstanding, you *can't* "do anything you put your mind to."

Next chapter rethinks education from a social point of view. When you invest in your own education, how well does your investment pay off for *everyone*—yourself included? Given the power of signaling, the social case for education is dramatically weaker than the private case. The self-help guru who says, "You need more education" and the policy wonk who says, "We need less education" may both be right.

The Selfish Return to Education: A Primer

Imagine you could raise your income 0.1% from now until retirement by singing *Mary Poppins*. You only have to sing it once. In this world, researchers who knew people's income and musical history would detect a 0.1% "Poppins premium." Is that a good payoff? Yes! Singing the musical takes three hours. With an annual salary of $50,000, a 0.1% premium means $50 extra every year for your entire working life. Not bad, even if you hate classic Disney.

The answer would tilt, naturally, if you had to sing *Mary Poppins* on a full-price Disney cruise. Unless you already planned to take this vacation, you presumably value the cruise less than the fare. Say you value the $2,000 cruise at only $800. Now, to capture the 0.1% premium, you have to fork over three hours of your time plus the $1,200 difference between the cost of the cruise and the value of the vacation. To further sour the deal, imagine the 0.1% income premium only kicks in five years after your performance.

The point: When you weigh the value of education, knowing the benefits of education is not enough. You also need to know *costs* and *timing*.

If you invest in education, how much comes back (or "returns") to you—and how long must you wait to collect? Economists answer both questions with one number. They call that number the "rate of return to education" or just the "return to education."

Laymen cringe when economists use a single metric—rate of return—to evaluate bonds, home insulation, and college. Hasn't anyone ever told them money isn't everything! The superficial response: Economists are by no means the only folks who picture education as an investment. Look at students. The Higher Education Research Institute has questioned college freshmen about their goals since the 1970s. The vast majority is openly careerist and materialist. In 2012, almost 90% called "being able to get a better job" a "very important" or "essential" reason to go to college. Being "very well-off financially" (over 80%) and "making more money" (about 75%) are almost as popular. Less than half say the same about "developing a meaningful philosophy of life."[2] These results are especially striking because humans exaggerate their idealism and downplay their selfishness.[3] Students probably prize worldly success even more than they admit.

The deeper response to laymen's critique, though, is that economists are well aware money isn't everything—and have an official solution. Namely: *count everything people care about*. The trick: For every benefit, ponder, "How much would I pay to obtain it?" For every cost, ponder, "How much would I pay to avoid it?" Maybe you value a fulfilling job at $5,000 a year, or disvalue boring classes at $3,000 a year. While most things don't come with *visible* price tags, you can slap *mental* price tags on absolutely anything. A cynic isn't someone who puts a price on the sacred; a cynic is someone who puts a *low* price on the sacred.

After you've priced education's every benefit and cost, you can analyze it like any other investment. The world's simplest investment is a one-year loan. You lend $100. A year later, you recoup your $100 investment plus some interest. Your rate of return equals the interest divided by your initial investment. If you get back $7 in interest on a $100 loan, your return is 7%. If you get back $2 in interest, the return is 2%. If you earn no interest, the return is 0%. If you earn no interest and only recover $90 of your original investment, your return is negative 10%. The worst-case scenario is complete default, where you lend $100 and get $0 back—earning a return of negative 100%.

A simple one-year loan is the Rosetta Stone of investing. Once you grasp the return on a one-year loan, you can decipher the return on any investment whatsoever. Suppose a complex investment "has a 7% return." Translation: the complex investment is precisely as lucrative as earning 7% interest on a series of one-year loans, reinvesting every penny of interest earned along the way.

Picture a $1,000 investment that takes ten years to mature. It pays nothing for five years. Starting in year six, you recoup $300 a year for five years. Whenever another $300 check arrives, you lend it out. At the end of the tenth year, you call all your loans in and count your cash. To compute your return, imagine an alternate scenario where you repeatedly make one-year loans of $1,000, reinvesting every penny of interest. Then ask yourself: What interest rate makes both investing strategies equally rewarding? Any spreadsheet spits out the answer: 5.2%. At 5.2%, traveling either road leaves you with $1,665 at the end of your ten-year journey.

Educational investments are messy. Just listing the main benefits and costs is an endurance test. In practice, most economists take the easy way out. When they calculate the selfish (or "private") return to education, they focus on one benefit—the education premium—and two costs—tuition and foregone earnings.[4]

The education premium. Even after scrupulously correcting for ability bias, education raises earnings. The crucial question is: How much? When they answer, economists conventionally assume all years of education are created equal, and plug in "the" education premium.[5]

Tuition. Tuition is the most blatant cost of education, but you should carefully distinguish tuition from room and board. Nonstudents have living expenses too, so they aren't really a "cost of education." To be precise, you should count only the *difference* between the cost of living at school and the cost of a comparable lifestyle outside of school.

Foregone earnings. Going to school makes it harder to hold down a job. Few do both full time. So another major cost of education is the extra income you would have earned if you weren't in school.

As long as these three factors are the whole story, computing the return to education is straightforward. Start with the yearly sum you can now earn full time—say $50,000. Plug in a good ability-corrected estimate of the premium for a year of school—say 10%. Find the cost of a year of tuition—say $10,000. Then you're essentially investing $60,000—$50,000 foregone earnings plus $10,000 tuition—in order to earn an extra $5,000 every year for the rest of your working life. Assume you'll retire forty years from today. Then math savants know enough to compute the return to education in their heads—and the rest of us can consult a spreadsheet. The answer is 7.9%. Intuitively, you would end up equally rich if you'd stayed in the labor force for the year, saved all $60,000, then repeatedly invested that nest egg at 7.9%.

No primer on the return to education is complete without a technical admonition: *estimates of the return to education arrive adjusted for inflation*. In economic jargon, returns to education are "real" not "nominal." Published returns on everyday investments, in contrast, rarely arrive adjusted for inflation, so you must adjust them yourself. In recent years, the nominal rate on a 30-year Treasury bond has been about 4%; subtracting forecasted inflation leaves a real return of only 2%.[6] The oft-quoted "10% long-run return on stocks," similarly, falls to around 7% after subtracting long-run inflation.

One last question: What's a good rate of return? A bad rate? The evasive will tell you, "It depends on current interest rates, risk, risk tolerance, liquidity, leverage, the rest of your portfolio, and beyond." So true, yet so useless. In lieu of this evasive answer, I employ these helpful rules of thumb: An inflation-adjusted return of 10% is excellent. A 7% return is very good—about average for stocks. Five percent is pretty good. Three percent is so-so. Two percent is poor. One percent or less is awful.

The Selfish Return to Education: Counting Everything that Counts

Enough with the primer. Drastically simplifying the return to education is fine on a homework problem. If you seek practical guidance, however, you can't blithely assume education has precisely one benefit and exactly two costs. Instead, you must strive to count everything that counts.

This open-ended calculation begins with brainstorming—identifying every semiplausible benefit and cost of education.[7] Fortunately, an army of researchers has been brainstorming for decades. Education conceivably enhances not only compensation and employment, but job satisfaction, health, happiness, and beyond. Obtaining these benefits, though, requires more than tuition and foregone earnings. You might also miss valuable job experience and endure agonizing classroom boredom. And there's a big catch: you can pay some, most, or all the costs of education yet fail to earn your degree.

When brainstorming, *double-counting* is the key pitfall to avoid.[8] Education leads to higher income, and higher income leads to nicer stuff—better homes, better cars, better medicine. When summing the benefits of education, though, "income" and "goodies income buys" are not two distinct benefits. They are two perspectives on the same benefit. The same conceivably holds for any putative benefit of education—job satisfaction, health, whatever.

After placing a multitude of benefits and costs on the table—and vetting them for double-counting—researchers are ready to start their real work. Namely: investigating whether each alleged effect of education is genuine. If genuine, we must measure the size of the effect, scrupulously correcting for ability bias. Next, we must ballpark the dollar value of each and every effect. Then, at last, we possess the ingredients to fairly compute the return to education.

This task is so arduous I split it into two separate legs. First leg: methodically analyzing the return to education for a cartoonish "Good Student." Second leg: methodically analyzing the leading causes of higher and lower returns. By the end, you'll be armed with numerate, customized educational advice for anyone—yourself included.

Be aware: there is a chasm between *numerate* advice and *definitive* advice. Crunching numbers on the return to education is not like measuring Planck's constant. All our calculations require guesswork, yielding averages or "expected values," not precise predictions. But don't be alarmed. Whenever possible, guesswork builds on canonical data and careful academic research. Such data and research are available for every major building block in the calculations. For minor building blocks, however, data and research are often thin. Rather than pleading agnosticism—as academics are wont to do—I use my best judgment. If my "best judgment" on a component of the calculation seems off, substitute your own. Waiting for omniscience is not an option. Educational decisions confront students, workers, voters, and policy makers here and now. Instead of imagining we can live without guesswork, let us strive to guess with care.

The Selfish Return to Education: The Case of the Good Student

If a ninth-grader asks for educational advice, you should give a straight-up answer. Otherwise they won't listen. Yet this is no excuse for intellectual laziness on your part. A quality advisor carefully weighs complexities and subtleties on the advisee's behalf. That way, the counsel is not only digestible, but insightful. Let's methodically walk through the intricate benefits and costs of education, do some math, and see what insight we can offer our Good Student archetype.

What precisely *is* a Good Student? "He" is equally likely to be a man or a woman. He keeps busy: he's either a full-time student or—job market permitting—a full-time worker. He's single and childless. He attends nearby public schools at all levels of education. Most critically, picture the Good Student as someone who *fits the profile* of the B.A. who did *not* continue on to graduate or professional school. "Fits the profile" is deliberately all-inclusive: the Good Student has B.A.s' *average* cognitive ability, character, background, and everything else. In practice, we never know all this information; we have to do our best with what's available. In terms of measured cognitive ability, the Good Student stands at the 73rd percentile.[9]

By construction, a Good Student who finishes his B.A. enjoys outcomes that *match* those of the average college graduate in the real world. If the Good Student quits high school, however, he gets the outcomes for a high school dropout who fits the profile of the typical B.A.[10] If the Good Student finishes only high school, he gets the outcomes for a high school graduate who fits the profile of the typical college graduate. If he completes a master's degree, he gets the outcomes for a master's degree holder who fits the profile of the typical B.A.

Compensation. We've already learned three vital facts about the effect of education on compensation. First, thanks to ability bias, education's financial benefits—cash and noncash—are smaller than they look. A reasonable estimate is that only 55% of the apparent premium is genuine.[11] Second, most of education's financial benefits are sheepskin effects. In percentage terms, the last year of high school is worth about 3.4 times as much as a regular high school year, and the last year of college is worth about 6.7 times as much as a regular college year. Since sheepskin results for the master's are sparse, I assume they match the bachelor's ratio.[12] Third, noncash benefits are a big deal. Compensation exceeds income by an average of 44%.[13] While more educated workers earn higher benefits, the ratio of benefits to income mildly *falls* as education rises.[14]

What does this imply for a Good Student? If he stops his education after finishing college, then by definition he earns the average compensation for a college graduate. What if our Good Student stops school sooner or stays in school longer? Then we can estimate education's effect on income by taking Table 3.1's raw earnings for full-time, year-round workers, then adjusting them for ability bias and sheepskin effects.[15] To reach education's effect on noncash benefits, calculations start with the Congressional Budget Office's benefit/income ratios for private sector workers, then assume ability bias and sheepskin effects for benefits match those for income.[16]

Figure 5.1 shows the output. A regular school year—in high school, college, or graduate program—boosts annual compensation by two or three thousand dollars. Crossing academic finish lines, however, is far more lucrative: the annual bonus is $9,000 for a high school diploma, $20,000 for a bachelor's degree, and $13,000 for a master's.

Employment. Figure 5.1 shows income for full-time, year-round workers, who by definition work at least 50 weeks per year.[17] Yet in the actual labor market, people who *want* to work year-round sometimes struggle to work at all.

Labor statisticians distinguish two ways to lack a job. If you're hunting for a job but have yet to find one, you're "unemployed"; if you're not even hunting for a job, you're "out of the labor force." When calculating the return to education, some researchers adjust for *both* forms of idleness.[18] On reflection, this is a mistake. Reducing your risk of unemployment is a clear gain; it means you're likely to have a job when you want one. Reducing your risk of being out of the labor force, in contrast, is not a clear gain; it only means you're more likely to *want* a job.[19]

While all workers risk unemployment, the risk falls with education. From 2000 to 2013, the average unemployment rate was 10.0% for dropouts, 6.3% for high school grads, 3.4% for college grads, and 2.7% for

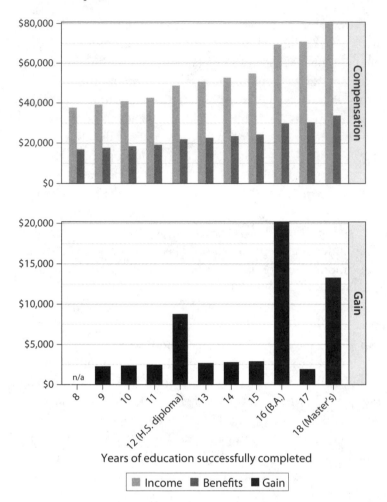

Figure 5.1: The Effect of Education on Compensation for a Good Student (2011)
Source: United States Census Bureau 2012d, 2012e, assuming:
(a) Full-time, year-round employment.
(b) 50/50 gender balance.
(c) 45% ability bias.
(d) Private sector ratios of overall compensation to cash compensation by education level from Falk 2012, pp. 6, 10.
(e) Finishing the last year of high school has 3.4 times the percent effect of one ordinary high school year, finishing the last year of four-year college has 6.7 times the percent effect of one ordinary college year, and finishing the last year of a master's has 6.7 times the percent effect of one ordinary master's year.

those with a master's.[20] By definition, a Good Student who only finishes a B.A. gets the average unemployment rate for college grads: 3.4%. To predict unemployment for Good Students with other education levels, I adjust raw gaps for ability bias and sheepskin effects. Unfortunately, few papers estimate ability bias for unemployment, and—to the best of my knowledge—no papers estimate sheepskin effects for unemployment.[21] Given this sparse evidence, the natural approach is to assume education affects employment the *same* way it affects compensation (see Figure 5.2).

Taxes and transfers. When a new degree lands you a higher-paying job, you don't pocket the entire raise. Uncle Sam demands his cut. When your lack of a degree leads to a layoff, you don't starve in the streets. Uncle Sam sends you an unemployment check. How do these taxes and transfers sway education's payoff?

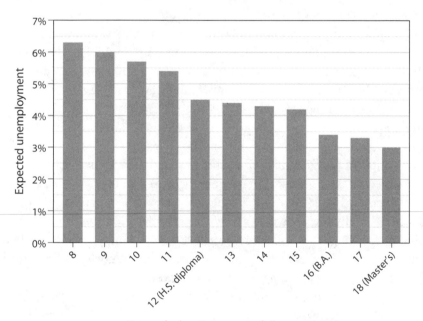

Figure 5.2: The Effect of Education on Unemployment for a Good Student
Source: Federal Reserve Bank of St. Louis 2015, assuming:
(a) 50/50 gender balance.
(b) 45% ability bias.
(c) Sheepskin breakdown from Figure 5.1.

The complexity of U.S. tax code and welfare state is legendary. To ballpark federal taxes, I apply the 2011 tax code to workers' *expected* income.[22] Calculations assume workers take the standard deduction and pay an additional flat rate of 10% in state and local taxes. Noncash benefits are untaxed. Since the Good Student is by assumption a single, childless, full-time worker, he is eligible for only one important transfer: unemployment benefits.[23] Calculations assume unemployed workers receive the *average* 2011 unemployment benefit of $300 per week.[24] While state-by-state formulas pay larger benefits to workers with higher earning histories, statutory floors and ceilings on benefit levels keep payments for full-time workers within fairly narrow bounds.[25]

Job satisfaction. I have a dream job for life. I get paid to think my thoughts, share my ideas with students, and eat lunch with my best friends. I owe this job to my education; without my Ph.D., I would not be at George Mason University. If I never went to grad school, I might earn more in another line of work, but my job satisfaction would crash.

I'm apparently atypical. More educated workers are marginally happier with their jobs. For the most part, however, this stems from higher income. When you compare workers with equal incomes but *un*equal educations, education has no clear effect on job satisfaction.[26] Some researchers actually find job satisfaction goes down as education goes up.[27] One plausible reason: education raises expectations. College graduates are harder to please because they compare themselves to fellow college grads and feel *entitled* to a "good job." But on balance, we should stick to the moderate position that—income aside—education has zero average effect on job satisfaction.

Happiness. Better-educated people are, on average, happier.[28] Does education really turn you into a happier person? As long as you eschew double-counting, the evidence is weak. Education may slightly boost happiness, even correcting for income. One team reports that college graduates are two percentage points more likely to be happy than high school grads, and high school grads four percentage points more likely to be happy than dropouts.[29] Research correcting for both income and health, however, finds education could actually *reduce* happiness.[30] Again, perhaps education inflates expectations: college graduates must be more objectively fortunate to avoid the subjective feeling the universe is against them. Since the evidence is mixed and weak, calculations set the happiness benefit of education to zero.

The agony and ecstasy of learning. People who hear I'm a college professor often reminisce about their time in school, living the life of the mind. Few tell me, "I'm happy *now* because I went to college." But many yearn for the good old days: "How wonderful to be a student again, savoring fascinating new ideas every day!" When I look at college students, though, I see little savoring. Excruciatingly bored students fill the classrooms. Well, "fill" isn't quite right, because so many don't bother to show up.

Objecting, "Some students love school, some hate it. The end," is a cop-out. On average, students are painfully bored. The High School Survey of Student Engagement, probably the single best study of how high school students feel about school, reports that 66% of high school students say they're bored in class *every day*. Seventeen percent say they're bored in *every* class *every* day. Only 2% claim they're never bored in class. Why so bored? Eighty-two percent say the material isn't interesting; 41% say the material isn't relevant.[31] Another research team gave beepers to middle school students to capture their feelings in real time. During schoolwork, students were bored 36% of the time, versus 17% for all other activities.[32] No wonder a major Gates Foundation study ranked boredom the *most* important reason why kids drop out of high school.[33]

Research on college boredom is thin but confirms the continuity of pain. A study of British college students found 59% were bored in half or more of their lectures. Only 2% claimed to find none of their lectures boring.[34] Since classroom attendance is usually optional in college, we can also reason from students' *behavior* rather than merely inquiring about their feelings. Look at attendance. Students loathe class so much that 25–40% don't show up.[35]

One could protest that for every disgruntled student who cuts class, there's an enthusiastic student sucking the marrow out of college. Wishful thinking. Remember: even though college students are generally free to unofficially attend any course, cutting classes is far more common than crashing classes. My teaching is highly rated, and I publicly announce all my courses are open to everyone on earth. Yet guests fill under 5% of my seats.

The harsh reality, then, is that most students suffer in school. Nostalgics who paint their education as an intellectual feast are either liars or outliers. In terms of *The Simpsons*, Barts vastly outnumber Lisas. The

Simpson family's most typical student, though, is Homer. From the episode "Two Bad Neighbors":

> HOMER: Marge, I'm bored . . .
> MARGE: Why don't you read a book, then?
> HOMER: Because I'm trying to *reduce* my boredom.[36]

When calculating the Good Student's return to education, we must count the pain he faced in the classroom. Key proviso: Since we're weighing school versus work, we shouldn't count *all* academic malaise. Instead, we should compare the agony of school to the agony of work—and assign a dollar value to the emotional *difference*. As long as work feels even worse than school, counting students' malaise actually improves the return to education.

The strongest available evidence on the relative pleasantness of work and school comes from the Princeton Affect and Time Survey (PATS). Surveyors phoned a random sample of Americans and walked them through the previous day to find out (a) how respondents spent their hours, and (b) how each activity made them feel at the time—happy, stressed, sad, interested, pained? All PATS emotion scales run from 0 (not feeling the emotion at all) to 6 (feeling the emotion very strongly).

Main result: ranking activities from most to least pleasant, work and education are both near the *bottom* of the list. Yet work has a slight edge. During work hours, people are a little less stressed and sad, equally bored, but feel slightly more pain.[37] The biggest difference is happiness. Work happiness averages 3.83—versus 3.55 for education. Education barely beats elder care, the depths of woe.[38]

What price tag should we put on school's emotional cost? Imagine you could make your primary task (work or school) a full step happier on a 0–6 scale. Five percent of your full-time income sounds like a reasonable deal. Then with a full-time income of $20,000, being in school feels $280 per year worse than being on the job. This is small enough to ignore, but initial calculations include it so we can swing back later and recalculate returns for students who love—or loathe—sitting in class.

Health. I've been hearing proeducation sales pitches since I was a small child. In all these years, I've *never* heard someone nag, "Finish high school or you'll get sick a lot," "College makes you live longer," or

"Health troubles? A master's degree could be the cure you're looking for." Yet despite public silence, decades of research in medicine, economics, and sociology find education does a body good. Higher-quality studies self-consciously measure the effect of education on health correcting for income, to see if education gives you a healthier body even if it *fails* to get you a better job.

While laymen tend to see education's apparent health benefit as spurious, the research consensus says otherwise. After correcting for income, intelligence, conscientiousness, time horizon, risk taking, and more, education still seems to make you live longer and feel healthier. Most of these benefits *don't* look like sheepskin effects; the health benefits of education—unlike the career benefits—are fairly smooth.[39]

Start with basic survival. Multiple research teams estimate the effect of education on U.S. mortality using the National Longitudinal Mortality Study.[40] Research designs vary, but all adjust for age, demographics, and income. Correcting for these traits, typical results imply a year of education increases life expectancy by .1 to .4 years.[41] But in all candor, the range is wide. One prominent study finds that, correcting for income and lifestyle, education might actually hurt life expectancy.[42] A study at the other extreme finds a year of education boosts life expectancy by "as much as 1.7 years."[43] Another research team detects large sheepskin effects for mortality; while most years make little difference, high school graduation boosts life expectancy by a year or more, with even larger effects for college completion.[44]

All these figures are probably inflated, as many of the sources themselves admit. One serious problem is that income, unlike education, jumps around from year to year. As a result, education "steals" some credit that rightfully belongs to *long-run* income.[45] Furthermore, some of the apparent effect of education and income on health probably reflects reverse causation: poor health impedes both scholastic and professional success.[46]

The deeper problem is that education often brings better health at onerous personal cost. To a large degree, the better educated are healthier because they have healthier lifestyles.[47] They drink less, smoke less, weigh less, and exercise more. Looming question: If people enjoy drinking, smoking, eating, and loafing, are healthier lifestyles truly a "benefit"? Suppose education caused celibacy, which in turn raised life expectancy

by eliminating all risk of venereal disease. Hailing celibacy-induced longevity as a clear-cut "benefit of education" would still be odd. Why isn't
it equally odd to name higher exercise—or lower drinking, smoking, or
eating—as clear-cut "benefits of education"?

The most tempting response is that the "health benefits of education"
are not healthier lifestyles per se, but *better-informed* health decisions.
The more you know about health, the lower the personal cost of being
healthy. Yet when researchers directly measure health knowledge, they
find little effect on lifestyle.[48] If this seems implausible, note that to this
day, smoking rates fall sharply with education, even though knowledge of the dangers of smoking has been near-universal for decades.
The same goes for the health effects of alcohol, obesity, exercise—and
celibacy. Taking all these caveats together, my best guess is that the true
survival benefit of a year of education is somewhere between nothing
and a fifth of a year. Subsequent calculations use the midpoint, .1 years.

Since health is more than survival, researchers also scrutinize education's effect on "wellness." Usual method: present a health scale, then ask
people to place themselves. The General Social Survey asks, "Would you
say your own health, in general, is excellent, good, fair, or poor?"—a
four-step scale. Other surveys use five-step or seven-step scales; the bigger the scale, the less impressive a one-step gain. While this approach
may seem hopelessly subjective, self-rated health is a good predictor of
objective health outcomes—and mortality itself.[49]

As education rises, so does self-rated health. On the General Social
Survey's four-step scale, for example, an extra year of education raises
self-rated health about .08 points. Correcting for competing factors cuts
the measured effect, but some health benefit almost always remains. In
the General Social Survey, correcting for income and demographics
halves the benefit of education from .08 points per year to .04 points per
year.[50] Research teams using other data sources find similar magnitudes.
Correcting for income, demographics, and a range of other factors, estimates of the health gain of a year of education range from a high of
.07 steps on a five-step scale to a low of .01 steps on a seven-step scale.[51]

All these self-rated health effects are inflated for the same reason
lifespan effects are inflated. Income jumps around from year to year, so
education is partly a proxy for long-run income. Part of the measured
"effect of education on health" is probably an "effect of health on edu-

cation."[52] And to a fair degree, education makes people feel healthier via puritanical habits. When researchers adjust for lifestyle, the effect of education on perceived health falls by about a third.[53] Taking all these caveats together, my best guess is that the true health benefit of year of education is somewhere between nothing and .02 steps on a four-step scale. Subsequent calculations use the midpoint—.01 steps.

Since calculating the return to education is our goal, putting price tags on these health benefits is the last step. Start with longevity. Cost-benefit analysts' standard "value of a year of healthy life" is $50,000, but this absurdly treats leisure time as worthless.[54] Setting the value equal to *potential* annual earnings—roughly *two* full-time incomes—is more judicious. So if a year of education prolongs your life by .1 years, and your full-time income is $50,000 a year, the life expectancy benefit boils down to $10,000. Not $10,000 per year; $10,000 total.

For self-rated health, researchers have yet to settle on any "standard dollar value." Indeed, they rarely raise the issue. A plausible rule of thumb, though, is that a full step on a four-step health scale is worth 20% of your full-time income. So if a year of education improves self-rated health by .01 steps, and your full-time income is $50,000 a year, the quality of life benefit boils down to $100. Not $100 total; $100 per year.[55]

Tuition and other expenses. Elites pay shocking sums for education. Annual tuition and fees for high school students at Phillips Exeter Academy now run $37,000.[56] Harvard University's list price exceeds $45,000 a year.[57] Students who live on campus pay even more. A child of privilege can easily consume a half million dollars of education before landing their first job.

The cost for a Good Student, who by assumption attends nearby public schools, is drastically lower. Instead of $37,000 a year for Exeter, he attends high school free of charge. Instead of $45,000 a year for Harvard, he pays in-state tuition at his local college—and unlike the elite, receives a lot of financial aid. For the bottom line, turn to the College Board's annual *Trends in College Pricing*. This report tabulates the list price of college, then subtracts average financial aid to yield "net tuition." For our Good Student, the final numbers are shockingly affordable.[58] The out-of-pocket cost of a year of four-year college—tuition, fees, books, and supplies minus aid—sums to $3,662.[59]

Adding the cost of room and board more than triples this figure; the average price of on-campus living was another $8,890. Yet most researchers avowedly ignore such expenses. You have to live somewhere, and you have to eat something. Since we've already stipulated that a Good Student attends a *nearby* college, we may as well assume he lives with his family for free, setting the *extra* cost of college to $3,662 on the nose.

If you're elite or near-elite, $3,662 per year for college sounds like con artistry. You might scoff, "I don't know *anyone* who paid that." Rather than dismiss the numbers, though, know you live in a bubble. When folks like you go to public universities, you pay close to list price. That doesn't stop other kids from getting four-year degrees for less than the cost of a semester at Harvard.

Of course, college students who live at home miss the classic residential "college life" of daily socializing and recreation. Research is scarce, but many students clearly savor these nonacademic experiences. The downside, naturally, is the extra expense. To deal with this issue, I make two assumptions. First: students who live at home have as much fun as workers who live at home. Second: students who live on-campus value the residential experience at cost, so the *net* benefit of campus socializing and recreation is zero. This is overly pessimistic for extroverted and fun-loving students but could easily be too optimistic for students with the opposite temperament.

What about advanced degrees? While solid statistics on net tuition are scarce, financial aid is abundant.[60] Overall, setting graduate net tuition equal to undergraduate net tuition is a tolerable approximation—and we'll use it.

Foregone earnings. Even if tuition is zero, schooling is not free. Instead of attending school full time, our Good Student could have worked full time. Whatever compensation he *fails* to earn while in school is a cost of education. Indeed, given the affordability of net tuition, the compensation he fails to earn while in school is the *main* cost of education.

Can you really measure what you "fail to earn"? We already have. Revisit Figure 5.1. If you use it to guess how much a Good Student *will* earn if he spends more years in school, you can also use it to guess how much a Good Student *would have* earned if he spent fewer years in school.

Full-time workers earn full-time income and full-time benefits—unless, of course, they're unemployed. Is full-time compensation times probability of employment a fair measure of everything a student fails to earn? Almost. Main doubt: many full-time students have part-time jobs. We should subtract their pay from foregone full-time earnings. Still, part-time workers' low pay—not to mention the prevalence of unpaid internships—calls for only a modest adjustment—say 10% of full-time compensation.

Accounting for experience. When you have a job, you don't just earn income. Job experience improves your job skills—and the labor market rewards these extra skills with higher pay—also known as the "experience premium." The longer you stay in school, the longer you wait to learn skills on the job—and the longer you postpone the attendant raises.

The rewards of experience are . . . complicated. On average, an extra year raises earnings by 2–3%.[61] On closer look, though, the first years of career experience are several times as fruitful—and the last years are almost worthless.[62] Since more realistic earnings paths imply similar rates of return, my calculations stick to constant growth of 2.5%.[63]

Completion probability. Suppose a bank charges 10% interest on one-year loans. This doesn't mean the bank earns 10% interest on the average loan. Some borrowers default. They could spend the entire loan, then skip town or declare bankruptcy. Even rare defaults gut the lender's rate of return. When one borrower in twenty reneges, the bank's return falls by *55%*—from 10% to 4.5%.[64]

Educational investments face the same hurdle: *Trying* a year of school never ensures success. Students can and do pay tuition, kill a year, and flunk their finals. A small risk of failing a year of school, like a small risk of defaulting on a loan, sharply depresses education's return. Any respectable estimate of the return to education must account for these academic "bankruptcies."[65] The power of the sheepskin effect amplifies this truth. You cannot win the oversized prize for crossing the finish line unless you surmount *all* the intermediate obstacles. Of course, schools often allow students to repeat a failed year, but this gives students who waste a year's time and tuition only the chance to gamble another year's time and tuition. Every casino offers the same deal.

Unreflective researchers naturally overlook noncompletion because it falls far outside their personal experience. The researchers finished their degrees. So did almost everyone they personally know. How bad can attrition be? Dismal. Overall dropout or "noncompletion" rates are high at all levels of American education. About 25% of high school students fail to finish in four years. About 60% of full-time college students fail to finish in four years. Half of advanced degree students never finish at all.[66]

But these are only averages—and you shouldn't expect *Good* Students to have *average* completion probabilities. In high school, the Good Student is a big fish in a small pond, so his success rate is better than normal. In advanced degree programs, however, the Good Student is a small fish in a big pond, so his success rate is worse than normal.

How much better? How much worse? These are tough questions, and research is thinner than you'd expect. After reviewing available evidence, the Technical Appendix ends up assigning Good Students the following probabilities: 92.3% to finish high school in four years, 43.5% to finish a bachelor's degree in four years, and 32.7% to finish a master's in two years. Attrition, however, is gradual. To correct education's *annual* payoff, we need *annual* success probabilities. For simplicity, calculations assume constant failure rates.[67]

The punch line for Good Students. Time to pour all the numbers into a spreadsheet and crunch them. If you're a Good Student, how well does education pay? Figure 5.3 shows the results from two different angles: the Annual Return and the Degree Return. The Annual Return answers the question, "All things considered—risk of failure included—what is the value of trying the *current year* of education?" The Degree Return answers the question, "All things considered—risk of failure included—what is the value of continuing to pursue the *next degree on the horizon*?"[68] The Annual Return helps you decide, "If this were my last chance to spend a year in school, should I attend?" The Degree Return helps you decide, "If this were my last chance to earn a degree, should I stay in the program?"

Good Students plainly enjoy some hefty Annual Returns; remember, they're adjusted for inflation. High school and college graduation years are far more lucrative than stocks. Even the return for the final year of a master's roughly matches the stock market. The 4.8% rewards for intermediate high school years are pretty good. Intermediate college years, with a return around 2.5%, aren't awful. The only serious disappointment is the master's first-year negative return.

Degree Returns are also tasty. When a Good Student starts ninth grade, the next four years pay an average annual return of 7.4%. Every time he successfully completes a year of high school, the Degree Return ascends. Once he starts twelfth grade, the Degree Return equals the Annual Return of 16.2%. Why do Degree Returns rise as students progress? Because each year of educational success puts them one step closer to winning the pot of gold waiting over the finish line.

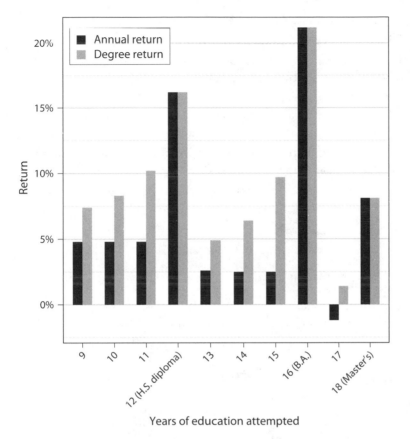

Figure 5.3: The Selfish Return to Education for Good Students
Source: Figures 5.1 and 5.2 and text.

College pays poorly by comparison, but it's still a great deal. When a Good Student starts college, the next four years pay an average annual return of 4.9%. Since that's adjusted for inflation, trying college is comparable to buying corporate bonds. Not a no-brainer, but a sound investment nonetheless. Master's degrees pay rather worse. On the first day of class, a Good Student can expect a paltry Degree Return of 1.4%.

The master's aside, education looks like such a good deal for the Good Student you may wonder, "Have all the doubts this book raises about education's selfish return been pointless pedantry?" Part of the answer, we'll soon see, is that education is less lucrative for the Fair Student, not to mention the Poor Student. The rest of the answer is that when you ignore my key doubts—ability bias and completion probability—

education is *astronomically* profitable. If dropouts and Ph.D.s had equal raw ability, and 100% of students finished whatever schooling they attempted, the selfish return to education would look like this—not just for Good Students, but for everyone (see Figure 5.4).

Check those double-digit financials. Every graduation year has an Annual Return over 20%. When starting high school, students can look forward to Degree Returns of 13%. For college, it's 15%. For a master's, 12% again. Dealing with my doubts hardly turns education into a bad deal. *Failing* to deal with my doubts, however, turns education into a full-blown get-rich-quick scheme. Hopefully you've heard the aphorism, "If it seems too good to be true, it probably is."

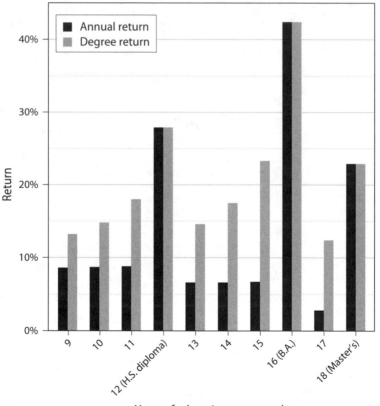

Figure 5.4: The Naive Selfish Return to Education for All Students
Source: Figures 5.1 and 5.2 and text.

The Selfish Return to Education: The Case of Everyone Else

We have reached a way station. Brainstorming and evidence collection have led us to estimates of the selfish return to education for Good Students. Now we're ready to push on to our final destination: computing the selfish return to education for virtually anyone. The journey remains treacherous, so we'll take it one step at a time, investigating how the selfish return varies by ability, choice of major, school quality, feelings about school versus work, gender, marital status, and more. All underlying spreadsheets are online, so readers can not only audit the math, but edit the assumptions for personal guidance.[69]

Ability and the selfish return to education. The Good Student, by definition, fits the profile of a typical B.A. who did *not* continue on to graduate or professional school. Now let's define three more ability archetypes: the Excellent Student, the Fair Student, and the Poor Student. The *Excellent Student* fits the profile of the typical master's degree holder. The *Fair Student* fits the profile of the typical high school graduate who does *not* try college. The *Poor Student* fits the profile of the typical high school dropout. Ideally, to repeat, "fits the profile" is all-inclusive, covering cognitive ability, character, background, and every other trait. In terms of measured cognitive ability, Excellent Students are around the 82nd percentile, Good Students the 73rd, Fair Students the 41st, and Poor Students the 24th.[70] Figure 5.5 shows expected compensation (earnings plus benefits) for each archetype.

The *absolute* benefits of education are larger for abler students. The Poor Student who drops out after eighth grade instead of forging ahead to a master's loses about $40,000 per year. The Excellent Student who does the same loses over $65,000 per year. Yet this does not imply Poor Students get a smaller *return* on their investment than Excellent Students. A Poor Student who quits work to study full time loses far less income than an Excellent Student who walks the same path.

This reasoning has led noted labor economists to urge education—especially college—regardless of student ability.[71] There is serious flaw in their logic. Figure 5.5 shows what happens only when students *successfully complete* a year of education. The harsh reality is that academic success is never certain and heavily rides on academic ability. How heavily?

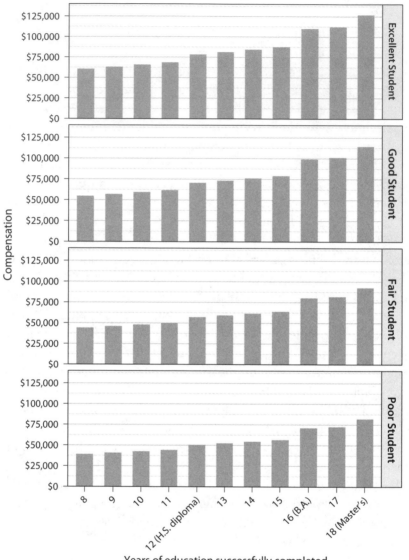

Figure 5.5: The Effect of Education on Compensation by Student Ability (2011)
Source: Figure 5.1 and text.

The Technical Appendix sifts through the less-than-ideal evidence. Figure 5.6 shows my best estimates.

Using these completion probabilities, Figure 5.7 shows Degree Returns by ability.

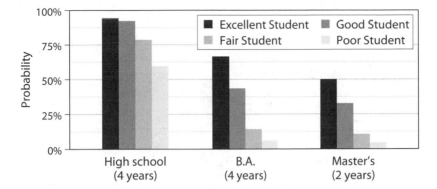

Figure 5.6: Degree Completion Probability by Student Ability
Source: See Technical Appendix.

Results closely match common sense. High school is lucrative for all four archetypes. Even Poor Students can reasonably expect the resources they invest in high school to out-perform high-yield bonds.[72] College, in contrast, is a solid deal only for Excellent and Good Students. Largely owing to their high failure rate, Fair Students who start college should foresee a low 2.3% return on their investment. For Poor Students, it's a paltry 1%. Master's degrees, finally, are a so-so deal for Excellent Students, a bad deal for Good Students, and a money pit for Fair and Poor Students.

Major and the selfish return to education. Talking about "the" return to education is handy but misleading. Your payoff hinges on *what* you study. While this presumably holds at all levels, researchers have largely focused on college students' academic majors.[73] Rather than cover all leading majors, I compare business—the archetypal "average" major—to two cases with infamously divergent career prospects: electrical engineering and fine arts (see Figure 5.8).[74]

The results are parental wisdom incarnate. The electrical engineering degree pays very well, especially for stronger students. The fine arts degree pays very poorly, especially for weaker students. Remember: zero and negative returns don't mean fine arts degrees are *worthless* in the labor market. A fine art degree raises expected income over 20%. What zero and negative returns mean, rather, is that capturing that raise is more trouble for Fair and Poor Students than it's worth.

Financially, anyway. If you love studying the arts—and yearn for an artistic career—you may welcome a seemingly ruinous rate of return.

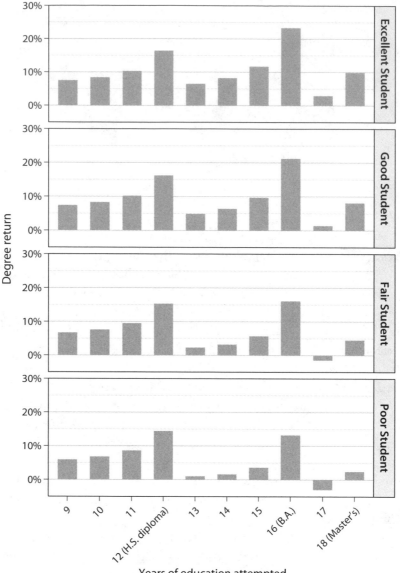

Figure 5.7: Selfish Degree Returns by Student Ability
Source: Figures 5.5 and 5.6 and text.

Put a dollar value on your feelings, edit my spreadsheets, and recrunch your customized numbers. When you do, remember you're more likely to find a major you love than a job that *uses* the major you love.

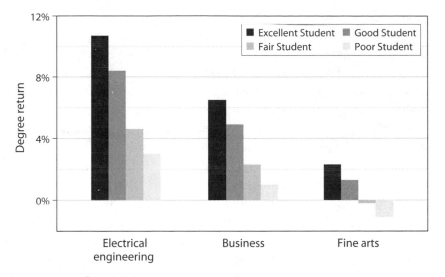

Figure 5.8: Freshmen's Selfish Degree Returns by Major
Source: Figure 5.7 and text.

College quality and the selfish return to education. What you study has a big effect in the labor market. What about *where* you study? Tiger Moms and Dragon Dads strive to place their kids in "top schools." How much does your alma mater's rank matter? Research is oddly mixed.[75] The consensus point: where you study is less important than what you study. As some early researchers said, "While sending your child to Harvard appears to be a good investment, sending him to your local state university to major in Engineering, to take lots of math, and preferably to attain a high GPA, is an even better investment."[76]

Deeper expert agreement is elusive. Students from top schools enjoy great success, but the specter of ability bias looms. Ivy League kids are so promising you'd expect them to excel with diplomas from Podunk State. To cope with this ability bias, researchers compare graduates of diverse colleges after statistically equalizing SATs, high school GPAs, family backgrounds, and so on. Further hurdle: "College quality" (also known as "selectivity") is vaguer than it sounds. Some researchers use average SAT scores, others Barron's ratings or tuition.

Answers dramatically vary. Two prominent papers by Stacy Dale and Alan Krueger find collegiate pedigree is almost worthless.[77] While they focus on a subset of largely selective schools, they get similar results in a representative sample.[78] Their most amazing discovery is that students who *submit* lots of applications to high-quality schools enjoy exceptional career success whether or not they attend such schools.[79] The reason presumably isn't that employers base salaries on what workers mailed when they were seventeen years old. The sensible tale is that college applicants who shoot high and cover their bases are full of ambition and determination—two traits the labor market handsomely rewards. If Dale and Krueger's results feel implausible, picture all the faculty attention and support the University of Delaware would shower on a student good enough for Harvard.

Intriguing as Dale and Krueger's studies are, they remain outliers. Virtually all other specialists detect *some* payoff for college pedigree. Indeed, whenever Dale and Krueger discard what they know about college applications, they detect payoffs for college pedigree, too. Researchers who measure quality with Barron's ratings typically find graduates from "top" schools out-earn graduates of "bottom" schools by about 20%.[80] Researchers who measure quality with average SAT scores find raising average SATs by 100 points raises graduates' income by anywhere from 1% to 11%.[81] Researchers who measure quality with tuition find raising it by $1,000 raises graduates' earnings by 0–1%, and raising it by 10% raises graduates' earnings by 0–1.4%.[82] Studies also compare graduates of private versus public schools, with mixed results.[83] The most impressive research carefully merges diverse measures into an overall index of college quality.[84] Punch line: moving from the bottom to the top quartile raises male earnings by about 12% and female earnings by about 8%.[85]

Does this mean a money-grubbing college-goer should attend the most selective school that will have them? Not necessarily. Intuitively, you would expect better schools to be harder, and harder schools to have lower completion probabilities. Could you even survive at Caltech? A glance at graduation rates shows that students at better schools have unusually *high* completion probabilities,[86] but there's an obvious explanation: students at top schools are awesome enough to surmount the toughest coursework with ease.

Strangely, most experts on this topic ultimately reject this common-sense story. The consensus, instead, is that top schools are a free lunch. Hand Princeton a random student, and it *boosts* their graduation probability along with their salary after graduation.[87] How? Maybe studying and slacking are contagious; if you're surrounded by diligent students, you're slacking alone. Personally, I suspect students at top schools have extra advantages that researchers overlook.[88] Still, in light of the evidence, my rates of return treat college quality and completion probability as unrelated.

What then is the return for graduating from a top school instead of a bottom school? Since research is mixed, Figure 5.9 builds on low, middle, and high estimates of the quality premium. The low estimate is no quality premium. The middle estimate is that top schools lead to 5% higher—and bottom schools to 5% lower—compensation.[89] The high estimate is +10% for top schools and −10% for bottom schools. For the time being, keep assuming tuition is locked at $3,662 a year.

As long as extra quality neither raises tuition nor depresses completion, every student has but two choices worth considering: go to the best college that accepts you, or don't go at all. The curious implication: as the quality premium goes up, college becomes an even better deal for Excellent and Good Students, and an even worse deal for Fair and Poor Students. Why? Because strong students can get into the good schools—and weak students have to settle for not-so-good schools. The best school that accepts a weak student probably isn't good enough to attend.

Out-of-pocket costs and the selfish return to education. My calculations for bachelor's and master's degrees assume everyone pays public institutions' average net price of $3,662 a year. How do returns change if a student gets a full scholarship—or pays list price at a private university?[90]

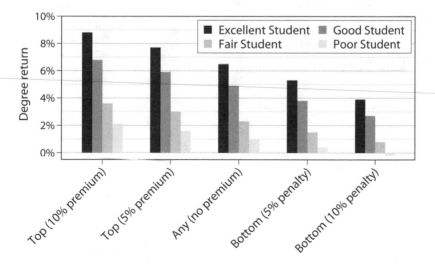

Figure 5.9: Freshmen Selfish Degree Returns by College Quality
Source: Figure 5.7 and text.

Figure 5.10 shows how out-of-pocket costs sway returns *if* college quality does not depend on cost (or the labor market doesn't pay for college quality).

The numbers are much as you'd expect. For Fair and Poor Students, even full scholarships can't make college a good deal. Paying list price at public schools is a good deal for Excellent Students, a pretty good deal for Good Students, and a lousy deal for Fair and Poor Students. Unless you're an Excellent Student, private school is a mediocre investment at best—even counting the standard rebates.[91] Added complication: the most elite colleges often have *very* generous financial aid for top students from low-income families. If your family income is less than $75,000, for example, Harvard normally charges less than official in-state tuition at George Mason University.[92] Excellent Students from poor families are well advised to apply to top schools—and go with the lowest bidder.

Doesn't higher tuition buy better degrees? Far from clear. Measured by Barron's ratings or average SAT scores, many public schools—such as UC Berkeley, the University of Virginia, and the University of

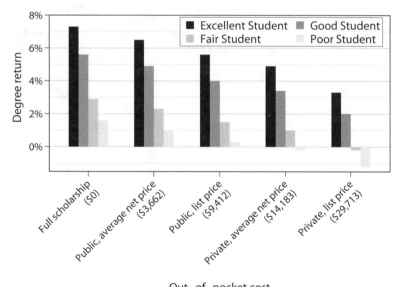

Out—of—pocket cost

Figure 5.10: College Freshmen's Selfish Degree Returns by Out-of-Pocket Costs
Source: Figure 5.7, S. Baum and Ma 2011, and text. "List price" = "Tuition and Fees" + "Books and Supplies"; "Average Net Price" = "List price" – "Federal Grants and Tax Benefits" – "State Grants" – "Institutional Grants" – "Outside Grants" (S. Baum and Ma 2011, pp. 6, 15).

Michigan—approach the top of the pecking order. As long as your state's best public school admits you, there's no solid reason to pay more.[93]

Final point: while many parents willingly cover tuition, few ask their kids, "Would you prefer the cash, no strings attached?" Owing to this earmarked parental subsidy, education can be an awful investment for your family *and* a great investment for you. Suppose you're a Good Student at a private school, and your parents pay full fare. Your *family's* Degree Return is 2%. Selfishly speaking, however, you get Figure 5.10's "full scholarship" return of 5.6%—or better if your parents toss in some spending money.

School-versus-work feelings and the selfish return to education. My favorite students live and breathe economics, but my favorite students are weird. Most human beings dislike both work and school but dislike work a little *less*. Many quit school and find a job because school is so boring; few quit work and find a school because work is so boring. What happens, though, if we forget averages and ponder outliers?

This chapter posited that making your primary task (work or school) a full step happier on a 0–6 scale is worth 5% of your full-time income. So picture two characters. One maximally loves school and maximally hates work—enough to pay 30% of full-time income to stay in school. The other maximally hates school and maximally loves work—enough to pay 30% of full-time income to stay *out* of school. How do extreme pro- and antischool feelings shift Degree Returns (see Figure 5.11)?

The clearest lesson: dropping out of high school is imprudent for virtually all shapes and sizes. Even Poor Students who *loathe* school should foresee returns near 5%. Other lessons: Higher education is a good deal for Excellent Students even if they despise school. For Good Students, though, deep-seated hostility makes higher education a close call. The flip side: College is a so-so deal for Fair Students who truly love school. Otherwise, higher education for Fair and Poor Students is a hail-Mary pass. Unless they get lucky, they can better prepare for their future by getting a job and saving money. The master's degree, finally, is an okay deal for Excellent Students who adore school. Everyone else, beware.

Sex and the selfish return to education. Hewing to our assumption that all workers stay in the labor force from graduation until retirement, how does men's return to education compare to women's? Women's rate of return is normally *higher*. Women's big edge is they're more likely to

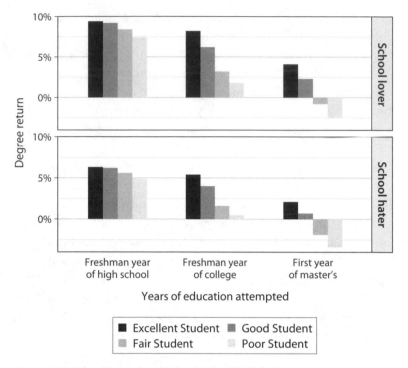

Figure 5.11: School Lovers' and School Haters' Selfish Degree Returns
Source: Figure 5.7 and text.

finish whatever education they start. Their overall high school graduation rate is now about 8% higher than men's. Their four-year B.A. graduation rate is *33%* higher than men's.[94] Women out-finish men even when their prior academic records match.[95] Women continue to earn smaller paychecks at every education level, but high school and college enrich women by a slightly higher *percent*, and that's what counts for returns. Figure 5.12 snaps the facts together.

Women's advantage is largest in high school—over two percentage points for every ability level. Their premium ramps down in college: men's higher total salaries are more likely to outweigh tuition. For the master's degree, men seize the advantage: they're less likely to finish, but their salary rises more if they make the grade.

Marriage and the selfish return to education. From the outset, I stipulated that the Good Student was single. Yet most folks eventually marry—and marriage drastically shifts education's return. The main reason is

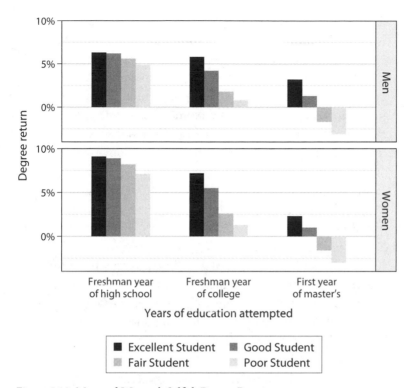

Figure 5.12: Men and Women's Selfish Degree Returns
Source: Figure 5.7 and text.

timeless: like marries like. When your education rises, you shouldn't merely foresee yourself with a higher salary. You should foresee a *spouse* with a higher salary. This is good news for strong students, because marriage is one of the purest forms of trickle-down economics. A lot of your spouse's extra money becomes *your* extra money by financial osmosis.

Conscious on-campus gold-digging may be rare, but extra schooling still *improves your odds of striking gold*. Life could hardly be otherwise. Mating requires meeting.[96] In our society, the further you advance in school, the more likely you are to spend your days surrounded by folks who are—or will be—well-off. Even if you *randomly* marry an acquaintance, extra education makes you more likely to pair up with a high-income spouse.

And few marry randomly. Instead, humans are attracted to partners like them in age, religion, ethnicity, class, hobbies . . . and education.[97] The mutual attraction is strong. If you have one more year of education, your spouse typically has an extra .5 or .6 years.[98] About 80% of this effect persists correcting for intelligence, age, year, race, sex, and religion.[99] Using the General Social Survey, we can actually detect sheepskin effects *of* sheepskin effects. High school graduation makes you almost *30* percentage points more likely to marry a high school grad. College graduation makes you another *25* percentage points more likely to marry a college grad. American marriage is a diploma-based caste system.[100]

Traditionally, the marital return to education was sizable only for women, many of whom married soon after graduation and never pursued a career. When I was an undergrad at Berkeley, kids still rudely joked about academically marginal female students earning their "M.R.S. degrees." Today's world is starkly different—not because modern women stopped earning M.R.S. degrees, but because modern men started earning "M.R. degrees."[101]

How lucrative is education's marital payoff? The research is oddly thin for women, and barely existent for men.[102] While scholars are well aware high-income men increasingly match with high-income women,[103] they rarely wonder, "How much will spending another year in school help your odds of marrying money?" Still, the few scholars who *do* mine such questions unearth piles of gold.[104]

One explanation for the research shortage is that marital payoffs seem zero-sum. If married couples divide their family income equally, then consume their shares separately, the lower-earner's financial gain automatically implies an equal financial *loss* for the higher-earner. If Wife earns $60,000 and Husband earns $40,000, marriage makes Husband $10,000 richer by making Wife $10,000 poorer.

Yet on reflection, married couples save a bundle by sharing their consumption. The adage, "Two can live as cheaply as one" exaggerates. Compared to two one-person households, though, one two-person household plainly saves on housing, furnishings, transportation, utilities, chores, and even groceries, thanks to stores like Costco. How much do couples save? Academics analyze this prosaic question with an array of methods.[105] They find savings of 20–40%, with the most credible estimates around 35%.[106] Marriage automatically enriches the lower-earning spouse and potentially enriches the higher-earning spouse.

I ballpark education's marital return using the General Social Survey. First, I estimate how much your education *raises* the education of the person you marry. Next, I figure out how much your education raises your *spouse*'s income if your spouse is average *given* their education.[107] Third, assuming married couples share equally and save 35% on their cost of living, I calculate your education's Degree Return. To keep the number crunching tractable, I focus on couples that (a) marry at 25, (b) always work full time, and (c) stay married (see Figure 5.13).

As expected, marriage pumps up the return to education for both genders and all abilities. Marriage raises returns by roughly one percentage point for men and two percentage points for women. This change is often enough to resolve educational toss-ups . . . as long as you *know* you'll marry young.

Incidentally, the marriage market is probably the strongest reason to pay for expensive private schools. Going to Harvard may not get you a better job but almost certainly puts you in an exclusive dating pool for life. Admittedly thin research on this topic confirms the obvious: one research team finds that *over* half of women's financial payoff for college quality comes via marriage.[108] There is nothing counterintuitive about

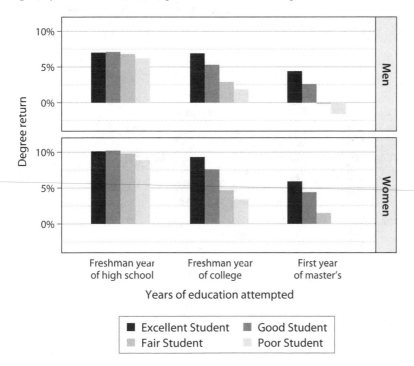

Figure 5.13: Married Men and Women's Selfish Degree Returns
Source: Figure 5.12 and text.

the idea that schools improve your spouse more than they improve you. If you go to Harvard, you'll *be* the same person, but you'll *meet* the elite.

Folk wisdom says, "Don't marry for money. Go where the rich people are, and marry for love." This mindset may sound old-fashioned, but remains as true as ever. As the gender gap narrows, women's marital return matters less, but men's marital return comes into its own. As a professor married to a lawyer, I ought to know.

Workforce participation and the selfish return to education. Until now, I've assumed every student desires to work full time without interruption from graduation until retirement. In technical terms, all estimates assume "100% workforce participation" and "100% full-time work"—graduates occasionally struggle to find a job but don't stop *trying* to work regular hours until they hit 65. The presumption: anyone who bothers to ask, "Is my education worth it?" wants a full-blown career after graduation.

This presumes too much. The most motivated of students may exit the labor market to raise a family, "find themselves," or cope with chronic illness. More importantly, if you dispense educational advice, many of your advisees will *not* be highly motivated. Some will stop trying to capitalize on

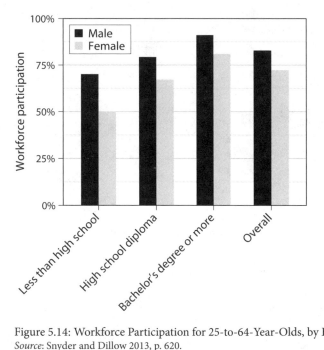

Figure 5.14: Workforce Participation for 25-to-64-Year-Olds, by Education (2011)
Source: Snyder and Dillow 2013, p. 620.

their education—and others won't even start. Workforce participation rises with education but is always noticeably below 100% (see Figure 5.14).[109]

Further complication: a sizable minority of workforce participants—about 9% of males and 22% of females—work only part time.[110] Part-timers earn a small fraction of full-time pay: 31% as much for males, 38% for females.[111] For simplicity, my calculations treat part-time workers as fractional full-time workers: a part-time male counts as 31% of a full-timer, a part-time female counts as 38% of a full-timer.[112]

The part-time complication aside, one shouldn't take participation numbers at face value. Part of the gap surely reflects ability bias: people who keep studying before graduation also tend to keep working after graduation. Unfortunately, research on workforce participation and ability bias is extremely thin. The most credible approach is to apply standard corrections for ability bias and sheepskin effects, then recalculate (Figure 5.15).[113]

Basic math ensures across-the-board decline in Degree Returns. What's remarkable is the size of the fall. Taking participation into ac-

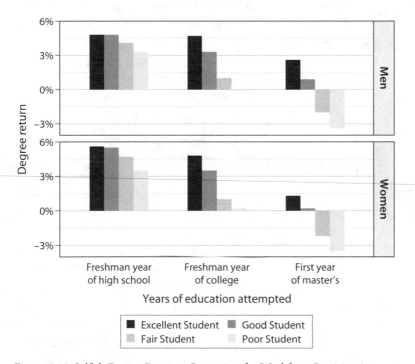

Figure 5.15: Selfish Degree Returns, Correcting for Workforce Participation
Source: Figures 5.12 and 5.14 and text.

count largely wipes out the female educational edge. "Career women" gain markedly more from high school and college than "career men." But the *average* woman's advantage over the *average* man is modest for high school, and near zero for college. Also notable: High school ceases to be a no-brainer for Poor Students. For female Poor Students, the Degree Return plummets from 7.1% to 3.5%. Why the big change? Because less than half of such women cash in on their education with full-time jobs.

Practical Guidance for Prudent Students

Teachers hate when students groan, "Can't you just tell us the answer?" For academics, a short, sweet solution is indecent unless clothed in a thorough explanation. For educational decisions, however, the stakes are so high I'm willing to set decency aside. And since my calculations *include* nonmonetary values, the advice is stronger than it sounds. The world is full of chance, every individual is unique, no strategy is foolproof, and every generalization has exceptions, but some academic paths really are more prudent than others. Namely . . .

Go to high school unless you're a terrible student (or don't want a full-time career). High school is a good deal for almost any student who wants a full-time career after graduation. On the first day of high school, Excellent, Good, Fair, and even Poor Students can count on a Degree Return of at least 5%. Since uncredentialed, inexperienced workers earn low salaries, teens can cheaply bet on their own academic success even if they usually lose the bet.

High school's payoff remains healthy even in bleak scenarios. While school is less fruitful for confirmed bachelors, Poor Students, and people who hate sitting in class, a male Poor Student who rules out marriage and hates school has a Degree Return of 4%. There are only two main groups who should skip high school in favor of low-skilled jobs. The first group: Poor Students who don't plan to work full time after graduation. The second group: students who are worse than Poor. If you're in the bottom 10–15% of the academic pecking order, your graduation odds are so slim that you should quit school and start work. Whatever you do, don't bother with a GED. It sounds like an appealing middle way, but its chief function is to tell employers, "I have the brains but not the grit to finish high school."[114]

Go to college only if you're a strong student or special case. College is a square deal for Excellent and Good Students who follow three simple rules. First, pick a "real" major. STEM is obviously "real"; so are economics, business, and even political science. Second, go to a respected public school. It probably won't charge list price, and even if it does, you get your money's worth. Third, toil full time after graduation. Working irregularly after finishing college is like failing to harvest half the crops you plant. Those who stray far from these rules get burned.

For weaker students, college is normally a bad deal. If you're a Fair Student, go only if you're a special case. Will you major in something like engineering? Did an elite school miraculously offer a cushy scholarship? Are you a woman who firmly plans to marry? Then despite your spotty academic record, college may be for you. Otherwise, skip college and get a job. Poor Students, finally, should not go to college, period.

Don't get a master's degree unless the stars align. On the day they start a master's degree, even Excellent Students can expect a lousy Degree Return of 2.6%. You should enroll, then, only if you have a great reason—or several good reasons—to believe you'll beat the odds. For starters, your academic ability must exceed Excellent. Failure in graduate programs is so prevalent only the top 5–10% of the population can confidently expect to cross the finish line. Field also matters enormously. While data on graduate earnings by subject are scarce, there is little doubt engineering, computer science, and economics have far higher returns than fine arts, education, and anthropology. The latter degrees make sense only if you're a gushing fan of your subject compared to your fellow master's students. For women, finally, marital plans are also crucial. As long as she's an Excellent Student, the master's is a fine deal for the woman who marries, but a lousy deal for the woman who stays single.

My counsel rubs many the wrong way. Some dismiss it as "elitist," "philistine," or "sexist." The correct label is candid. It's not my fault education's rewards hinge on graduation. It's not my fault past academic performance strongly predicts graduation. It's not my fault fine arts degrees pay poorly. It's not my fault married women profit far more from education than single women. It's not my fault so many graduates don't work full time. I am only a messenger. My job is to honestly report the facts, especially unwelcome facts of great practical importance.

The most common visceral reaction to my advice, however, is to accuse me of hypocrisy: "Sure, he advises other people's kids to think twice before they go to college. But he'd never say that to his own kids." They don't know me. I advise my kids the same way I advise anyone else: tailoring my message to the student. I learn their academic track record, motivation, intended field of study, marital plans, and so on. Then I tell them how various paths typically pan out for people who fit their profile. My first two sons are outstanding students interested in economics, so of course I'll urge college. My younger two are just starting school, so the jury is still out. If either turns out to be a C student, I will gently but emphatically advise them to find a full-time job right after high school.

Finally, none of my maxims assumes human beings base their educational decisions on careful calculations of the return to education. Quite the opposite. If human beings based their educational decisions on careful calculations of the return to education, they wouldn't need my advice because they'd already be following it! My assumption, rather, is that our educational decisions are deeply corrupted by inexperience, conformity, and pride. My goal is to save readers time, money, and grief by rooting out—or at least curbing—this corruption.

Doubts

Thousands of papers calculate the selfish return to education. Why should we prefer my numbers to anyone else's? First, to the best of my knowledge, I am the only researcher to account for ability bias, sheepskin effects, and completion probability at the same time. All three forces are so mighty that ignoring even one discredits the answer. Second, to the best of my knowledge, my numbers are the most comprehensive. I investigate every semiplausible benefit and cost of education, and my calculations incorporate whatever I find in the return. Third, I never retreat to agnosticism. I strive to compile the best available evidence from every relevant field. Yet when the best evidence is mixed or weak, I explicitly state my best guess and run with it.

My refusal to meet uncertainty with reticence may horrify fellow academics. The real world, however, denies us the luxury of waiting for certainty. If researchers withhold our best guesses from students, students have to act on their *own* best guesses—corrupted as they are by inexperience, conformity, and pride. Still, I'm enough of an academic to crave penance for building on imperfect evidence. To ease my intellectual conscience, I now confess my greatest doubts about my efforts.

Completion probabilities. Probabilities are definitely low, especially for weaker students, but the evidence is surprisingly thin. I end up relying on one model for high school and one for the bachelor's. I wish I had ten canonical models of completion probability for each educational level, but to the best of my knowledge, they aren't accessible.

How school and work feel. There isn't enough research on how students emotionally experience school versus work. Most adults have done both for years, but few researchers seriously compare the two. The same goes for job satisfaction.

Education and health. Research on the health effects of education is sprawling. My concern: their numbers look small to me, even though many health economists call their effects "big." The disparity could be driven by the dollar values I pin on health outcomes. If you think people value a year of life at more than double their yearly full-time income or if you think people in "good" health would give up more than 20% of their total full-time income to have "excellent" health, education's return is understated.

The neglected master's. Evidence on the master's degree is sparse. Estimates of the sheepskin effect are scarce and vary widely, so I stipulate that the master's sheepskin breakdown matches the bachelor's. Completion rates for the master's are lower than the bachelor's. But I failed to locate any statistical models that estimate how master's completion varies by prior academic performance. While broad outlines are not in doubt, I also located no solid evidence on how, correcting for student ability, the master's payoff varies by discipline.

Sins of omission. To keep my write-up manageable, I gloss over three major credentials: the associate degree, the professional degree, and the Ph.D. My assessments, however, are no surprise. The associate completion probability is abysmal. The degree officially takes two years, but the *six*-year graduation rate for exclusively full-time students is only 58%.[115] And even if you finish, the labor market only modestly rewards the associate credential—with the important exception of vocational programs like nursing.[116] The professional degree and the Ph.D., in contrast, pay well for most disciplines. Unfortunately, the vast majority of students lack the ability to survive these programs. Most Ph.D. students have spent their entire lives at the top of the class, yet half wander off before they defend their dissertations. Professional completion rates tend to be higher; for example, over 80% of medical students finish their degrees on time.[117] To maintain such numbers, however, professional schools rely on brutal admission standards. They don't even give the average college grad the chance to flunk.

Quantification fosters illusions of certainty and precision. I disclaim both. My estimates of the selfish return to education are educated guesswork, nothing more. The crucial fact to remember: *no* important decision can be based on anything better than educated guesswork. The question is not whether you should rely on educated guesswork, but whether you should rely on *mine*. I obviously think you should. If you demur, check out my competitors and note all they ignore.[118]

The Spreadsheet of You

Your career hinges on your educational path. Wherever you turn, you're betting years of your life—and often tens of thousands of dollars. As a decision maker, you're perfectly free to follow your gut or follow the herd. Yet given the prevalence of "subprime" educational investments, you shouldn't trust either. Audit your gut. Audit the herd. Crunch the numbers until you have numbers to live by.

True, prudence and dollars are not the same. But the prudent course is to assign dollar values to everything you care about—and maximize the dollar value of *that*.[119] Do you like term papers, art history, or strolling Princeton's idyllic grounds? Do you hate lectures, sitting still, or failure? Great; put dollar values on each and every facet you care about. Give your future a few hours of undivided attention. Personalize my spreadsheets until they fit you like a glove, then compare your options.

No matter how long you scrutinize these spreadsheets, remember you're calculating education's *selfish* return. Irreproachable numbers won't resolve whether your education enriches mankind. To calculate education's *social* return, you have to rethink every number. You have to drop questions like "How much does my schooling cost *me*?" in favor of questions like "How much does my schooling cost society?" Above all, you must remember the power of signaling. My estimates of the selfish return to education are only moderately pessimistic. Taking signaling seriously moves us from this moderate pessimism to my admittedly radical case against education.

CHAPTER 6

We Care If It's Signaling

The Social Return to Education

The selfish rate of return concisely values personal investments. How fruitful were your sacrifice of time and money? For some purposes, this amoralism is defensible. I wouldn't trust an academic advisor who harangued my children about "what's best for society." Talk about what's best for my child, or don't talk at all.

Yet for other purposes, looking out for number one is a lousy guide. As a college professor, I would immensely profit if federal, state, and local governments launched a "War on Ignorance" by tripling their spending on higher education. But enriching Bryan Caplan is a terrible argument for a War on Ignorance. To persuasively evaluate such a crusade, we have to count everyone's interests, not mine alone.

"Counting everyone's interests" sounds like a green light for holistic thinking, but it's not. Broad social concern is a reason to carefully rework our calculations, not throw away our calculator. To measure the selfish rate of return, we put dollar values on everything one student cares about. To measure an analogous social rate of return, we put dollar values on everything *anyone* cares about.

Signaling barely made a peep last chapter. The omission was intentional: selfishly speaking, the critical question is "How well will my education pay?" not "Why will my education pay?" In this chapter signaling brashly returns. Remember: once employers know enough to rank job candidates, further signaling is pure redistribution. When you calculate education's *selfish* return, you can ignore this truism. Money's money, even if it ultimately comes out of others' paychecks. From a social point of view, however, redistribution is sterile. When you calculate education's *social* return, you should presume signaling's payoff is illusory— because socially speaking, it normally is.

The Social Return to Education: A Primer

Calculating education's selfish return was challenging. Calculating its social return is daunting. In practice, most economists take the easy way out. They start with the selfish return, tweak it in two simple ways, then call it a day.[1] Why start with the selfish return? Because most economists tacitly embrace human capital purism. If your education raises your income by $1,000, your education made you $1,000 more productive. What about signaling? Meh, that's only a theory.

Still, even human capital purists recognize social and selfish returns diverge. Students don't pay the full cost of their education: taxpayers fully subsidize public K–12, heavily subsidize public colleges, and partially subsidize private colleges. Neither do workers receive the full benefit of their education: when education helps you in the labor market, your taxes go up—and your government transfers (such as unemployment insurance) go down. To handle these wrinkles, researchers routinely (a) count taxpayers' support as a social cost of education, and (b) count workers' full *market* compensation as a social benefit of education.

These adjustments are steps in the right direction. But if you seek serious estimates of education's social return, they're woefully insufficient. We didn't take shortcuts to education's selfish return, and we won't take them to its social return. Instead, we'll go back to square one: brainstorming, then investigating education's every semiplausible benefit and cost.

The Social Return to Education: Recounting Everything that Counts

Fortunately, half our brainstorming is already done. Last chapter inventoried education's alleged private benefits and costs, so we can skip to their investigation phase. How, item by item, do social and private effects diverge? To take an obvious case: education has a hefty marital return. Socially speaking, however, this is zero-sum. Your degree helps you hook a rich spouse; but if you hadn't earned your degree, your rich spouse would have married—and enriched—someone else instead. By this logic, social returns should omit education's marital payoff.

But rethinking education's private effects from a social perspective isn't enough. When figuring education's selfish return, many conceivable benefits never come up because—genuine or not—they're *purely* social. If education reduces violent crime, it's not the *student* who benefits; it's everyone they would have victimized—not to mention taxpayers who fund police, courts, and prisons. To extract education's social return, then, we must also brainstorm for purely social effects, then examine each in turn.

From compensation to productivity. The selfish return to education hinges on compensation: How much pay do you forfeit while you're in school, and how much extra pay do you capture after you finish? The social return to education, in contrast, hinges on *productivity*: How much stuff does society forfeit while you're in school, and how much extra stuff does society capture after you finish?

In a pure human capital story, compensation and productivity are equal case by case: employers won't want you if you ask more than you produce and can't get you if they offer less than you produce.

In a pure signaling model, in contrast, compensation and production are equal only *on average*. When your credentials match your ability, your productivity matches your pay. Otherwise, pay and productivity diverge. If your credentials are unusually weak for someone of your ability, you earn *less* than you produce. If your credentials are unusually strong for someone of your ability, you earn *more* than you produce.[2]

To calculate education's social return, then, you must know *why* education raises pay and benefits. If education boosts compensation solely by *raising* worker productivity, society's gain equals the worker's gain. If education boosts compensation solely by *revealing* worker productivity, society gains far less. For most purposes, in fact, society gains zero. True, the economy is more productive—and society richer—when employers know which workers are good and which workers aren't.[3] Knowledge is wealth, so ranking students has social value. But once students have been properly ranked, the social value ends. Employer's knowledge of worker quality would be essentially identical if everyone had one less degree, right? In economic jargon, the *marginal* social benefit of signaling is roughly zero even though its total social benefit is substantial.[4]

Precisely what share of education's effect on earnings and employment stems from signaling? Evidence reviewed in earlier chapters leads to a Cautious and a Reasonable view of signaling's role (see Figure 6.1).

The Cautious view hands signaling full credit for the sheepskin effect, but no more. Given our sheepskin breakdowns, this implies signaling shares of 38% for high school, 59% for the bachelor's, and 74% for the master's.[5] More plausibly, though, part of the ordinary year-to-year return is signaling as well. An extra year of education may not say a lot about you, but it says *something*. How much? Multiple approaches point to a Reasonable estimate of 80% signaling overall. If the sheepskin effect is all signaling, this implies a year-to-year signaling share of 57% for high school, 47% for the bachelor's, and 25% for the master's.

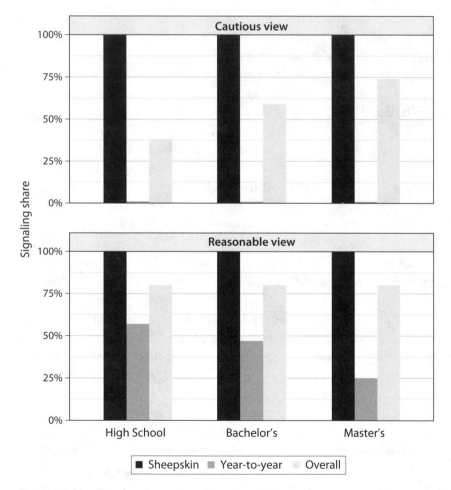

Figure 6.1: Two Signaling Scenarios
Source: See text.

When deriving education's effect on productivity, the driving assumption is that workers *on average* earn what they're worth. A Good Student with a B.A. earns what he produces because a Good Student, by definition, has the ability of an average worker with a B.A. If the same student goes straight to work after high school, however, the market doesn't merely pay him less; it pays him *less than he produces*. Why? Because his credentials make him look worse than he really is. If the Good Student gets an M.A., similarly, the market doesn't merely pay him more; it pays him *more than he produces*. Why? Because his credentials make him look better than he really is. As signaling's share ascends, so do the spreads between productivity and pay. Figure 6.2 shows the patterns for Good Students.

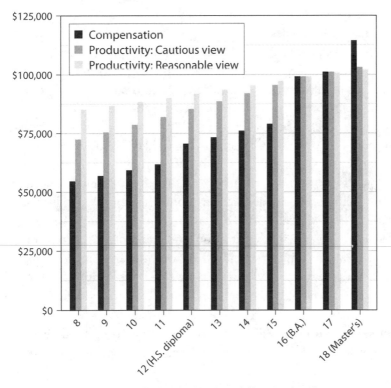

Figure 6.2: The Effect of Education on Compensation and Productivity for a Good Student (2011)
Source: Figures 5.1 and 6.1.

From a selfish point of view, the pay you miss while you're in school and the raise you get once you're out of school are symmetric. The pay you miss is all selfish cost. The raise you get is all selfish benefit. From a social point of view, however, what counts is productivity, not pay. The social cost of school is the stuff you fail to produce. The social benefit of school is the extra stuff you learn to produce. If education's payoff is 80% signaling, and a year of education raises annual earnings by $5,000, only $1,000 is a true gain to society. The other $4,000 is your reward for *convincing* employers they've been underestimating your value.

Employment. Suppose four years of college cut your unemployment risk from 9% to 4%. If education's rewards are 80% signaling, this means 20% of college grads' reduced risk of unemployment—one percentage point—stems from their enhanced productivity. The rest is zero-sum. Your college degree lowers your unemployment risk by raising the risk for your unadorned rivals.

Taxes and transfers. As extra education advances your career, government takes more of your money and gives you less of its help. Yet from a social point of view, such modifications are zero-sum. If your education boosts your productivity $1,000, society is $1,000 richer—even if you keep only $500 after taxes. If your education prompts the government to cut your welfare payment $1,000, society is no poorer—even though you're $1,000 in the hole. In one way, then, social returns are more straightforward than private returns. The byzantine tax code and patchwork welfare state are distractions from what counts: production.[6]

Job satisfaction, happiness, and the joy of learning. Though the better-educated have greater job satisfaction and happiness, the reason is largely material: the educated enjoy their jobs and lives more because they make more money, not because their careers feel more fulfilling.[7] Does education have *any* independent impact on job satisfaction or happiness? While some researchers detect mild benefits, others discover that—money aside—the well-educated feel worse about their lives. If you drive a cab for a living, a college diploma makes you see a failure in the rear-view mirror.

From a social point of view, education's effect on job satisfaction and happiness is even more questionable. Humans savor status—a high rank in the pecking order. In our society, status heavily depends on education.[8] Unfortunately, status is, almost by definition, zero-sum.[9] As society's education rises, so does the education one needs to feel socially superior. The disturbing implication: even if education were a path to personal happiness, it could remain a dead end for social happiness.

Research on this fear is sparse but intriguing. In the General Social Survey, education slightly lifts individuals' job satisfaction and happiness—even if income stays the same. How? By pushing them up the hierarchy. Correcting for status, education's effect on job satisfaction vanishes, and its effect on happiness shrinks by two-thirds.[10] If there's little reason to think education makes one human happier with their job or life, there's even less reason to think education makes humanity happier with its jobs or lives. Since my selfish returns already set education's effect on job satisfaction and happiness to zero, my social returns do the same.

What about the classroom experience? On average, as last chapter reported, school is one of people's least-liked activities. They're not fond of work either but resent school slightly more. From a social point of a view, there is every reason to take their feelings at face value. If your teacher bores you to death, the knowledge that millions of other kids are equally bored is scant consolation.

Health. Health researchers normally treat education like hygiene: everyone will be healthier if everyone passes their exams, just as everyone will be healthier if everyone washes their hands. Still, scholars intermittently wonder if "the effect of education on health" is a covert "effect of *status* on health." Animal experiments confirm status does a body good: altering an animal's rank in the pecking order shifts its health in the same direction. Human health could work the same way.[11] Selfishly speaking, this is idle curiosity; as long as education invigorates you, who cares about the mechanism? Socially speaking, however, the interplay between education, status, and health is all-important. Insofar as schooling makes you healthier by raising your status, its health benefits are zero-sum: you can't raise your rank without dragging others down, so you can't make yourself well without making others sick.

When researchers check, they consistently verify that human health and status go hand in hand.[12] Furthermore, education's health benefits are—at least in part—status benefits in disguise.[13] Correcting for status, anywhere from 20% to 60% of education's apparent effect on self-reported health vanishes.[14] On the General Social Survey's four-point health scale, correcting for status halves my earlier estimate of education's health benefit from .04/year to .02/year.[15]

Last chapter named multiple reasons to think education's true health benefit is even smaller than it looks.[16] From a social standpoint, the status evidence calls for one last downgrade. Since the selfish health benefit is small, and the status effect substantial, I mark education's *social* health benefits down to zero. Academic achievement is unlike hygiene. If everyone had a B.A. or more, people who had only B.A.s would stand on the lowest rung of the social ladder—with health woes to match.

Tuition and other expenses. Selfishly speaking, the standout cost of education is foregone earnings—not tuition or other student fees. Public high school remains free of charge. Although public colleges' average list price now exceeds $9,000, their typical student pays under $4,000 thanks to a smorgasbord of discounts and subsidies. But socially speaking, the relevant number is not cost to the student, but cost to *everyone*—especially public education's Forgotten Man, the taxpayer.

Start with the full cost of public K–12. The per-student bill varies massively from state to state. In 2009–10, the latest available year, Utah spent $7,916. Washington, DC, tripled that, for a grand total of $23,816. The U.S. average was $12,136.[17] This figure is all-inclusive, counting cost of instruction, support services, food, enterprise operations, capital outlays, and interest payments.[18] When calculating the social cost of the *typical* high school student's education, however, this number isn't quite right.

The big glitch: official figures include special education—and special education is expensive. Schools now classify about 13% of their students as disabled, and standard estimates say special education is twice as costly as regular education.[19] Taking official statistics at face value, the social cost of educating students who *aren't* disabled is only 88% of the average.[20] Yet common sense balks at the idea that 13% of U.S. students are meaningfully disabled. Critics back up this commonsense skepticism, arguing schools have strong incentives to inflate their disability numbers.[21] If we subtract out the most elastic special education category—"specific learning disability," the disabled fraction falls to a more creditable 8.2%.[22] Using this toned-down figure implies the typical high school student costs 92% of the average, for a total of $11,165.[23]

A smaller glitch: the social cost of K–12 should exclude food, for the same reason the selfish cost of college excludes room and board; kids eat whether or not they're in school. Subtracting food costs, per-student social cost falls another $405 to $10,760, or $11,298 in 2011 dollars.[24]

Calculating the full social cost of college has its own complications. Using list price is tempting, but misguided. Colleges' standard financial strategy is to combine an exorbitant list price with ample discounts. While schools frame this discounting as high-minded do-gooding, it amounts to what economists call "price discrimination"—tailoring prices to squeeze extra profits out of richer and less flexible customers.[25] Price discrimination is the standard story about why travelers pay vastly more for same-day plane tickets. List tuition does not capture the "true cost of schooling" any more than same-day plane fare captures the "true cost of flying."

From this vantage point, there is a fundamental divide between "institutional grants"—tuition breaks offered by schools themselves—and federal, state, private, and employer grants. Institutional grants don't really burn social resources; schools offer them precisely because education costs *less* than list price to provide. Federal, state, private, and employer grants, in contrast, burn social resources by making students unable or unwilling to defray the cost of their own education profitable to admit.

To measure the full social cost of college, then, I start with list price, then subtract average institutional grants. The College Board again provides all the relevant figures. Public four-year colleges offer $1,133 in institutional grants per student.[26] Since list price is $9,412, this implies a social cost of $8,279.[27] Financial data on master's programs is sparse, so I continue to equate the cost of graduate and undergraduate education. If anything, this is optimistic, because small graduate classes imply high per-student costs.

Accounting for experience. A trained worker returns to school reluctantly. The more experience they have, the more money they make; the more money they make, the more they sacrifice on hiatus. Socially, the story is the same. The more experience a worker has, the more they produce; the more they produce, the more society sacrifices when the worker takes time off. My social return numbers therefore stick with last chapter's 2.5% annual experience premium.

Completion probability. Social investments, like private investments, always risk failure. A percentage point of risk slices 1% off *expected* benefits. Suppose an investment, if successful, yields $1,000 of selfish benefits and $200 of social benefits. Given a 20% risk of abject failure, expected selfish benefits fall to $800, and expected social benefits fall to $160. Last chapter already estimated completion probabilities; social returns must continue to factor them in.

What if a government program shears the risk of educational failure? All else equal, selfish and social returns rise. But "all else equal" is key. The cheapest and surest way to raise high school graduation rates is indiscriminately awarding diplomas to all. Before long, however, this infinitely merciful system erases the selfish and social gains of graduation: if everyone gets a diploma, no one does. Chapter 7 ponders constructive ways to boost completion probabilities.[28] For now, the goal is evaluating education as it really is, not education as it might be.

The Social Return to Education: Purely Social Benefits

Economists' educational bean counting can come off as annoyingly narrow. Normal human beings—also known as noneconomists—lean holistic. We can't measure education's social benefits by tweaking its selfish benefits. Instead, we must ask ourselves, "What kind of society do we want to live in—an educated society or an ignorant one?"

Normal human beings score a solid point: we can and should investigate education's broad social implications. But that is a poor excuse for discarding what we already know. Evidence on education's broad social effects should *supplement*, not supplant, evidence on its narrow effects. In any case, looking at the big picture is no excuse for innumeracy. If education curtails murder, that is a point in its favor. But it's a lame point until you ballpark (a) how much extra education costs, and (b) how many murders it prevents. Instead of scorning bean counters, we should scrupulously count beans of every description.

Economic growth. New ideas are the root of progress. People today live far better than they did in 1800 because people today *know* far more than they did in 1800. Earth in 1800 contained all the materials required to make an airplane or iPad. But until the right ideas came along, the materials lay fallow. Why did mankind have to wait so long for the right ideas to arrive? Part of the answer is that ideas, once created, are cheap to copy. As a result, innovators glean only a sliver of the value they create.[29]

These truisms lead straight to the stirring sermon, "Education, Foundation of a Dynamic Society." While most students are not creative, heavy K–12 investment fertilizes society's creative potential by giving everyone the mental tools to innovate. Heavy investment in colleges and universities, similarly, brings top students up to the research frontier and provides innovation leaders with employment and funding. If consistently investing 10% of national income in education elevates the annual growth rate from 1% to 2% without *any* further benefits, the social return is a hefty 11%.[30]

Unfortunately, this stirring sermon is wishful thinking. Chapter 4 already reviewed research on the national education premium.[31] While the evidence is messy, education seemingly does *less* for countries than individuals. At the national level, it's not clear that education increases living standards at all, much less that education makes countries' living standards increase at a faster rate. If you can't tell if your machine moves, you may safely assume it's *not* a perpetual motion machine. Researchers who specifically test whether education accelerates progress have little to show for their efforts.[32]

One could reply that, given all the flaws of long-run macroeconomic data, we should ignore academic research in favor of common sense. But what does common sense really say? "An educated people is an innovative people" sounds plausible—until you recall the otherworldliness of the curriculum. In high school, students spend only about a quarter of their time on math and science. In college, about 5% of students major in engineering, 2% in computer science, and 5% in biology and biomedical science.[33] "Giving students the mental tools they need to innovate" is, at best, an afterthought. In the modern world, moreover, the brightest minds often end up as university professors, applying their creativity to topics of academic interest rather than commercial value. True, ivory tower self-indulgence occasionally revolutionizes an industry. Yet common sense insists the best way to discover useful ideas is to search for useful ideas—not to search for whatever fascinates you and pray it turns out to be useful.[34]

Workforce participation. As education rises, so does workforce participation—the likelihood of wanting a job. In other words, as education goes up, *voluntary* unemployment goes down.[35] This partly reflects ability bias. Some people are stayers, unwilling to abandon their commitments; others are quitters, who walk away when the going gets tough. Still, there is every reason to think education's apparent effect is *partly* genuine. Extra education reinforces the desire to work.

Selfishly speaking, this is no cause for celebration. What's so great about changing your own priorities? Suppose education caused us to spend less time with our families and more time working. It's unclear why this shift would count in education's favor. Socially speaking, however, the welfare state makes even voluntary unemployment a burden to others. Idlers get more than they produce via programs like Medicaid and food stamps; workers get less than they produce owing to levies like income and payroll taxes. This doesn't mean it's "best for society" to make everyone work. Stay-at-home parents, retirees, and slackers are *part* of society, after all. The point is that extra workforce participation *can* simultaneously be a bad deal for the individual and a good deal for humanity. When education boosts workforce participation, social returns have to count what individuals selfishly ignore: all the taxes they start paying and all the transfers they stop collecting.[36] Intuitively, suppose the government gives you $10,000 a year while you're out of the labor force. If you worked, your pretax productivity would be $30,000, but you'd pay $5,000 in taxes and forfeit your $10,000 in transfers. If you care only about yourself, you'll work if you value your time less than $15,000. If you care about everyone, you'll work if you value your time less than *$30,000.*[37]

Tallying taxes is straightforward, but transfers are messy. As long as workers are full time and childless, even those with eighth-grade educations normally earn too much to collect anything beyond unemployment insurance. Once workers exit the job market, however, their labor earnings fall to zero. Most instantly become eligible for government programs we've hitherto managed to ignore.

The big transfer programs are Medicaid, TANF (Temporary Assistance to Needy Families, or "welfare"), and SNAP (Supplemental Nutrition Assistance Program, or "food stamps"). Since the passage of the Affordable Care Act, a single childless adult with zero income can definitely get

Medicaid. Valued at cost, this is worth $4,362 a year.[38] TANF is limited to households with kids, so single childless adults cannot collect. SNAP's rules are complex: childless adults face time limits or work requirements, but state governments can make exceptions. In 2011, an eligible single adult with zero income collected roughly $2,192 in food stamps.[39] My social return calculations assign the sum of these Medicaid and SNAP payments to anyone out of the labor force.

Signaling, as usual, is the final wrinkle. Give an individual more education, and they get better offers so they're more likely to want a job. Give *everyone* more education, and you ignite credential inflation. Implausible? Ponder this: in 1950, only 33% of adult males had finished high school, but male workforce participation was higher than today.[40]

Crime. About 65% of American inmates never earned standard high school diplomas.[41] In 2006–7, 8.7% of male dropouts aged 16–24 were incarcerated.[42] Around 15% of white male dropouts and 70% of black male dropouts spend some time in prison by their mid-30s.[43] All these rates are roughly two-thirds lower for men who finished high school, and miniscule for college graduates. Dwelling on such vast disparities raises high hopes: Maybe society can prevent crime with school instead of punishing crime with prison. Don't the numbers imply universal high school graduation would eradicate half of all crime?

Hardly. As usual, there is less to education than meets the eye. Dropouts' troubles emerge long before they quit school. They don't just have low IQs and poor grades; they're precocious troublemakers.[44] Future dropouts are much more likely to be suspended from school and get arrested. They smoke more, drink more, use more drugs, and have more sex—and start their risky habits younger. Before crediting education for observed crime differences, then, you must account for ability bias in all its forms. Instead of asking, "How law-abiding are dropouts compared to high school grads?" you should ask, "How law-abiding are dropouts compared to high school grads with identical IQs, grades, personalities, and juvenile behavior?"

Correcting for IQ and grades makes education look only mildly less effective at preventing crime.[45] The game changer is the criminal personality. Future criminals, like future dropouts, are impulsive, aggressive, and defiant—and act accordingly.[46] Their illegal careers usually start when they're still in school.[47] When researchers correct for early antisocial attitudes and behavior, the measured effect of education on crime plummets.[48] In naive estimates, an extra year of education reduces expected lifetime jail time by about four weeks, and the probability of serving *any* time by about two percentage points. But correcting for demographics, intelligence, class rank, personality, and early deviance, an extra year of education cuts expected lifetime jail time by less than *one* week, and the probability of serving any time by about *half* a percentage point.[49]

Yet even such vestigial effects may be of great social value, because the all-inclusive social cost of crime is titanic. The current budgetary cost of imprisoning a criminal is about $30,000 a year.[50] But crimes committed vastly outnumber sentences served. Murder aside, offenses rarely lead to arrest, much less prison. Only 3–5% of rapes, robberies, and aggravated assaults—and less than 1% of property crimes—lead to jail time.[51] Yet for each and every violent and property crime, at least one victim suffers—often horribly. Everyone who takes costly precautions to *avoid* victimization shoulders an additional burden. Setting aside victimless crimes, the most comprehensive tally of crime's social cost comes out to $3,728 per American per year in 2011 dollars.[52]

The total cost of the crime members of society suffer must equal the total cost of the crime members of society inflict. As long as criminality is proportional to incarceration, then, we can compute yearly average crime costs by education (see Figure 6.3). Raw gaps are so huge that social benefits remain sizable after subtracting 75% ability bias.

Yet there's a subtler reason to dial down estimates of the pacifying power of education: signaling. If signaling is potent, education can defuse *individual* criminality with little impact on *society's* criminality. The mechanism should be painfully familiar. Hand one delinquent a high school diploma, and they look better to employers. Hand *every* delinquent a high school diploma, however, and the credential loses all worth. It no longer boosts legal income and therefore leaves crime as attractive as ever. Think that's a stretch? Back in 1950, when adult male dropouts outnumbered high school grads two to one, the U.S. murder rate was no higher than today.[53] Signaling's elegant explanation: Back in 1950, the average dropout stood at the 33rd percentile of achievement, so employer stigma against dropouts was mild. Today, the average dropout stands at the 10th percentile of achievement, so the employer stigma against dropouts is severe, making crime an appealing substitute for honest toil.

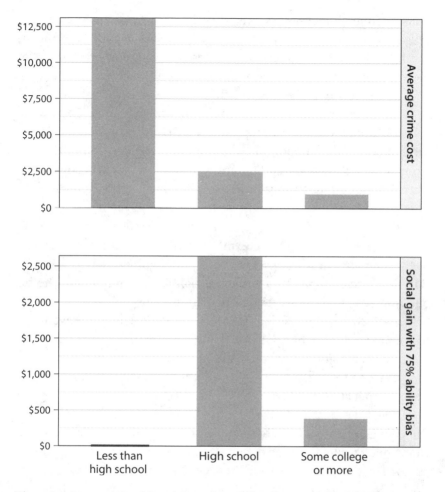

Figure 6.3: Average Annual Social Cost of Crime by Education (2011 Dollars)
Sources: D. Anderson 1999 for aggregate crime costs; Harlow 2003 for incarceration by education level.

Recall that sheepskin effects—oversize gains for crossing academic finish lines—are a telling symptom of signaling. If education truly instilled respect for law and order, there would be nothing special about graduation. In crime data, however, high school's senior year stands out like a sore thumb. According to the U.S. Census, men who quit high school are almost as likely to be jailed as men who finished only middle school. But when men pass the twelfth-grade finish line, their chance of incarceration crashes nearly 50%.[54] Research on this criminal sheepskin effect is virtually nonexistent. But extending published work yields a stark result: correcting for ability bias in all its forms, *only* the senior year of high school cuts crime.[55] Since this evidence is thin, I assume the sheepskin breakdown for crime matches the sheepskin breakdown for income: the last year of high school counts as much as 3.4 regular years, and the last year of higher degrees counts as much as 6.7 regular years.

Final complication: crime is a young person's game, so if education restrains crime, most of the restraint kicks in quickly. Since social returns place heavier weight on earlier payoffs, returns must take this "front loading" into account. Coming calculations handle this wrinkle by merging arrest statistics by age with the age breakdown of the population.[56]

Politics. Democratic participation rises with education. The well-educated are more likely to vote, more interested in politics, and more likely to join political groups. For the sake of argument, suppose education deserved full credit for the extra political engagement.[57] The big question remains: Does more participation make public policy better or worse? To answer that big question, unfortunately, you have to (a) figure out the best public policies, then (b) measure whether education increases voter support for these policies. No matter what your policy views happen to be, the social value of participation hinges on the *quality* of participation.[58]

Throughout this book, I've stood against intellectual buck-passing. But trying to figure out the best public policies in the middle of an education book would be a mad detour. There's no remotely plausible way to resolve such vast issues between these covers. Chapter 9 analyzes education's effect on values—including political values. These effects are, as usual, smaller than they look. But small or big, I leave their evaluation to the reader.

Think of (the quality of) the children. If you compare children of college graduates to children of high school dropouts, there's one glaring difference: children of college graduates enjoy far more academic success. Take Americans adults born after 1950. Only 37% of children of two dropouts finished high school, and a mere 2% earned a B.A. In the same era, 98% of children of two college grads finished high school, and 56% earned a B.A.[59] These academic success gaps eventually translate into financial, career, and marital success gaps.[60] Education conceivably has torrential ripple effects.

Unfortunately, no one can tell if the ripples are genuine without facing an ancient debate: nature versus nurture, heredity versus upbringing. Children resemble their parents in every measurable way. Tall parents have tall kids; successful parents have successful kids. Why? Successful parents might have successful kids because of the way they raise them. But there's a competing theory. Successful parents might have successful kids because of the genes they gave them. In a 100% nurture story, the ripple effects of success are as big as they look. If two high school sweethearts graduate, they transform their home into an incubator for achievement. In a 100% nature story, the ripple effects of success are illusory. If two high school sweethearts graduate, they'll live in a nicer neighborhood, but the genes they pass on remain unchanged.

For most of intellectual history, the nature-nurture debate was stuck in a ditch. In typical families, kids are raised by their biological parents, so nature and nurture are hopelessly intertwined. A few decades ago, however, scientists started intently studying atypical families— especially families with adoptees or twins—to tow the science of nature and nurture back to the road. Researchers studied adoptees, to isolate the power of upbringing. If you randomly assign children to biologically unrelated families, yet clear family resemblance emerges, the mechanism almost has to be nurture. Researchers studied identical and fraternal twins, to isolate the power of genes. If identical twins are *more* similar than fraternal twins, the mechanism almost has to be nature.

This approach, called "behavioral genetics," consistently finds strong, pervasive effects of nature, and weak, sporadic effects of nurture. In developed countries, nature doesn't merely dwarf nurture on physical traits like height, weight, and longevity; nature also dwarfs nurture on psychosocial traits like intelligence, happiness, personality, education, and income.[61] The genes your parents give you at conception have a much larger effect on your success than all the advantages your parents give you after conception.

Behavioral geneticists have isolated the effects of upbringing on years of education, grades, and income.[62] Both adoption and twin studies typically find that being raised by an adoptive parent with an extra year of education boosts your education by about five weeks.[63] In other words, each generational ripple shrinks by a factor of ten. Similar studies find *zero* effect of upbringing on grades.[64] Scholastic performance runs in families because performance hinges on students' talents, attitudes, and behavior, all of which revolve around genes. Adoption and twin studies also surprisingly find upbringing has an even tinier effect on income than education. Growing up in a family with 10% higher income raises your adult income by somewhere between 0% and 1%.[65]

In light of all this evidence, a reasonable guess is that whatever raises your income by 10% will raise each of your children's income by 0.5%, with near-zero effect on later descendants. And there's a catch: the labor market won't reward your children for your efforts until they actually start working. Nowadays this means a multidecade delay, so the ripples have a microscopic effect on education's social rate of return. My calculations round it down to zero.[66]

Think of (the quantity of) the children. Family size goes down as education goes up. Demographers often measure "completed fertility"—the total number of children women have by the time they're 40. In 2012, women who dropped out of high school had almost 50% more kids than women who finished college. Only 12% of dropouts were childless, versus 21% of college grads.[67]

For the sake of argument, suppose education is the sole cause of these fertility gaps. The question remains: Is thinning society's membership a social benefit—or a social cost? This is no technocratic issue. You can't begin to answer without taking sides on a litany of controversies.

Conventional thinkers emphasize the environmental dangers of higher population, but critics highlight offsetting economic advantages—especially for innovation.[68] New ideas are the engine of economic growth—and ideas come from people. Picture a world where half your favorite writers, musicians, scientists, and entrepreneurs had never lived. Critics of population also often complain about "crowding." But if crowding is so awful, why are urban rents so high? Because crowding has glorious side effects like opportunity, choice, and excitement. Even the birth of a clear-cut "drain on society" can be a net social benefit if, like most of us, the "drain" is glad to be alive.

I raise these issues not to settle them, but to quarantine them. A book on education is not the place to judge whether human beings are more trouble than they're worth. Chapter 9 narrows down education's true effect on family size.[69] Yet the reader must judge if and when lower fertility is good, bad, or neutral.

Crunching Society's Numbers: Cautious Signaling

We have reached another way station. After rethinking education's self-ish effects in a socially minded way, we brainstormed and sifted the evidence on education's purely social effects. Now on to our final destination: computing the social return to education for virtually anyone. As always, my underlying spreadsheets are online, so readers can check the work and play with the assumptions.[70]

As expected, social returns hinge on the power of signaling. Remember: the higher signaling's share, the lower education's social return. As you near the pure signaling pole, the social return to education falls to zero—then goes negative. For clarity, let's begin with the relatively pro-education Cautious signaling assumption. Remember: according to the Cautious assumption, all benefits of education *except* sheepskin effects reflect human capital.

The case of the Good Student revisited. Good Students, by definition, have the raw ability of the typical B.A. We've already scrutinized their selfish return to education. How worthwhile is Good Students' education taking *everyone's* interests into account? Figure 6.4 compares selfish returns to social returns implied by Cautious signaling.

Social returns differ from selfish returns in two striking ways. Unlike selfish returns, social returns within each degree program are nearly flat. Graduation years are unusually lucrative for students, but are not especially constructive for mankind. More importantly, social returns are *way* lower than selfish returns. Factoring in a modest role for signaling, Social Degree Returns are less than half of Selfish Degree Returns. The social return for high school is a so-so 3.4%. The social return for college is poor—less than 2%. The social return for the master's is a ruinous *negative* 4%.

Low returns are the rule even though education provides an array of benefits for society as a whole. All computations grant that education boosts worker productivity and workforce participation, and cuts unemployment and crime. Why the low social return? Because of the meager value of the combined benefits. The world overflows with better ways to invest. The government could pour more money into roads, cancer research, policing, baby bonuses, or debt repayment. Or it could

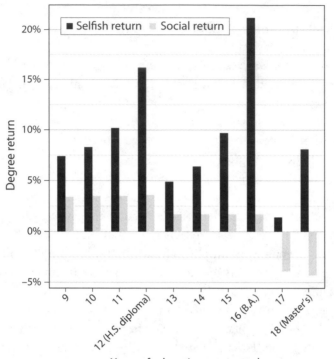

Figure 6.4: Degree Returns to Education for Good Students with Cautious Signaling
Source: Figure 5.3 and text, assuming:
(a) 45% ability bias for income, benefits, unemployment, and participation effects.
(b) 75% ability bias for crime effects.
(c) Sheepskin effects of education reflect signaling; all other effects of education reflect human capital.

let taxpayers keep more of their own money. Private investors are almost sure to beat 3.4% over the long haul.

Social returns by ability. There's nothing especially awful about investing educational resources in Good Students. Under the Cautious assumption, educational investments usually pay poorly regardless of student ability. The return to college ranges from poor to ruinous, and the return to the master's is negative across the board (see Figure 6.5).

Social returns, like selfish returns, usually rise with student ability. Higher-ability students are more likely to complete whatever education they attempt, and use whatever education they complete. The one stark exception: sending Poor Students to high school is the *best* so-

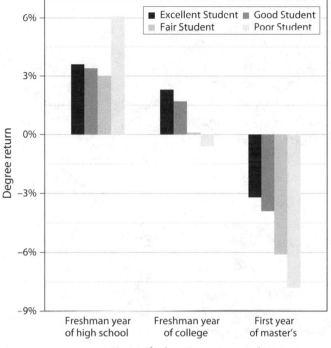

Figure 6.5: Social Degree Returns to Education with Cautious Signaling
Source: Figure 5.7 and text, assuming:
(a) 45% ability bias for income, benefits, unemployment, and participation effects.
(b) 75% ability bias for crime effects.
(c) Sheepskin effects of education reflect signaling; all other effects of education reflect human capital.

cial investment of all, reaping a handsome 6.1%. Since Poor Students incline to crime, crime has massive social costs, and most offenders are young, mildly curbing Poor Students' criminality more than pays for itself.

With Cautious signaling, education is a markedly worse use of social resources than almost everyone pictures. Sending kids to high school is tolerably rewarding, but hardly a no-brainer. Sending kids to college when they're likely to *succeed* is a bad investment. Sending kids to college when they're likely to *fail* is an awful investment. Encouraging college graduates to continue on to the master's is folly.

Crunching Society's Numbers: Reasonable Signaling

The trouble with the Cautious signaling assumption, as argued earlier, is it's too cautious. Every year of education—not just graduation—signals *something* good. What happens to education's social return given what I dub the Reasonable view—namely, that signaling accounts for 80% of education's benefits (see Figure 6.6)?

The results are beyond bleak. Social returns are very low for *every* level of academic difficulty and *every* level of student ability. Sending Poor Students

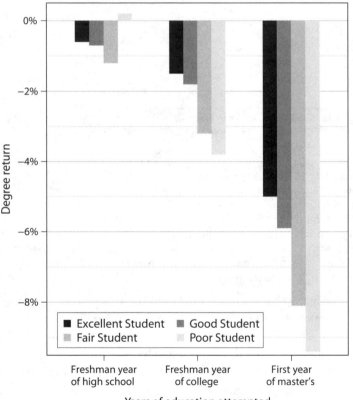

Figure 6.6: Social Degree Returns to Education with Reasonable Signaling
Source: Figure 5.7 and text, assuming:
(a) 45% ability bias for income, benefits, unemployment, and participation effects.
(b) 75% ability bias for crime effects.
(c) 20% of the effects of education reflect human capital.

to high school earns a wretched .2%. Every other educational investment yields a *negative* return. To repeat, this does not mean schools fail to improve their students. They do. What it means, rather, is that students typically die of old age long before society recoups the initial outlay of time and money. Schooling's numerous social benefits pale before its staggering social cost.

How can social returns be so low when selfish returns are pretty decent? Because signaling is a *redistributive* game, serving you a larger piece of the pie without enlarging it. Asking "How can there be too much education if education is lucrative?" is like asking "How can there be too much air pollution if cars are convenient?"

Crunching Society's Numbers: You Call That Reasonable?

Your best guess about signaling's share likely varies from mine. Indeed, while I'm confident that signaling is high, my 80% "Reasonable" estimate remains fluid. How sensitive are pessimistic results to the ubiquity

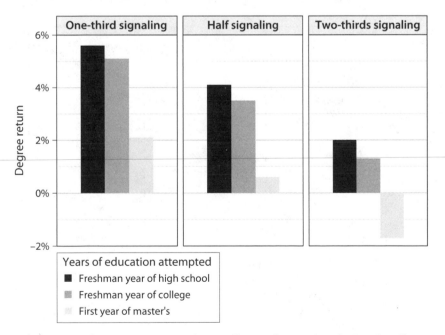

Figure 6.7: Social Degree Returns to Education for Excellent Students by Signaling Share
Source: Figure 6.6 and text.

of signaling? Figures 6.7 and 6.8 show what happens to social returns for strong students as signaling's share rises from a third to a half to two-thirds.[71]

With only one-third signaling, high school is a good deal, college is pretty good, and the master's a waste. This doesn't sound too bad for education until you recall we're discussing strong students. When signaling's share hits 50%, high school still looks like a decent deal, college is so-so, and the master's is ruinous. As signaling's share moves to two-thirds, social returns for even Excellent and Good Students crash. Despite its privileged place in our social mythology, high school as we know it turns out to be a poor use of social resources.

For weak students, results are grimmer still (see Figures 6.9 and 6.10). With one-third signaling, high school is good or great, but further education dubious or worse. With half signaling, high school's social return remains tolerable for Fair Students and ample for Poor Students. Anything more, though, is a waste. Pushing on to two-thirds signaling wipes out remaining pockets of hope. Sending Poor Students to high school isn't a terrible idea, but the rewards are nothing to write home about.

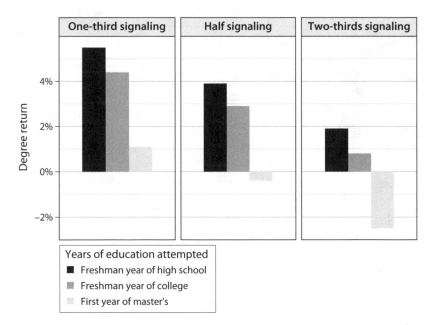

Figure 6.8: Social Degree Returns to Education for Good Students by Signaling Share
Source: Figure 6.6 and text.

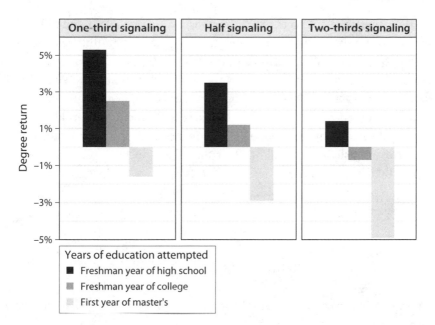

Figure 6.9: Social Degree Returns to Education for Fair Students by Signaling Share
Source: Figure 6.6 and text.

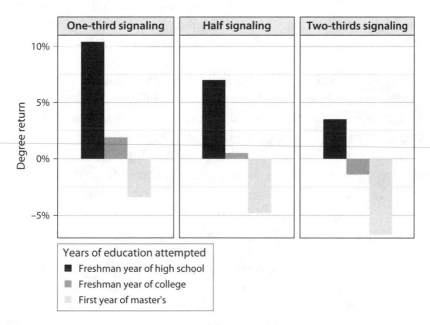

Figure 6.10: Social Degree Returns to Education for Poor Students by Signaling Share
Source: Figure 6.6 and text.

Thus, one need not accept 80% signaling as "Reasonable" to be unfashionably pessimistic. By mainstream standards, even one-third signaling shames education. While almost everyone should try high school, college is a good deal only for Excellent Students, and a disaster for Fair and Poor Students. The master's, moreover, is a bad deal across the board. Fifty percent signaling raises doubts about college for Excellent Students and undermines the social value of high school. High school's only clear social dividend is embarrassing: slightly curtailing Poor Students' shocking propensity for crime. By the time signaling hits two-thirds, the case against education is nearly complete. High school for Poor Students pays tolerably, but returns on every other level-ability combination range from poor to ruinous.

Searching for Social Returns

Averages conceal a lot. Do any educational investments enrich society despite the power of signaling?

Major, selectivity, attitude, and social returns. Parental wisdom distinguishes "real" majors that teach marketable job skills from "Mickey Mouse" majors that teach irrelevant fluff. As expected, workers with "real" majors fare better in the job market and rack up higher selfish returns. It is tempting to infer the major premium is all about skills: signaling may explain why fine arts majors earn more than high school grads, but human capital explains why engineers earn more than dance majors.

On inspection, however, the skill acquisition story is overrated. About three-quarters of STEM majors—and half of engineers—end up in jobs that *don't* use their specialized training.[72] STEM degrees impress a wide swath of employers, opening doors to careers in not only technology, but finance and business. What does this mean for social returns? With Cautious signaling, Excellent and Good Students in high-earning majors like electrical engineering still do well. With Reasonable signaling, however, the *most* qualified students studying the *most* lucrative majors remain burdens to society.[73] The same goes for students at highly selective but affordable colleges, and students who love school: social investments in their education are relatively rewarding but absolutely wasteful.[74]

Gender and social returns. Working women usually get a higher selfish return to education than working men. Socially speaking, however, two weighty offsetting factors arise. First, women are less likely to apply whatever job skills they learn in school because fewer women seek jobs. Second, women, regardless of education, commit virtually no crime. Male *college graduates* are more criminally inclined than female *high school dropouts*.[75] The social value of curbing female criminality is therefore low (see Figure 6.11).

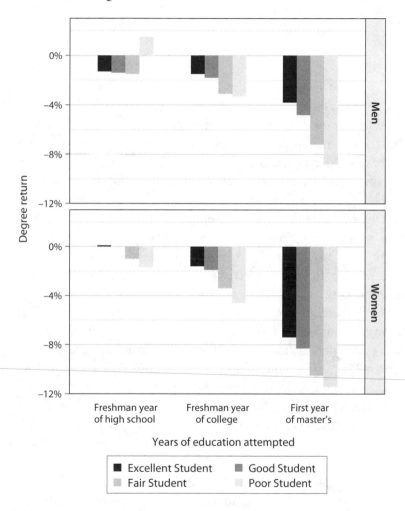

Figure 6.11: Social Degree Returns to Education by Sex with Reasonable Signaling
Source: Figure 5.12 and text, assuming:
(a) 45% ability bias for income, benefits, unemployment, and participation effects.
(b) 75% ability bias for crime effects.
(c) 20% of the effects of education reflect human capital.

How do the sexes' social returns compare when you snap the pieces together? In high school, investing in women usually pays better, with the key exception of male Poor Students. This isn't because female Poor Students are less morally deserving. Quite the opposite: investing in women is socially unprofitable because women avoid wrong-doing of their own accord. Beyond high school, educational investments in men perform better across the board—though "better" only means "not as wasteful."

Doubts

Every section in this chapter builds on interdisciplinary study of the evidence. When the evidence is mixed or weak, however, I state my best guess and proceed. Fellow academics may recoil, but candor trumps caution. If we researchers withhold our best guesses from voters and policy makers, voters and policy makers must act on their *own* best guesses— corrupted as they are by popular pieties about the glories of education.

But candor is more than the open statement of conclusions. It is also the open admission of doubts. My social return numbers have all the shortcomings of my selfish return numbers, plus several bonus shortcomings. Think of them not as "red flags," but as "yellow flags": lingering concerns meriting further investigation.

Signaling's share. My best guess says signaling accounts for 80% of education's return; I even anoint this the "Reasonable" position. Still, I am open to revision. A few outstanding studies could talk me down to as little as 60% or up to as much as 90%. While the Cautious assumption puts a high floor on signaling's share, future work on the sheepskin effect might show it's smaller than it looks. Like any competent forecaster, I do not *plan* to downgrade signaling, but signaling is so understudied that energetic researchers could quickly double the totality of our knowledge, warranting major rethinking.

Participation and ability bias. Social returns hinge on "workforce participation"—the fraction of graduates who want to work. Educated workers have relatively high participation rates. Some of this stems from ability bias, but how much? Social returns require a straight answer. Unfortunately, straight answers are scarce. Papers asking, "If the average college grad didn't go to college, how much money would they make?" are plentiful. Papers asking "If the average college grad didn't go to college, what are the odds they'd be in the workforce?" are nearly nonexistent. To bridge this research gap, I set ability bias for participation equal to ability bias for earnings, but a few good papers could show this shortcut is way off.

Crime, signaling, and sheepskin effects. The social benefits of schooling weak male students hinge on crime control. My crime numbers start with the all-inclusive cost of crime. Next, they incorporate the distribution of criminal behavior by education, age, and gender. They finish with corrections for ability bias and signaling. While there's nothing I'd do differently, I cannot banish two key doubts.

First, careful tallies of the full social cost of crime are scarce. The most comprehensive study covers 1997, when violent crime was about 50% higher than today. Second, crime researchers rarely test for sheepskin effects, so I set sheepskin effects for crime proportional to sheepskin effects for earnings. However, preliminary research suggests the sheepskin effect accounts for *all* of education's effect on crime. Since Cautious signaling treats sheepskin effects as socially worthless, the social benefits my calculations attribute to crime control may be a mirage—making the case against education more monolithic than ever.

The Educational Drake Equation

In Carl Sagan's awestruck words, each galaxy holds "billions upon billions" of stars.[76] Yet out of the galaxy's countless solar systems, we see but one with life: our own. How can the galaxy fall so desolately short of its potential? Astronomer Frank Drake publicized an elegant equation to clarify the matter. It's called the Drake Equation.[77] To simplify, the equation says the mind-boggling *requirements* for life must offset the mind-boggling *opportunities* for life. Humanity has the technology to speak to other worlds only because our solar system has a planet able to support life, because life in fact arose on this planet, because life evolved into intelligent life, because intelligent life developed the technology of interstellar communication, and because we've yet to destroy ourselves. We'll never speak to an alien civilization unless another solar system satisfies each and every one of these conditions. No wonder the cosmos looks so lonely.

In the right frame of mind, education statistics, too, inspire Saganian awe. Look at the lives of high school dropouts: their poverty, their joblessness, their attraction to crime. Compare that to the lives of college graduates with engineering degrees: their affluence, their devotion to their careers, their law-abiding ways. The distance between their lives is astronomical. Imagine the utopia our society would be after transforming every high school dropout into an engineer. Former Harvard president Derek Bok once quipped, "If you think education is expensive, try ignorance."[78] With gains this massive, why fret about cost?

Because education's powers of social transformation are galactically overrated. The observed gap between, say, dropouts and engineers, is only one term in what could be called the Educational Drake Equation. For workers, education's social benefit equals the observed dropout-engineer gap, times the probability of successfully completing the education, times the fraction of the gap *not* due to preexisting ability differences, times the fraction of the gap *not* due to signaling.

Suppose the average engineer contributes, on balance, three times as much to society as the average dropout, but each of the other terms in the Educational Drake Equation equals 50%. Then education's true effect is the +200% observed gap, times the 50% completion rate, times the 50% not due to ability bias, times the 50% not due to signaling. Grand total: a mere +25%.

Why does my approach deliver unfashionably wretched social returns? Despite the gory details, it boils down to the Educational Drake Equation. I start with the same observed gaps as other education researchers. But my competitors—usually tacitly, occasionally explicitly—set every other term in the Educational Drake Equation to 100%. Everyone who starts school finishes, none of the gap is due to ability bias, none of the gap is due to signaling, and everyone works. This is like rounding all the terms in the original Drake Equation up to 100%, then announcing that our galaxy contains billions of advanced civilizations. Yes, the well-educated are model citizens—skilled, employed, and law-abiding—but education is not a path to a model society. Indeed, plugging sensible numbers into the Educational Drake Equation shows the path to a model society starts with a U-turn. Deep education cuts won't transform us, but we can work wonders with the billions upon billions of dollars we save.

CHAPTER 7

The White Elephant in the Room

We Need Lots Less Education

> white elephant: a property requiring much care and expense and yielding little profit
>> —*Merriam-Webster's Collegiate Dictionary*

> elephant in the room: an obvious major problem or issue that people avoid discussing or acknowledging
>> —*Merriam-Webster Dictionary*

Every government on earth supports education.[1] They support it rhetorically with high praise, and financially with tax dollars. The ideal of "free and compulsory education"—schooling kids free of charge whether they like it or not—spans the globe. Democracies and dictatorships fund different kinds of education but spend at comparable levels.[2] Industrial policy—picking "winning" industries to protect and subsidize—is usually contentious. Yet industrial policy for education is wildly popular the world over. In a major international survey, clear majorities in *every* country favor bigger education budgets.[3] To the best of my knowledge, there is no country on earth where most people clamor for educational austerity.

American opinion is typical. In the General Social Survey, 74% favor *more* education funding, 21% favor the status quo, and only 5% favor cuts. Education enjoys bipartisan allegiance. Liberals say, "Spend more on health care and education," not "Spend more on health care *instead of* education." Conservatives say, "Spend more on defense and education," not "Spend more on defense *instead of* education." Avowed opponents of Big Government make an exception for education: 60% of *strong* Republicans hew to the conventional pro-spending wisdom, and only 12% are contrarian enough to claim we overspend.[1]

Even my fellow education critics normally argue *against* spending *more*, not *for* spending *less*.[5] Take Alison Wolf, Baroness of Dulwich and author of *Does Education Matter?*

> So it would be bizarre to see our education systems as just a collection of huge white elephants. But then no one is seriously advocating closing down all publicly funded education, or even cutting 25 per cent off its budget.[6]

What inspires this panideological affection? Proeducation industrial policy is so popular advocates have little need to share their reasons. When pressed, laymen's justifications are emotionally powerful but logically pitiful. "We need to invest in people!" (Reply: We usually rely on the free market to provide crucial investments. We can do the same for education.) "Nothing is more important than education!" (Reply: Food's more important, and we rely on the free market for that.) "Government has to make sure even the poorest children receive a good education!" (Reply: Means-tested vouchers can cheaply handle this problem. There's no need for government to run schools or subsidize tuition for kids who *aren't* poor.) Laymen's arguments almost never confront the question, "At what point would education spending be excessive?" "We've done enough for education" is as heretical as "We've done enough for paralyzed veterans."

Since politicians compete for laymen's favor, they parrot these populist clichés. Recall that *both* George Bushes wished to be known as "the education president."[7] Who could oppose investment in our children, our people, our nation, and our future? *The Onion*, the best parody site ever, once ran an article titled, "U.S. Government to Discontinue Long-Term, Low-Yield Investment in Nation's Youth."[8] In it, Secretary of Education Rod Paige takes a calmly analytical approach that would cost any politician their job:

> "Testing is exactly the sort of research the government should do before making spending decisions," Paige said. "How else will we know which individuals are sound investments and which are likely to waste our time and money?"

The article amuses by being oblivious to the very existence of populist sentiments to which successful politicians piously pander.

The Best Proeducation Arguments: What's Wrong with Them

In all fairness, views should be judged by the *best* arguments in their favor—and popular arguments are rarely the best. Education researchers craft a far sturdier case for educational industrial policy than laymen or politicians. Despite countless variants, their arguments fit into three big intellectual boxes: irrationality, credit constraints, and positive externalities. Irrationality and credit stories tacitly equate selfish and social returns, then argue free markets leave selfishly profitable, socially valuable educational investments unexploited. Externalities stories explicitly distinguish selfish and social returns, then argue free markets fail to exploit socially valuable educational investments because they aren't selfishly profitable.

Irrationality. In irrationality stories, the free market fails to *convince* students to make selfishly profitable educational investments.[9] Maybe students underrate education's payoffs; maybe they're too myopic to care about payoffs far in the future; maybe they're too young to grasp what an "investment" is. Whatever the reason, irrational students left to their own devices short-change themselves and us by finishing school prematurely. Government support for education helps confused students spot the golden opportunities by making education's benefits too massive to miss.

Credit constraints. In these stories, the free market fails to give students the *opportunity* to make selfishly profitable educational investments.[10] Suppose the normal market rate of interest is 4%. Inferring, "Students will stay in school as long as the return to education exceeds 4%" is dogma. In the real world, plenty of students can't afford living expenses, much less tuition—and their credit rating is too poor to borrow the difference. For minors, this is undeniable: Who wants to extend a $50,000 line of credit to a 14-year-old to pay for high school? The lender could *know* the return to education exceeds 4%, yet still reject the loan for lack of collateral. Left to their own devices, credit-constrained students short-change themselves and us by finishing school prematurely. Government support for education hands strapped students the seed capital to invest in themselves.

Externalities. The last best argument for education subsidies says the free market fails to give students the *incentive* to make socially valuable educational investments. Rational students with good credit hungrily exploit selfishly profitable educational opportunities. Trouble arises when their education benefits *bystanders*—people with no earthly reason to reward them for their help. Unless students are saints, they'll repay bystanders' ingratitude by ignoring their interests. Before responding, "Tough luck for them," remember we're *all* somebody's bystanders. Left to their own devices, selfish students short-change us—but not themselves—by finishing school prematurely. Government support for education entices these students to prolong their socially valuable stay.

Irrationality, credit constraints, positive externalities: all three stories are plausible. In a vacuum, each bolsters the case for proeducation industrial policy. There's just one small problem: we're not in a vacuum. An intellectually serious case for industrial policy must account for offsetting forces. Student irrationality cuts two ways: Students who underestimate education's return could easily *over*estimate their probability of graduation.[11] Students too myopic to care about payoffs in the far future might pursue long-shot degrees to impress their friends or avoid disappointing their parents. The same goes for externalities. In technical terms, signaling implies *negative* externalities: when students stay in school to impress employers, they hurt bystanders in the labor market who look worse by comparison. Honest defenders of proeducation policies must pool *all* factors and look at the grand total.

In a free market, evaluating the case for *some* proeducation policies would be straightforward. Estimate education's social return, then see if it exceeds the market interest rate. If it doesn't, doing nothing for education is better than doing something. Otherwise, doing something for education *may* be better than doing nothing. Why only "may"? Because government might overshoot. Instead of delicately fostering education until its social return reaches the market rate, government might spend money like a drunken sailor, driving social returns *below* the market rate.

Since no government leaves education to the free market, there is no straightforward way to evaluate the case for the very existence of proeducation policies. Sure, we can estimate education's social return, then see if it exceeds the market interest rate. Given our position, however, this comparison tells only whether government support for education is *currently* too high, too low, or just right. If, despite massive industrial policy, education's social return continues to exceed the market rate, government still isn't doing enough. If education's social return is less than the market rate, government has gone too far.

Last chapter, we methodically tabulated education's benefits and costs. We didn't just tabulate financial effects for students; we tabulated comprehensive effects for society. Result: education's social return ranges from mildly below market to dramatically below market. Given a modest role for signaling, government overinvests in high school and severely overinvests beyond high school. Given a plausible role for signaling, government severely overinvests in high school and beyond. Either way, government investment in weaker students is especially wasteful, male Poor Students in high school excepted.

Education researchers' arguments for proeducation policies could be valid as far as they go. My own calculations incorporate multiple positive externalities. What low and negative social returns show is that standard proeducation arguments are *incomplete*. They fail to face the Educational Drake Equation in all its dismal splendor. Counting everything that counts, industrial policy for education has clearly gone too far. The United States—and probably the rest of the world—is overeducated.

Schoolcraft as Soulcraft?

Some of the most prominent and heartfelt proeducation arguments don't talk about selfish *or* social returns. Instead, they praise education for instilling admirable values and uplifting the human personality. Education is good for the soul. How can you put a price on that? Economists may scoff, "Unless your budget is infinite, you *have* to put a price on everything." But most people—including me—still find "schoolcraft as soulcraft" a compelling ideal.

The ideal is so compelling, in fact, that it warrants a full chapter of its own. If you wish to see it addressed before reading policy recommendations, skip ahead to Chapter 9. In any case, if you think "schoolcraft as soulcraft" is the decisive objection to the proposed education reforms of this chapter and the next, please remember that I do face up to this challenge in the end.

How Big Is Your Elephant?

A classic bumper sticker muses, "It will be a great day when our schools get all the money they need and the air force has to hold a bake sale to buy a bomber." By most measures, this great day arrived in the United States long ago. The air force may not hold bake sales, but total education spending far surpasses total military spending. For the 2010–11 school year, education was 7.5% of the American economy, versus 4.7% for defense. Spending came to over $1.1 trillion on education, and a bit over $700 billion on defense. Schools overtook the military back in 1972 and sharply widened their lead after the Cold War.[12]

From a conventional point of view, this is great news. Even ardent hawks rejoice we're not sacrificing our children's future to protect their present. Who could oppose ample funding for education? Anyone who takes signaling seriously. $1.1 trillion a year is a royal sum— $1,100,000,000,000 in longhand. That's nearly $3,600 for every person in America—not every *student*, mind you, but every person. Chanting "investment" doesn't make it so. If half is wasteful signaling, we're wasting over half a trillion dollars a year. And that's only budgetary cost. A full damage report would include tens of billions of emotionally taxing, socially fruitless classroom hours.

One notable difference between defense and education is that *all* defense spending is government spending, but education spending is partly private. If government spent zero on education, education spending wouldn't disappear—and neither would wasteful signaling. Yet without government support, modern education would be unrecognizable. Like a rich uncle, government *helps us waste*. Whenever we can't or won't waste our *own* money on schooling, federal, state, and local governments are standing by to waste taxpayers' money on our behalf.

How much do U.S. governments really spend on education? A tough question. We can't blithely equate public schools with government spending and private schools with individual spending. Some public schools receive hefty private funding. Some private schools receive hefty government funding. Neither can we blithely sum federal, state, and local spending, because higher-level governments often turn their education budgets into grants for lower-level governments. That risks double- or triple-counting: if the feds give California $10 billion for education, and California hands every penny to local schools, total gov ernment education spending is not $30 billion, but $10 billion.

The best path to a solid measure begins with the U.S. Census. The cen sus estimates state and local governments' direct education spending— including all spending on K–12, higher education, plus "assistance and subsidies to individuals, private elementary and secondary schools, and private colleges and universities, as well as miscellaneous education ex penditures."[13] The 2010–11 figure is $861 billion. This counts all state and local spending funded by federal grants, but *not* direct federal edu cation spending or assistance to *individuals*.

Direct federal education spending is hard to pin down, but probably small enough to ignore. Federal assistance to individuals, in contrast, ex ceeds $100 billion. Main complication: the federal government chiefly of fers loans, not grants. If it charged market interest rates, you could claim student loans cost taxpayers nothing. Yet despite loud complaints about usury, even "unsubsidized" student rates are well below market. Loan guarantees have no visible upfront cost, but you probably don't want to cosign my personal loans for free. The Congressional Budget Office finds an average subsidy rate of 12%: every dollar of student "loan" contains a hidden taxpayer gift of 12 cents.[14] Figure 7.1 tallies the census numbers, federal grants to individuals, and implicit student loan subsidies.

Many Americans imagine public education operates on a shoestring budget. Private education, in contrast, looks so pricey it's implausible government does much to make it affordable. Both perceptions are wildly at odds with the facts. Figure 7.2 puts the numbers in perspective. Government provides more than four-fifths of all education spending. Government support for education comfortably exceeds notoriously bloated defense spending. Even at the height of the War on Terror, there was more government money for education than the military. Govern ment spending on education is about 6% of the whole economy.[15]

Where does the money go? The U.S. government, like governments around the world, prioritizes K–12 over college. But higher education is more dependent on taxpayers than it looks, because so much "pri vate" tuition has government fingerprints on it. In 2010–11, government spent at least $565 billion on K through 12—that's 87% of the total—and at least $317 billion on higher education—67% of the total.[16] The "bake

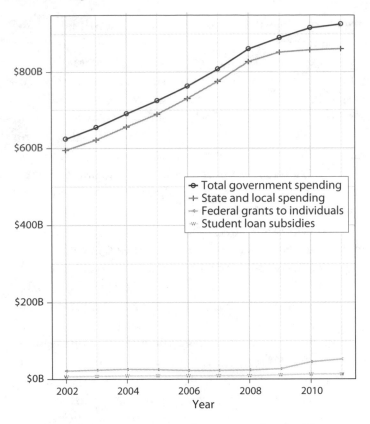

Figure 7.1: Total U.S. Government Education Spending (in $B)
Sources: Snyder and Dillow 2015, pp. 58, 60–61, Snyder and Dillow 2013, p. 57, S. Baum and Payea 2012, p. 10. State and local education spending excludes public libraries; in years that count them, I subtract average library budget share of 1.3%. Grant and loan numbers converted from constant to current dollars.

sale" bumper sticker has misled a generation. The U.S. doesn't starve schools to feed its war machine. It serves both a resplendent banquet.

Citizens are understandably nervous when they picture a government war on educational investment. Fortunately, no crusade against an external enemy is necessary because, as the cartoon *Pogo* famously quipped, "We have met the enemy, and he is us."[17] Governments have a nearly foolproof remedy for educational waste: spend less. Cut budgets for public education; cut subsidies for private education. Once citizens embrace educational austerity, the central question isn't "How?" but "Where do we start?"

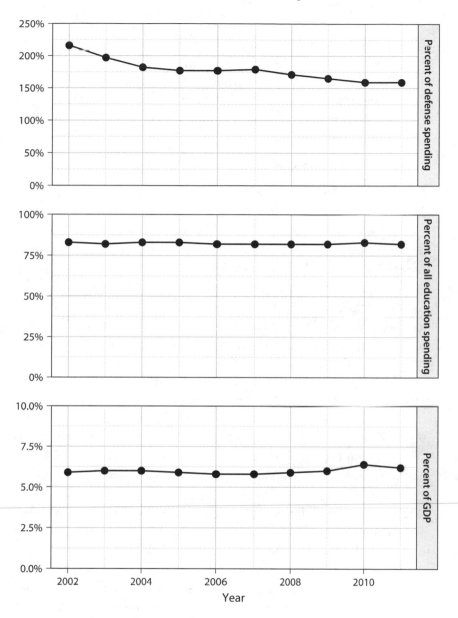

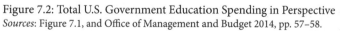

Figure 7.2: Total U.S. Government Education Spending in Perspective
Sources: Figure 7.1, and Office of Management and Budget 2014, pp. 57–58.

Cutting Education: Why, Where, How

> When once asked at a public lecture in St. Louis how large the
> state should be, Coase answered: "If you see a man who weighs
> over 400 pounds, and you ask me how much he should weigh, my
> answer would be . . . less."
>
> John Nye, "Ronald Coase: An Appreciation"[18]

When I argue education is largely wasteful signaling, most listeners yield. Popular resistance doesn't kick in until I add, "Let's waste less by cutting government spending on education." You might think conceding the wastefulness of education spending would automatically entail support for austerity, but it doesn't. The typical reaction is to confidently state, "Education budgets should be redirected, not reduced."

Such confidence is misplaced. The discovery of wasteful spending does not magically reveal constructive alternatives. Prudence dictates a two-step response. Step 1: Stop wasting the resources. Step 2: Save those resources until you discover a good way to spend them. *Not* wasting resources is simple and speedy. Don't just stand there; do it. Finding good ways to use resources is complex and slow. Don't just do it; think it through. Remember: you can apply saved resources *anywhere*. Time and money wasted on education could pave roads, cure cancer, cut taxes, subsidize childbearing, pay down government debt before our Fiscal Day of Reckoning, or allow taxpayers to buy better homes, cars, meals, and vacations.

Suppose I prove your toenail fungus cream doesn't work. I counsel, "Stop wasting money on that worthless cream." Would you demur, "Not until we find a toenail fungus remedy that works"? No way. Finding a real remedy could be more trouble than it's worth. It might take forever. Continuing to waste money on quackery until a cure comes into your possession is folly. Saying, "There *must* be a cure!" is childish and dogmatic. Maybe your toenails are a lost cause, and you should use the savings for a trip to Miami.

The signaling model highlights two desirable forms of educational austerity. The first: cutting fat from the curriculum. The second: cutting subsidies for tuition. Let's explore both.

Cutting fat from the curriculum. Anyone who scrutinizes modern schools with a mildly cynical eye witnesses piles of material students are laughably unlikely to use in adulthood. The fat emerges in kindergarten: history, social studies, art, music, foreign language. By high school, as we've seen, students spend at least half their time on fat. In college, many majors are made of fat: think history, communications, or "interdisciplinary studies." About 40% of graduates earn degrees in comically—or tragicomically—useless subjects. Even the hardest majors burn ample time on high theory and breadth requirements.

From a selfish point of view, as I've said many a time, the most useless coursework can pay off. Yet from a social point of view, these selfish rewards don't count. Purging the useless material is the socially responsible remedy. Return the hours we seize from the young at great taxpayer expense. When they're too little to release on their own recognizance, schools can still save a bundle by giving students more active time on the playground or more quiet time in the library. Once they no longer need babysitting, society can save even more by ending the school day the minute useful learning is done.

A moderate reform is to stop *requiring* useless coursework. Make history, social studies, art, music, and foreign language optional. The main problem with this moderation: pursuing material you're *allowed* to skip sends a favorable signal. Many students—urged on by their parents—will leap to outshine their peers. To defuse this wasteful arms race, we must do more than make armaments optional. We must constrain opportunities for combat.

One constructive constraint is raising standards so high most students quickly fall by the wayside. This is a bad idea for subjects students use postgraduation: weak readers are more productive than full-blown illiterates. For subjects students forget postgraduation, however, unforgiving standards stealthily save time and money. Take music. When music is optional, lots of students waste years on it. Most of the waste vanishes, however, if intro music teachers cull the bottom 80% of the class. Students who repeatedly survive such weedings might even have a prayer of a future in music.

The cleanest approach, naturally, is to discontinue classes that teach impractical material at taxpayer expense. There really is no need for K–12 to teach history, social studies, art, music, or foreign languages.

This is especially clear if you recall how much students forget: despite years of schoolwork, American adults can't date the Civil War, name their congressman, draw, sing, or speak French. Why not redouble our pedagogical efforts instead? The standard reasons: expected benefits of success are low, and the cost is high.

The same logic holds for college majors. Why should taxpayers fund the *option* to study fine arts at public expense? Instead, shut down the impractical departments at public colleges, and make impractical majors at private colleges ineligible for government grants and loans. Deprived of impractical options, some students will switch to practical subjects. Won't plenty of others respond to narrower options by cutting their schooling short? Hopefully. If students refuse to stay in school unless they're allowed to waste public money, taxpayers should call their bluff.

In practice, admittedly, "fat" is a matter of degree. Most students will foreseeably never use advanced mathematics or science after graduation. For budding quants, though, these subjects are deeply practical. How should curriculum reformers respond? Sequentially. Cut all obvious fat posthaste. Next, briefly review the near-obvious fat, and cut whatever fails to vindicate itself. Then carefully examine the debatable fat, and cut with greater caution. Above all, we shouldn't dither on straightforward cases because ambiguous cases perplex us.

As fat disappears from the curriculum, students will inevitably find other ways to signal excellence to the labor market. Does this make curriculum reform self-defeating? No, because some forms of signaling are less socially wasteful than others. Cutting fat leaves students with one well-lit path: work harder in their "real" classes. Given American adults' woeful deficiencies in reading, writing, and math, that's progress.

Cutting subsidies for tuition. Curriculum reform has one big drawback: education officials have little incentive to cut fat. As long as their funding holds steady, why should they confess that many subjects and majors are undeserving of taxpayer support? They've already opted for the status quo, so trusting them to pare down the very system they've built is naive. Voters could replace existing leaders with earnest austerians, but the public's attention will eventually wander, and the old regime will reemerge.

These fears highlight a less gameable way to cut education: shift the *cost* of education from taxpayers to students and their families. Raise tuition for public colleges. Cut subsidies. Turn grants into loans. Charge borrowers market interest rates. Impose at least *some* tuition for public high school. From a normal perspective, such proposals provoke the horrified reaction, "Attendance could fall!" From a signaling perspective, the right response is, "Lower attendance is what we're going for."

How does cost shifting raise education's social return? Supply and demand. Raising the price of school reduces attendance. The more attendance falls, the scarcer educated labor becomes, and the pricier it gets. Owing to signaling, the social benefit rises *less* than the selfish benefit, but social and selfish benefits still move in tandem. At some point, the education premium gets high enough to transform the marginal student into a good social investment.

How much must the education premium rise to hit a respectable inflation-adjusted social return—say 4%? A thorny question, because social returns have so many moving parts. When the education premium goes up, for example, students likely work harder to graduate, raising completion rates. Still, rough-and-ready numbers show the education premium must go *way* up. Suppose reducing the supply of educated workers affects only compensation, leaving all other outcomes the same. Further assume compensation for high school dropouts stays constant because the rising quality of dropouts offsets rising supply. Figure 7.3 shows what education premiums have to look like to hit a 4% Social Degree Return.

Signaling's severity governs the results. Given Cautious signaling, the high school premium needs to rise only modestly. For Poor Students, a lower premium would serve, because crime reduction overshadows their minimal acquisition of job skills. Any education past high school, however, requires unprecedented premiums: at least 100% for both the bachelor's and the master's. With Reasonable signaling and Excellent Students, the high school premium must more than double, the college premium nearly triple, the master's premium more than quadruple. Justifying education for weaker students requires bigger run-ups still.

How will we know when we've cut deeply enough? As long as my "Reasonable" signaling assumption is worthy of its name, the quick answer is: when high school grads earn twice as much as dropouts, B.A.s earn three times as much as high school grads, and M.A.s earn twice as much as B.A.s. How much will schooling have to fall before premiums reach such heights? A prominent but oversimplified model of the labor

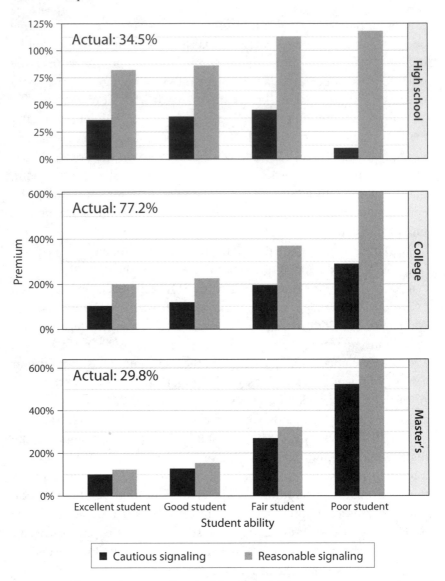

Figure 7.3: Education Premiums Required for 4% Social Return
Source: Figures 6.5 and 6.6 and text.

market implies America's high school and college completion rates are both about 20 percentage points too high.[19] For changes of this enormity, though, don't take the models too literally. What's clear is that attendance must plummet.

Can attendance radically fall? Sure—as long as government sternly cuts financial support. Researchers intently study the effect of subsidies on educational attainment. Since K–12 is already free, they focus on college.[20] When financial cost rises, how much do college attendance and completion fall? Answers land in a fairly narrow range: in modern dollars, cutting tuition or raising grants by $1,000 per student per year increases college graduation rates by 2–4 percentage points.[21] Student loan subsidies are comparably effective.[22] *Un*subsidized student loans, in contrast, do little for enrollment or graduation.[23]

College finance specialists often announce they're searching for cheap ways to "build the stock of college-educated labor."[24] But we can repurpose their projections. If cutting tuition or raising grants by $1,000 per student per year increases college graduates as a share of the population by 2–4 percentage points, we can cut that rate by 20 percentage points by raising the annual cost of college by $5,000 to $10,000. Not the "list price"—the actual price. Assuming equal price-sensitivity, the same goes for high school: To cut the ratio of high school graduates to population by 20 percentage points, annual tuition must rise by $5,000 to $10,000. Caveat: this is a very long-run solution. Raising tuition by $5,000 to $10,000 swiftly reduces the flow of new graduates, but the "overstock" of existing graduates will remain for generations.

What about the effect of higher tuition on fertility? Anyone who fears overpopulation should be eager to shift the cost of raising children from taxpayers to parents. But even the staunchest natalist should recognize that subsidizing education is a poor substitute for subsidizing fertility itself. Education cuts could easily fund large child tax credits, or outright baby bonuses.[25]

Yes, cutting education sounds outrageous to most Americans. They'll call it awful, crazy, mean, and foolish. Educational austerity is a secular heresy, a view no "decent" member of our society entertains. In the face of this profound resistance, I too feel tempted to sugarcoat. But I'd rather be clear than pleasing. Give heresy a chance. Once we grant the ubiquity of educational signaling, my main conclusions logically follow.

Are draconian education cuts really a good idea, especially for a society as rich as our own? Calling them "draconian" begs the question. If we're not getting good value for our educational investments, we shouldn't call deep cuts "draconian." We should call the status quo "profligate." Rich societies can *afford* to waste trillions. But why settle for that? Rich societies face countless opportunities. The trillions we spend boring youths might cure cancer, buy driverless cars, or end world hunger. Collective complacency seems harmless, but it kills by omission.

The Hidden Wonder of High Tuition and Student Debt

High tuition and student debt naturally disturb education's defenders: education is a great investment, so government should make it accessible for all. Strangely, though, education's *critics* often join the chorus against high tuition and student debt: education is a bad investment, so government shouldn't expect people to fund it themselves. Take critic Peter Capelli:

> Using loans to pay for college is an idea with great appeal to economists because the people getting the financial benefit—the graduates who get good jobs—are the ones paying for it, presumably in the future when they have those well-paying jobs. If there is not a good payoff from the degree, then that argument falls apart.[26]

But what would happen if lawmakers made college free of charge? Everyone now deterred by tuition bills and student loan payments would rethink their decision, sharply boosting attendance. If, as critics contend, too many students already go to college, this is bad. Instead of joining the populist alliance against tuition and debt, critics of education should rise to their defense.

Tuition does more than curb fruitless attendance. It improves the *mix* of majors. Practical majors already tend to be more selfishly and socially lucrative than impractical majors, but tuition rarely varies by field of study. As tuition inches up, then, impractical majors are the first to become losing ventures. Maybe would-be fine artists will rethink their major; maybe they'll rethink college altogether. Either way, across-the-board price hikes point students in less wasteful directions.

Student debt has the same upsides. Students who know they'll eventually pay for their education may still make foolish decisions. But at least they have an incentive to weigh their options—and wonder how they'll repay their debts with an anthropology degree. Contrary to populists, student loan programs are one of the *least* dysfunctional parts of the status quo. Subsidized loans definitely encourage college attendance, but subsidies are too low to encourage it much. Compared to overall taxpayer support for education, loan programs are a rounding error—in part, no doubt, because student debt survives bankruptcy.[27]

Critics of student loans occasionally appeal to the "Bennett Hypothesis": student loans pump up demand, perversely leading to higher tuition.[28] What's the point of expanding access with loans if schools respond by restricting access with tuition? From a signaling point of view, however, we should hope for perversity. The root problem with education is not too little access but too much attendance. The more loans inflate tuition, the less they inflate credentials.

Student loan programs could be improved. Government should charge higher interest rates, or leave lending to the free market. But most reformers want to head in the opposite direction: cut interest rates; replace loans with grants; forgive debts at taxpayer expense. Education's fans understandably favor such reforms; they want to make college cheaper so more kids go. It's baffling, though, when education's critics echo the fans' proposals. If too many kids go to college, *publicizing* bankruptcy law pushes enrollment in the right direction: "Remember, kids: student debt is almost impossible to discharge." *Relaxing* bankruptcy law pushes enrollment in the wrong direction: "Hey kids, guess what? If you ever find yourself struggling to repay your student debts, you might not have to pay at all."

Raising Completion Rates?

Education's social return would spike if students finished every academic program they started. Researchers have found some promising ways to boost completion rates.[29] Instead of cutting education spending, shouldn't we spend more to get students over the finish line?

No. While completion rates can be nudged, they chiefly reflect past academic success.[30] Better retention efforts will not make Poor Students perform like Fair Students, Fair Students like Good Students, or Good

Students like Excellent Students. Even if they did, they would make education's social returns only a bit less awful, because returns are bad across the board. The only realistic way to sharply raise completion rates is to slash academic standards—a self-defeating path in human capital and signaling stories alike.

When optimistic reformers protest, "Raising completion may seem elusive, but we've pinpointed special programs that work wonders," it's tempting to scoff, "That's what they all say." But there's a deeper reply. Namely: completion rates have been low for decades. If wonder-working programs remain unadopted, the system is too dysfunctional to trust with extra money. The wise path begins with cuts. Get rid of all the programs that *don't* work wonders. Then—and only then—allocate some of the savings to the shiny outliers. This is common sense—and a token of good faith to taxpayers whose money has been so squandered for so long.

The strongest objection to making school more expensive is that it's self-defeating. Suppose economic hardship distracts students from their studies, depressing completion rates. Then cutting financial aid would make education's social return worse than it already is. Maybe the best way to get taxpayers a decent return is to spend whatever it takes to make school completely affordable, so students can focus on their studies.

Or not. Maybe making students bear the cost of school *improves* their academic motivation by giving them "skin in the game." Consistent with these doubts, evidence on the link between financial aid and completion is mixed. According to a review of research up to 2005, most studies find grants modestly improve completion, but quite a few find no effect or the opposite effect.[31] A 2013 review finds mixed evidence for no-strings grants, but positive effects of performance-based grants (like scholarships that make recipients maintain a B average).[32] Even performance-based effects are moderate: scholarships that cover most or all tuition boost college graduation rates by 3 or 4 percentage points.[33] Performance-based funding is less wasteful than no-strings funding, but slightly higher completion rates aren't enough to tip the scales in education's favor. Not even close.

Signaling and Social Justice

> In a very few moments, I will put my signature on the Higher Education Act of 1965. . . . It means that a high school senior anywhere in this great land of ours can apply to any college or any university in any of the 50 States and not be turned away because his family is poor.
>
> —Lyndon Johnson, November 8, 1965[34]

Most of us don't merely oppose shifting the cost of education from taxpayers to students. We *recoil* at the idea. When rising tuition curbs attendance, who is most likely to be curbed? The poor. Instead of fretting about education's social *return*, shouldn't we fix our gaze on social *justice*—our commitment as a society to our least fortunate members?

These concerns would be well-founded if education were largely about teaching useful job skills. In such a world, raising tuition doesn't just make the workforce less skilled. It amplifies the *inequality* of skill: The poorer you are, the less you learn and the less you earn.

Since education is mostly signaling, however, the social justice catechism is wrong. Yes, awarding a full scholarship to one poor youth makes that individual better off by helping send a fine signal to the labor market. Awarding full scholarships to all poor youths, however, changes what educational signals *mean*—and leads more affluent competitors to pursue further education to keep their edge. The result, as we've seen, is credential inflation. As education rises, workers—including the poor—*need* more education to get the same job. Where's the social justice in that?[35]

Imagine the government subsidized wedding rings for the poor.[36] Anyone ready for marriage can go to any jewelry store in the country, knowing—whatever their income—they can buy a diamond ring. The snag: diamond rings are largely a *signal* of marital commitment. If diamonds were cheap as plastic, other gems would adorn our rings. They're valuable because they're costly. Once the government makes them affordable to all, then, diamond rings signal little or nothing. Doesn't this "level the playing field"? Only for a heartbeat. Once the nonpoor see diamond rings don't signal what they used to, they procure a snazzier ring to separate themselves from the pack. Thanks to government sub-sidies, every suitor can afford a wedding ring, but so what? Society is *functionally* as unequal as ever.

Subsidies don't just hurt the poor by fueling credential inflation. They reshape hiring and promotion to the poor's detriment. Picture a society where half the population can't afford college. In this setting, reserving good jobs for college grads is bad business. "There are plenty of qualified candidates who didn't go to college" is not wishful thinking, but literal truth. Education still signals something, but *lack* of education is not the kiss of death. When asked, "Why didn't you go to college?" "I couldn't afford it" is a great excuse. Heavy subsidies take it off the table. Indeed, what excuses are left? "I'm a bad test taker"? "I didn't feel like going to college"? "I figured I could learn better on the job"? Once the good ex-cuses are gone, employers have little reason to stay open-minded.

More technically, subsidies *raise the correlation between educational attainment and employability*. By itself, this helps high-ability, low-income students—exactly as Lyndon Johnson suggests. Unfortunately, as the correlation between education and talent rises, education be-comes more convincing to employers—and hence more lucrative. Rich rewards in turn spur students to amass even more education. If paren-tal income were the sole determinant of educational success, education would signal little to employers and therefore entice little waste.

I grant that subsidies *seem* to promote social justice. My best friend in my Ph.D. program came from a poor rural family. If a top state school hadn't given him a full ride for his B.A., he probably wouldn't have been sitting next to me at Princeton. Anyone who wanders a college campus will find equally visible success stories. To detect subsidies' downside for social justice, you must dwell on the opportunities the poor have *lost* because of credential inflation. When most Americans didn't finish high school, dropouts faced little stigma in the labor market. The stigma is now severe. When few Americans finished college, high school grads could plausibly work their way up the corporate ladder. No longer. The main difference isn't that "the economy changed," but that education rose, so workers need higher credentials to compete.

None of this philosophically undermines the quest for social justice. The point is that trying to speed up the academic treadmill is a misguided distraction from this quest.[37] The planet is full of blatant social injustice:

hungry kids, hopeless adults, refugees from war and tyranny. The hundreds of billions our society fritters away on education every year could make a giant dent in these dire problems. Even if your quest for social justice stops at the nation's borders, why not fork over the hundreds of billions saved to America's underclass? Human capital purists may protest that this squanders our country's seed grain. But letting the poor eat the seeds is better than burning the seeds signaling to each other.

What I Really Think

> Whenever you find yourself on the side of the majority, it is time to pause and reflect.
>
> —Mark Twain[38]

This is a book about education policy, not political philosophy. My top policy recommendation—austerity—is less jarring for some political philosophies than others. Yet once you buy my central thesis—education has a low social return because it's mostly signaling—almost every political philosophy urges cuts. Liberals and conservatives may decry each other as evil incarnate, but both affirm that wasting taxpayer dollars is bad.

Yet political philosophy is ultimately unavoidable, because philosophy sets *presumptions*. Some philosophies have a presumption in favor of education; others, in favor of the status quo. From these perspectives, the burden of proof rests on advocates of cuts. This burden is surmountable. Social return estimates amply justify spending 20% less on education *given* a presumption in favor of education or the status quo. But such presumptions still block radical reforms, because there is minimal concrete experience with radical reforms. We can speculate that cutting spending by 80% would be a great boon, but when the burden of proof is against you, speculation can't surmount it.

I favor radical reforms nonetheless. Philosophically, I am staunchly libertarian. While not absolutely opposed to taxpayer support for education, I have a strong moral presumption against taxpayer support for *anything*. Why? Because I have a strong moral presumption in favor of leaving others alone—and consider taxation to be a prime example of failing to leave others alone. Even if a tax has full democratic support, the burden of proof properly rests with the majority that wants to tax, not the minority that demurs. This burden, too, is surmountable. When taxation is the only way to avert clear-cut disaster, tax away. But taxing people to fund programs with modest or debatable social benefits strikes me as deeply wrong.

I know libertarianism is out of step with modern political thought. If you're curious why anyone would hold my eccentric view, I outsource the job to philosopher Michael Huemer's *The Problem of Political Authority*.[39] Still, when readers ask, "What is the ideal education policy?" responding "It depends on your philosophy" is a cop-out. Readers deserve full disclosure, even if it provides a convenient excuse to ignore the unphilosophical core of my case against education.

All things considered, I favor full separation of school and state.[40] Government should stop using tax dollars to fund education of any kind. Schools—primary, secondary, and tertiary alike—should be funded solely by fees and private charity. Such policies (lack of policies?) are extreme even by libertarian standards. Most libertarians dream of a voucher system, where schools are private but funding is public.[41] Yet to my mind, vouchers—and "school choice" more generally—only marginally improve over the status quo. Since education is mostly signaling, the chief problem is not low quality, but high quantity. America's schools, like its sport stadiums, are white elephants. The main drawback of massive government backing isn't that these white elephants are poorly managed or uncompetitive, but that they're far too numerous and lavish. Government should leave both industries to the free market, and view mass bankruptcies not as market failure, but market correction.

Full separation of school and state may seem doctrinaire, but it has a pragmatic advantage over more moderate proposals. To quote humorist P. J. O'Rourke, "Giving money and power to government is like giving whiskey and car keys to teenage boys."[42] Publicly funded education has an awful track record, wasting hundreds of billions every year. Full separation *transparently* keeps governments' untrustworthy hands away from the industry's control panel. A "95% separation" policy, in contrast, is tricky to monitor, leaving education open to renewed abuse. By analogy, suppose a teenage boy has a track record of driving drunk. You could take away 95% of his driving privileges. To get behind the wheel, he has to pass a breathalyzer test, drive during daylight hours, and refuse teenage passengers. Yet in light of the ongoing risk he'll squirm out of whatever rules you impose, confiscating the wayward motorist's car keys is the wiser course.

Advocates of separation of school and state often compare their position to separation of church and state. The comparison is strange yet reasonable. State-supported religion has a terrible track record. You could respond by limiting government to a "small" religious role. But "small" is fuzzy, hence open to abuse. The wiser course is to cut the cord between government and religion once and for all. Opposing *any* government religious policy may sound dogmatic in theory but works well in practice. Once you concede government has been wasting hundreds of billions of dollars year in, year out, separation of school and state is a measured response.

The case against government funding of primary education is definitely weaker than the case against high school and beyond. Since almost everyone in the United States at least *starts* high school, there is no clean way to calculate the selfish return for earlier grades. Nationally representative data on K–8 curricula are also wanting, so there's no clear way to ballpark its signaling share—or estimate its social return. If I had to leave tax-funded education one final toehold, I'd pick a modest, means-tested voucher program for primary education.

Still, I'd be mildly opposed even if the exception were hermetically contained. Private charity apparently did a good job of educating the poor in nineteenth-century Britain and the United States.[43] When Britain first made education compulsory for 5-to-10-year-olds in 1880, over 95% of 15-year-olds were already literate. Mid-nineteenth-century American literacy was comparable, at least outside the South.[44] Since modern society is vastly richer, private charity is abler than ever to rescue the needy from ignorance. Yes, vouchers are arguably a more effective remedy. But "arguably a more effective remedy" fails to surmount my strong moral presumption in favor of leaving taxpayers alone.

Disagree? Almost everyone does, and that's okay. You can reject my scruples without rejecting my story. You certainly don't need to be a libertarian to buy the social science. Autobiographically, my doubts about the social value of education long predated my discovery of political philosophy. What undermined my faith? Firsthand experience. Soon after starting kindergarten, I started to realize, in a childish way, that

I'd never use most of the material my teachers taught. Yet I also knew a bright future was waiting for me as long as I went through the motions. Once I was old enough to grasp that employers are greedy but not stupid, my rendezvous with the signaling model was almost unavoidable.

Why Not Tax Education?

> I have not changed my view that higher education has some positive externality, but I have become much more aware that it also has negative externalities. I am much more dubious than I was when I wrote Capitalism and Freedom that there is any justification at all for government subsidy of higher education. The spread of PC [political correctness] right now would seem to be a very strong negative externality, and certainly the 1960s student demonstrations were negative externalities from higher education. A full analysis along those lines might lead you to conclude that higher education should be taxed to offset its negative externalities.
>
> —Milton Friedman, "Letter to Richard Vedder"[45]

If discouraging education is such a good idea, why stop when subsidies hit zero? Why not go further by taxing it? The idea may be "politically impossible," but so are all the best reforms we've explored. Unpopularity aside, is there anything wrong with taxing education?

The straightforward objection is that education is not *100%* signaling. My best guess, to repeat, is that education is about 80% signaling and 20% skill creation. Taxing all education risks throwing out the skill creation baby with the signaling bathwater. Yet on reflection, this is a weak response. True, an education tax might throw out the skill creation baby with the signaling bathwater. But cutting subsidies has exactly the same drawback. Imposing a 1% tax should discourage skill creation every bit as much as removing a 1% subsidy.

A stronger antitax argument begins by noting government has long and heavily sponsored wasteful education. Given this track record, trusting it to do the opposite is naive. Thus, even if an ideal government would actively discourage education, giving *real* governments the power to do so is folly. Picture the complexity of the tax code—and opportunities for abuse—if the education tax varied by major or school ranking. The transparent alternative is to bar government from the business of education.

The decisive argument against this novel tax, however, is that almost all moral presumptions stand against it. Taxing education doesn't just butt against conventional presumptions in favor of education and the status quo. It runs afoul of the libertarian presumption in favor of leaving people alone. Since the proposal is untried, its effects remain speculative—and we shouldn't try it unless we *know* it works wonders.

The False Savior of Online Education

We lived through the stock market bubble and the housing bubble. Investments paid off for years, then collapsed. Will education share the same fate? Plenty of parents and pundits suspect so. For a rising generation of technophiles, however, the debate is over. They're convinced our education bubble is ready to burst, starting with higher education.[46] Why now? Because today's Internet teaches more effectively than old-school schools for a fraction of the cost. Online competition has already crushed traditional record companies, newspapers, and retailers. Brick-and-mortar schools are next in line.

If the technophiles are right, squabbling about education spending is pretty pointless. Taxpayers are wasting billions on obsolete business models, but why fight over a sinking ship? Government cannot stop the power of disruptive innovation. If you want to make a difference, forget about education policy. Found an online education startup, and become the change you wish to see in the world.

When I explain the centrality of signaling, audiences often think I'm endorsing the technophiles' story. This utterly misunderstands me. Education is not a bubble, but *stable waste*. As long as traditional education receives hundreds of billions of taxpayer dollars every year, the status quo will stand. Online education will slowly carve out a niche, but that is all.

Technophiles would have a compelling case if education's sole function were teaching job skills. Online education has clear pedagogical advantages over traditional education. Coursera, Khan Academy,

Marginal Revolution University, and their rivals hire the best teachers in the world.[47] Students can learn at their own pace—pausing whenever they need to reflect, rewinding whenever they need review, fast forwarding as soon as they master the material. Anyone who's lost can drop a level without looking like a loser. Anyone's who's bored can jump a level without looking like a nerd. Online education is an awesome way to build human capital.

Unfortunately, students aren't hungry for human capital. They're hungry for signals. Why? Because the labor market mainly pays for credentials acquired, not skills learned. After years of hype, sophisticated technophiles are finally coming to terms with this fact. Kevin Carey of the New America Foundation explains the intellectual evolution: "Three years ago, technology was going to transform higher education. What happened?"

> The failure of MOOCs [Massive Open Online Courses] to disrupt higher education has nothing to do with the quality of the courses themselves, many of which are quite good and getting better. Colleges are holding technology at bay because the only thing MOOCs provide is access to world-class professors at an unbeatable price. What they don't offer are official college degrees, the kind that can get you a job. And that, it turns out, is mostly what college students are paying for.[48]

Fans of online education are blessed with can-do spirit, so Carey's epiphany leaves them unfazed. Education is mostly about signaling? Fine. Then online education will soon let students send the labor market more accurate and detailed signals than brick-and-mortar schools ever dreamed. Employers want to know how smart you are? How conscientious? Great. Online schools will devise world-class tests of intelligence and conscientiousness, credibly communicate scores to employers, then sit back and watch their alumni prosper and their enrollment skyrocket.

There's just one glaring problem: testing traits *off*line has been dirt cheap for decades. Major companies spread test-writing expenses over millions of students. The marginal cost is a few hours of students' time, plus a little paper and ink. This is a pittance compared to all the time and money students burn in school. Why do students keep throwing fuel on the fire? Because employers don't take standardized tests from uncredentialed applicants seriously. Testing will be cheaper online than offline, but how does making cheap tests even cheaper change the

way employers think? Technophiles shouldn't predict an online testing revolution until they can explain why there *wasn't* an offline testing
revolution.

My explanation, you may recall, is that education signals more than
brains and work ethic. It also signals *conformity*—submission to social
expectations. This traps students in a catch-22: trying to unconvention-
ally signal conformity signals *non*conformity. In our society, you're *supposed* to go to college if you value success. When otherwise promising
teens refuse to attend, they demonstrate they don't know or don't care
what they're supposed to do. Protesting "Why can't I signal my conformity online instead?" is further proof a kid can't or won't conform. In
principle, social expectations can evolve over time. Still, as long as the
first wave of students who jump ship from traditional to online education is weird, evolution will be slow at best. The revolution will begin
when promising students say, "I've decided to drop out of school and
study online" and adults unsarcastically respond, "Good idea!"

Why believe me rather than the technophiles? They haven't merely
been wrong a few years in a row. Broadly construed, they've been wrong
for ages. Videotapes of the world's best teachers could have replaced mediocre meatspace lecturers forty years ago. They didn't. Employers could
have substituted standardized tests for traditional diplomas a century
ago. They didn't. This is not an all-purpose "If your new idea was good,
we'd already use it" argument. Any new idea takes time to get rolling.
The point is that slight variations on the technophiles' ideas have been
tried for decades, and *none* gained momentum.

Online education is rapidly growing in two distinct directions. It is
growing inside brick-and-mortar schools, so students can take *some*
courses from home or dorm. It is also growing on countless educational websites. Yet neither form of growth poses much threat to the
educational status quo. Offering traditional students online options is
a convenience but leaves the fixed costs of campus almost unchanged.
Educational websites primarily compete with blogs, podcasts, and other
forms of online edutainment. Without a conventional diploma, "I took
a bunch of online classes" is almost as worthless in the labor market as
"I read lots of blogs."

Though techno-optimists will dismiss my critique as stodgy fatalism, we need not sigh "Let's agree to disagree." Anyone who confidently

predicts imminent radical change should be eager to profit from my tunnel vision. On my blog, I've repeatedly challenged believers in the "education bubble" to bet me. Standard terms: "Ten years from now, the fraction of 18-to-24-year-olds enrolled in four-year colleges will fall no more than 10%" at even odds. Only one person has accepted—and the offer's still on the table.

The Politics of Social Desirability Bias

Americans relentlessly gripe about schools and colleges, but virtually *no one* wants to cut spending on education. If education is as wasteful as I claim, why is it universally popular? The "Wisdom of Crowds" is fallible, but are we really supposed to believe billions of people from every major culture have converged on a common error? That's quite a bullet to bite.

When you chew this bullet, however, it melts in your mouth. Collective folly is inherently plausible. Weigh the intellectual payoffs. When spending our *personal* resources, we retain a clear incentive to second-guess popular ideas. Consumers who discover a best-selling product is junk can unilaterally save their own money. Don't like it? Don't buy it. When spending *collective* resources, in contrast, second-guessing popular ideas is selfishly futile. Taxpayers who discover a beloved program is junk must pay their taxes like everyone else. Don't like it? You're only one person. Without the prominence and charisma to reverse public opinion, nay-saying won't save you money but will make you enemies.

The moral: in politics, critical thinking is an act of charity. Objective truth has to beg for spare change to survive. Owing to these perverse incentives, almost any political idea that *becomes* popular tends to remain popular.[49] Even if it's false. Even if it's always been false.

Why would the false become popular in the first place? *Because human beings don't like expressing—or believing—ugly truths.* Instead, we gravitate—in word and thought—to views that "sound good." Psychologists call this Social Desirability Bias.[50] "There's no such thing as a stupid child" sounds better than "10% of children are stupid." "We will win the War on Terror" sounds better than "There's a 50% chance the War on Terror reduces terrorism, a 30% chance it makes no difference, and a 20% chance it makes terrorism worse." Isn't "what sounds good" occasionally true? Certainly. When skinny people ask "Am I fat?" the unbiased response is "No." Social Desirability Bias distorts responses to "Am I fat?" because we want to say "No" to *everyone*.

Social Desirability Bias takes many forms. The bald lie—declaring "I love you" when you feel no love—is only one. More typically, the bias works through intellectual laziness. It's not a lie if you believe it—and if you avoid calm deliberation, you can believe almost anything.

What does this have to do with education? Education and Social Desirability Bias are a perfect fit. "Give a man a fish, and he'll eat for a day; teach him to fish, and he'll eat for a lifetime" sounds lovely. So does "In a modern society, every child needs the best possible education." "Education is the most important investment we make in our children's future" leaves a warm glow. "We have to ensure everyone who might benefit from college attends" is music to our ears.

Such statements aren't blatant falsehoods. But we're inclined to hastily accept them regardless of their truth because they're *emotionally appealing*. With intellectual security this lax, we should expect proeducation slogans to permeate our culture, whatever their merits. The only way to sort out the mess is to put crowd pleasing aside and crunch the numbers.

How can Social Desirability Bias explain the ubiquity of proeducation sentiment? There are three top stories. One appeals to human universals. Underneath our diverse cultural baggage, we're much alike.[51] Homo sapiens around the world cotton to motherhood, sugar, clear skin—and caring, future-oriented, idealistic slogans like "In a modern society, every child needs the best possible education." Populism is pretty similar all over the world because what's popular is pretty similar all over the world.

A complementary account: calling *any* popular view a "fallacy" is socially undesirable—and the human mind is naturally prone to the fallacy of composition. Since education has pretty good selfish returns, humans hastily infer matching social returns; what's true for the part must be true for the whole, right? Social Desirability Bias deters us from using our firsthand knowledge of the irrelevance of the curriculum to challenge this fallacy—even in the privacy of our own minds.

The final story appeals to global elite culture. Non-Western elites straddle two worlds: Western elite culture, and their own traditional cultures. After Western elites fell in love with education in the nineteenth century, they won over Western masses and non-Western elites. Non-Western elites, in turn, gradually spread the gospel of education to their own cultures. The global ubiquity of proeducation sentiment is no more puzzling than the global ubiquity of Abrahamic religions.

What's so bad about Social Desirability Bias? It is the fountainhead of wasteful and counterproductive policies. You know the mechanism. Almost all governments on earth crave popularity. In democracies, leaders who fail to remain popular fail to remain leaders. In dictatorships, leaders who fail to remain popular can cling to power, but cling they must. Either way, leaders have a strong incentive to do whatever's popular—to be crowd pleasers.

Responding "That's all for the best" is wishful thinking. Look at the world, then think about human emotions. Many good policies sound bad. Many bad policies sound good. Politicians' natural response is not to counter Social Desirability Bias but pander to it—to demagogue. "In a modern society, every child needs the best possible education"? Great. Let's spend a trillion dollars a year for the children. What about all the other goods we could have enjoyed instead? Oh, there's no trade-off. The more we spend on education, the richer we'll be. A maverick politician could call shenanigans on this wishful thinking, but joining the demagogues is far easier than beating them.

CHAPTER 8

▬▬▬▬▬▬▬

1 > 0

We Need More Vocational Education

> As anyone who has ever taught high school will attest, even
> among teens who attend the very best high schools, many simply
> hate school. They have never done well in school, see no relevance
> in it, never do assignments, and habitually cut classes or are tru-
> ant. . . . Why do policy makers seem to want to deny the existence
> of students who exhibit these attitudes and behaviors?
>
> —Kenneth Gray, "Is High School Career and Technical
> Education Obsolete?"

Human capital enthusiasts normally defend education as it is: existing schools greatly enhance students' job skills.[1] They accordingly perceive the signaling model as an attack on a system that enriches us all. In principle, however, a human capital enthusiast could accept the ubiquity of signaling, then cry out for reform. Instead of treating the human capital model as an accurate description of education, they could treat it as a noble *prescription for* education. Let's transform our schools from time sinks to skill factories.[2]

How can we make this happen? Finding better ways to teach students reading, writing, and math is the conventional path. Since an army of researchers and practitioners are already working on this problem, I have little constructive to add. Yet overall, we should be pessimistic about improving basic skills. Why? Because the goal has long been popular, the research has long been ample, yet basic skills remain mediocre.[3] The logical inference is either (a) pinpointing ways to improve basic skills is elusive, or (b) schools spurn the methods that work. Intellectually, for example, the case for firing bad teachers is solid, but who expects it to prevail?[4] While there are signs of academic progress,[5] they mostly look like "teaching to the test." Until *uncoached adults* score better on reading, writing, and math tests, we should presume basic skills remain static.

Rather than ride the basic skills bandwagon, this chapter high-lights a neglected yet promising alternative: vocational education. Vocational education, also known as "career and technical educa-tion," takes many guises—classroom training, apprenticeships, on-the-job training, and straight-up work experience—but they have much in common. All vocational education teaches specific job skills, and all vocational education revolves around learning-by-doing, not learning-by-listening.

"Prepare students for the future by teaching them how to do a job" sounds unobjectionable. The most successful forms of vocational education—especially Germany's marvelous apprentice system—are the envy of almost everyone who scrutinizes them.[6] Yet vocational edu-cation has long been on the defensive. Flowery arguments against vo-cational education drown out the prosaic arguments in its favor—and Social Desirability Bias infects the whole debate.

The standard case *for* vocational education starts with bitter facts. Plenty of kids find academics daunting and dull. College graduation—not to mention elite careers—is unrealistic for such students.[7] Hence, they're better off training to be plumbers, electricians, or mechanics. The standard case *against* vocational education, in contrast, starts with sweet slogans. College prep readies students for "whatever they choose to do with their lives." The world is full of "late bloomers." Every child can grow up to be president.

While the friends of vocational education stand on firmer ground, both sides normally take human capital purism for granted: if two forms of education are equally lucrative, they equally benefit society. Signaling raises the debate to a new level—and heavily tilts it toward vocationalism. The signaling model begs us to ask, "*Why* is this edu-cation lucrative? Does it teach students how to *do* a better job—or merely help students *get* a better job?" Education that builds job skills is more socially valuable than education that merely impresses employers—*even if both forms of education are equally profitable for the students themselves.*

Why Vocational Education Rules

> Career and Technical Education is to some students what Advanced Placement and honors courses are to others.
>
> —Kenneth Gray, "Is High School Career and Technical
> Education Obsolete?"[8]

Fans of college love to contrast the average college graduate to the average high school graduate. Fans of vocational education love to contrast successful plumbers, electricians, and mechanics to debt-ridden baristas with English degrees. Such comparisons don't just stack the deck. Worse, they lose sight of social returns. The search for desirable education policies should *start* by measuring effects on students' careers. Yet no search is complete without a guesstimate of signaling's share.

The selfish return to vocational education. In proponents' eyes, vocational education raises pay, reduces unemployment, and increases high school completion. Research, though a bit sparse, supports proponents on all counts. Core insight: vocational students are typically "academic underachievers" *before* entering the vocational track. The right metric isn't, "How do vocational students compare to average students?" but rather, "How do vocational students compare to *comparable* students who didn't study a trade?" Vocational ed fares well by this metric. It raises pay more than academic coursework.[9] It reduces unemployment more than academic coursework.[10] It even boosts high school graduation: the academically uninclined are less prone to quit school when they don't detest all their classes.[11] Vocational education even seems to deter crime.[12] Those who search for the most lucrative *mix* of academic and vocational education normally discover students are too academic for their own good. Most will earn more if they replace some—but not all—of their standard courses with vocational alternatives.[13]

Researchers do sporadically detect long-run drawbacks of vocational education. A notable paper finds that once workers reach their fifties, vocational backgrounds mildly retard employment rates.[14] Given all the advantages of vocational ed for workers *under* fifty, though, this is praising with faint damnation. Higher wages, higher employment, higher completion rates: snap all three pieces together, and the selfish return to vocational education in high school is at least a percentage point higher than normal. Weak and disgruntled students enjoy especially rich rewards.

The social returns to vocational education. Signaling isn't the only reason selfish and social returns diverge. Public funding, taxation, redistribution, crime, and more play a role. Yet signaling's share is the axis around which all else revolves. What fraction of vocational ed's selfish benefits stem from signaling?

The lowest estimates, strangely, come from vocational education's *critics.* Many inadvertently set its signaling share below zero. How so? Critics fear that vocational education bears a stigma.[15] Specializing in auto shop tarnishes your image because society infers you "lack the talent for anything better." Restated in the language of signaling: the vocational path sends bad signals about raw ability.

In this scenario, vocational education enriches society *more* than it enriches vocational students. Society gains the extra productivity, but students capture the extra productivity less the stigma. Imagine you're an average student contemplating the vocational track. With academic training, you produce $100 a day; vocational training boosts your productivity to $120 a day. Unfortunately, the average vocational student's raw ability is $10 below average. If you go vocational, employers assume you fit this profile. Skills and stigma are a package deal, so you earn $110 a day—the productivity of the *average* vocational student—even though you personally produce $120 a day (see Table 8.1).

Table 8.1: Selfish Benefits, Social Benefits, and Stigma

	Academic Track	Vocational Track	Gain
Income	$100	$110	+10% selfish gain
Productivity	$100	$120	+20% social gain

Does vocational study really so tarnish your image? While it's tempting to declare, "The jury is still out," the truth is more like, "The jury has yet to be convened." To my knowledge, this lamented stigma remains unmeasured. Still, the critics probably go too far. In our society, even incurable snobs rank vocational students above high school dropouts. The signal vocational ed sends is *weak*, not bad.

In any case, matching course content to job openings remains the most direct way to ballpark vocational ed's signaling share. All classes prepare students for *some* job. Auto shop teaches students how to repair cars; history teaches students how to do history. From a signaling standpoint, the issue is always, "How often do students use the skills they learn?" Vocational ed stands out because it prepares students for *common* jobs. According to the Bureau of Labor Statistics, the United States has roughly 900,000 carpenters, 700,000 auto mechanics, and 400,000 plumbers. Classic college-prep classes like literature, foreign language, and history fall short because they prepare students for *rare* jobs. The whole U.S. employs only 129,000 writers, 64,000 translators, and 3,800 historians.[16]

What then is vocational education's signaling share? Bearing both stigma and job relevance in mind, *half of normal* is a reasonable guess. Suppose my earlier 80% signaling figure is correct, so 40% of vocational education's payoff stems from signaling. Then *ignoring* the selfish advantages of learning a trade—extra income, higher employment, better high school completion rates—the social return for vocational ed surpasses regular high school's by at least four percentage points. The social return for Poor Students—especially male Poor Students—exceeds 7%. Fiddling with the signaling assumption naturally shifts the bottom line, but as long as conventional schooling's signaling share exceeds 50%, halving it dramatically boosts social returns.

What makes vocational ed's social return so ample? Status is zero-sum; skill is not. Conventional education mostly helps students by raising their status, but average status cannot rise. Vocational education mostly helps students by building their skills—and average skill *can* rise. Why are social returns especially ample for Poor Students? Because vocational ed trains these crime-prone students for productive work without igniting severe credential inflation.[17]

What's Wrong With Child Labor?

> Child labor has not always been thought of as an evil. There have
> been times when it was treated as unpleasant to the child, but
> nevertheless desirable, somewhat akin to our contemporary view
> of education.
>
> —Kaushik Basu, "Child Labor"[18]

School is not vocational education's only venue. If learning job skills in
the school is good, wouldn't learning job skills on the job be better? Unfortunately, we have an innocuous yet infamous label for kids learning
job skills on the job: "child labor."

Civilized adults recoil at the name. Children with joy in their hearts
don't belong in gray workshops, toiling all day long, cogs in the machine. They're kids, not robots! Well, unless the gray workshop is called
a "school" and the cogs earn zero wages. No one cares if kids devote
every free minute to basketball or violin, but gainful employment is
for grown-ups. Hostility to child labor admittedly mellows as "children" approach adulthood, but we're still supposed to spurn the idea of
16-year-olds quitting school to work full time.

Child labor laws reflect these popular sentiments. Federal regulations do more than exclude minors from dangerous jobs. Outside
of family businesses, farming, newspaper delivery, and performing
arts, work for kids under 14 is all but prohibited. U.S. federal law
caps 14- and 15-year-olds' work at three hours a day on school days
and eighteen hours a week on school weeks.[19] Plenty of states have
stricter regulations. Under California law, 16- and 17-year-olds may
not work without school permission or more than four hours on a
school day.[20]

When children languish in school, adults rush to rationalize. Making
kids sit at desks doing boring busywork may seem cruel, but their pain
trains them for the future. Why then is child labor so reviled? Toil may
not be fun, but it too trains kids for their future.

Child labor has a dark side.[21] Then again, so does book learning.
When my mom was a schoolgirl, the nuns in charge freely hit kids with
sticks. Judging either activity by long-gone creepy abuses is folly. In

modern times, is there any decent reason to discourage kids from getting jobs and learning job skills?

The silliest objection is that businesses "exploit" our children, handing them a pittance for their toil. No one expects schools to pay their students; the training kids receive is payment enough. Why hold firms to a higher standard? College students ferociously compete for unpaid internships because training is valuable compensation—and total compensation, not cash alone, is what counts.[22] In any case, if the young were really grossly underpaid, employing them would be extraordinarily profitable—and thanks to competition, few business models stay extraordinarily profitable for long.

Another complaint is that children are too immature to know a bad deal when they see it. As a father of four, I don't demur. But we normally rely on parents to protect kids from their own childishness. Under current U.S. law, moms and dads can already employ their sons and daughters on almost any terms they please.[23] The natural rationale is that few *want* to mistreat their flesh and blood. Exceptions notwithstanding, parents are children's best guardians. Once we trust them to decide whether they're fairly compensating their kids, why not trust parents to decide whether someone *else* is fairly compensating their kids?

A more thoughtful objection is that work is good, but school is better. Child labor distracts youths from their primary mission: academic success. The critical premise is that the academic path is so reliably superior that leaving students the *option* to prioritize work over school is dangerous. On cursory look, the facts fit: working students average lower grades, worse behavior, and more trouble with the law.

But a closer look tells another tale altogether. *Working students' visible shortcomings predate their employment.* When researchers compare working students to comparable nonworking students, work has a clear upside and no clear downside. Early job experience has durable dividends, boosting postgraduation earnings by 5, 10, or even 20% for at least a decade.[24] The link between work and academic success, in contrast, is weak.[25] The same goes for crime and other bad behavior.[26] According to one intriguing study, looser child labor laws cut education *and* crime; locking work-oriented students in school makes them "act out."[27] The two-thirds of 16-to-19-year-olds who don't even try to work during the school year are missing a major opportunity.[28]

To be clear, none of this research urges teens to quit high school to get full-time jobs. Researchers who hail the long-run career benefits of youthful employment remain skeptical of "intense" work—30 or 40 hours a week. For selfish returns, they're probably right. In our society, high school dropouts bear a savage stigma.

For public policy, however, selfish returns are a distraction; social returns alone matter. Since stigma hurts only selfish returns, wise policy analysts ignore it. Instead, they compare skills students learn in class to skills students learn on the job. Frankly, there's no comparison. Doing *any* job teaches you how to do a job.[29] If this seems a low bar, recall that almost half of dropouts and a third of high school graduates these days aren't even *looking* for work. Acclimating them to any form of employment would be a step up.

Since the minimum wage doesn't vary by age or experience, we shouldn't worry that youths will be "exploited." We should worry that youths—especially Poor Students—won't be hired at all.[30] Under current law, untrained workers must produce the cost of their training plus $7.25 an hour to be profitably employed.[31] Quite a catch-22, especially for slow learners: you need training to become a productive worker, but firms won't train you unless you already *are* a productive worker.

Aren't unpaid internships a massive loophole? Not taking the law literally. In the for-profit sector, the U.S. Department of Labor allows unpaid internships only if "the employer that provides the training derives no immediate advantage from the activities of the intern."[32] A bizarre rule. Why would a *for-profit* firm bother hiring workers from whom it derives zero immediate advantage? If you sought to convince a CEO to start an internship program, your pitch wouldn't be, "Let's hire a bunch of inexperienced workers to provide our firm with no immediate benefits whatsoever."

Unpaid internships survive because authorities hypocritically fail to enforce the letter of the law. As long as interns are college students or recent college grads learning a college-like job, government turns a blind eye. If McDonald's hired unpaid trainees, prosecution would be swift. Unlike orthodox observers, I hasten to add, I say we need *more* hypocrisy. Instead of ending the unofficial exemption for college interns, we should grant it to everyone.

What else should policy makers do? Deregulate and destigmatize child labor. Early jobs are good for kids and good for society. Parental oversight isn't a perfect way to root out abuses, but we rely on it in virtually every other sphere of life. Parents can make their kids devote their childhoods to sports and music—no matter how much they hate playing. Parents can sign their kids up for mountain climbing. Parents can take their kids to dangerous countries. Holding nonfamilial employment to stricter standards than mountain climbing is senseless.

Once child labor is legal, some teens will take full-time jobs. As long as they have their parents' permission, let them. If this means dropping out of high school, we should set our phobias aside and allow that too. Selfishly speaking, the average dropout is making a mistake. Plenty of students, though, are not average, starting with the silent minority who like work and loathe school. Working enthusiastically probably has a higher selfish return than studying apathetically, because the labor market rewards graduation, not attendance. In any case, education policy should never lose sight of signaling. Students who quit school to work curb credential inflation, opening doors for peers who stay in school because, "You can't get a good job without a diploma." When Bill Gates dropped out of Harvard, he didn't just strike it rich; he struck a blow against credential inflation.

What about setting up a formal apprenticeship system? The best regimes are jewels, but they're notoriously difficult to emulate. Most countries can't be Germany. Internationally, apprenticeship programs consistently outshine adult job training programs, but that's faint praise indeed.[33] Before using taxpayer dollars to jumpstart apprenticeships, government should get out of the way and take stock of all the opportunities the labor market provides.

Misvocational Education, or 1 > 0

> Perhaps no greater mistake in terms is made in our educational practice today than to say that the high-school student who has had four years of Latin, three of Greek, four of English, two of ancient and mediaeval history, two of mathematics, and one year of mathematical physics has pursued a "liberal-culture" course

of study. As a matter of fact his course has been narrowly technical, in that it leads to but a few selected occupations; and he is in
no sense liberally educated, for he knows little about the modern
world in which he lives.

—Ellwood Cubberley, "Does the Present Trend toward
Vocational Education Threaten Liberal Culture?"[34]

Most education experts remain leery of vocational ed. Chief objection:
it's shortsighted. The vocational track teaches students specific skills
they need for their first job. The academic track teaches students general
skills they need for *every* job. The wise approach is to set everyone on
the academic track. Let kids max out their general skills before targeting
any particular vocation.

This objection is confused. While literacy and numeracy are genuinely general skills, most academic classes amount to vocational training for ultrarare vocations. Think about classic college prep in literature,
history, social science, and foreign language. Only a handful of occupations use the skills these classes teach. Science and higher mathematics
are more relevant, but even college grads rarely apply them on the job.[35]
STEM is vocational training for quants and scientists, not general training for workers.

Ultimately, then, the debate is between two *kinds* of vocational education. "Traditionalists" want to train everyone for long-shot, prestigious
careers like author, historian, political scientist, translator, physicist, and
mathematician. So-called vocationalists want to train students for careers they're likely to enter. The traditional route is painless for educators: teach your students whatever your teachers taught you. The vocational route is painful for educators: to follow it, we must keep tabs on
student aptitudes and the job market. So be it. To prepare youths for
plausible futures, educators must feel the pain.

Defenders of traditional academics often appeal to the obscurity of
the future. The labor market is mercurial mutation. What's the point of
prepping students for the economy of 2015, when they'll be employed in
the economy of 2025 or 2050? Fair enough, but this is no argument for
old-school academics. Ignorance of the future is no excuse for preparing
students for occupations they almost surely *won't* have. And if we know
anything about the future of work, we know that demand for authors,

historians, political scientists, translators, physicists, and mathematicians will stay low.

The crowd-pleasing objection to vocationalism, though, is not epistemic, but egalitarian. Placing everyone on the academic track seems more equal than sorting children by "aptitude" and assigning them to "suitable" training. You could say equality is already an illusion; despite the fiction of college prep for all, colleges count only honors and A.P. as the genuine article. Yet the ambitious egalitarian would retort, "Then let's have honors and A.P. coursework for all."

This sounds lovely but works poorly. Egalitarians picture college prep as a free lunch: anyone who fails academically can switch to the vocational track, so everyone might as well start with academics. This ignores the disturbing possibility that after academic students crash, they'll be too embittered to learn a trade.[36] When such students start on the academic route, they learn how to do *zero* jobs. When they start on the vocational route, in contrast, they probably learn how to do *one* job.

The vast American underclass shows this disturbing possibility is more than theoretically possible. Keeping bored, resentful kids on the academic track backfires. Instead of "downshifting" to vocational training, they settle for unskilled labor—or worse. Remember: about 20% of Americans never earn a standard high school diploma.[37] Training likely dropouts to do a midskill job when they're 12 or 14 is no panacea, but it's more realistic than hoping they're "late-blooming" stars. Does this deprive such students of the chance to rise high up the social ladder? Debatably. Yet it slashes their risk of starting adulthood bereft of marketable skills.[38]

High school dropouts aren't the only kids who learn how to do zero jobs. After graduation, plenty of high school and even college students taste how unqualified they are. Think of the timeless question, "What can you do with an English degree?" For many, as we've seen, the answer is: be a bartender, cashier, cook, janitor, security guard, or waiter. Literally speaking, of course, no one uses their English degree to guard a warehouse. The real story is their education prepared them for no realistic occupation, so they learned how to guard warehouses on the job.

Historically, teachers trained students for three specific professions: the clergy, law, and medicine. The modern curriculum is more versatile but has changed far less than educators like to think. Today's schools prepare students for careers as authors, poets, mathematicians, scientists, artists, musicians, historians, translators, and professional athletes. Yet the fraction of students who enter these occupations is trivial. Contrary to popular proeducation rhetoric, schools devote little time to "general skills." Instead, students spend their days training for jobs few want and even fewer get. As a result, many leave high school, college, and even grad school with zero realistic career options. Thankfully, most recover by absorbing useful skills on the job. Inexcusably, a sizable minority do not. All the years kids sit in school are more than enough to teach everyone how to do at least one job—and knowing one job is vastly better for the individual and mankind than knowing none. $1 > 0$.

Youth Reimagined

> Pig farmers, electricians, plumbers, bridge painters, jam makers, blacksmiths, brewers, coal miners, carpenters, crab fisherman, oil drillers . . . they all tell me the same thing over and over, again and again—our country has become emotionally disconnected from an essential part of our workforce. . . .
>
> Even as unemployment remains sky high, a whole category of vital occupations has fallen out of favor, and companies struggle to find workers with the necessary skills. The causes seem clear. We have embraced a ridiculously narrow view of education. Any kind of training or study that does not come with a four-year degree is now deemed "alternative." Many viable careers once aspired to are now seen as "vocational consolation prizes," and many of the jobs this current administration has tried to "create" over the last four years are the same jobs that parents and teachers actively discourage kids from pursuing. (I always thought there was something ill-fated about the promise of three million "shovel ready jobs" made to a society that no longer encourages people to pick up a shovel.)
>
> —Mike Rowe, "The First Four Years Are the Hardest"[39]

In backward nations, youths work. In advanced nations, youths study. As civilization advances, the young spend ever more years sequestered from paid employment. The modern fear is that work might interfere with school, never that school might interfere with work. These rules are so ingrained they seem like laws of nature.

The logic is elusive. As society evolves, teaching the young *different* occupations is common sense. Teaching them *no* occupations and hoping they adapt to the job market after graduation is not. It doesn't matter how futuristic our society becomes. Making kids study irrelevant material for a decade-plus is timelessly dysfunctional.

What's the alternative? Reboot vocational education. Sticking with the classic curriculum instead of trying to forecast the job market is looking for your keys under the streetlight because it's brighter there. Sure, teach the genuinely general skills: reading, writing, math. But otherwise, schools should make educated guesses about future career opportunities, measure students' aptitudes, then expose them to plausible occupations. Instead of viewing youth employment as "exploitation" or a risky distraction from school, we should celebrate work as vocational education in its purest form. When the young quit school to work full time, we should not mourn. Such kids will never cure cancer, but at least they'll be self-supporting members of society.

Isn't this a grim dystopian vision? Not at all. Visualize a world where 16-year-olds have real job skills and earn enough to provide for themselves. Visualize a world where academically uninclined preteens look up to apprentices instead of delinquents. Visualize a world where students find their lessons either practical or interesting. If we could raise a new productive, independent, engaged generation, wouldn't that be a great improvement over the bored, infantilized youth of today?

Instead of fearing a dystopian future, we should gawk at our dystopian present. In modern societies, achievement-oriented kids spend almost two decades in school. Most find the curriculum dreadfully dull. During this drawn-out ordeal, students are either poor or financially dependent on their parents. When they finally join the "real world," graduates apply only a sliver of what they studied. Once they have kids of their own, they reexperience extended immaturity from the parent's side. Our status quo isn't *1984* or *Brave New World*. But if we weren't used to our education system, who would wish for it?

CHAPTER 9

Nourishing Mother

Is Education Good for the Soul?

College graduates often proudly name-drop their alma mater, but few realize the phrase contains a worldview. In Latin, "alma mater" means "nourishing mother." A rich metaphor. A nourishing mother doesn't merely teach you practical skills or help you land a well-paid job. She nurtures your whole person, teaches you right from wrong, and shows you the magic of life. As William Bowen, former president of Princeton, and Derek Bok, former president of Harvard, attest:

> Education is a special, deeply political, almost sacred civic activity. It is not merely a technical enterprise—providing facts to the untutored. Inescapably, it is a moral and aesthetic enterprise—expressing to impressionable minds a set of convictions about how most nobly to live in the world.[1]

Most economists are dedicated fans of education but still roll their eyes at such lofty words. They push education because they think it has a high social return, not because they think it good for the soul . . . whatever that means. Once in a while, philosophical economists muse education might be a "merit good"—a product with value above and beyond customers' willingness to pay.[2] But such musings rarely sink in with their pragmatic peers.

Economists' philistine ways expose them to a sharp humanist critique. An old-school fan of liberal arts education could chide, "You base your support for education on its high social return. But Caplan convincingly shows this 'social return' is poor at best. Those who live by the sword die by the sword." The humanist could then turn to me and add, "You don't win either. You may have beaten your fellow economists at their own game, but that game isn't worth playing. The humanist tradition remains the most meaningful perspective: Ideas and culture matter more than dollars and cents."

I sincerely take the humanist critique to heart. For all my iconoclasm, I love ideas and culture. "Impractical" ideas and "uncommercial" culture are my life. The journey from ignorance to enlightenment moves me. Consider Malcolm X's spellbinding story about teaching himself to read in prison:

> I saw that the best thing I could do was get hold of a dictionary—to study, to learn some words. . . .
>
> I spent two days just riffling uncertainly through the dictionary's pages. I'd never realized so many words existed! I didn't know *which* words I needed to learn. Finally, just to start some kind of action, I began copying. . . .
>
> I woke up the next morning, thinking about those words—immensely proud to realize that not only had I written so much at one time, but I'd written words that I never knew were in the world. . . .
>
> I was so fascinated that I went on—I copied the dictionary's next page. And the same experience came when I studied that. With every succeeding page, I also learned of people and places and events from history. Actually the dictionary is like a miniature encyclopedia. Finally the dictionary's A section had filled a whole tablet—and I went on into the B's. That was the way I started copying what eventually became the entire dictionary. . . .
>
> I suppose it was inevitable that as my word-base broadened, I could for the first time pick up a book and read and now begin to understand what the book was saying. Anyone who has read a great deal can imagine the new world that opened.[3]

Unlike most economists, moreover, I think the value of ideas and culture reflects more than my personal tastes. Philosophy and opera really are merit goods. Reading David Hume's *Enquiry concerning Human Understanding* is intrinsically better than reading E. L. James's *Fifty Shades of Grey*. Hearing Richard Wagner's *Tristan und Isolde* is intrinsically better than hearing Toby Keith's "White Trash with Money." Humanist fans of education grasp profundities typical economists carelessly dismiss.

Old-school humanists nevertheless overstate their case. Education definitely *can* be good for the soul. But that hardly shows actually existing education achieves this noble end. In practice, education often turns out to be a neglectful or abusive mother rather than a nourishing one.

Meritorious Education

> The Master said, "In ancient times, men learned with a view to
> their own improvement. Now-a-days, men learn with a view to
> the approbation of others."
>
> —Confucius, *The Analects*[4]

Practical education has no need to be uplifting. As long as students
graduate with skills to apply outside the classroom, even academic
drudgery serves a worthwhile purpose. When you have instrumental
value, you don't need intrinsic value. To be a worthwhile end-in-itself,
though, education must meet higher standards. To plausibly qualify as a
merit good, it needs three ingredients.

The first ingredient: worthy content. Learning about great ideas
and glorious culture uplifts the soul. Learning about half-baked ideas
and so-so culture, not so much. While the liberal arts tradition wisely
prizes the value of grappling with error, this holds only for *well-argued,
thoughtful* errors.

The second ingredient: skillful pedagogy. Learning from enthusiastic teachers who have mastered their subjects uplifts the soul. Learning
from uninspired teachers who parrot the textbook, not so much. Mediocre instruction is tolerable for practical training, but worthless for
intellectual or artistic inspiration.

The third ingredient: eager students. Sharing great ideas and glorious culture with students who find them fascinating uplifts their souls.
Force-feeding great ideas and glorious culture to students who couldn't
care less, not so much. Indeed, the charade degrades students, teachers, and the subjects themselves. Opera is divine, but herding rock fans
into opera houses is not only futile, but cruel. Many educators assuage
their consciences by insisting youthful force-feeding will in time blos-
som into mature fascination. Even if they're right, the force-feeding is a
regrettable pathway to the merit good of mature fascination, not a merit
good in itself.

How does actually existing education measure up against these
standards of merit? As long as you've had a vaguely typical education, you already know the answer. The content of education is mixed

at best: pockets of greatness, surrounded by insipid busywork. The pedagogy is poor: frankly, most teachers are boring. The students are worse: no matter how great their teachers, few yearn for the life of the mind. Private education is arguably slightly better, but it's cut from the same cloth as public education. Harvard University's Steven Pinker sadly reports that the best students in the world yawn at the best teachers in the world:

> A few weeks into every semester, I face a lecture hall that is half-empty, despite the fact that I am repeatedly voted a Harvard Yearbook Favorite Professor, that the lectures are not video-recorded, and that they are the only source of certain material that will be on the exam. I don't take it personally; it's common knowledge that Harvard students stay away from lectures in droves, burning a fifty-dollar bill from their parents' wallets every time they do.[5]

When I judge our education hollow, it isn't just my opinion; it's very likely your opinion, too. Honestly, how many educators do *you* find fascinating? Do you really think kids find them any more fascinating than you do? Even those who refuse to voice the unseemly answers speak the unvarnished truth with their behavior. Modern education's staunchest fans don't nourish their souls by watching YouTube videos of average teachers. No one does. The empirics on student boredom we've covered underscore the obvious: stimulating education is the exception that proves the rule.[6]

While the humanist critique of philistine economists rings true, economists have a punchy comeback: cost matters. Suppose opera really is good for the soul, and education genuinely promotes love of opera. These facts mean little until we know the per capita cost of conversion. "Exposing a single person to opera is worth any expense" is bravado. Cost matters whenever you spend your own money. How could cost cease to matter when you spend taxpayer money? Every dollar spent is a dollar that could have been repurposed.

This economistic comeback is now more compelling than ever. Ours is an age of science fiction. Almost everyone in rich countries—and about half the earth's population—can access machines that answer virtually *any* question and teach virtually *every* subject.[7] The Internet doesn't merely satisfy our curiosities; it connects us to global communities that share our curiosities. These global communities are more than clubs of novices; they include many of the greatest teachers on the planet.[8] The Internet provides not just stream-of-consciousness enlightenment, but outstanding formal coursework. This ceaseless intellectual feast is, with rare exceptions, free of charge. If education is a merit good, the Internet is the Merit Machine.

On reflection, this Merit Machine is swiftly making traditional humanist education policy obsolete. Once everyone can enrich their souls for free, government subsidies for enrichment forfeit their rationale. To object, "But most people don't use the Internet for spiritual enrichment" is actually a damaging admission that eager students are few and far between. Subsidized education's real aim isn't to make ideas and culture accessible to anyone who's interested, but to make them mandatory for everyone who *isn't* interested.

The rise of the Internet also undercuts the Machiavellian line that intellectual force-feeding ultimately blossoms into sincere appreciation. Today's adults are the product of over a decade of mandatory exposure to abstract ideas and high culture. If educational force-feeding worked well, most educated adults would adore these nerdy realms—and eagerly tap the Internet to revisit them. To understate, they rarely do. "Kim Kardashian" gets about twenty times as many Google hits as "Richard Wagner" and about two hundred times as many as "David Hume."[9] Insisting "the end justifies the means" is comical when progress toward the end is barely visible.

A philistine could reply: "Of course adults rarely bother studying ideas and culture online. There's no money in it." But this chapter is not aimed at philistines, but at anyone who defends actually existing education as good for the soul. The rise of the Internet has two unsettling lessons for them. First: the humanist case for education subsidies is flimsy today because the Internet makes enlightenment practically free. Second: the humanist case for education subsidies was flimsy all along because the Internet proves low consumption of ideas and culture stems from apathy, not poverty or inconvenience. Behold: when the price of enlightenment drops to zero, enlightenment remains embarrassingly scarce.

The Soulful Fallback

> Education does not have to be justified solely on the basis of its
> effect on labor productivity. This was certainly not the argument
> given by Plato or de Tocqueville and need not be ours. Students
> are not taught civics, or art, or music solely in order to improve
> their labor productivity, but rather to enrich their lives and make
> them better citizens.
>
> —Andrew Weiss, "Human Capital vs. Signalling
> Explanations of Wages"[10]

There are intermediate positions between "philistine" and "humanist." Restrained educational idealists could fault the humanist tradition for overemphasizing students' inner lives. Sure, students rarely *feel* their souls being enriched. But why not pragmatically equate "enriching the soul" with fostering desirable adult attitudes and behavior? From this perspective, "Education is good for the soul" counts as true as long as education appreciably shifts society in the right direction.

This is a tempting fallback position, so let's delve into it. Identifying the "right direction" for societal change is up to the reader. Ballparking education's effect on society, however, is up to me.

To preview: education does seem to shift students' values, though less than teachers and parents advertise. To isolate education's influence on society, however, you must unpack *how* education sways students. Is the mechanism "leadership"—planting teachers' ideas in students' heads? Then education remolds society. Is the mechanism "peer effects"— sorting kids into distinct groups? Then education mainly *reshuffles* society without remolding it.[11]

Suppose you funnel an extra kid into college. The student's peer group seismically shifts. Given human conformity, the freshman will likely try to blend in with these new peers. College youths are less religious, for example, so one would expect the student to veer in a secular direction. This does not imply, however, that college makes *society* less religious. The existence of college splits kids into two subcultures with opposing peer effects. If college kids are less religious than average kids, then non-college kids must be *more* religious than average kids. Members of each subculture adjust their behavior to locally fit in. Religious conformity pressure in the noncollege pool offsets secular pressure in the college pool. Net effect on society's religiosity: unclear, even if college demonstrably makes students less religious.

Leadership and peer effects both exist, but there are three hefty reasons to think peer effects outweigh leadership. First: on dimensions where academic leadership seems most intense, education's effect on attitudes and behavior is mild. Second: although schools focus their preaching on a handful of issues, education sways attitudes and behavior on *many* dimensions. Indeed, as we shall soon see, educated opinion occasionally spurns the pedagogical consensus. Third: individual and social effects rarely "add up." Boosting an individual's education usually changes that individual far more than boosting a society's education changes that society.

High Culture Falls on Deaf Ears

Educators hope to enrich the soul in a hundred different ways. But there's one form of enrichment high school and college pursues more explicitly and energetically than any other: instilling appreciation for high culture. English classes push classic novels, plays, and poetry: William Shakespeare, Washington Irving, Edgar Allan Poe, Mark Twain, Edith Wharton, Sinclair Lewis, Robert Frost. Music classes push traditional music, especially classical: Antonio Vivaldi, Ludwig van Beethoven, Wolfgang Amadeus Mozart, and above all, John Philip Sousa. Art classes are more hands-on but still try to raise the status of visual works in top museums. Even schools' iconoclasm is conservative: academic curricula often cover Kurt Vonnegut, Arnold Schoenberg, or Jackson Pollock, but rarely George R. R. Martin, Lady Gaga, or Frank Miller. Though some schools promote high culture more energetically than others, curricula are plainly tilted against pop culture.

How effectively has this tilt fostered high culture? Earlier in the book, I appealed to the truism that education can't be responsible for more than 100% of what we know. The same principle allows us to set an upper bound on education's cultural impact: education can't be responsible for more than 100% of the high culture our society consumes.

Let's start with books. Consumer demand is shockingly low overall: Americans spend 0.2% of their income on *all* reading materials, barely more than $100 per family per year.[12] Americans used to spend more on reading but never spent much: back in 1990, well before the rise of the web, reading absorbed 0.5% of the family budget.[13] Today's Americans spend about four times as much on tobacco and five times as much on alcohol as they do on reading.[14] Within this small pond, high culture is no big fish. Table 9.1 shows three rankings of the best-selling English-language fiction of all time. Sales figures include school purchases and assigned texts, so they *overstate* sincere affection for the canon.

Table 9.1: Best-Selling English-Language Fiction of All Time

Rank	Wikipedia	Ranker	How Stuff Works
1	*The Lord of the Rings* (Tolkien)	*A Tale of Two Cities* (Dickens)	*A Tale of Two Cities* (Dickens)
2	*Harry Potter and the Philosopher's Stone* (Rowling)	*The Lord of the Rings* (Tolkien)	*The Lord of the Rings* (Tolkien)
3	*And Then There Were None* (Christie)	*The Hobbit* (Tolkien)	*Harry Potter and the Sorcerer's Stone* (Rowling)
4	*The Hobbit* (Tolkien)	*And Then There Were None* (Christie)	*And Then There Were None* (Christie)
5	*She: A History of Adventure* (Haggard)	*The Lion, the Witch, and the Wardrobe* (Lewis)	*The Lion, the Witch, and the Wardrobe* (Lewis)
6	*The Lion, the Witch, and the Wardrobe* (Lewis)	*She: A History of Adventure* (Haggard)	*The Da Vinci Code* (Brown)
7	*The Da Vinci Code* (Brown)	*The Da Vinci Code* (Brown)	*Harry Potter and the Half-Blood Prince* (Rowling)
8	*Harry Potter and the Half-Blood Prince* (Rowling)	*The Catcher in the Rye* (Salinger)	*Harry Potter and the Chamber of Secrets* (Rowling)
9	*The Catcher in the Rye* (Salinger)	*Anne of Green Gables* (Montgomery)	*The Catcher in the Rye* (Salinger)
10	*Harry Potter and the Chamber of Secrets* (Rowling)	*Black Beauty* (Sewell)	*Harry Potter and the Goblet of Fire* (Rowling)

11	*Harry Potter and the Prisoner of Azkaban* (Rowling)	*Charlotte's Web* (White)	*Harry Potter and the Order of the Phoenix* (Rowling)
12	*Harry Potter and the Goblet of Fire* (Rowling)	*The Tale of Peter Rabbit* (Potter)	*Harry Potter and the Prisoner of Azkaban* (Rowling)
13	*Harry Potter and the Order of the Phoenix* (Rowling)	*Harry Potter and the Deathly Hallows* (Rowling)	*Ben Hur* (Wallace)
14	*Harry Potter and the Deathly Hallows* (Rowling)	*Jonathan Livingston Seagull* (Bach)	*Lolita* (Nabokov)
15	*Lolita* (Nabokov)	*Angels and Demons* (Brown)	*Harry Potter and the Deathly Hallows* (Rowling)
16	*Anne of Green Gables* (Montgomery)	*Kane and Abel* (Archer)	
17	*Black Beauty* (Sewell)	*To Kill a Mockingbird* (Lee)	
18	*The Eagle Has Landed* (Higgins)	*Valley of the Dolls* (Susann)	
19	*Watership Down* (Adams)	*Gone with the Wind* (Mitchell)	
20	*Charlotte's Web* (White)	*The Thorn Birds* (McCullough)	

Sources: Wikipedia 2015c, Ranker 2015, HowStuffWorks 2015. Nonfiction and non-English works omitted.

While sales figures are plainly flawed, all three lists paint similar pictures of the public's long-run literary tastes. High culture is but a niche market. Dickens's *A Tale of Two Cities* tops two of the three lists. *The Catcher in the Rye, Ben Hur, To Kill a Mockingbird, Gone with the Wind*, and *Lolita* all appear on at least one list. But fantasy—Tolkien, Rowling, Lewis—dominates. The point is not that fantasy lacks literary merit; by my lights, *Lord of the Rings* towers over *Catcher in the Rye*.[15] The point is that the books high school and college hail for their supreme literary merit lose out to much less prestigious genres. By and large, literature teachers fail to "get through" to their captive audiences: they rarely spark love of reading, much less love of the genres they urge their students to admire.

In music, pop culture's victory over high culture is even more decisive. *The Three Tenors in Concert* is the best-selling classical album ever.[16] With twelve million copies sold, it does not even break into the top *fifty* albums of all time.[17] Looking at overall sales, classical music is only 1.4% of the U.S. music market. Country is eight times as popular, and rock/pop over thirty times as popular.[18] Classical does better globally but still only commands a 5% share of the world's music marketplace. Well, at least it beats jazz.[19] The point is not that classical music alone is aesthetically worthwhile. Bad Religion isn't Bach, but it's good. The point is that schools' aesthetic priorities have negligible cultural impact. Even if American schools cause *all* U.S. consumption of classical music, their combined efforts boost its market share only from 0% to 1.4%.

Why is high culture so marginalized? Humanists may be tempted to blame poor salesmanship: students would love Shakespeare and Brahms had they only the right teachers. The straightforward story, though, is that high culture requires extra mental effort to appreciate—and most humans resent mental effort. Students are overwhelmingly bored by Shakespeare, and the rare fans of high culture would probably have come to love the Bard on their own. Students sample a little high culture when their grades depend on it. Once they submit their final exams, however, the vast majority of students rush back to their low-brow comfort zone.

Anyone reading this book is probably a bird of a different feather. You may even remember the names of the teachers who opened your eyes to the finer things in life. I owe my love of classical music to Mr. Zainer (General Music, seventh grade), and my love of literature to Mrs. Ragus (Honors English, eleventh grade). A quick look at the basic facts, however, shows our experiences are abnormal. The vast majority of our classmates emerge from years of cultural force-feeding with their aesthetic palates unchanged.

The Paper Tiger of Political Correctness

American educators lean left. There's no denying it. The party breakdown for K–12 public school teachers is lopsided: roughly 45% Democrat, 25% independent, and 30% Republican.[20] The breakdown for college faculty is starkly lopsided: a nationally representative study of all professors—including professors in two-year colleges—finds 51% Democrats, 35% independents, and 14% Republicans.[21] A similar study of four-year college faculty reports 50% Democrats, 39% independents/other, and 11% Republicans.[22] Left-wing dominance seems even stronger at elite schools.[23]

Colleges are least balanced in the most politically charged subjects, with about five Democrats per Republican in the humanities, and eight Democrats per Republican in the social sciences.[24] As recently as 2006, 5% of humanities professors and 18% of social scientists were self-described "Marxists."[25] The ratio of liberals to conservatives is less extreme, presumably because—unlike party affiliation—these are relative terms.[26] When 18% of their colleagues are Marxists, many mainstream Democrats understandably feel "moderate" by comparison.

None of this proves teachers and professors use their classrooms to "enlighten" or "brainwash" their students. But the conditions for enlightenment/brainwashing are most auspicious. Educators' distinctive worldview provides a compelling *motive* to mold students' minds. Captive student audiences provide a golden *opportunity* to mold students' minds. Even if teachers avoid blatant proselytizing, ideological neutrality requires Vulcan self-discipline. Won't the subtlest slant, maintained year after year, win students' hearts and minds in the end?

Apparently not. In the data, the well-educated are only microscopically more liberal. In the General Social Survey, people place themselves on a seven-step scale, where 1 is "extremely liberal," 4 is "moderate," and 7 is "extremely conservative." An extra year of education seems to make people .014 steps more liberal.[27] Taken literally, over seventy years of education are required to shift ideology a single step. Statistical corrections make this effect look stronger, but it stays weak.[28]

If the effect on ideology is slight, the effect on partisanship is perverse: as education rises, people grow slightly *less* Democratic. The General Social Survey's respondents place themselves on a seven-step scale, where 0 is "strong Democrat," 3 is "independent," and 6 is "strong Republican." An extra year of education seems to make people .071 steps more Republican.[29] Statistical corrections make this effect look weaker, but education still appears to mildly boost support for the party that teachers and professors *dis*favor.[30]

The plot thickens when you analyze education's effect on specific opinions. Abundant research confirms education raises support for civil liberties and tolerance, and reduces racism and sexism.[31] These effects are only partly artifactual. Correcting for intelligence cuts education's impact by about a third.[32] Correcting for intelligence, income, occupation, and family background slices education's impact in half.[33] All corrections made, education fosters a package of socially liberal views.

At the same time, abundant research also confirms education *raises* support for capitalism, free markets, and globalization.[34] These effects, too, are partly artifactual. Correcting for intelligence cuts education's impact by about 40%. Correcting for intelligence, income, demographics, party, and ideology halves it.[35] But when all corrections are done, education fosters a package of economically conservative views.[36]

If educators are as left-wing as they seem, why would education have such contradictory effects on students' stances? The charitable story is that educators keep their politics out of the classroom. The more plausible story, though, is that educators are unpersuasive. The Jesuits say, "Give me the child until he is seven and I'll give you the man."[37] Society gives liberal educators the child until he's fifteen, eighteen, twenty-two, or thirty. But issue-by-issue, teachers are about as likely to repel their students as attract them. Educators could protest, "The problem isn't that we're unpersuasive, but that students are stubborn," but students revise their opinions all the time. The longer they stay in school, the more they revise. They just don't revise in a reliably liberal direction.

Critics who highlight educators' leftist leanings usually have an ideological ax to grind (or swing): "Leaving education of the young in the hands of 'politically correct' ideologues endangers our democracy. School should be a vibrant marketplace of ideas, not a center for indoctrination." Though they're right about the imbalance, it's a paper tiger. Even extreme left-wing dominance leaves little lasting impression. Contrary to the indoctrination story, education doesn't progressively dye students ever brighter shades of red.[38]

Since education raises social liberalism *and* economic conservativism, neither liberals nor conservatives should cheer *or* jeer education's effect on our political culture. What about people who are both socially liberal and economically conservative? Should they admit that education really is "good for the soul" after all? It's complicated. If teachers aren't molding their students, the logical inference is that students are molding each other. But peer effects, to repeat, are double-edged. When schools cluster socially liberal, economically conservative youths inside the Ivory Tower, they inadvertently but automatically cluster socially conservative, economically liberal youths *outside* the Ivory Tower. If education is good for the souls of the former, it's bad for the souls of the latter. Net effect on the polity? Ambiguous.

But doesn't knowledge of history lead us to support wiser policies, both foreign and domestic? This is true almost by definition: someone who understood history *deeply enough* would be able to sift through their knowledge of the past, find the relevant parallels, and skillfully apply it to the issues of the day. Yet this hardly shows that actually existing historical education has these wondrous effects. Indeed, we already have two strong reasons to doubt the political benefits of history classes.[39] First, despite years of study, most adults are historically illiterate. Either they never learned basic history, or they swiftly forgot what they learned. If a world of historical ignorance is scary, you should be scared already, because that's where we live. Second, humans' ability to transfer knowledge from one domain to another—such as from history to policy—is poor. When Bush invaded Iraq, was he ignoring the lesson of the Vietnam War or heeding the lesson of the Korean War? So even if citizens knew the details of history, it is far from clear they'd fruitfully apply their knowledge.

Getting Out the Vote

Voting is a bipartisan tenet of our secular religion. "It doesn't matter how you vote, but vote": educators say it loud, proud, early, and often. Staunchly partisan teachers plead with their students to vote, silently hoping they'll "vote correctly." Genuinely apolitical teachers are often equally insistent: democracy is at stake. K–12 teachers probably preach the duty to vote more energetically than college professors, but the whole education system reads from the same prayer book.

Do their sermons work? It's complicated. Voter turnout rises sharply with education. Substantial effects of education on turnout usually linger after statistically correcting for income, demographics, intelligence, and so on.[40] Despite some thoughtful naysayers, limited experimental data also show extra education boosts turnout.[41]

The catch: education has sharply risen over the last century, but turnout has gently fallen. This could mean offsetting factors masked education's provoting effect.[42] But several prominent researchers instead conclude that turnout depends on *relative* education.[43] People vote not because they're educated, but because they're *more* educated than others. This once again suggests peer effects: the longer you stay in school, the more politically active your social circle, and the more politically active you become to fit in.

Suppose you're convinced voting enriches the soul. As long as relative education is what counts, education redistributes the enrichment rather than creating it. Schooling one more person makes them more likely to experience the wonder of democratic participation but also makes the rest of the citizenry less likely to partake in the wonder.

The Modern Lifestyle

Culture and politics aside, we have stereotypes about education's effect on lifestyle: the well-educated favor the "modern" way of life; the less-educated, the "traditional" way of life. The modern are secular and bohemian, with few children; the traditional are religious and stodgy, with many children. Schools may not loudly favor modernity over tradition, but perhaps they subtly turn their students into Modern Men and Modern Women nonetheless. Education could be good for the soul because it frees us from the dead hand of the past.

Or not. For all their appeal, stereotypes about education and modernity are unreliable. By the numbers, the well-educated are more modern in some ways, more traditional in others.

Religion. Stereotypes say the well-educated are less religious, but this is a half-truth. The well-educated are less religious *theologically.* As education goes up, faith in God and the literal truth of the Bible recedes. Yet the well-educated are more religious *sociologically.* As education goes up, so do church membership and church attendance. These are well-established patterns, at least in the United States.[44]

Statistical corrections make education's theological effect look smaller but its sociological effect look bigger. The General Social Survey measures Americans' confidence in God's existence on a 1–6 scale (1="I don't believe in God," 6="I know God really exists and I have no doubts about it") and religious attendance on a 0–8 scale (0="never," 8="more than once a week"). After correcting for income, intelligence, social status, demographics, and time, a year of education reduces faith in God by .04 steps, but increases religious attendance by .06 steps.[45] Global studies of religion typically conclude *intelligence* reduces both forms of religiosity, but education's effect on religion remains fuzzy. The only clear-cut evidence that education seriously undermines religion comes from former Communist countries, where curricula—not to mention governments themselves—were harshly atheistic.[46]

How can education—including college—matter so little for religion? Sociologists Uecker, Regnerus, and Vaaler paint a plausibly cynical picture:

> Some students have elected not to engage in the intellectual life around them. They are on campus to pursue an "applicable" degree, among other, more mundane pursuits, and not to wrestle with issues of morality or meaning. They instead stick to what they "need to know"—that which will be on the exam. Such students are numerous, and as a result students' own religious faith (or lack of it) faces little challenge. . . . *What is not contested, then, cannot be lost* [emphasis added].

All this is unsurprising given how little youths know about their religions in the first place:

> While higher education opens up new worlds for students who apply themselves, it can, but does not often, create skepticism about old (religious) worlds, or at least not among most American young people, in part because students themselves do not perceive a great deal of competition between higher education and faith, and also because very many young Americans are so undersocialized in their religious faith (before college begins) that they would have difficulty recognizing faith-challenging material when it appears.[47]

None of this shows education is *inherently* religiously impotent. Perhaps heavy-handed parochial or atheistic education would spur widespread conversion or apostasy. Actually existing education's religious effects are, however, mixed and weak.

Marriage and divorce. Since the 1940s, lifelong marriage retreated as education advanced.[48] Have schools sapped our traditional values in favor of bohemian permissiveness? Unlikely. Despite bohemian trends, education, marriage, and divorce are tenuously linked.

In the modern United States, *getting* married is slightly more common for male college grads, but slightly less common for female college grads. *Being* married is more common for all college grads, because graduates of both sexes are now less likely to divorce. Yet on closer look, the patterns blur. Americans who start college but fail to finish are *less* likely to marry and *more* likely to divorce than Americans who avoid college altogether. American women with advanced degrees are *less* likely to be married than American women who stop after the B.A.[49] Looking back in time or around the world further blurs the story.[50] Until recent decades, educated American women tended to stay single.[51] Internationally, the well-educated are less likely to marry in some countries, but more likely to marry in others; the same holds for divorce.[52]

How much of education's surface effect is genuine? Evidence is thin, but researchers who try to statistically isolate education's effects usually learn that—at least in the modern United States—education truly fosters marriage.[53] In the General Social Survey, estimated effects are small but solid—at least for the last two decades. Correcting for demographics, intelligence, church attendance, and era, each year of education raises the chance of being married by 0.7 percentage points, and reduces the chance of being divorced by 0.3 percentage points.[54]

Overall, then, friends of traditional marriage have little to fear from education. While its effect is uneven, time in school now seems to make Americans *less* bohemian. As usual, peer effects are the go-to mechanism. Humans care far more about how their "social equals" are living today than what their teachers said or insinuated years ago. Consistent with this story, social class fully accounts for education's effects on marriage and divorce in modern America.[55] Staying in school gets individuals into the elite club, which in turn helps them get married and avoid divorce. When everyone stays in school longer, however, the elite club jacks up its membership requirements, leaving the prevalence of marriage unchanged.

Fertility. Educated people have fewer kids. Few demographic laws are more strictly enforced. This law doesn't fit just the modern United

States.[56] High-education countries are less fertile than low-education countries, and countries' fertility erodes as education advances, at least since 1900.[57] Fertility gaps are big: Averaging over the world, low-education women outbreed high-education women by about one-third.[58] Nation-by-nation, disparities of a full child or more are common.[59]

In principle, education could be a mask for income, intelligence, status, democratization, or modernization. When statistically challenged, though, education stays strong.[60] To illustrate, take the United States from 1972 to 2012. During this era, each year of education seems to cut Americans' fertility by .12 children. After statistically correcting for income, intelligence, demographics, and era, one year of education still seems to prevent .10 births.[61] While education cools fertility for both sexes, it cools women's more: wives' education matters three or four times as much as husbands'.[62]

Does education sway childbearing via leadership or peer effects? The leadership story is straightforward: Almost all schools—even schools that never mention birth control—explicitly urge students to *delay* childbearing. And most schools at least insinuate that high-powered careers are better than big families. Peer effects make sense, too: look at the Baby Boom. Globally, the mix remains unclear.[63] At least in the modern United States, however, peer effects seem weak. Even though social class fully explains education's effects on marriage and divorce, social class explains *none* of education's effect on fertility.[64] Dropouts who climb into the upper class still breed like dropouts; Ph.D.s who stumble into the lower class still breed like Ph.D.s.

When schools prompt their students to have fewer kids, then, they're plausibly prompting society to have fewer kids, too. Education leads society toward a less populous future. Out of all the educational consequences we've scrutinized, this is the most impressive. The key question: are these consequences impressively *good* or impressively *bad*?

If you're convinced every country on Earth is overpopulated, education's antinatal effect is a great point in its favor. Anyone who accepts the dangers of low fertility, however, should tremble. Almost all developed countries are below replacement fertility. Germany, Japan, and Russia's populations have fallen already.[65] Many other lands will join them in coming decades. Even worse, education doesn't just sap overall population. It targets the educational elite, because the people most inclined to linger in school restrict their childbearing the most. Whatever weight you put on human capital versus signaling, or nature versus nurture, this is demographically perverse. The flip side, happily, is that governments can apparently make babies with budget cuts, arresting their demographic troubles for less than nothing.[66]

Broadening Horizons

I've been griping about curricula since kindergarten. Whenever teachers gave "stupid" assignments, I voiced my malcontent to teachers and parents alike. Their standard response: even the "stupidest" assignments serve the higher purpose of broadening horizons. The world is rich with possibilities, yet most students are poor in curiosity. Teachers have a sacred duty to make closed-minded youths sample this cornucopia. Academic "tasting menus" don't just enrich students emotionally. They enrich students vocationally by exposing them to overlooked career paths.

In hindsight, the teachers' and parents' theory was sound. Kids *are* closed-minded, and schools *can* help them by nudging them to try new things. Unfortunately, educators misapply this noble theory. Rhetoric aside, educators are as narrow-minded as kids. Most of the items on the academic tasting menu have the same stale flavor—unsurprising since teachers typically teach whatever they were taught. When schools decry "narrow-mindedness," their real goal is to replace students' narrowness with their own.

Think about what passes for "broadening students' horizons." Teachers expose students to an ossified list of subjects: music, art, poetry, drama, foreign language, history, government, dance, sports. Some kids respond eagerly, especially to music and sports. Yet the greater their excitement, the greater their ultimate disappointment: almost no one grows up to be a violinist, painter, poet, actor, historian, politician, ballet dancer, or professional athlete. More importantly, all the kids who respond eagerly to none of the above must wait until college for the mandatory "broadening" to relent.

The alternative? For starters, give students numerous and diverse options. Instead of making students study yet another American poem, expose them to Japanese graphic novels. Rather than forcing kids to perform one more play, show them a few films from the 1980s. When you run out of ideas, assign a random Wikipedia article. If you want to help kids discover what emotionally "clicks" for them, trial and error beats academic tradition cold. Anyone who calls Japanese comic books and old movies "useless" should check their double standard. How are comic books and movies any *more* useless than poems and plays?

All else equal, of course, exposing students to plausible careers is better than exposing them to mere hobbies. To live the adage "Do what you love, and you'll never work a day in your life," students must learn what lovable jobs are available. Give students numerous, diverse, yet *realistic* options. Start with the Bureau of Labor Statistics' figures on "employment by major occupational group" and "occupations with the most job growth."[67] Expose boys to nursing. Introduce strong math students to insurance. Tell upper-middle-class kids what plumbers and electricians do and earn. See how many students try Python programming if it fulfills their foreign language requirement. When you run out of ideas, have students check out an unfamiliar job from the Bureau of Labor Statistics' *Occupational Outlook Handbook*.[68]

The fact that schools probably won't try any of these reforms teaches us a sad truth about actually existing education: "broadening horizons" is a slogan educators use to squelch students' sensible doubts. If educators really wanted to broaden students' horizons, curricula would give students a tour of what the world has to offer—not a tour of what educators were forced to learn when they were students.

The Merit of Play

> Rather than give children 30 minutes to while away the time as they please, he said, it makes more sense to teach them a skill, like dancing or gymnastics.
>
> —*New York Times* on Atlanta schools superintendent
> Dr. Benjamin Canada[69]

Education can be glorious. At its best, to quote Roman philosopher Lucretius, it is a "voyage in mind throughout infinity."[70] But education is not the *sole* glorious experience. Since students have only twenty-four hours a day, even the finest studies risk crowding out competing experiences of greater worth.

What could possibly outshine the wonders of education? It is tempting to focus on prestigious activities like writing a killer app or training for the Olympics. Students' most relevant competing experience, though, is *play*—savoring the joys of youth. The more time and effort students devote to their studies, the less remains for carefree exploration of their world. Recall the classic back-to-school essay, "What I Did on My Summer Vacation." Some kids fritter away their free months watching reality TV in a lonely basement. But plenty of others bond with grandparents or cousins, collect seashells, play Dungeons and Dragons with friends, or travel the country. If kids spent more time in school, some of this enrichment would be lost. If kids spent *less* time in school, can there be any doubt that *more* of this enrichment would be gained?

Psychologist Peter Gray could well be the world's greatest spokesman for the merit of free play. Kids have more fun and learn vital lessons when adults give them their space.

> "Playing well and having fun are more important than winning" is a line often used by Little League coaches after a loss, rarely after a win. But with spectators watching, with a trophy on the line, and with so much attention paid to the score, one has to wonder how many of the players believe that line, and how many secretly think that Vince Lombardi had it right. The view that "winning is the only thing" becomes even more prominent as one moves up to high school and then to college sports. . . .
>
> In informal sports, playing well and having fun really are more important than winning. Everyone knows that; you don't have to try to convince anyone with a lecture. And you can play regardless of your level of skill. The whole point of an informal game is to have fun and stretch your own skills, sometimes in new and creative ways that would be disallowed or jeered at in a formal game. . . . If you are a better player than the others, these are ways to self-handicap, which make the game more interesting for everyone. In a formal game, where winning matters, you could never do such things; you would be accused of betraying your team.[71]

The lesson isn't that all play and no school are best for kids. The lesson is that champions of academic soulcraft shouldn't *fixate* on education. Instead, they should seek out what *mix* of school and play is best for the soul. Unfortunately, thanks to the high status of education and the low status of play, we tend to compare school at its best to play at its worst: another hour of Angry Birds can't compete with a Shakespeare lecture from the teacher Robin Williams played in *Dead Poets Society*. The smart way to discover the best mix of school and play, though, is to compare school and play as they really are. Both fall short of their promise, but it's unclear which falls shorter.

Still, there's little reason to favor a dominant role for education over play—and in our society, education dominates children's days. School and study time has been high and growing for decades. According to leading tabulations of 6-to-12-year-olds' schedules, weekly school and study time rose from about 31 hours in 1981 to 37 hours in 1997 and 2003. Playtime is small by comparison, about 10 hours a week. "Play" counts computer games but excludes TV time, which fell from over 18 hours in 1981 to 14 hours in 2003.[72] Outdoor play has atrophied over the last generation: 70% of mothers say they played outside every day when they were kids, while only 31% of their children do the same.[73] Only a small minority of elementary schools have abolished recess, but one major study found 20% of school districts trimmed it during the first five years of the No Child Left Behind Act. Virtually no district made recess longer.[74]

Longer school days do serve one socially useful function: they warehouse kids so both their parents can work. But more hours *in* school needn't mean more hours *of* school. Schools could have used kids' extra campus hours to expand recess. Indeed, if they wanted kids to keep some independence, they could have offered an array of fun yet frugal options in lieu of extra class time. My pet cause: keep the school library open so studious and intellectually curious kids have a tranquil place for free reading. Until college, every school I ever attended had a well-stocked library that was almost never open to the student body. Free play takes many forms. Why not turn the library into a bookworms' sanctuary?

For college kids, you may recall, playtime is now longer than ever.[75] The college workload slimmed down as K–12's bulked up. Most critics of modern education take this as a tragic fall in standards. But once you accept the merit of play, the rise of Leisure College, USA, is a blessing in disguise. College gives students ample time for carefree exploration— time they rarely had in childhood. Plenty of undergrads fritter away their opportunity in a drunken stupor. Yet others sample a medley of fascinating options, acquiring passions that last a lifetime. My under graduate years were my favorites precisely because classes were so un-demanding. Every day was packed with hours for play, and play I did. I read philosophy, listened to opera, wargamed with my friends, and argued politics with strangers past midnight. I owe my soul to lax academic standards.

The Cynical Idealist

Economists are a cynical bunch. Most are tone-deaf to the humanist thesis that education enriches the soul. They studiously measure education's career benefits. They grant education has consumption benefits. Yet most balk at claims about education's intrinsic worth. When humanists face my calculations of education's selfish and social returns, my calls for educational austerity and vocational training, they assume I'm being a typical cynical economist, oblivious to the transformative ideals so many educators hold dear.

I am an economist and I am a cynic, but I'm not a typical cynical economist. I'm a cynical idealist. I embrace the ideal of transformative education. I believe wholeheartedly in the life of the mind. What I'm cynical about is *people*.

I'm cynical about students. The vast majority are philistines. The best teachers in the universe couldn't inspire them with sincere and lasting love of ideas and culture. I'm cynical about teachers. The vast majority are uninspiring; they can't convince even *themselves* to love ideas and culture, much less their students. I'm cynical about "deciders"—the school officials who control what students study. The vast majority think they've done their job as long as students obey.

Anyone who searches their memory will find noble exceptions to these sad rules. I know plenty of eager students and passionate educators, and I know of a few wise deciders. They're the salt of the earth. Still, my forty years in the education industry—many at the "best schools in the world"—leave no doubt that eager students, passionate educators, and wise deciders are hopelessly outnumbered. Meritorious education survives but does not thrive.

I don't hate education. Rather I love education too much to accept our Orwellian substitute. What's Orwellian about the status quo? Most fundamentally, the idea of compulsory enlightenment. Educators routinely defend compulsion on the ground that few students *want* to explore ideas and culture. They're right about the students' tastes but forget a deeper truth: intrinsically valuable education *requires* eager students. Mandatory study of ideas and culture spoils the journey.

Even if you bite the end-justifies-the-means bullet, compulsory enlightenment yields little enlightenment. For all their Orwellian self-congratulation, schools are unconvincing. Despite auspicious conditions, they fail to make either high culture or liberal politics noticeably more popular. Regimentation may be a good way to mold external behavior, but it's a bad way to win hearts and minds—and a terrible way to foster thoughtful commitment. As Stanford education professor David Labaree remarks, "Motivating volunteers to engage in human improvement is very difficult, as any psychotherapist can confirm, but motivating conscripts is quite another thing altogether. And it is conscripts that teachers face every day in the classroom."[76]

Even top students respond to incentivized soulcraft by gaming the system, not reforming their priorities. Unlike those in the United States, British universities essentially base admissions on academic performance. When British professor Greg Clark began teaching at Stanford University, his elite American students looked like better human beings than their British counterparts. He soon learned Americans' superiority was a ruse:

> In my second year as an assistant professor at Stanford University, I was assigned the task of mentoring six freshmen. Each appeared on paper to have an incredible range of interests for an eighteen-year-old: chess club, debate club, history club, running team, volunteering with homeless shelters. I soon discovered that these supposed interests were just an artifact of the U.S. college admission process, adopted to flesh out the application forms and discarded as soon as they have worked their magic.[77]

Still, humanists should not despair. The savior of transformative education has arrived: the Internet, the Merit Machine. Though online education isn't poised to put brick-and-mortar schools out of business, it already beats traditional education in the quest for enlightenment. The Internet enlightens the money-poor: out-of-pocket cost is near zero.

The Internet enlightens the time-poor: commuting cost is normally zero, too. The Internet enlightens the intellectually isolated: search engines and ratings mark the most promising autodidactic paths.

Many idealists object that the Internet provides enlightenment only for those who seek it. They're right, but petulant to ask for more. Enlightenment is a state of mind, not a skill—and state of mind, unlike skill, is easily faked. When schools require enlightenment, students predictably respond by feigning interest in ideas and culture, giving educators a false sense of accomplishment.

When enlightenment is optional, in contrast, educators' failure to transform their students is undeniable. Cynics may lose whatever hope they had left, but cynical idealists will wonder, "How can we do better?" The obvious responses are better pedagogy and better marketing. This isn't wishful thinking: online education, broadly defined, refines pedagogy and marketing every day. Educators' less obvious response is broadening the audience. Most humans intrigued by abstract ideas and high culture are working adults. Instead of lamenting youthful apathy, passionate educators should redirect their energy to humans who are *ready* for enlightenment. There is little money in blogging, podcasting, or uploading lectures to YouTube. But if, like me, you love education to the depths of your soul, such efforts are their own reward.

CHAPTER 10

Five Chats on Education and Enlightenment

I've learned much about education by experience. I've learned more by reading research. Neither experience nor research feels complete, however, without discussion and argument. Conversations about education are reliably engaging because—unlike conversations about, say, offshore oil drilling—no one's in the dark. Few read education research, but virtually every adult's been to school and had a job.

Unfortunately, most arguments about education are insular. Researchers pay little attention to laymen's firsthand experiences. Indeed, they're dismissive on principle: "You can't believe what people *say*." Laymen pay even less attention to researchers' high-tech analyses: "You can prove anything with statistics." My ambition in *The Case against Education* is to merge *all* the evidence—the testimony of students, parents, workers, teachers, and employers as well as research in economics, psychology, sociology, and education.

Though I can heed everyone, I cannot please everyone. Rather than try to placate any one faction, this chapter brings them all together for a battle royale. The following dialogues are inspired by three decades of arguments about education. I'm the only real character. The rest are archetypes, composites—though hopefully not caricatures—of my favorite critics.

The Cast

Bryan Caplan, professor of economics at George Mason University. Highest credential: Ph.D. in economics from Princeton University.

James Cooper, freshman at the University of Kansas; major: undeclared. Highest credential: diploma from Topeka High School.

Frederick Dodd, columnist for the *Wall Street Journal*, blogger for the *Chronicle of Higher Education*. Highest credential: M.A. in journalism from New York University.

Alan Lang, professor of economics at the University of California, Berkeley. Highest credential: Ph.D. in economics from MIT.

Gillian Morgan, freelance tech journalist. Highest credential: B.S. in computer science from UCLA.

Cynthia Ragan, English teacher at Woodrow Wilson High School, New Jersey. Highest credential: B.A. in English from the College of New Jersey.

Derek Romano, recent high school dropout. Highest credential: none.

Gretchen Simpson, student loan activist. Highest credential: M.A. in sociology from the University of Florida.

Daria Stein, entrepreneur and parent of a high school junior. Highest credential: B.S. in engineering from the University of Texas.

Chat #1: Education, What It's Good For

DEREK: Let me get this straight. You're a teacher who admits school is a big waste of time. *I'm* the smart one for quitting high school after every adult in my life told me not to.

BRYAN: Not quite. Selfishly speaking, you shot yourself in the foot. Though you'll never need to know most of what you missed in school, you'll still bear an ugly stigma in the job market.

ALAN: He's going to "bear an ugly stigma" because he quit school before he learned the basic skills workers need in the modern economy.

CYNTHIA: Right, Alan. Bryan's position is plain irresponsible. Kids like Derek need to know school is the path out of poverty.

BRYAN: I don't deny schooling pays decently in the job market. I claim, rather, that schooling pays mainly by signaling employability, not by raising employability. If Derek obtained his high school diploma *without* learning anything he doesn't already know, his job prospects would be much brighter.

CYNTHIA: Odd claim for a professor with a Ph.D. from Princeton.

BRYAN: I'm a whistle-blower. Without my prestigious credentials, would you even listen to my "case against education"? And what I'm saying is anything but odd. You see it with your own eyes. Tell me, Cynthia: What are you teaching your kids this week?

CYNTHIA: [pause] The poetry of T. S. Eliot.

BRYAN: Ah, "the hollow men." When will your students ever use T. S. Eliot on the job?

CYNTHIA: Who knows? Any one of them could become a poet or literary critic.

BRYAN: I'm guessing you've taught about 3,500 students in your lifetime. As far as you've heard, have *any* of your students found employment in poetry, literary criticism, or anything else that taps their knowledge of Eliot's oeuvre?

ALAN: Not a fair question. Who knows what job skills poetry builds? Instead of relying on our intuition about what subjects are "useful," we should see what passes the market test. If employers are more interested in applicants with good grades in English, who are you to deny the "usefulness" of Eliot's work?

BRYAN: His poetry passes *a* market test. The nature of the test, however, is ambiguous. While knowing Eliot's poetry is conceivably a useful job skill, it's more likely to *signal* preexisting job skills.

CYNTHIA: Why does it matter? My students won't use Eliot on the job, but they need good grades to get a job—and if they don't do the assigned work, they won't get good grades.

ALAN: It doesn't matter for your students, but it matters for society. If teachers only affix labels to students' foreheads, we might as well cut the labeling process short, save a pile of time and money, and let students assume their adult roles earlier. Once we concede Bryan's signaling nonsense, it's game over.

BRYAN: How is it "nonsense"?

ALAN: School is packed with useful material. Reading, writing, math. It's not "all signaling."

BRYAN: I never said "all"! My thesis is that the education premium is *mostly* signaling, not *entirely* signaling. That's why I spill so much ink trying to quantify the human capital/signaling breakdown.

DEREK: You're reminding me why I dropped out. Professor, please speak English.

BRYAN: Sorry, I picked up bad habits from my teachers. Derek, you agree extra education can help you get a better job and make more money, right?

DEREK: Yea, because employers care more about a scrap of paper than what you can do.

BRYAN: You're getting ahead of me. When education raises your income, economists call that "the education premium."

Part of the premium exists because school makes you more productive. That's the human capital share.

The rest of the premium exists because school makes you *look* more productive. That's the signaling share.

The "human capital/signaling breakdown" is both shares, side by side; 70/30 means "70% human capital, 30% signaling."

CYNTHIA: So you're saying employers use academic records kind of like Yelp reviews?

BRYAN: Largely.

DEREK: You say "Yelp reviews," I say discrimination. High school dropouts can't get a decent job because employers look down on us.

BRYAN: Conceivable, but doubtful. If most employers refused to hire dropouts out of sheer snobbery, fair-minded employers could get rich quick. Fire all the overpaid graduates, replace them with equally competent dropouts, then pocket the difference.

CYNTHIA: Sounds too good to be true.

BRYAN: Exactly. While competent dropouts exist, they're hard to pinpoint during the hiring process, so employers rely on credentials instead. Sure, they miss a few diamonds in the rough, but granting every applicant a chance to prove themselves is too troublesome.

ALAN: Come on. If that's what's going on, there's got to be a cheaper way.

BRYAN: Federal, state, and local governments massively tilt the scales toward the status quo. Without hundreds of billions of annual subsidies, who knows what alternative worker certification systems would have arisen?

ALAN: [dubious] So it's all government's fault?

BRYAN: No, but government subsidies aggravate deeper problems.

CYNTHIA: At least you don't blame everything on public education. What are these "deeper problems"?

BRYAN: Most fundamentally, credible signals *have* to be expensive. To echo the King James Bible: signaling have ye always. If diamonds were suddenly cheap as plastic, suitors would switch to pricier gemstones to prove their devotion. If an innovative new testing service cost half as much as regular education, students would need extra years of tests to convince employers they've got the right stuff.

ALAN: People like you always insist employers would hire based on IQ tests if the courts allowed it.

BRYAN: Then I disagree with "people like me." The law against hiring practices with "disparate impact" is vague and laxly enforced. If businesses thought IQ testing was a great way to find high-quality, uncredentialed workers, they'd already be using it.

ALAN: But if it's all signaling, IQ testing would be the killer app.

BRYAN: I keep telling you *it's not all signaling.* Eighty percent signaling is my best guess. That said, you'd have a strong point if education signaled intelligence alone. In the real world, however, education signals a *package* of desirable employee traits: intelligence, work ethic, and sheer conformity for starters.

ALAN: Fine. Then why don't elite firms like Goldman Sachs poach high school seniors as soon as they're admitted to Harvard, instead of waiting four years for them to graduate?[1] Harvard's completion rate is near 100%, so admission and graduation are virtually equivalent.

BRYAN: Not so fast. If Goldman Sachs tried poaching, they'd get the dregs of the Harvard barrel. Harvard admittees struggle their whole lives to get into top colleges. In their social circles, the Ivy League is the One True Way. What kind of a rising Harvard freshman would even *consider* skipping college altogether? A misfit. A weirdo. Goldman Sachs doesn't want misfits and weirdos. It wants outstanding conformists.[2]

ALAN: Adverse selection, eh? If you were right, labor markets would have sorted out this problem ages ago.

BRYAN: Really? Last time I checked, you still believed ten million able-bodied workers were involuntarily unemployed. Have labor markets suddenly sorted out the problem of mass joblessness?

ALAN: [sigh] Even well-qualified unemployed workers have a devil of a time convincing employers they're worth hiring.

BRYAN: Now *you're* appealing to adverse selection . . . not that there's anything wrong with that. If adverse selection can prevent able-bodied workers from getting a job at all, why can't it prevent talented workers from getting good jobs without impressive credentials?

Chat #2: College and Catch-22s

GILLIAN: [bemused] This argument has been mildly entertaining, but you're all living in the past. Online education is exploding as we speak. So is scientific measurement of job skills. In a few years, IQ tests will look like eight-track tapes.

ALAN: I've heard such predictions for years. Online education is carving out a niche for itself, but I fail to see the revolution.

GILLIAN: That's what the record companies and book stores thought. Rest assured, the tsunami of online education is on its way.

BRYAN: What makes you so sure?

GILLIAN: Economic logic. The Internet can provide customized education for a fraction of the cost of one-size-fits-all brick-and-mortar schools. Why mortgage your house to build job skills you can learn over the Internet for pennies?

BRYAN: You know my answer: signaling. Education pays primarily by certifying worker quality, not job training.

GILLIAN: Maybe now, but that's all going to change.

BRYAN: Have any close relatives in high school?

GILLIAN: Sure, my little brother is 17.

BRYAN: Would you advise him to skip college in favor of online education?

GILLIAN: Not yet. Give it five years.

BRYAN: But in your view, isn't online education *already* superior to traditional education?

GILLIAN: Online education is a better way to learn, but employers still don't take it seriously.

BRYAN: Exactly. And employers don't take it seriously because the "early adopters" flout social convention.

GILLIAN: A transitional problem. Once online education dominates the market, students at *traditional* schools will be stigmatized as "nonconformists."

BRYAN: Alas, there's a catch-22. Online education won't escape the nonconformist stigma until it dominates the market, but it won't dominate the market until it escapes the nonconformists stigma.

GILLIAN: You're kidding yourself, professor. No industry is immune to the power of disruptive innovation. Including your own.

BRYAN: "Immune" is a strong word. But schools have weathered such storms for centuries. Conformity signaling elegantly explains their resilience. I wish you were right about the future, but you're the one who's kidding herself.

CYNTHIA: You keep insisting that school "signals conformity." You're wrong. Teachers like me constantly tell our pupils to "be your own person." I even gave them a term paper on Emerson's "Self-Reliance": "Whoso would be a man, must be a nonconformist."

BRYAN: I love that essay. [pause] Tell me: What happens if a student, taking Emerson to heart, leaves their seat without permission? Or refuses to write their term paper? Derek might know.

DEREK: Funny. The worst thing about school is all the stupid rules. The second-worst thing is all the hypocrisy about "being yourself."

ALAN: I hate to sound like an adult, Derek, but your negative attitude will get you nowhere. Bryan, would *you* want to hire him?

BRYAN: Derek's been snubbed enough for the last ten years, but Alan makes a fair point. Businesses need conformity to function. Still, in Derek's defense: if he'd apprenticed at 12 instead of suffering through school, we wouldn't need to convince him conformity serves a purpose. He'd know from experience.

FREDERICK: Let me step in here. Bryan and Alan are talking past each other. Bryan's talking about college, where kids learn seventeenth-century Danish poetry; Alan's talking about K–12, where kids learn reading, writing, and math. I think we all agree K–12 builds human capital; let's focus on how much signaling there is in college.

ALAN: Bryan's more extreme than you realize. He sees signaling at every academic level.

BRYAN: Verily. Think about all the nonacademic classes K–12 requires: music, dance, art, P.E. Think about all the academic classes K–12 students rarely use on the job: history, foreign language, poetry, civics. My book is *The Case against Education*, not *The Case against Higher Education*. Still, I'm still happy to zero in on college.

FREDERICK: [taken aback] Well, there are plenty of useless college classes, but isn't the system reforming itself as we speak? Liberals arts are in steep decline. Modern college students seek out majors that teach job skills. STEM is the future.

BRYAN: STEM majors earn *moderately* more than non-STEM majors, but it's not because they're acquiring great job skills. Most STEM majors end up in non-STEM jobs. Signaling is the obvious explanation: earning a STEM degree impresses employers regardless of what concrete skills the job requires.

FREDERICK: If "signaling is the obvious explanation," why is your view so unpopular?

BRYAN: Social Desirability Bias. Education sounds great to liberals and conservatives alike. Blinded by panideological love, people rush to embrace theories that praise education and reject theories that criticize education.

FREDERICK: You're psychologizing. Just tell me the top substantive objections to the signaling model.

BRYAN: Frankly, critics grasp the model so poorly that most "refutations" point to facts the model specifically predicts. If only I had a nickel for every time I heard, "The signaling model says education doesn't matter" or "The signaling model says it doesn't matter if students skip class."

ALAN: [sarcastic] "Specifically predicts." Ha. You can explain *anything* with signaling.

BRYAN: I want to reply, "You can explain anything with human capital," but then we'd both be wrong. There are lots of ways to distinguish human capital from signaling.

FREDERICK: Such as?

BRYAN: My favorite is the sheepskin effect. While social scientists endlessly talk about "years of education," most of the education premium stems from *graduation*. The human capital explanation is hazy. Do schools wait until senior year to teach practical jobs skills? The signaling explanation, in contrast, is straightforward. In our society, you're supposed to finish high school and college. Failure to do so shouts, "I lack the ability or motivation to meet society's expectations."

FREDERICK: I get you. I still have nightmares about accidentally missing my final exams a day before graduation.

ALAN: Now dreams are "evidence"? The sheepskin effect could be selection. Perhaps graduates would be nearly as successful if they hadn't finished their degrees.

BRYAN: Doesn't look like it. When researchers statistically correct for preexisting ability, the education premium falls for both years of education and diplomas, leaving their *ratio* roughly constant. But stats aside, the sheepskin effect is visible to the naked eye. Picture your career if you cancelled your dissertation defense at the last minute. Without your Ph.D., you couldn't be a professor at Podunk State, much less Berkeley. And like every caring academic advisor, you urge your students to finish their degrees so they can get good jobs.

ALAN: You're fond of appeals to "common sense."

BRYAN: Guilty as charged. Unlike most researchers, I take laymen's observations with utmost seriousness. A decade-plus of firsthand educational experience has to count for something.

DEREK: Then what's the point of all the statistics?

BRYAN: Unlike most laymen, I take research very seriously. When smart people devote their lives to a topic, you've got to respect that. The best way to explore a complex topic is to give everyone a hearing, not look for methodological excuses to exclude most of the testimony.

FREDERICK: You're an enthusiastic debater, but how can I take your side over the dozens of other labor economists I've interviewed?

BRYAN: Reread their exact words. Like most academics, they target their brilliance on a few narrow questions. The problem isn't that labor economists' research on signaling is wrong. The problem is they dodge the issue.

ALAN: Why not be agnostic?

BRYAN: Because solid evidence exists; labor economists just fail to connect the dots. Still, I might be agnostic if I hadn't spent forty years in the education industry. I simply cannot reconcile those four decades with anything close to human capital purism. Can you?

Chat #3: How Educational Investments Measure Up

DARIA: Do you mind if we get a little less academic, professor? My daughter's applying to colleges next year. I want to know the best way to invest in her future.

BRYAN: Happy to help. Would neutral observers call her an "excellent student"?

DARIA: [short pause] They would. She's got the right stuff to earn an advanced degree if she wants.

BRYAN: Has she decided on a major?

DARIA: I'm trying to sell her on engineering, but she's more into biology.

BRYAN: Then selfishly speaking, a four-year degree is a good investment for her. Biology is less lucrative than engineering, but her expected return, correcting for inflation, is around 7%.

JAMES: What about me? I barely got into the University of Kansas. I'm only a freshman, but I'm already bored out of my mind. None of my classes inspire me. Daria wants her daughter to be an engineer, but my parents would be happy if I settled on *any* major . . .

ALAN: [interrupts] Bryan's probably going to advise you to drop out. Don't listen to him.

JAMES: Why not? I don't feel like I'm getting much out of college.

ALAN: Your feelings are a poor guide to the modern economy, James. Anytime you're tempted to drop out, compare college grads' average earnings to high school grads.'

BRYAN: James' feelings are indeed a poor guide to the modern economy. But Alan's thoughts are even worse. James, how would you compare yourself to other high school students? Other college students?

JAMES: [glum] I was slightly above average in high school. Now I feel below average.

BRYAN: Then don't compare average college earnings to average high school earnings. Compare *below*-average college earnings to *above*-average high school earnings.

ALAN: A needless complication.

BRYAN: [exasperated] Needless? Absurd, but suppose you're right. James's *expected* payoff is still subpar because—as a marginal student—his odds of graduation are poor. Students like James frequently flunk out or give up, rendering vain all their sacrifices.

DARIA: You're penny-pinching. Shouldn't we give every kid a chance?

BRYAN: Every society rations educational opportunities eventually. What makes "one shot at college" the magic cut-off?

DARIA: I know it's a cliché, but a mind is a terrible thing to waste.

BRYAN: Yes, but a mind isn't the *only* terrible thing to waste. Every education system navigates between two evils: Overlooked Potential and False Hope. The evil of Overlooked Potential: the stricter your standards, the more qualified students you fail to teach. The evil of False Hope: the laxer your standards, the more unqualified students you teach to fail. Why are we so obsessed with the first evil and so indifferent to the second?

DARIA: James should stop making excuses and work harder.

BRYAN: If I were James's father, I'd agree. But I wouldn't encourage my son to go to college unless he buckled down *first*. I base my advice on James as he is, not James as we'd like him to be.

ALAN: Plenty of kids like James finish college. He can too.

BRYAN: When industrialists weigh whether to build a factory, you warn them against best-case thinking. When a teen weighs whether to go to school, you strangely *urge* best-case thinking. Alan, you're a good enough economist to evaluate both investment plans coolly.

ALAN: Appealing to my vanity, I see.

BRYAN: [smirks] You're also a good enough economist to know money isn't everything.

ALAN: Did the fact slip my mind?

BRYAN: Kind of. The median garbage collector makes almost $34,000 a year.[3] Many college grads would be happy with that salary. Would you advise James to become a garbage collector?

ALAN: [peeved] The answer to your patronizing question is no. Garbage collection pays well, but it's nasty.

BRYAN: Have you considered the possibility that for kids like James, attending school is, like garbage collection, a nasty way to make a buck?

ALAN: A ridiculous comparison.

BRYAN: Ridiculous for nerds like us. Not so ridiculous for the multitudes who find their classes painfully dull.

JAMES: You're losing me, professors. If Bryan's right, what's my bottom line?

BRYAN: You should expect about a 3% return to starting college. Selfishly speaking, that's no disaster, but you can do better. Quit school, get a job, and invest your savings in stocks and bonds.

JAMES: There's no guarantee stocks and bonds will pay off.

BRYAN: [animated] There's no guarantee college will pay off, either! Even if you finish, a college degree doesn't ensure a college job. It's only a hunting license.

ALAN: There's something big Bryan's not telling Daria or James. He doesn't want kids to attend college even if it *is* great for them. When he tells you, "Education is a good investment selfishly speaking," he tells himself, "Education is a bad investment socially speaking."

BRYAN: There's no conflict. Sending Daria's daughter to college will be good for her daughter. Sending James to college is bad for James. Society's return on investment is less than zero for both.

DARIA: What does "society's return on investment" even mean?

BRYAN: Good question. A regular ("selfish") return measures how beneficial an investment is for *the investor*. A social return measures how beneficial an investment is for *everyone*.

DARIA: I'm an engineer. Measuring what's "beneficial for everyone" sounds annoyingly touchy-feely.

BRYAN: Like all investment forecasts, social returns are guesswork plus math. One possible benefit of education, for example, is crime reduction. To count it, we have to put a dollar cost on crime, estimate education's effect on crime, then multiply the two. Signaling reduces social returns because it means some of the selfish benefits of education are zero-sum.

DARIA: Why zero-sum?

BRYAN: In the signaling model of education, students try to impress employers by jumping through academic hoops. When you jump through a hoop and your competitors don't, you look better but they look worse. Picture how bachelor's degrees evolved during your lifetime.

DARIA: When I finished college, a bachelor's degree opened exciting career doors. Now my firm won't interview a would-be secretary without one.

BRYAN: Credential inflation at work. When average education levels rise, employers jack up educational requirements.

FREDERICK: Isn't that because the economy is so much more high-tech?

BRYAN: Jobs are a *little* higher-tech than they used to be, but workers are *much* more educated than they used to be. When researchers disentangle the "technological change" and "credential inflation" stories, the breakdown is roughly 20% tech, 80% credentialism.

FREDERICK: Your case against education is so one-sided. Regardless of signaling's share, doesn't education have major offsetting social *benefits*?

BRYAN: Sure. Crime is the biggest. Education also helps the Treasury by raising the taxes people pay and cutting the benefits they collect.

FREDERICK: Then intuitively, why is education so bad on balance?

BRYAN: Suppose you arbitrarily hand one dropout a diploma. On the surface, the social effects are pleasing. Armed with their new diploma, the dropout finds a better job and makes more money. As a result, they pay extra taxes and consume less welfare. They're also likely to commit less crime, because they've got more to lose.

FREDERICK: Plausible.

BRYAN: What happens, though, if you arbitrarily hand a diploma to *every* dropout?

FREDERICK: Credential inflation?

BRYAN: Bingo.

FREDERICK: You exude confidence but repeatedly admit that you're "guessing." I find that most odd. Shouldn't you spend more time researching to resolve the key uncertainties?

BRYAN: Unfortunately, that would take many lifetimes. I've been able to write this book only by piggybacking on the efforts of hundreds of other scholars. I can't single-handedly complete the work they've left undone.

FREDERICK: When I read other researchers, they rarely share their "guesses."

BRYAN: That's because most academics proverbially "look for their keys under the streetlight because it's brighter there." They target questions they can definitively answer instead of questions that really matter.

DARIA: Last question. I hear you're a big fan of big families, and a father of four. If I'd had to pay for all my kids' K–12, I honestly might have stopped at two. Aren't you worried lower education subsidies will lead to smaller families?

BRYAN: Definitely. But there's a clear remedy: use some of the money we save on schools to fund fertility. I'm a fan of hefty, front-loaded tax credits, but baby bonuses serve a similar function.

DARIA: Do those work?

BRYAN: Very well. As a general rule, effective policies pointedly target desired outcomes: if you want more babies, pay more for babies. And according to the best research, modest tax credits don't just noticeable raise fertility. In the long-run, they more than pay for themselves, because babies eventually grow up and start paying taxes.[4]

DARIA: So what are your educational plans for your four kids? Somehow I can't picture you telling *them* to skip college.

BRYAN: I'll tailor my advice to the child. My older sons are excellent students, so college is their best path.

ALAN: "Selfishly speaking."

BRYAN: Yes, selfishly speaking. When people I love are stuck in a rat race, I don't worry about the social value of the race. I cheer, "Run!"

DARIA: What about your younger kids?

BRYAN: They're seven and five, so it's too soon to tell. If they're average high school students, I'll urge them to study more. If their academic rank remains average, I'll level with them: college isn't for every Caplan.

Chat #4: Why Do You Hate Education?

GRETCHEN: I can't believe how seriously the rest of you are taking Bryan's lunacy. He's the reductio ad absurdum of the right-wing education "reform" movement. His fellow right-wingers pretend to care about education; they want only to "improve" it with vouchers. Bryan hates education openly. When an author calls his book *The Case against Education*, we need not read between the lines.

CYNTHIA: Sometimes officials in my teachers' union claim their critics "hate education." That's unfair. Most critics love education as much as I do; we just have a conflict of visions. Bryan's the exception that proves the rule. He doesn't strike me as a hateful person, but if he doesn't hate education, who does?

BRYAN: Seriously, I harbor no hate for education. Why would I? The system has been exceedingly kind to me. My teachers praised me, top schools accepted me, and a fine university gave me a dream job for life. To fairly evaluate education, I must put personal feelings aside. When I do, education looks grossly overrated.

FREDERICK: Education often disappoints me, too, Bryan. But you seem more interested in gutting education than fixing it.

GRETCHEN: No kidding. If education is as bad a deal as he says, why does he propose *zero* policies to make the deal *better*? Half the grad students I know owe over $50,000 in student loans. Bryan's solution: "Raise tuition."

BRYAN: I see myself as a voice of moderation. Education is so universally beloved—and so lavishly funded—that my skeptical words and austerian proposals seem hateful *by comparison*. Suppose I opposed government subsidies for football stadiums. Would it be fair to accuse me of hating football?

FREDERICK: Bryan, I know moderates. Moderates are friends of mine. You're no moderate. You aren't calling for slight budget cuts. Your first choice, as you clearly state, is "separation of school and state." What could possibly be more extreme?

BRYAN: Well said. By temperament, I'm an extremist.

FREDERICK: Pretend you were a moderate at heart. Then what would you recommend?

BRYAN: For elementary and secondary school, means-tested vouchers. Taxpayers fund education for poor children. Otherwise, parents pay.

GRETCHEN: What about higher ed?

BRYAN: End the taxpayer subsidies. To preserve access for poor students, government could offer *un*subsidized student loans, outsourcing collection of delinquent payments to the IRS.

GRETCHEN: [exasperated] What is wrong with you?

BRYAN: [speechless]

GRETCHEN: You favor higher tuition. How does that make education a *better* deal?

BRYAN: "Better deal" for whom? Higher tuition intentionally makes education a worse deal for *students*. Since students spend most of their time jumping through meaningless hoops, though, higher tuition makes education a better deal for *society*.

FREDERICK: How?

BRYAN: Higher tuition spurs youths to waste fewer years in school signaling and more years in the workforce producing.

GRETCHEN: [sarcastic] No doubt the "waste" includes my degrees in sociology.

BRYAN: [earnest] Sociologists have taught me a great deal, and I thank you. Still, what practical job skills do you have to show for all your years of study?

GRETCHEN: [pause] I know how to teach sociology and do sociological research. If higher education were adequately funded, there'd be a bustling market for these skills.

BRYAN: Okay, so you've learned how to be a sociology professor. For what other jobs have your studies prepared you?

GRETCHEN: I could teach K–12 social studies. I could work for the census. I know statistics, so I guess I could be a quant somewhere.

BRYAN: How much of your sociological training would you use in these nonprofessorial careers?

GRETCHEN: [reluctant] Only a little. I can't teach Bourdieu to eighth-graders.

BRYAN: If you knew you were going to end up in one of these other careers, you could have left school years ago.

GRETCHEN: Not really. The decent positions require advanced degrees.

BRYAN: Why would employers require these superfluous credentials?

GRETCHEN: Sociology 101. There's a status hierarchy, and we can't all be at the top. Credentials are a superficially meritocratic way to ration status.

BRYAN: Then we have common ground after all. Signaling is intellectually reinforced Sociology 101.

FREDERICK: All right, I'll bite.

BRYAN: Suppose workers with advanced degrees were actually no more productive than workers without advanced degrees. Every employer would have a foolproof way to "make money fast": fire expensive workers with advanced degrees, and replace them with equally qualified workers without advanced degrees.

FREDERICK: So workers with advanced degrees must be more productive.

BRYAN: On average. This need not mean, however, that advanced degrees boost productivity. They might just *certify* workers' preexisting productivity.

GRETCHEN: What's "sociological" about this?

BRYAN: In the signaling model, certification is socially relative. To stay on top of the social hierarchy, elites need credentials that most people *don't* obtain.

GRETCHEN: None of this changes the fact that young people *need* tertiary degrees to get good jobs in the modern economy.

BRYAN: For now. But hefty budget cuts would bring credential inflation to its knees. The less affordable education is, the less students get; the less students get, the less workers need.

GRETCHEN: So according to you, the student loan crisis is all in our heads?

BRYAN: Here's the real crisis: every year, over a million students who *won't* graduate start college. Their failure is foreseeable; high school students with poor grades and low test scores rarely earn B.A.s. Instead of tempting marginal students with cheap credit, we should bluntly warn them that college is stacked against them.

DARIA: What do we advise all these "marginal" high school students to do with their lives after graduation?

BRYAN: We shouldn't wait until senior year to advise them. Instead, we should steer academically uninclined kids toward vocational education when they're 12 or so. Teenage workers may not discover their "calling," but at least they'll get used to gainful employment.

DARIA: Seems like a recipe for a class society.

BRYAN: [quizzical] Unlike the classless society we inhabit today?

GRETCHEN: We're terribly unequal, but it can get worse. If we listen to you, it will. Shunting so-called weaker students into vocational ed excludes them from high-end jobs—especially kids from lower- and working-class families.

BRYAN: I'm surprised to see a sociologist lose sight of social realities. Think about the vast American underclass. Most don't even finish high school. Does *college* really strike you as a viable path out of poverty for them?

GRETCHEN: It would be if they enjoyed the same advantages your kids do.

BRYAN: Suppose you care about a 12-year-old boy with poor grades and low test scores. He stubbornly hates school. You don't want him to end up in poverty. You can either leave him on the conventional college track, or "shunt" him into vocational training. Which do you choose?

GRETCHEN: [long pause] Fine. Vocational.

BRYAN: Because you think he's more likely to escape poverty that way.

GRETCHEN: Our education system already molds kids for their future roles in the capitalist system. Vocational education takes this probusiness bias to a higher level.

BRYAN: If you're right, why is it so hard for high school grads to get good jobs? You'd think capitalists would leap at the chance to hire graduates who spent the preceding thirteen years learning to serve them.

GRETCHEN: No system's perfect.

BRYAN: From employers' point of view, K–12 is dysfunctional, not "imperfect." The schools are all but oblivious to their manpower needs. Frankly, if perpetuation of capitalist hierarchy were my goal, I'd model schools after military academies. I'd drill every student to conform and obey, imposing harsh discipline and tough standards. I'd drop fine arts, literature, and history from the curriculum. Whatever social studies remained would trumpet the theme, "What's good for business is good for the country."

GRETCHEN: Dystopian.

BRYAN: True. I wouldn't send my kids to a school like that. Still, if schools were designed to mold kids for their future roles in the capitalist system, that's how they'd look.

    The point of vocational education, in contrast, isn't to brainwash kids to serve their corporate paymasters. It's to teach kids marketable skills so employers court *them*.

FREDERICK: Vocational education may be better economically, but you're cutting kids' childhoods short. Our society is rich enough to let teenagers delay the drudgery of adult jobs and adult responsibilities.

BRYAN: What about the drudgery of *school*?

FREDERICK: It's all part of life.

BRYAN: Such a double standard. When kids feel bored and resentful at work, we pity them as victims and call for regulation. When kids feel bored and resentful in school, we roll our eyes and tell them to suck it up. The wise question to pose, for young students and young workers alike, is whether the pain is worth the gain.

FREDERICK: Kids are too ignorant to make that call.

BRYAN: While the young have notoriously poor judgment, paternalism has a disappointing track record too. Today's schools force every kid to "prepare for college," but only a third cross the collegiate finish line.

FREDERICK: You make your reforms sound pragmatic, but isn't libertarian ideology right below the surface?

BRYAN: It's complicated. My heterodox views on education long precede my interest in political philosophy. I've believed in something like signaling since kindergarten.

FREDERICK: [ironic] Strangely enough, the facts all fit the theory you cooked up when you were five.

BRYAN: I had no "theory" in kindergarten. Just two epiphanies:

    First, I had to excel academically in order to get a good job when I grew up.

    Second, I would never use most of my book learning on the job. Though it took me years to see the tension between these two epiphanies, I (crudely) reinvented the signaling wheel sometime in junior high. Armed with my crude signaling theory, I gamed the system, working as little as possible to get A's in all the classes I deemed boring and useless.

FREDERICK: So you were a rebel, not a reformer?

BRYAN: Right, until my senior year of high school. Once I discovered libertarianism, education reform came naturally. Why on earth should government subsidize socially wasteful education?

FREDERICK: Then you admit your education reforms are ideologically driven.

BRYAN: No. I only admit that my political philosophy—or "ideology" if you prefer—sways the *questions* I ask.

FREDERICK: But surprise surprise, the facts are in perfect harmony with your ideology.

BRYAN: Hardly. Libertarians rarely challenge the beloved education sector. Instead, they promise, "Free markets will make education even better."

FREDERICK: Well, why *don't* you say that?

BRYAN: Because I disbelieve it. It goes against everything I've seen. I've attended both public and private schools. They're cut from the same cloth.

DARIA: Like it or not, government support for education is mighty popular. Bluntly rejecting it is no way to win over the public.

BRYAN: You're probably right. I have a whole book on this theme called *The Myth of the Rational Voter*. Popular policies aren't good, and good policies aren't popular.

DARIA: You're cynical about more than education.

BRYAN: I prefer "realistic," but have it your way. Voters favor—and governments adopt—policies that sound good, even if they work poorly. That's what I call the "politics of Social Desirability Bias." Cutting education spending sounds awful despite its merits, so it will remain unpopular and untried.

DARIA: Why advocate policies that will never happen?

BRYAN: As an economist, my answer is: we should always think at the margin. My arguments are astronomically unlikely to transform education but may slightly tilt the policy scales by handing budget hawks a little extra intellectual heft.

Yet ultimately, I meet the challenge as a humanist. Understanding and improving the world are both meritorious. Hopefully my work will save society time and money and ease the plight of long-suffering taxpayers. But figuring out the best policy is inherently worthwhile even if the world won't listen.

Chat #5: Education versus Enlightenment

CYNTHIA: The more Bryan and Alan argue about education, the more I think they miss the point. Education deserves our love no matter what it does for GDP. Enlightening eager young minds is a thing of beauty.

BRYAN: Cynthia, we're more in sync than you think. I'm a teacher too—and I love what I do.

CYNTHIA: It scarcely comes across.

BRYAN: Remember, I usually argue with people like Alan. When my fellow economists make overblown claims about education's economic rewards, and I debunk them, we all sound like philistines by omission. There *is* more to life than GDP.

FREDERICK: Then why call your book *The Case against Education*? You should have stuck to economics.

BRYAN: Because my contrarian take goes beyond economics. Unlike a lot of economists, I glorify enlightenment for its own sake.

FREDERICK: Shouldn't that make you *more* proeducation, not less?

BRYAN: Only given three conditions that real schools rarely meet.

FREDERICK: Namely?

BRYAN: First, worthy content. The material should be genuinely worth knowing.

FREDERICK: Trivial.

BRYAN: You never had to memorize the fifty state capitals? Anyway, the second requirement is skillful pedagogy.

CYNTHIA: Who's decides what's "skillful"?

BRYAN: You're a teacher, I'll trust your verdict . . . as long as your coworkers aren't eavesdropping. Everyone who's taught knows a few stellar teachers. The rest are uninspiring at best. College professors' frequent complaints about teaching "load" expose their mindset: educating students is not a calling, but a chore.

CYNTHIA: You can't expect every teacher to be "inspiring."

BRYAN: I don't. Uninspiring education is worth enduring as long as it teaches useful skills. Only inspiring education, however, is valuable for its own sake.

FREDERICK: Your last requirement?

BRYAN: Eager students. Ordering resentful kids to shut up and do their work may provide useful training for their future. Without students who hunger for knowledge, though, education lacks intrinsic value. In the real world, such students are sadly rare.

CYNTHIA: No doubt you've had some bad experiences, but you paint with a broad brush.

BRYAN: Actually, like most professors, I enjoyed a lot of my classes. My classmates' faces told a different story. So do the faces of my students today. Most are bored.

CYNTHIA: Sure, kids find school boring. Enlightenment is an uphill battle.

BRYAN: "Uphill"? How often do you summit?

CYNTHIA: What do you mean?

BRYAN: On the first day of class, what fraction of your students find literature boring?

CYNTHIA: Ugh, 80%.

BRYAN: At the end of the semester, what fraction of your students continue to find literature boring?

CYNTHIA: I don't know. Seventy-eight percent? Are you so much better?

BRYAN: I wish! In my experience, I "reach" only the rare students who *want* to be reached. The rest put in a little effort, take the tests, and move on with their lives.

CYNTHIA: What's the alternative?

BRYAN: Teach curious students about ideas and culture. Leave the rest in peace and hope they come around.

CYNTHIA: If students find reading boring, should they learn to read?

BRYAN: Yes, because reading is a practical skill. Even if they suffer now, they'll profit in the long run.

CYNTHIA: Why can't you say the same about poetry?

BRYAN: Because poetry isn't a practical skill. The vast majority of students who find poetry painful never "recoup their losses."

CYNTHIA: Not materially, but it still enriches their lives.

BRYAN: Very rarely.

CYNTHIA: How can you possibly know that?

BRYAN: Look at sales of poetry books. Almost everyone has to study poetry in school. Almost no one voluntarily continues to study poetry in adulthood. Poetry is an acquired taste that almost no one acquires.

CYNTHIA: I acquired it.

BRYAN: Me too. But outliers like us are a poor reason to push poetry on everyone.

CYNTHIA: If schools don't teach it, we outliers will go extinct.

BRYAN: No we won't. Remember: plenty of ideas and culture receive *no* tax-payer support. Public schools don't teach religion, yet religion endures. Few schools public or private push rock-and-roll, but rock-and-roll thrives. When I was growing up, I explored my many interests at the library. Today's kids enjoy the divine bounty of the Internet.

FREDERICK: You're awfully negative for someone who denies he hates education.

BRYAN: I love education too much to accept our Orwellian substitute.

FREDERICK: Your standards are impossibly high.

BRYAN: No they aren't. Look at online learning. It's packed with great material taught by the best teachers on earth to students who sincerely yearn for enlightenment. If traditional schools can't match that, so much the worse for them.

GILLIAN: I'm confused. I thought your signaling story makes you pessimistic about online education.

BRYAN: Signaling makes me pessimistic about online education as a *business model*, but I'm one of online education's biggest fans. Never mind the future. Online education has *already* made enlightenment virtually free for anyone with an Internet connection. This is a sci-fi triumph of the human mind.

GILLIAN: [disgruntled] So online education wins a moral victory, but traditional schools stay the dominant business model.

BRYAN: Exactly.

CYNTHIA: Tell us something *positive* about school. The reality must live up to the hype once in a blue moon.

BRYAN: You're right. As a father of four, I keep reliving education through my kids' eyes. Do you know what impresses me the most?

CYNTHIA: Math?

BRYAN: No. Preschool.

CYNTHIA: You believe all the research about preschool's lifelong benefits?

BRYAN: Not really. Still, I'm sincerely impressed by the preschool experience. Toddlers learn letters and numbers, both useful skills. Teachers expose them to a sampler of plausibly enjoyable activities. And the tots have ample time for free play. When I drop my daughter off at preschool, she's happy—and I'm happy for her.

CYNTHIA: I like preschool too, but it can't go on forever.

BRYAN: Nor should it. I praise preschool because it has the right priorities. Teach everyone skills they're likely to use later in life. Gently introduce students to a wide range of enrichment opportunities. If something sticks, great. Otherwise, leave them in peace to do their own thing.

FREDERICK: End result: Appreciation of ideas and culture becomes rarer than it already is.

BRYAN: Maybe, but I doubt it. Force-feeding ideas and culture to recalcitrant youths often sparks resentment rather than appreciation. Did you ever listen to glum high school students read Shakespeare aloud? [shudders]

FREDERICK: [shudders] What alternative is there?

BRYAN: Patience. Young philistines have a lifetime to reconsider their intellectual apathy.

FREDERICK: That's wishful thinking.

BRYAN: When free machines provide instant access to the totality of human knowledge, humanists should count their blessings. The life of the mind is now open to all. I'm not convinced that mandatory enlightenment ever made sense, but either way, it's obsolete.

Conclusion

For I have neither wit, nor words, nor worth,
Action, nor utterance, nor the power of speech,
To stir men's blood. I only speak right on;
I tell you that which you yourselves do know.
—Shakespeare, *Julius Caesar*

The vast majority of us lack the insight to reinvent the wheel.[1] Without education, every generation would have to reinvent *all* the wheels. This isn't pedants' puffery. Private and public sector employers gladly pay hefty upcharges for educated workers. Given these truths, how dare anyone—let alone a professor—mount a "case against education"?

Concisely: for all its wonder, education is grossly overrated. It's grossly overrated in the United States and around the globe. You don't have to be a professor to see it, but only a professor can credibly *say* it.

The overrating is starkest from a social point of view. Students forget most of what they learn after the final exam because they'll never need to know it in real life. The heralded social dividends of education are largely illusory: rising education's main fruit is not broad-based prosperity, but credential inflation. Crunching the numbers, social investment in education underperforms stuffing money under mattresses.

Education does better from a selfish point of view, but it's still not what it's cracked up to be. Though high school pays well for almost everyone, the average person shouldn't go to college. Indeed, the average *college student* shouldn't go to college.

What makes the rule true? First: ability bias. The typical college graduate owes their success to a "dream team" of credentials, intelligence, motivation, and attitude, not just their college diploma. Second: completion probability. Starting college, like starting a business, is a gamble—with the odds stacked in favor of "nerds" and "teacher's pets." Pushing college on the failure-prone majority is cruelly misleading. You might as well urge them to buy lottery tickets because jackpot winners live in luxury.

Education is even grossly overrated from a humanist or "spiritual" point of view. While great teachers sporadically inspire lifelong love of ideas and culture, few teachers are great. We need no clever statistics to prove this. Basic facts suffice. If schools caused *all* consumption of fine art, high-brow music, and classic literature, it would still be a pittance. Education's effects on political and social attitudes are also overrated. Time in school does little to promote leftist ideology or undermine traditional lifestyles. While there are some credible peer effects, they often push in counterintuitive directions. Education makes people appreciate capitalism more, not less.

Is there some way to redeem education, to make it live up to the propaganda we've borne since childhood? Conceivably, but to quote Eomer from *The Lord of the Rings*, "Do not trust to hope. It has forsaken these lands."[2] The propaganda is too jubilant, the reality too grim. The prudent response is to act on the known. Stop throwing good money after bad. Cut education budgets. Shift the financial burden of education from taxpayers to students and their families. Vocational education is promising, but "get out of the way" is the place to start. Plenty of extra vocational education is waiting to happen if and when its detractors relent.

If You See Something, Say Something

Where does the idea that school is a waste of time come from? Personal experience. Most of what we learn in school doesn't *feel* relevant to the real world. My case against education doesn't put common sense on trial. As long as you describe your school years *unromantically*, you're a friendly witness.

Unconvinced? Think about all the school time you burned studying irrelevancies. Notice how often you asked yourself, "What do I need to graduate?" instead of "How can I maximize my learning?" Recall all the ways you gamed the system: cramming for exams, seeking lax instructors, skipping assignments because "I already have an A." Count the times your peers asked, "Will this be on the test?"—but never "Will this be on the job?" Picture all the overqualified graduates you've encountered waiting tables and working in bookstores. You've seen a world of academic oddities with your own eyes. Signaling elegantly explains them all.

If research and common sense are both on my side, who's the defendant? The party line—what we're *supposed* to believe about education. You've been enmeshed in the irrational exuberance since preschool. "School prepares us for our future." "School is fun." "Nothing is more important than education." We've all heard it, and we've all repeated it.

If the party line is so false, why is dissent so scarce? Social Desirability Bias. Calling school a rat race verges on nihilism. When students challenge the party line, teachers and parents get upset. When graduates challenge it, they seem immature. Even those who don't care to preen don't want to get stomped. Education's like John Gotti, the legendary "Teflon Don": guilty as sin, but everyone's petrified to testify against it.

The Case against Education aims to reassure the witnesses. Standing up to Social Desirability Bias is inherently scary, but you're not alone.[3] Most people who reflect on their time in school privately agree with you. Research in economics, psychology, sociology, and education itself has your back. Testifying against education is safer than it looks.

Strangely, the scariest scenario for me is that my case *prevails* in the court of public opinion. I teach at Virginia's largest public university, and love what I do. Though I call my academic position a "dream job for life," it's not absolutely guaranteed. If taxpayers elected politicians as committed to education austerity as I am, I wouldn't just say goodbye to a plum job; my beloved circle of nerds would scatter to the four winds.

Why promote policies so dreadful for me? A blend of idealism and cynicism. Idealistically, I'm duty-bound to blow the whistle on my industry's vast, ongoing abuse of the taxpayer. Voters need to know they're not getting the human capital they've been promised—and who will tell them if I don't? Cynically, I doubt the majority will heed my warnings. Fulfilling my duty is painless because even the most intellectually compelling arguments won't convert the typical voter to distasteful conclusions.[4]

The Punch Line

An old joke says, "Those who can, do. Those who can't, teach."[5] Insinuation: we should *expect* our education system to fail, because teachers lack the skills they're hired to impart. The truth is stranger and funnier . . . if you're blessed with a twisted sense of humor. In the real world, teachers rarely teach practical skills they can't do. They teach *im*practical skills they *can* do. While schools undeniably cover reading, writing, and math, students spend the bulk of their time on esoteric studies they'll never use unless they become teachers themselves. You might think employers and other "doers" would respond by scorning academic credentials. Instead, they make credentials the foundation of their pecking order.

All very weird, yet it all makes sense. Employers can't afford to give every applicant a chance. They need rough-and-ready ways to decide whom to interview and whom to hire. In our society, academics are the focal metric. It's intrinsically appealing, since academic success calls for a blend of brains, toil, and submission. And over time, this intrinsic appeal has fed on itself. Education is now *the* way the adult world measures the promise of youth. Scholastic failure doesn't merely reveal a lack of talent and drive; it signals deviance. Kids willing to quit school *despite* this stigma are deviant indeed—and employers shun them accordingly.

Why then do schools waste so much time? As long as academic success leads to career success, neither parents nor students have much motive to critique the curriculum. How do educators decide *which* irrelevant subjects to emphasize? The path of least resistance: we teach what we learned when we were students. The fingerprints of the dead hand of the past, the time when school prepared elite youths for medicine, law, and ministry, are all over our pedagogy.

How stuck are we? Given the near-trillion dollars government annually heaps on the status quo, we're nearly immobilized. Never-ending cosmetic changes create the illusion of fluidity. Schools adopt a new history textbook or add Mandarin to the course catalog. They toy with technology. Instead of playing on their phones in class while the professor lectures, college students can play on their phones in their dorm rooms while the professor streams the lectures over the Internet. Yet no matter how many cosmetic changes accumulate, the essence of school endures: students spend over a decade learning piles of dull content they won't use after graduation.

There is a way to sever this Gordian knot: slash government subsidies. This won't make classes relevant but will lead students to spend fewer years sitting in classrooms. Since they're not learning much of use, the overarching effect will not be "deskilling" but credential *deflation*. Though this unprecedented reversal sounds like social science fiction, the logic is clear: the less education applicants have, the less applicants *need* to convince employers they're worth hiring.

Will the Gordian knot be cut? I fear not. Unlike grandstanding politicians and pundits, I expect no vindication by future events. Social Desirability Bias rules government. Policies don't triumph and endure because they work well. They triumph and endure because they sound good. "Every child deserves the best education in the world" sounds great to citizens the world over, ruinous social returns notwithstanding.

Why fight political psychology? Instead of being a soloist crying for *less* education, I could join the megachorus crying for *better* education. Alas, my arguments hold me back. What I've shown is that otherworldly education is overrated. The commonsense response is to cut otherworldly education, and spend the savings on something worthwhile—*with no presumption that "something" should be another form of education.*

Education is so integral to modern life we take it for granted. *Of course* youths have to leap through interminable academic hoops to secure their place in adult society. This is how civilized societies work. My thesis, in a single sentence: civilized societies revolve around education *now*, but there is a better—indeed more civilized—way. We can switch as soon as adults collectively admit we're making childish mistakes. We have to admit academic success is a great way to *get* a good job, but a poor way to learn how to *do* a good job. If everyone got a college degree, the result would not be great jobs for all, but runaway credential inflation. Trying to spread success with education spreads education but not success.

Back in the 1980s, a sign hung in my junior high school's main office. It read: "Teenagers! If you're tired of being harassed by unreasonable parents, now is the time for action. Move out and pay your own way while you still know everything!" I didn't appreciate the sign then, and I still don't. Kids have much to learn, but they grasp key facts more clearly than their seniors. Above all, kids know adults are forcing them to learn mountains of boring material most adults have long since forgotten. This doesn't mean, of course, that individual students can blow off school with impunity. But even bad students are more sinned against than sinning. If adults had voted for educational austerity, adulthood would start years earlier. "Move out and pay your own way" would then be a viable option instead of a cruel taunt.[6]

Completion Probability and Student Quality

High school completion. Over the last two decades, about 25% of high school students failed to graduate on time.[1] Many of these dropouts eventually get a GED. For job purposes, however, a GED is *not* equivalent to high school graduation. Indeed, the labor market treats GED holders as if they were high school dropouts.[2] In the end, about 20% of American adults never earn a standard high school diploma.[3]

How should we expect Excellent, Good, Fair, and Poor Students to compare to the average? Hundreds of studies statistically analyze high school completion.[4] Unfortunately, only a tiny minority provide enough details to allow readers to calculate completion probabilities by type of student.[5] Furthermore, major data sets often inappropriately pool GEDs with regular high school graduates.[6] In the end, I rely on Herrnstein and Murray's analysis of high school graduation in the NLSY.[7] They provide enough information to compute exact probabilities—and separately analyze high school dropouts and GEDs. Despite their controversial reputation, their results on this topic are quite mainstream.[8]

Herrnstein and Murray use cognitive ability and parental socioeconomic status to predict probabilities of (a) permanently dropping out of high school, and (b) earning a GED instead of a regular diploma.[9] To derive a four-year noncompletion rate from overall noncompletion rate, I assume the observed *ratio* of four-year noncompletion to overall noncompletion (25%/20%=1.25) does not vary by student ability.

How can we use Herrnstein and Murray's equations to calculate high school completion probabilities for my four archetypes? For cognitive ability, I plug in my standard percentiles: 82nd percentile for Excellent Students, 73rd for Good, 41st for Fair, 24th for Poor.[10] What about socioeconomic status? In the NLSY, cognitive ability and socioeconomic status have a .55 correlation. I use this correlation to derive students' predicted socioeconomic status from their cognitive ability. Figure A1 brings all the results together.

By default, this book analyzes rates of return for "balanced" populations—half male, half female. Since young males slightly outnumber females, Figure A1's probabilities are not quite right; we must separately compute

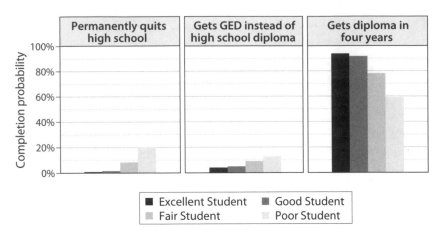

Figure A1: High School Completion Probabilities by Student Ability
Source: Herrnstein and Murray 1994, pp. 146–51, 597–98.

completion rates for men and women, then take the average. While Herrnstein and Murray do not break high school diploma results down by gender, both of their predictors—cognitive ability and parental socio-economic status—are uncorrelated with gender. As a result, we can adjust their predicted success rates to fit the latest cohort's real-world gender gap: 3.9% below average for men, 4.2% above average for women, then take the average to get balanced completion probabilities (see Figure A2).[11]

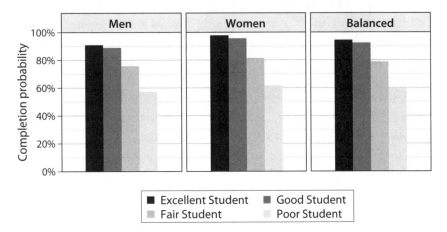

Figure A2: Four-Year High School Completion Probabilities by Student Ability and Sex
Sources: Herrnstein and Murray 1994, pp. 146–51, 597–98, adjusted by percentage gender gaps from Heckman and LaFontaine 2010, p. 254, table 3, latest cohort (born 1976–80).

B.A. completion. Finishing college is far more challenging than finishing high school. At first glance, the Department of Education's numbers show success is unbelievably rare. Out of students who started four-year public institutions in 2005, a measly 32% finished on time, and only 56% finished in *six* years.[12] However, these numbers mislead in two big ways. First, they count graduation only from students' *initial* colleges, even though many students transfer. Second, they lump full- and part-time students together. Expecting a part-time student to earn a B.A. in four years is senseless.

Fortunately, the National Student Clearinghouse (NSC), an association that includes virtually all American institutions of higher education, has recently created a huge comprehensive data set (over two million students) that handles both problems. Out of full-time students who started at four-year public institutions in 2007, the NSC reports that 72% possessed a bachelor's degree from that school six years later. Eighty-two percent, however, possessed a bachelor's degree from *somewhere*.[13] That's far above 56% but still implies *most* full-time students fail to finish their degree on time.

To repeat, that's an average. How should we expect my student archetypes to measure up? Once again, a multitude of studies statistically analyze college completion, but few provide enough details to allow readers to calculate completion probabilities by type of student.[14] Even the best studies typically lump full- and part-time students together.[15] In the end, I rely on UCLA's Higher Education Research Institute's (HERI) analysis of the NSC numbers.[16] In particular, I use HERI's simple model that predicts full-time students' four-year completion as a function of SAT scores and high school GPA. For SAT scores, I plug in my standard percentiles— 82nd for Excellent Students, 73rd for Good, 41st for Fair, and 24th for Poor.[17] For GPA, I assign Excellent Students an "A+/A," Good Students a B+, Fair Students a C+, and Poor Students a D. Although the NSC data takes student transfers into account, HERI's analysis does not.[18] To remedy this problem, I raise HERI's probabilities by 14%.[19] Figure A3 reports results broken down by gender, along with the implied balanced results.

Master's degree completion. While data on master's completion is sparse, the overall rate for graduate and professional school is a mere 50%.[20] Researchers often focus on specific types of programs, including law degree, medical degrees, and Ph.D.s.[21] Rare wider-ranging studies fail to report enough details to allow readers to calculate completion probabilities by type of student.[22]

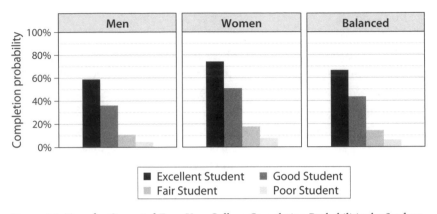

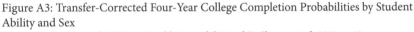

Figure A3: Transfer-Corrected Four-Year College Completion Probabilities by Student Ability and Sex
Sources: DeAngelo et al. 2011, p. 17, table 8, model 3, and D. Shapiro et al. 2013, p. 12.

Given these lacunae, I simply assign Excellent Students the average completion rate of 50%. This may seem odd. If advanced degree students are a mixture of Excellent, Good, Fair, and Poor, shouldn't the Excellent have *above*-average success rates? But remember: Excellent Students by construction fit the profile of the average person with an advanced degree, so some students *must* be better than Excellent. To fill in the rest of the numbers, I assume completion probabilities are proportional to Figure A3's. Figure A4 brings the results together.

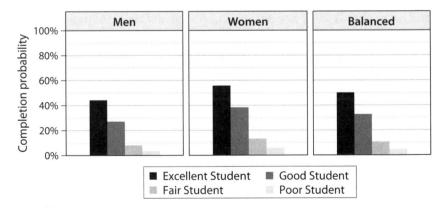

Figure A4: Two-Year Master's Completion Probabilities by Student Ability and Sex
Source: Balanced sample of Excellent Students are assigned the average of 50%; other probabilities are proportional to Figure A3's.

Notes

Introduction

1. Epigraph: Wendy's Wizard of Oz 2015.
2. See, e.g., Robinson and Aronica 2015, D. Goldstein 2014, Beck and Olson 2014, Ravitch 2011, Murray 2008, Horowitz 2007, Latzer 2004, B. Shapiro 2004, and D'Souza 1991.
3. These are the U.S. education premiums for 2011 for full-time, year-round workers. U.S. Census Bureau 2012a.
4. In 2011, 33% of all workers had bachelor's degrees or higher. United States Census Bureau 2012a.
5. See the calculations in Chapter 7, in the section "How Big Is Your Elephant?"
6. The phrase is Robert Frank's, though he would very likely reject its application to education (Frank 1999, pp. 146–58).
7. 83.3%, to be precise. T. Snyder and Dillow 2011, p. 234.
8. The correlation between grades and both salary and job performance is modest but robust (Roth and Clarke 1998, Roth et al. 1996).

Chapter 1: The Magic of Education

1. Epigraph: B. Collins 1997, p. 36.
2. United States Census Bureau 2012a.
3. See, e.g., Card 1999 for the effect of education on cash income, and Oreopoulos and Salvanes 2011 for the effects of education on noncash income, quality of life, and unemployment.
4. Thurow 1972, p. 71.
5. Draper and Hicks 2002, p. 5.
6. Granada Hills Charter High School 2015.
7. To graduate, students need at least 230 credits for grades 9–12. A full load of six courses is 30 credits per semester (Granada Hills Charter High School 2015).
8. Granada Hills Charter High School 2015. The main difference is that CSU and UC colleges require a C or better in *all* required classes.
9. Bahrick and Hall 1991, p. 22, surprisingly find that adults who took calculus or beyond rarely even use algebra on the job.
10. University of California Berkeley 2015b.
11. University of California Berkeley 2015a.
12. For an overview, see Angrist and Pischke 2017.
13. For an overview, see Spence 2002. Seminal works include Arrow 1973a, Phelps 1972, Schelling 1980, Spence 1974, 1973, and Stiglitz 1975. Nobel laureate Paul Krugman isn't closely associated with the idea, but he too has found signaling worthy of his attention (Krugman 2000).
14. Nobel Prize 2015.

15. Besides the aforementioned seminal works, see also Riley 2001, Stiglitz and Weiss 1990, and Weiss 1995.

16. On "answering easier questions," see Kahneman 2011, pp. 97–108.

17. See Arrow 1998, 1973b, Fang and Moro 2011, and Phelps 1972.

18. Posner 2008.

19. In the National Longitudinal Survey of Youth, the correlation between education and intelligence is +.59. On intelligence and occupational attainment, see, e.g., Schmidt and Hunter 2004.

20. Richards 1988.

21. Belley and Lochner 2007 and Light and Strayer 2000 both confirm that family income predicts higher education, even correcting for many other factors.

22. My junior high and high school in the Los Angeles Unified School District all but officially embraced this trinity; our report cards separately assessed academic performance, "Work Habits," and "Cooperation." The system continues to this day (Pérez and Loera 2015).

23. Heckman and coauthors argue at length that the high school equivalency exam (the GED) provides a "mixed signal": "GED recipients are smarter than other dropouts, but their character skills are as bad or worse than those of other dropouts. Both cognitive and character skills are valued in the market and in schools. Hence, the net signal sent by a GED certificate is inherently ambiguous" (Heckman, Humphries, and Kautz 2014b, p. 179).

24. See Chapter 4, section "The Sheepskin Effect," for detailed discussion.

25. See Caplan 2012a, 2012b.

26. Hornby 2009.

27. Arrow 1973a, p. 194.

28. See, e.g., Deary 2001, Jensen 1998, and Herrnstein and Murray 1994.

29. Despite common claims to the contrary, hiring based on IQ tests is basically legal and surprisingly common. See Chapter 3, section "Is Credentialism a Creature of the State?"

30. Indeed, Arrow elaborates on this distinction from page one: "From the viewpoint of formal theory, it does not matter how the student's productivity is increased, but implicitly it is assumed [by most economists] that the student receives cognitive skills through his education. Educators on the other hand, have long felt that the activity of education is a process of socialization; the latent content of the process, the acquisition of skills such as the carrying out of assigned tasks, getting along with others, regularity, punctuality, and the like, being at least as important as the manifest objectives of conveying information" (1973a, p. 194).

31. Wiles 1974, p. 50.

32. Cowen 2008, p. 83.

33. Becker 2006.

34. Leading papers include Farber and Gibbons 1996, Belman and Heywood 1997, Altonji and Pierret 2001, Altonji 2005, Lange 2007, and Arcidiacono et al. 2010.

35. See Altonji 2005, p. 112: "The implication is that the market may be slow to learn that a worker is highly skilled if the worker's best early job opportunity given the information available to employers is a low-skill-level job that reveals little about the worker's talent."

36. Hayes 1995 tantalizingly claims to teach "strategies for competent people without college degrees," but his advice is underwhelming (Caplan 2011f).

37. See, e.g., Sweet 1989, Granholm 1991, Cox and Kramer 1995, Klaas and Dell'Omo 1997, Folger and Skarlicki 1998, and Segalla et al. 2001. Many managers dislike firing enough to outsource it, creating a multibillion-dollar market in "outplacement services" (Rogers 2010).

38. Popowych 2004.

39. See, e.g., Tess-Mattner 2004 and McCord 1999.

40. Caplan 2013.

41. Kling 2006.

42. Princeton University 2015.

43. See, e.g., Sabot and Wakeman-Linn 1991, and Bar et al. 2009.

44. See, e.g., Epstein 2006. For this point, I am indebted to Omar Al-Ubaydli.

45. For this point, I am indebted to Alex Tabarrok. See Tabarrok 2012.

Chapter 2: The Puzzle Is Real: The Ubiquity of Useless Education

1. Epigraph: Schneider 1993.

2. Autor 2010.

3. Summing T. Snyder and Dillow 2011, p. 412, on 2008–9 graduation numbers for biological/biomedical sciences, computer/information sciences, engineering, engineering technologies, and physical sciences/science technologies yields 225,852 science and engineering graduates out of a total of 1,601,368, or 14.1%. In the same year, 34.0% of American high school graduates 25 and up held a bachelor's degree, along with 34.5% of American high school graduates aged 25–29 (T. Snyder and Dillow 2011, pp. 24–25).

4. In the General Social Survey, 88% of respondents who claim to speak a foreign language "very well" say they learned to speak it in the home. GSS variable identifiers OTH-LANG, GETLANG, and SPKLANG.

5. The category also includes special education, which arguably instills basic life skills its students might otherwise fail to acquire (Hocutt 1996).

6. Algebra II is more common than Algebra I because so many students take Algebra I in junior high or middle school.

7. "Rigorous" economics undergraduate programs rely heavily on calculus, but most aren't rigorous.

8. Kahneman 2011.

9. I owe this observation to economic historian Mark Koyama.

10. Bureau of Labor Statistics 2014f. Employment data comes from 2014, so the mismatch between degrees and jobs is probably even worse than it looks. As a practical matter, you need a graduate degree to actually work as a psychologist; as the BLS notes, "Although psychologists typically need a doctoral degree in psychology, a master's degree is sufficient for some positions."

11. Bureau of Labor Statistics 2015g.

12. Bureau of Labor Statistics 2014c.

13. Research assessing K–12 learning is voluminous; see, e.g., Glewwe et al. 2014, Pritchett 2013, Hanushek and Woessmann 2011, Hanushek 2003, Pithers and Soden 2000, and Ceci 1991. For learning in college, see Pascarella and Terenzini 2005, pp. 65–

212 (a comprehensive though slightly dated review), along with Arum and Roksa 2011 and Lederman 2013.

14. Prominent experimental or quasi-experimental research on learning includes Carlsson et al. 2015 and Chetty, Friedman, Hilger, et al. 2011.

15. See generally Cooper et al. 1996.

16. See, e.g., Jacob et al. 2010 and the literature review in E. Cascio and Staiger 2012. Dickens and Flynn 2001 propose a model where lasting intelligence gains require a lastingly enriched cognitive environment.

17. Bahrick and Hall 1991.

18. Kutner et al. 2007. The survey was also conducted in 1992, with similar results (Kirsch 1993).

19. Kutner et al. 2007, p. iii.

20. Kutner et al. 2007, pp. 87, 88–89.

21. The "composite score" for an education category is just the average prose, document, and quantitative score for each literary level. E.g., high school grads are at the Intermediate level 44% of the time for prose, 52% for documents, and 29% for quantitative, so their composite score for intermediate is (44+52+29)%/3=42%.

22. Only 1% of native-born Americans aged 25–34 dropped out before the ninth grade (U.S. Census Bureau 2012b).

23. Berry et al. 2009, p. 8.

24. Cribb 2008, p. 2.

25. Romano 2011, p. 56.

26. Somin 2013, pp. 33–34. Somin reports that the average respondent correctly answered 14.3 out of 30 questions (48%)—six more than the 8.3 out of 30 (28%) they would get from guessing.

27. See Somin 2013, Caplan 2007, and Delli Carpini and Keeter 1996 for surveys.

28. The correction works as follows. Let x=the share of the population that *knows* the answer, y=the share of the population that doesn't know the answer but guesses something, z=the share of the population that says "don't know," R=the share of the population that says the correct answer, and N=the number of response options. Assume the ignorant are equally likely to guess every option. Then we have:

$$x+y+z=1 \text{ (the three groups are mutually exclusive and jointly exhaustive)}$$

and

$$x+y/N=R$$

By substitution:

$$x+(1-x-z)/N=R$$

So:

$$x=(RN-1+z)/(N-1)$$

If a study does not report "don't know" answers, I set z=0. For the Bill of Rights question, R=.57, N=4, and z=.06, implying x=.447. I thank Jim Schneider for spelling out this formula.

29. See National Science Board 2012, pp. 7-19 to 7-27 for further discussion.

30. This simply divides number of questions known by 3.3, the average number of years high school students study science (T. Snyder and Dillow 2011, pp. 228–30).

31. GSS variable identifier BIBLE.

32. GSS variable identifiers OTHLANG, SPKLANG, and GETLANG. See also Caplan 2012c.

33. For overviews, see Singley and Anderson 1989, Detterman and Sternberg 1993, McKeough et al. 1995, and Haskell 2001. Susan Barnett and Ceci 2002 is an excellent critical review of this massive literature.

34. Perkins and Salomon 2012, p. 248.

35. See Gick and Holyoak 1983 and Reed 1993 for general discussion, and Gick and Holyoak 1983, pp. 3–5, for more details.

36. Gick and Holyoak 1983, p. 3.

37. Gick and Holyoak 1983, p. 4.

38. Detterman 1993, p. 10.

39. Chi and VanLehn 2012, p. 178.

40. See Arthur et al. 1998, Baldwin and Ford 1988, Cormier and Hagman 1987, and L. Burke and Hutchins 2007, especially p. 275. Psychologists call this "decay"; for general discussion, see Georghiades 2000.

41. L. Burke and Hutchins 2007, especially pp. 275–76, and Cormier and Hagman 1987. Psychologists call this "interference"; for general discussion, see M. Anderson 2003.

42. Ceci 2009, pp. 36–40.

43. Spencer and Weisberg 1986, pp. 445–47.

44. Haskell 2001, p. xiii.

45. Huber and Kuncel 2016. Over the last fifty years, however, the effect of college on critical thinking seems to have greatly declined (Huber and Kuncel 2016, pp. 452–55).

46. Huber and Kuncel 2016, p. 458, end their exhaustive literature review with, "The present study demonstrates that college students learn critical thinking skills, but this does not guarantee that they retain these skills long after college or apply them in other contexts. . . . Our search did not reveal any studies that followed up with college graduates to determine their levels of critical thinking skill or disposition later in life." But many of the studies I subsequently discuss in this section seem on point.

47. Perkins 1985.

48. Perkins 1985, p. 564.

49. Both maturation (youth's reasoning skills may improve with age) and selection (worse students are more likely to drop out) tend to *overstate* measured improvement. However, Perkins's results barely change after he statistically corrects for age and IQ.

50. Leshowitz 1989, p. 1160.

51. Leshowitz 1989, p. 1160.

52. Bassok and Holyoak 1989.

53. Fong et al. 1986.

54. Students who avowed little or no knowledge of sports were excluded from the experiment.

55. Fong et al. 1986, p. 280.

56. "Many previous demonstrations of people's difficulties with statistical principles are based on problems to which no subjects, or almost no subjects, apply statistical

reasoning. . . . Quite deliberately, we avoided such difficult problems for the present investigations" (Fong et al. 1986, p. 281).

57. Lehman and Nisbett 1990. One hundred sixty five students took the pretest, but only 121 took the posttest owing to attrition and changes in major (p. 955). Hence, the reported effects of education could be *over*stated.

58. Lehman and Nisbett 1990, p. 959.

59. Lehman et al. 1988.

60. Lehman et al. 1988, p. 441.

61. Quoted in Perkins and Salomon 2012, p. 255.

62. Gardner 1991, p. 3.

63. Strictly speaking, there is also a token amount of air resistance.

64. Clement 1982, p. 67.

65. Gardner 1991, pp. 152–72, Voss et al. 1986.

66. Gardner 1991, p. 18.

67. Detterman 1993, p. 17.

68. Susan Barnett and Ceci 2002 and Salomon and Perkins 1989 are two notable examples.

69. See, e.g., Haskell 2001, Perkins and Salomon 2012, and Salomon and Perkins 1989.

70. Sports medicine calls this "detraining." See Mujika and Padilla 2000a, 2000b for an overview.

71. See especially Ceci 1991, pp. 705–8.

72. Jensen 1998, pp. 333–44.

73. For a thorough introduction, see Winship and Korenman 1997.

74. See Carlsson et al. 2015 and Stelzl et al. 1995.

75. Hausknecht et al. 2007, p. 381.

76. Hausknecht et al. 2007, pp. 380–81. Commercial claims about the effectiveness of SAT preparation classes are nevertheless overstated: see, e.g., Powers and Rock 1999.

77. See, e.g., Jensen 1998, pp. 333–44, Te Nijenhuis et al. 2001, and Williams 2013, pp. 759–60.

78. Freund and Holling 2011.

79. Ceci 1991, p. 717 (references omitted).

80. Ceci 1991, p. 718.

81. Carlsson et al. 2015.

82. Keyes 2005.

83. Jensen 1998, p. 341.

84. Steven Barnett 2011, p. 975.

85. Steven Barnett 2011, p. 976.

86. Cooper et al. 1996. Most of this research focuses on "achievement tests" rather than "IQ tests," but the content closely overlaps. Math and reading questions are staples on both kinds of tests.

87. Cooper et al. 1996, p. 259.

88. Chua 2011, p. 86. Chua is approvingly quoting her daughter's violin teacher.

89. G. Jones and Schneider 2010, p. 746, partially reviews the literature. Correcting for education, estimates of the effect of 1 IQ point on earnings range from +.7% to +1.4%. Papers excluded from Jones and Schneider's overview find comparable IQ effects. Za-

gorsky 2007, pp. 493, 496, finds 1 IQ point raises the average person's income by .9%. Cebi 2007, pp. 923, 930, finds 1 IQ point raises income by .8%. Gould 2005, pp. 173, 175, an outlier, finds 1 IQ point raises income by .3–.5%. All calculations normalize to give IQ a standard deviation of 15.

90. Kambourov and Manovskii 2009 intriguingly report a high financial reward for sticking to an *occupation*, but little for sticking with a firm or industry.

91. Ericsson 2008, p. 991.

92. Ericsson, Prietula, and Cokely 2007, p. 116.

93. Ericsson, Krampe, and Tesch-Romer 1993, pp. 366, 391–92. They also make the stronger claim that deliberate practice is virtually the *sole* cause of expertise: "We attribute the dramatic differences in performance between experts and amateurs-novices to similarly large differences in the recorded amounts of deliberate practice. Furthermore, we can account for stable individual differences in performance among individuals actively involved in deliberate practice with reference to the monotonic relation between accumulated amount of deliberate practice and current level of performance" (p. 392). This research inspires Malcolm Gladwell's famous "10,000 Hour Rule" (Gladwell 2008). But subsequent work shows deliberate practice is only one vital factor among many. Starting age, intelligence, personality, working memory, and beyond are also influential (Hambrick et al. 2014, Macnamara et al. 2014).

94. McDaniel et al. 1988 find the effect of job experience on job performance is especially strong for workers with under three years of experience. For more experienced samples, the effect substantially shrinks, suggesting most workers approach their peak performance after a few years' practice.

95. In Quiñones et al. 1995, all measures of work experience predict job performance, but direct measures of the amount of practice are markedly more predictive than mere time on the job.

96. Toole 1980, p. 44.

97. Quoted in Kirkland 1964, p. 86.

98. Babcock and Marks 2010, 2011.

99. Babcock and Marks 2011, p. 475.

100. Arum and Roksa 2011, p. 98.

101. Arum and Roksa 2011, p. 98.

102. Arum and Roksa 2011, p. 76.

103. Mincer 1974, pp. 64–82, is the seminal source. Modern estimates almost always include quadratic and higher order terms to capture the initially large but gradually declining effect of additional experience on income. See especially Heckman, Lochner, and Todd 2003, and Murphy and Welch 1990.

104. See, e.g., Mouw 2003 and Ioannides and Loury 2004.

105. See, e.g., Obukhova 2012.

106. Mouw 2003, pp. 882–88.

107. Loury 2006, esp. pp. 308–12.

108. See, e.g., Montgomery 1991, Mouw 2003, Ioannides and Loury 2004, Loury 2006, Pellizzari 2010, and Obukhova and Lan 2013.

109. Marmaros and Sacerdote 2002.

110. Lahelma 2002, p. 369. Reprinted by permission of the publisher, Taylor & Francis, Ltd., http://www.tandfonline.com.

Chapter 3: The Puzzle Is Real: The Handsome Rewards of Useless Education

1. United States Census Bureau 2012a. This compares full-time, year-round workers.
2. Heckman 1995, p. 1111.
3. See Jencks and Phillips 1999 for general discussion.
4. Wikipedia 2015a.
5. See, e.g., Jensen 1998, Sternberg et al. 2001, Deary 2001, and Gottfredson 1997.
6. See the references in Chapter 2, note 89.
7. Bowles et al. 2001, pp. 1149–51.
8. Heckman 1995, p. 1111, reports that after correcting for AFQT "the returns to education sometimes fall by as much as 35 percent, but they do not go to zero." Blackburn and Neumark 1995, p. 221, finds that correcting for ASVAB (AFQT plus some other military tests) reduces the education premium by 28%. Cebi 2007, p. 930, reports a 32% decline in the education premium correcting for AFQT. Gould 2005, p. 175, reports smaller effects of correcting for the AFQT: a 13% decline in the education premium for 1978, a 20% decline for 1992. In Taber 2001, p. 669, correcting for AFQT score reduces the college attendance premium by 29% for 1982–84, 26% for 1985–87, and 21% for 1988–90. Note: Statisticians routinely rely on the approximate equality between logged variables and percentages. However, when coefficients are large, this approximation breaks down, so I convert results to percentages for clarity.
9. Murnane, Willett, and Levy 1995, pp. 257–58. However, an earlier study (Taubman and Wales 1973, p. 36) found that correcting for mathematical ability cut the education premium by only 15–25%.
10. Hanushek, Schwerdt, et al. 2015, p. 112.
11. Altonji 1995, pp. 422–23 (columns 0 and 7), reports that after correcting for these five measures of ability, the financial reward for 10 course-hours each in math, science, and foreign language falls 50%. Altonji 1995, p. 417, describes his aptitude and achievement measures and argues reverse causation from high school curriculum to aptitude is not a serious problem because "previous studies that contain information on 9th grade and 12th grade test scores suggest that 12th grade test scores are dominated by the effects of prior ability and achievement rather than by experiences during high school."
12. See Barrick and Mount 1991 for survey of the links between personality and job performance.
13. Heckman, Stixrud, and Urzua 2006, p. 418, supplemented by e-mail communication with author Sergio Urzua. The "fatalism" measure is a short Rotter Locus of Control test.
14. Gensowski 2014, p. 25. All the subjects in this data set have high IQs, so correcting for IQ *and* personality reduces the education premium by only 16%. Many studies estimate the effect of personality on earnings, but to the best of my knowledge, only Gensowski estimates how correcting for a full set of personality measures affects the measured education premium.
15. Bowles et al. 2001, p. 1164. Duncan and Dunifon 1998, the original paper that studied the effect of these attitude and behavior measures, did not report the 37% figure. Duncan and Dunifon provided the 37% figure to Bowles et al. at their request. In e-mail correspondence with me, Dunifon confirmed the estimated education premium falls 37% relative to an estimate that already controls for cognitive ability plus other background variables. This implies, for example, that if correcting for cognitive ability

and background reduces the education premium by 25%, correcting for cognitive ability, background, and noncognitive ability reduces the education premium by a total of (1− [1−.25]*[1−.37])=53%.

16. Bowles et al. 2001, p. 1155. The authors were able to determine whether the test predated or postdated completion of schooling for about two-thirds of studies reviewed.

17. Blackburn and Neumark 1995, p. 228. Neal and Johnson 1996, p. 893, reinforces this result: correcting for AFQTs, an additional year of pretest schooling has a *larger* effect on earnings than an additional year of posttest schooling. Taber 2001, p. 673, similarly remarks, "In particular, if attending college improves AFQT scores, and since students in the older cohorts may have enrolled in college prior to taking the test, one would expect AFQT to have more predictive power for the older cohorts than for the younger ones. However, at least with a probit specification not reported here, this does not appear to be the case."

18. Murnane, Willett, Duhaldeborde, and Tyler 2000, p. 559. Results converted from log dollars to percentages. The 3% figure for women is the strongest evidence in favor of reverse causation. Note, however, that the researchers used two separate data sets. One implied female ability bias of only 3%, the other 18%.

19. Cebi 2007, p. 930, uses tenth- and eleventh-graders' fatalism to predict their adult wages. Correcting for cognitive ability alone reduces the education premium by 32%, correcting for noncognitive ability alone reduces the education premium by 3%, and correcting for both reduces the education premium by 34%. Groves 2005, pp. 835, 839, shows (a) correcting for childhood fatalism reduces the education premium by 7% in the United States, and (b) correcting for childhood aggression and withdrawal reduces the education premium by 4% in the United Kingdom. See also Heckman, Stixrud, and Urzua 2006.

20. Card 1999, pp. 1843–44.

21. See, e.g., Caplan 2011b, Jensen 1998, and Harris 1998.

22. See, e.g., Altonji and Dunn 1996.

23. Light 2001 highlights another seemingly large but largely ignored form of ability bias: Most researchers ignore the work experience students gain when they're officially enrolled. As a result, they falsely attribute the combined career benefit of (school plus work) to school alone.

24. Most strikingly, the standard measure of "fatalism," the Rotter Internal-External Locus of Control Scale, is a four-question personality test (Heckman, Stixrud, and Urzua 2006, p. 432).

25. See, e.g., Bowles et al. 2001, p. 1140.

26. For a summary, see Card 1999, p. 1855. Card's article currently has over 3,500 citations. See also Card 2001. For approachable reviews, see Angrist and Pischke 2015, pp. 209–9, and Oreopoulos and Petronijevic 2013.

27. A. Krueger and Lindahl 2001, p. 1106. Alan Krueger and David Card have repeatedly collaborated, but most of their education research is separately authored.

28. Greenstone and Looney 2011, p. 5.

29. Perhaps most notably, Georgetown's Center on Education and the Workforce has published a series of policy analyses implicitly setting ability bias at 0%; see especially Carnevale and Rose 2011 and Carnevale, Rose, and Cheah 2011. The United States Census does the same; see, e.g., Julian and Kominski 2011, 2012.

30. Card's 1999, p. 1834, otherwise exhaustive literature review explicitly makes this choice: "One strand of literature that I do not consider are studies of the return to schooling that attempt to control for ability using observed test scores."

31. Angrist and Pischke 2015, p. 213.

32. See Card 1999, pp. 1846–52, and Angrist and Pischke 2015, pp. 219–22.

33. See Card 1999, pp. 1837–38, and Angrist and Pischke 2015, pp. 228–34.

34. See Angrist and Pischke 2015, pp. 223–27, and Oreopoulos and Salvanes 2011.

35. Sandewall et al. 2014, Bound and Solon 1999, and Neumark 1999.

36. Bound, Jaeger, and Baker 1995, pp. 446–47.

37. Stephens and Yang 2014, esp. pp. 1784–88. On p. 1789, the authors note that quasi-experimental studies of compulsory attendance laws outside the United States detect little or no payoff.

38. Ashenfelter et al. 1999 also discovers signs that quasi-experimental studies reporting larger benefits of education are more likely to be published.

39. For an edifying summary, see Altonji et al. 2012a, pp. 197–202.

40. Altonji 1995, pp. 422–23, columns (5) and (7).

41. Levine and Zimmerman 1995.

42. Rose and Betts 2004, p. 505, column 1. Table 3 normally reports effects of individual courses; for foreign language, however, it reports effects of having 1–2 courses or 3–4 courses. My 1.6% effect equals column 1's coefficient for 3–4 foreign language courses (5.6%) divided by 3.5.

43. Dolton and Vignoles 2002, p. 426.

44. Joensen and Nielsen 2009, p. 191.

45. Altonji et al. 2012a, p. 217. Again, I convert from log dollars to percentages.

46. Since 1.78/1.40=1.27.

47. Arcidiacono 2004, p. 347.

48. To be more precise, the effect of major on the *logarithm* of earnings falls by roughly 50%. Hamermesh and Donald 2008, p. 489, find that almost exactly 50% of the gap in log dollars disappears after correcting for an extensive list of other traits. Altonji et al. 2012a, pp. 210–15, summarize the rest of this literature.

49. See Stinebrickner and Stinebrickner 2014, Ost 2010, and Arcidiacono 2004, pp. 348–51.

50. For more detailed analysis, see Black, Sanders, and Taylor 2003.

51. See Robst 2007, pp. 402–5.

52. Robst 2007, pp. 405–6.

53. Hamermesh and Donald 2008, p. 489, alludes to this joke. For precise wording, see Villain Instructional 2016.

54. Altonji et al. 2012b, p. 8, estimates that majors in "Philosophy and Religious Studies" earn .086 log dollars more than education majors. If half of this effect is causal, this translates into roughly 4% higher earnings than education majors.

55. Assaad 1997, p. 94.

56. Gregory and Borland 1999, pp. 3580–82.

57. Mayer 2011, p. 10.

58. Borjas 2002, p. 42.

59. See Falk 2012, Borjas 2002, pp. 14–16, Katz and Krueger 1991, and Bender 1998. Bender 2003, pp. 62–75, however finds mixed evidence of wage compression in Britain's public sector.

60. See Gyourko and Tracy 1988, pp. 238–39, Disney and Gosling 1998, pp. 353–63, Melly 2005, pp. 513–14, and Katz and Krueger 1991.

61. Unions compress wages, and government workers now have over five times the unionization rate of private-sector workers—37% versus 6.9% (Bureau of Labor Statistics 2015a). Gyourko and Tracy 1988 separately examines the education premium for (a) private nonunionized workers, (b) public nonunionized workers, (c) private unionized workers, and (d) public unionized workers. Correcting for union status, the education premium is *slightly* higher in the public sector, suggesting unionization is the driving force.

62. Mayer 2011, pp. 2, 9, provides the public/private and educational breakdowns by sector, allowing computation of the fraction of college grads employed in the public sector.

63. See Mayer 2004, p. 11, for unionization rates, and Kleiner and Krueger 2010, pp. 679–81, for licensing rates.

64. See Kleiner 2006, pp. 75–84, and Kleiner and Krueger 2010, pp. 681–84.

65. Kleiner and Krueger 2010, p. 680.

66. 32%*15% is roughly 5%.

67. From Figure 3.1's "reasonable" estimate. To the best of my knowledge, Kleiner and Krueger 2010, p. 683, are the only researchers to estimate the education premium, correcting for licensing. Their correction has no effect. But even if later research finds otherwise, the education premium is far too large to be a licensing premium in disguise.

68. The 1991 Civil Rights Act also bans race-norming, the lowest-cost way to retain IQ tests while avoiding any "disparate impact" on groups with low average IQs. See Wax 2011, pp. 704–7, and W. Cascio et al. 2009, pp. 282–84.

69. Last 2013, p. 164. For a detailed, more academic defense of the IQ laundering thesis, see O'Keefe and Vedder 2008.

70. On the disparate impact of IQ testing, see Wax 2011, Sackett et al. 2008, and Murphy 2002. On the literal interpretation of the business necessity standard, prominent during the 1970s, see Committee on Ability Testing 1982, and Wigdor 1982.

71. Leading *Griggs* critics are well aware of this point: see O'Keefe and Vedder 2008, p. 4–7, 19, and Wax 2011.

72. Even the EEOC now defers to credentials. *Griggs* notwithstanding, educational requirements are absent from its list of potentially Prohibited Policies/Practices (United States Equal Opportunity Commission 2015).

73. Wang and Yancey 2012, pp. 45–47.

74. L. Nielsen, Nelson, et al. 2008, p. 7, Koppel 2009.

75. L. Nielsen and Beim 2004, p. 252, finds an average award of $1,077,953. The *median* award, however, is only $125,000. Rare massive judgments make the average award far exceed the median.

76. Twenty-three thousand cases per year * $1.1M per case * 2% chance of winning=$506M.

77. L. Nielsen, Nelson, and Lancaster 2010, pp. 187–88.

78. Kotkin 2007, pp. 144–45, reports an average settlement for 1999–2005 of $54,651, about 5% of the average trial award from L. Nielsen and Beim 2004.

79. Twenty-three thousand cases per year * $54,651 per settlement * 58% chance of settling = $729M.

80. L. Nielsen, Nelson, et al. 2008, p. 11. Other sources cite even lower figures. Between 1970 and 1989, 1.4% of federal employment civil rights cases were brought under *Griggs* (Donohue and Siegelman 1991, p. 989). Schmidt (2009, p. 9), a prominent defender of IQ testing, states, "Currently, less than 1% of employment-related lawsuits are challenges to selection tests or other hiring procedures."

81. Finicky economic theorists might deny the relevance of this evidence. In theory, the "test tax" could be low because employers fully expect to be sued if they use IQ tests, and therefore almost never do. The real world, however, is full of unstrategic litigants and capricious juries, so the fact the test tax is low given current employer behavior is also good evidence the test tax would remain low if employers did more IQ testing. See Shavell 1987 for general discussion.

82. See also Schmidt 2009, pp. 9–10.

83. O'Keefe and Vedder 2008, p. 18. The authors argue such a delay should be expected: "There likely is a lag of several years between the time a court decision is made and the time it significantly affects labor markets. And if the *Griggs* decision affected the demand for college, we should expect an additional lag of four or five years, the time between deciding to go to college and actually obtaining a degree and entering the labor market" (p. 17). But if the IQ laundering story is true, we should see a totally different pattern. Initially, the college premium should *spike*, since *Griggs* suddenly raised the demand for college graduates without increasing their supply. Since the higher college premium entices more people to go to college, this initial spike should then gradually erode.

84. Goldin and Katz 2009, pp. 84–85.

85. Weiss 1983, p. 422.

86. Terpstra and Rozell 1997, p. 490, surveyed large firms' human resource departments to ask them why they *didn't* use various hiring methods. Cognitive ability testing was the hiring method firms most often avoided for "legal concerns." However, only 16% expressed legal reservations. Firms were far more likely to avoid such tests because they doubted their usefulness.

87. A. Ryan et al. 1999, pp. 375–77, surveyed firms in 20 countries about their hiring methods. On a 1–5 scale, where 1="never uses cognitive ability tests" and 5="almost always or always uses cognitive ability tests," the average U.S. firm scores 2.08, versus 2.98 for the whole sample.

88. According to Hersch 1991, pp. 148–51, for example, firms in class action employment suits see share prices fall an average of 15.6% around the time of the case.

89. Oreopoulos and Salvanes 2011, p. 163.

90. See, e.g., McArdle 2013, Hope 2012, and Rampell 2011.

91. Ritter and Taylor 2011, pp. 33–34.

92. See, e.g., Bureau of Labor Statistics 2015b, and Falk 2012, pp. 6, 10.

93. Falk 2012, p. 10.

94. Two unpublished papers (Leping 2007, Mok and Siddique 2011) use the NLSY to estimate the effect of race and ethnicity on employee benefits, controlling for education and AFQT scores. But neither reports the effect of education on employee benefits.

95. Author's computations on the NLSY.

96. See, e.g., Card 1999, pp. 1815–16.

97. A standard estimate for the reliability of measured education is .9, implying attenuation bias of roughly 10% (Card 1999, p. 1816).

98. Bronars and Oettinger 2006, p. 29, explicitly recognizes the problem of multiple forms of measurement error but ignores it for lack of a "plausible" solution. Full-length intelligence tests have a very high reliability; the reliability of the AFQT, for example, is .94 (ASVAB 2015). Short intelligence tests, in contrast, have markedly lower reliability—.74 in the case of the General Social Survey's ten-word IQ test (Caplan and Miller 2010, p. 645).
99. Notable exceptions include Drago 2011 and Groves 2005. The reliability of full-length personality tests is roughly .8, with slightly lower reliability for abbreviated versions (Donnellan et al. 2006, p. 199).
100. On the danger of correcting for mismeasurement of a single variable when multiple variables are mismeasured, see Garber and Klepper 1980 and Bound, Brown, and Mathiowetz 2001, pp. 3715–16.
101. See especially Blackburn and Neumark 1995, pp. 222–24, and Bishop 1989, pp. 180–82. The latter simultaneously adjusts for measurement error in IQ, education, and family background, finding that "correcting for measurement error increases the estimated effect of [IQ] by 74 percent and reduces the direct effect of years of education very slightly."

Chapter 4: The Signs of Signaling

1. Epigraph: International Lyrics Playground 2016.
2. To be fair, many data sets don't measure degree completion, only years of completed education. But nothing prevents researchers from using such data sets to see if *typical* graduation years (12 years of education for high school, 16 for college) are unusually lucrative. All the main papers that try this approach find spikes for years 12 and 16:

Table E1: Sheepskin Effect Estimates (No Explicit Degree Measures)

Data	Ave. Year 9–11 Premium	Year 12 Premium	Ave. Year 13–15 Premium	Year 16 Premium
Hungerford and Solon 1987, p. 177.				
Current Population Survey, 1978	+3.7%	+8.6%	+3.3%	+17.6%
Frazis 2002, p. 302.				
Current Population Survey, 1977–91	+5.5%	+15.1%	+5.2%	+22.0%
Lange and Topel 2006, p. 493.				
National Longitudinal Survey of Youth, 1999	+6.0%	+16.2%	+5.9%	+36.5%
Average	+5.0%	+12.7%	+5.5%	+23.1%

3. The two main exceptions: Kane and Rouse 1995, pp. 605–6, and D. Clark and Martorell 2014. Kane and Rouse measure course credits and diplomas, finding substantial sheepskin effects for men who complete B.A.s and women who complete A.A.s, but not women who complete B.A.s or men who complete A.A.s. Clark and Martorell look at earnings for high school students who just passed or just failed their high school exit

exam and find virtually no sheepskin effect for high school diplomas. For a critique of Clark and Martorell, see Caplan 2011a.

4. Here are all the main papers that "race" the financial payoff of diplomas against years of education.

Table E2: Sheepskin Effect Estimates (Explicit Degree Measures)

Data	Ave. Year 9–11 Premium	Year 12 Premium	Ave. Year 13–15 Premium	Year 16 Premium
Park 1994, p. 17, Park 1999, p. 239.				
Current Population Survey 1990	+8.0%	+18.1%	+3.9%	+26.2%
Jaeger and Page 1996, p. 735, column 2.				
Current Population Survey 1991–92	+5.5%	+17.4%	+5.9%	+39.1%
Arkes 1999, p. 139, column 1.				
National Longitudinal Survey of Youth, 1993	+6.9%	+13.0%	+7.4%	+30.1%
Ferrer and Riddell 2002, p. 893, column 3.				
Canadian Census 1996 (males)	+3.4%	+8.9%	+3.4%	+29.8%
Ferrer and Riddell 2002, p. 893, column 4.				
Canadian Census 1996 (females)	+5.7%	+12.3%	+5.7%	+35.9%
Riddell 2008, p. 26, column OLS 3.				
International Adult Literacy and Skills Survey 2003	+3.4%	+27.0%	+3.4%	+58.2%
Bitzan 2009, p. 762, column 2.				
Current Population Survey Merged Outgoing Rotation Groups 1999–2003 (white males)	+3.8%	+20.5%	+6.5%	+30.4%
Bitzan 2009, p. 762, column 3.				
Current Population Survey Merged Outgoing Rotation Groups 1999–2003 (black males)	+1.2%	+16.0%	+7.8%	+23.6%

Flores-Lagunes and Light 2010, pp. 456–57, column 1.				
National Longi-tudinal Survey of Youth 1979–2004 (starting wages)	+2.1%	+2.6%	+2.1%	+33.2%
Average	+4.4%	+15.1%	+5.1%	+34.1%
Median	+3.8%	+16.0%	+5.7%	+30.4%

Chevalier et al. 2004, p. F510, also finds large sheepskin effects for the key milestones in the British education system. Kane et al. 1999 argues that degrees are better measured than years of education, leading sheepskin estimates to overstate the effect of degrees relative to years. But in absolute terms, measurement of years of education is highly reliable (Card 1999, p. 1816), so it is hard to see this as a serious flaw.

5. Park 1994, p. 17 pools everyone with 18 or more years of education, making sheepskin calculations problematic. However, he finds one year of postgraduate education without a diploma raises earnings by a mere 1%, versus 14% for one year of postgraduate education plus a master's degree. Jaeger and Page 1996 report large sheepskin effects for professional degrees, but not the master's or Ph.D. Arkes 1999 and Bitzan 2009 find *all* advanced degrees' payoff comes from sheepskin effects. Ferrer and Riddell 2002 conclude master's and Ph.D. completion years are worth two to four times as much as ordinary years. Riddell 2008 finds postgraduate completion years are worth about three times as much as ordinary years. Flores-Lagunes and Light's 2010 results imply completion years for graduate degrees are worth more than fifteen times as much as ordinary years. In the General Social Survey, completion years for advanced degrees are typically worth at least five times as much as ordinary years.

6. These figures come from the 1991–92 Current Population Survey but are typical for all modern U.S. data sets (Jaeger and Page 1996, p. 734).

7. The diploma measures assume (a) everyone with a college diploma got their high school diploma, and (b) everyone with a graduate diploma got their bachelor's degree.

8. See, e.g., Lange and Topel 2006, pp. 492–96.

9. Light and Strayer 2004, p. 762, column 5, shows large A.A. and B.A. sheepskin effects remain correcting for AFQT scores. Kane and Rouse 1995, p. 606, shows female A.A. and male B.A. sheepskin effects persist correcting for standardized test scores, high school rank, and parental income. Kane and Rouse's sheepskin results always include these ability controls, so it is unclear whether correcting for ability makes male A.A. and female B.A. sheepskin effects go away, or if they were absent all along.

10. Arkes, 1999, p. 139, column 2, and Riddell 2008, p. 26, column OLS 6, both find *relative* payoffs for nondegree years versus degrees years stay roughly the same after correcting for ability. In Frazis 1993, p. 546, the college sheepskin effect actually gets larger controlling for IQ and high school GPA.

11. Raudenbush and Kasim 1998, pp. 48–50, reach even stronger findings. Correcting for literacy reduces the K–12 payoff by about two-thirds but reduces the payoff for high school graduation by about one-third.

12. Tabulations from Jaeger and Page 1996, p. 734.

13. Attewell et al. 2006, p. 886.

14. After correcting for ability bias, of course! You can't split more than exists.

15. Wood 2009 makes this mistake in an otherwise excellent piece: "The pure screening or credentialing theory of education does predict the sheepskin effect, as defined above, and it would be disproven by its absence."

16. For a review, see Hérault and Zakirova 2015.

17. See, e.g., Fogg and Harrington 2011, Harrington and Sum 2010a, and Vedder et al. 2013.

18. See Hartog 2000 for further discussion, and Groot and Van den Brink 2000, p. 150–53, and Fogg and Harrington 2011, pp. 54–55, for slightly different taxonomies.

19. This method usually classifies you as "overqualified" if your education is at least one standard deviation above either the *average* or *modal* education in your occupation.

20. See Groot and Van den Brink 2000, p. 154.

21. Groot and Van den Brink 2000, p. 154.

22. In many cases, government labor statisticians evaluate occupations' skill requirements. Researchers then convert those skill requirements into educational requirements.

23. Groot and Van den Brink 2000, p. 154.

24. The most prominent example of this definitional approach is Carnevale, Smith, and Strohl 2010a. For a critical exchange, see Harrington and Sum 2010a, 2010b, and Carnevale, Smith, and Strohl 2010b.

25. Fogg and Harrington 2011, pp. 56–58. While malemployment rates definitely fall during workers' careers, the problem is persistent. In a typical year, under 20% of malemployed workers switch to a job that matches their training (Rubb 2003, pp. 391–92).

26. F. Pryor and Schaffer 2000, pp. 41–45. For even longer-run figures, see Van de Werfhorst and Andersen 2005, pp. 328–29.

27. Vaisey 2006, pp. 844–46. Rodriguez 1978, pp. 61–63, reports nearly identical patterns for 1940–70.

28. Ehrenberg 2012, pp. 195–96.

29. Hard-line deniers of malemployment also often assert that even the "unskilled" jobs of the past require greater skill in our modern, high-tech economy. "The relentless engine of technological change, spurred onward by global competition, drives up skill requirements and demand for postsecondary education and training within occupations—all occupations, not just 'professional, technical, managerial, and high-level sales occupations'" (Carnevale, Smith, and Strohl 2010b). Researchers who directly study occupational skill requirements, however, find little evidence for it (see, e.g., F. Pryor and Schaffer 2000, pp. 52–59). Intuitively: while some jobs have grown more complex, others are simpler than ever. Scanning bar codes, for example, is less mentally challenging than running an old-fashioned cash register. Livingstone 1998, pp. 139–48, documents a large rise in objective skill requirements in the U.S. during the 1940s and 1950s, followed by near-stability from 1960 to 1990.

30. Joke borrowed from Vedder et al. 2013, p. 28.

31. Van de Werfhorst and Andersen 2005, pp. 322–23.

32. The main results appear in Carnevale, Rose, and Cheah 2011. Coauthor Stephen Rose generously shared his underlying data with me. Leonhardt 2011 builds on an earlier, incomplete version of Rose's underlying data.

33. College-educated bartenders and waiters are almost certainly more "polished," and hence more employable at higher-end establishments. But we should be even more hesitant than usual to give college much credit for *transforming* students into high-end serv-

ers. It's hard to believe that schooling is better at socializing workers than work itself. Ability bias (the well-polished are more likely to go to college in the first place) and signaling (employers correctly infer that college grads are more likely to be polished) are both more credible.

34. Occupational classifications available on request.

35. Carnevale and Rose 2011, p. 30. The authors then briefly acknowledge signaling but insist it only matters in the short run: "Since job recruitment can be hit or miss at identifying the best workers, employers often use educational credentials to maximize the chances of finding skilled employees. . . . However, once in the job, employers look to the production of each individual worker in rewarding promotions and pay advances. It is unlikely that employers would continue to use degrees as an indicator of performance if doing so did not consistently give them the results they wanted." See Chapter 1, section "Signaling 'Simply Doesn't Make Sense,'" for theoretical weaknesses in this position, and Chapter 4, section "The Speed of Employer Learning," for the empirics of employer learning.

36. Carnevale and Rose's omission is striking because malemployment researchers often appeal to signaling to explain their findings. See especially Vedder et al. 2013, pp. 7–9, and F. Pryor and Schaffer 2000, pp. 72–73.

37. Education's apparent payoff in nonacademic fields could also reflect mere location. Waiters in well-educated areas like New York City and Boston, for example, are unusually well paid. While the Georgetown data does not permit a test, some of education's alleged rewards could be locational rewards in disguise. I thank Greg Mankiw for raising this point.

38. See, e.g., Chevalier 2003, which finds the malemployed have lower academic ability and major in less academically demanding subjects. Robst 1995 similarly reports the malemployed have degrees from less selective schools.

39. Farber and Gibbons 1996, pp. 1026–27, column 6, and Altonji and Pierret 2001, p. 330, columns 2 and 4.

40. Lange 2007, p. 16.

41. Bishop 1992.

42. Arcidiacono et al. 2010, p. 77.

43. Arcidiacono et al. 2010, pp. 86–88. A methodologically similar study compares Israeli college graduates at the highly selective Hebrew University (HU) to graduates from the less-selective College of Management Academic Studies (COMAS). After graduation, COMAS students with high test scores take seven years to match the earnings of comparable HU grads (Lang and Siniver 2011, p. 776).

44. This is true as long as we statistically correct for IQ or other ability measures that are nonobvious to employers (Farber and Gibbons 1996, pp. 1010–18, Altonji and Pierret 2001, pp. 316–23). So we should expect sheepskin effects to gradually decline as long as employers initially know only workers' credentials, and gradually infer how many years of education they successfully finished.

45. Belman and Heywood 1997. This paper uses typical degree years as a proxy for credentials, an approach that *understates* sheepskin effects' true size.

46. Arcidiacono et al. 2010, pp. 86–88.

47. Two noteworthy exceptions: Farber and Gibbons 1996 has two measures of ability: AFQT scores, and whether anyone in your childhood home had a library card. Pasche

2009 has three measures: AFQT, self-esteem, and fatalism. An employer who knew *all* these facts would still have highly imperfect knowledge of your productivity.

48. See Hanushek and Zhang 2009, pp. 132–33, and the more detailed explanation in Hanushek and Zhang 2006, pp. 21–23, as well as Bauer and Haisken-DeNew 2001.

49. While research on this story is sparse, Heisz and Oreopoulos 2006 report the payoff for high-ranked M.B.A. and law degrees *increases* with experience, even correcting for individual ability, because high-ranked degrees lead to good first jobs, which lead to even better jobs down the line.

50. For overviews, see Bewley 1999, esp. pp. 70–75, Fehr and Gächter 1998, Rees 1993, Akerlof and Yellen 1990, and Baker et al. 1988.

51. See, e.g., Roehling and Boswell 2004, Roehling 2002, Segalla et al. 2001, Lind et al. 2000, Bewley 1999, esp. pp. 170–262, Folger and Skarlicki 1998, Klaas and Dell'Omo 1997, Akerlof et al. 1996, and Cox and Kramer 1995.

52. Bewley 1999, pp. 70–85.

53. Bewley 1999, pp. 153–69.

54. Altonji and Pierret 1998, p. 187. Calculations based on the 0.5 and .75 columns of their table 8.7's Mixed Model block.

55. Lange 2007, pp. 28–32. Pasche 2009 extends Lange's approach to employer learning for both cognitive and noncognitive ability, estimating lifetime human capital/signaling splits ranging from 39/61 to 95/5. At Lange's preferred 5% interest rate, Pasche's lifetime human capital/signaling splits range from 59/41 to 78/22.

56. Instead of building on the interaction between pay, experience, education, and ability, Fang 2006, p. 1180, relies on a complex theoretical model that yields a human capital/signaling breakdown of 70/30 for young college graduates, and 75/25 for older college graduates.

57. Start with Altonji and Pierret 1998, p. 187, table 8.7. Suppose the initial human capital/signaling split is 50/50. If the weight on productivity after 15 years experience is only .25, then lifetime signaling share is at least 43%.

Lange 2007's estimates, similarly, sharply depend on his preference for a 5% interest rate. With a more typical 3% interest rate, signaling would account for 26–47% of the education premium. In Lange's model, low interest rates counterintuitively imply a *larger* role for signaling because he assumes "workers choose schooling in order to maximize the present value of lifetime earnings" (2007, p. 3).

58. Education's personal and national effects also diverge if schools successfully teach socially wasteful skills (Wolf 2002, Pritchett 2001, pp. 382–84). Picture schools for crime, extracting bribes, suing competitors, or lobbying for bailouts. Given global schools' limited success in their core literacy/numeracy mission (Pritchett 2013), though, it's hard to believe they dramatically improve antisocial prowess. I thank David Balan for raising this issue.

59. Labor economists call the effect of personal education on personal income the "Micro-Mincer return to education," and the effect of national education on national income the "Macro-Mincer return to education." For introductions, see Pritchett 2006, and A. Krueger and Lindahl 2001.

60. OECD 2014, p. 146.

61. See D. Krueger et al. 2010, p. 4, and Acemoglu 2003, p. F123.

62. Trostel et al. 2002, p. 5. The Philippines has unusually low income and an unusually high education premium. If you drop it from the sample, the U.S. stands out even more.

63. Psacharopoulos and Patrinos 2004, p. 115, table 3.

64. Like almost all international studies of the education premium, Psacharopoulos and Patrinos 2004 fails to correct for any form of ability bias. Assuming ability bias is equally severe around the globe, the true education premium is at least 25% smaller than it looks. Hanushek and Zhang 2009, pp. 133–35, using data for the U.S., Chile, and eleven European countries, finds correcting for cognitive ability and family background cuts the education premium by 39%.

65. For overviews, see Pritchett 2006, Bosworth and Collins 2003, and A. Krueger and Lindahl 2001.

66. See, e.g., Pritchett 2001, pp. 367–91, Islam 1995, and Benhabib and Spiegel 1994.

67. A. Krueger and Lindahl 2001, p. 1125, columns (2), (3), and (5).

68. For a survey, see Lange and Topel 2006, pp. 462–70.

69. One major exception: D. Cohen and Soto 2007 emphasizes the high quality of their data and the low uncertainty of their results. But even their findings dramatically hinge on their sample. When they look at 59 countries over 1960–90, a year of education raises national income by 4.9%. When they look at 81 countries over 1970–90, a year of education raises national income by 9.0% (D. Cohen and Soto 2007, p. 68, columns 5 and 10).

70. De la Fuente and Doménech 2006a. De la Fuente kindly shared their unpublished appendix (de la Fuente and Doménech 2006b) reporting the measured effect of national education on national income.

71. Education measure #6 comes from D. Cohen and Soto 2007. Education measure #7 comes from de la Fuente and Doménech 2000. Education measure #8 comes from de la Fuente and Doménech 2006a.

72. Bosworth and Collins 2003, p. 140. The latest entry in the great data race is Barro and Lee 2013. To my knowledge, no one has yet used their data to estimate the effect of national education on national income.

73. Bosworth and Collins 2003, p. 139, remark: "The fact that macroeconomic analysis has had such difficulty finding a positive association between increased average years of schooling and economic growth, even in those studies that control for other factors, is puzzling." De la Fuente and Doménech 2006a, p. 1, concede, "Empirical investigations of the contribution of human capital accumulation to economic growth have often produced discouraging results. Education variables frequently turn out to be insignificant or to have the 'wrong' sign in growth regressions."

74. D. Cohen and Soto 2007, p. 72, subtitled "Good Data, Good Results," is the clearest case. The authors literally call their results "better" *because* they find an atypically large effect of education on national prosperity. "Our data performs better than Barro and Lee (2001) series in the standard cross-country growth regressions estimated in the earlier literature. Indeed when our data is entered into such regressions we find that it is significant, as opposed to the Barro and Lee (2001) series." Furthermore, they treat these "good results" as a reason to think they have "good data": "The significance of the schooling variable in growth regressions is one additional test for the quality of the data" (D. Cohen and Soto 2007, p. 64).

75. To be fair, a few prominent researchers report that—at least inside the United States—education's effect on state and city income equals or exceed its effect on personal income (Acemoglu and Angrist 2001, Moretti 2004, Ciccone and Peri 2006). Since migration of abler workers to high-earning areas is far easier within countries than

between countries, I put little weight on these results. The fragility of compulsory attendance "quasi-experiments" raises more doubts about Acemoglu and Angrist (Stephens
and Yang 2014).

76. See especially Lange and Topel 2006, pp. 467–69, A. Krueger and Lindahl 2001, pp.
1112–26, and de la Fuente and Doménech 2006a, pp. 21–29.

77. A. Krueger and Lindahl 2001, p. 1125, columns (5) and (6).

78. A. Krueger and Lindahl 2001, p. 1115, explicitly makes this assumption: "As is well
known, if an explanatory variable is measured with additive white noise errors, then the
coefficient on this variable will be attenuated toward zero in a bivariate regression. . . .
A similar result holds in a multiple regression *(with correctly-measure covariates)*" (em-
phasis added). The assumption is less blatant in de la Fuente and Doménech 2006a, but
de la Fuente confirmed it in personal correspondence.

79. See Garber and Klepper 1980, Bound, Brown, and Mathiowetz 2001, and Chapter 2,
section "Underrating the Benefits of Education?"

80. T. Snyder and Dillow 2011, pp. 15, 53, reports total K–12 enrollment of 55,282,000,
total public school spending of $600 billion, and total private school spending of $49
billion. Private spending per student is $886, public spending per student is $10,853.

81. On the lack of research on reverse causation, see Sianesi and Van Reenen 2003, p. 193.

82. Bils and Klenow 2000, p. 1177.

83. Methodologically, the authors rely on a host of conventional but rarely tested mathematical assumptions. Substantively, the authors implausibly assume countries increase
education spending not because they *had* income growth, but because they *foresee* income growth.

84. See Lange and Topel 2006, pp. 466–49, 482–88, and A. Krueger and Lindahl 2001,
pp. 1118–21. Most researchers prefer to interpret this as evidence that measurement
error is less serious over long time horizons. But A. Krueger and Lindahl 2001, p. 1120,
admit their findings could also reveal reverse causation: "It is plausible that simultaneity
bias [reverse causation] is greater over longer time intervals, so some combination of
varying measurement error bias and simultaneity bias could account for the time pattern of results." Caveat: both research teams ignore physical capital in these estimates,
heavily inflating education's apparent import.

85. What if we make some plausible corrections? A conservative correction for ability
bias pares the personal premium down to 6–9%. A conservative correction for reverse
causation pares the national premium down to 1–2%. The range remains large, but signaling always outshines human capital.

86. See especially Pritchett 2006.

87. *Los Angeles Times* 2016. Since value-added is measured in relative terms, the "least
effective" teachers correspondingly *reduce* their students' scores.

88. Chetty, Friedman, Hilger, et al. 2011. For a partial critique, personally fact-checked
by Chetty, see Caplan 2011e.

89. Chetty, Friedman, and Rockoff 2014. For a critique, see J. Rothstein 2015.

90. See Hanushek, Peterson, and Woessmann 2013 for an introduction, and Hanushek
and Woessmann 2008 for more technical discussion.

91. Hanushek and Kimko 2000. Hanushek, Peterson, and Woessmann 2013, pp. 21–25,
reports *no* effect of education on economic growth after correcting for national test scores.

92. Hanushek, Peterson, and Woessmann 2013, pp. 59–66.

93. Hanushek and Woessmann 2012.

94. See Bahrick and Hall 1991 for math.

95. G. Jones 2016 reports that IQ, like test scores, yields much bigger payoffs for nations than individuals. Schmidt 2009 documents the robust connection between intelligence and job performance.

96. Hanushek 2003, Hanushek, Schwerdt, et al. 2015.

97. Sociology has a long "credentialist" tradition—the idea that firms focus on formal credentials rather than skill. But sociologists tend to treat this focus as costly snobbery rather than a profit-maximizing response to imperfect information (Berg 1970, R. Collins 1979). Economists' signaling models steered sociologists in a new direction; see, e.g., Labaree 1997, 2012, Bills 1988, 2003, 2004, David Brown 2001, 1995, Rosenbaum and Jones 2000, Kerckhoff 2000, and Spilerman and Lunde 1991. Thurow 1972, which actually slightly predates both Arrow and Spence, straddles the economic and sociological approaches. For signaling's influence on psychology, see, e.g., Bangerter et al. 2012. For signaling's influence on education research, see Pascarella and Terenzini 2005, pp. 460–63.

98. The same goes for two of my mentors, William Dickens and Tyler Cowen. For their side of the story, see Dickens 2010, and Cowen 2013, 2011a, 2011b, 2010. Economist bloggers, however, are sympathetic to signaling (Caplan 2011c).

99. Lange and Topel 2006, p. 505.

100. Layard and Psacharopoulos 1974, pp. 989–90, one of the earliest tests of signaling, states, "The screening hypothesis implies that some aspects of a person's educational record are more useful to an employer than others.... This is the basis for the 'sheepskin' version of the screening hypothesis according to which wages will rise faster with extra years of education when the extra year also conveys a certificate." Their failure to detect sheepskin effects "is devastating, unless the hypothesis says that employers use years of education rather than certificates." In a subsequent critique, Hungerford and Solon 1987, p. 175, recounts, "A frequently cited article by Layard and Psacharopoulos ... dismissed the importance of the screening hypothesis on the grounds that several of its refutable predictions were not supported by available evidence. One of these was the 'sheepskin' prediction."

101. Lange and Topel 2006, pp. 492–95, is probably the best-developed example of this denialism. After conceding, "The existence of diploma effects ranks among the most persistent empirical findings in labor economics," they claim, "Those least capable to profit from schooling drop out before the completion of degree years." Lange and Topel then provide a careful theoretical model of their story, with zero empirical support. Stinebrickner and Stinebrickner 2012 find that low *grades* substantially raise college dropout rates, but this hardly shows that such students' job productivity improves at a subnormal rate.

Chapter 5: Who Cares If It's Signaling?

1. See Caplan 2007, pp. 148–51, for an overview of research on voter motivation.

2. J. Pryor et al. 2012, pp. 4, 43.

3. See, e.g., Krumpal 2013 and Randall and Fernandes 1991.

4. For background, see Heckman, Lochner, and Todd 2008, 2003.

5. Heckman, Lochner, and Todd 2008, 2003 criticize this convention.

6. As of January 2014. United States Department of the Treasury 2016.

7. For exceptionally thorough brainstorming, see McMahon 1998.

8. For more on double-counting, see McMahon 1998.

9. In the 1976–2012 GSS, 18-to-39-year-olds who concluded their education with their B.A. scored .61 standard deviations above average on the cognitive test, putting them at the 73rd percentile of their cohort. If this seems low, remember that top students tend to go on to graduate or professional school. B.A.s' average math percentiles in the NLS-72 and NELS-88 are almost the same (71st and 72nd percentiles respectively) (Bound, Lovenheim, and Turner 2010, p. 138).

10. The CPS reports average incomes for all high school dropouts. To calculate the payoff for finishing grades 9, 10, and 11, I assume the *average* dropout successfully completes tenth grade before leaving school. For recent high school dropouts, this is approximately correct (T. Snyder and Dillow 2015, p. 218).

11. Chapter 3, sections "Credit Where Credit Is Due: The Specter of Ability Bias" and "Correcting for Ability Bias: What You See Is More Than What You Get."

12. Chapter 4, section "The Sheepskin Effect." Since researchers often report that the return to advanced degrees is *entirely* a sheepskin effect, this assumption is conservative.

13. Bureau of Labor Statistics 2012, p. 3, calculates a cash/benefits breakdown of 69.4% /30.6% for all civilian workers, making benefits 44% of monetary compensation.

14. See Falk 2012, pp. 6, 10.

15. To follow my procedure, let's walk through one case. In the 2011 census, average year-round, full-time earnings are $46,038 for male high school grads, $32,249 for female high school grads, $80,508 for male college grads, and $58,229 for female college grads. Since our Good Student is equally likely to be male as female, average high school earnings are $39,144 for high school grads, $69,369 for college grads. The observed college premium is therefore 77.2%. Correcting for 45% ability bias, however, tells us that the true premium is only .55*77.2%=42.5%. Now recall my sheepskin assumption that each of the first three years raises earnings by equal percentages, and graduation provides 6.7 as much as a regular year. Given annual compounding, this implies that each of the first three years raises income by 4%, and the last year multiplies income by 26.7%, a cumulative 42.5% increase.

16. See Falk 2012, pp. 6, 10. The private sector benefit/income ratio is .46 for workers with high school or less, .43 for workers with bachelor's degrees, and .41 for workers with master's degrees.

17. In the CPS, "full-time" workers can be unemployed, but "year-round workers" must work 50–52 weeks per year. Bureau of Labor Statistics 2015j, p. 3.

18. See especially Greenstone and Looney 2011, 2012.

19. For further discussion, see Caplan 2014a.

20. All rates come from the Federal Reserve Bank of St. Louis (FRED) website for unemployment of labor force participants aged 25–64. Variable identifiers LNU04027675, LNU04027676, CGBD2564M, and CGMD2564M for men, and LNU04027679, LNU04027680, CGBD2564W, and CGMD2564W for women. Calculations continue to assume a 50/50 gender balance. I use average 2000–2013 unemployment because 2011 unemployment was atypically high owing to the Great Recession.

21. See Ritter and Taylor 2011 and Riddell and Song 2011.

22. Internal Revenue Service 2011, p. 273. Owing to the progressivity of the tax code (Congressional Budget Office 2013), taxes on average earnings are lower than average

taxes, so this modestly understates how much taxes depress education's return. Payroll taxes were temporarily reduced by 2 percentage points in 2011, but I use the standard 7.65% rate in my calculations.

23. For single, childless individuals, the 2011 Earned Income Tax Credit eligibility cut-off was $13,660 in adjusted gross income (Internal Revenue Service 2015). Furthermore, single, childless adults younger than 25 or over 65 are ineligible for the EITC (Internal Revenue Service 2016). Even after the passage of the Affordable Care Act, childless full-time workers are almost always ineligible for Medicaid (Kaiser Family Foundation 2013, Sebelius 2012).

24. According to Stone and Chen 2014, "the average unemployment benefit was about $300 per week in 2010, 2011, and 2012."

25. Eligibility rules also vary by state. For practical purposes, workers normally need at least two quarters of full-time employment to qualify, with reduced benefits if they have less than four quarters of full-time employment (United States Department of Labor 2014). My calculations assume workers are eligible for unemployment benefits after one full-time year in the labor force.

26. See Fabra and Camisón 2009, pp. 601–2, for a review of research on education's effect on job satisfaction. Oreopoulos and Salvanes 2011, pp. 163–64, is a noteworthy exception; in the General Social Survey, they find college grads are about 3 percentage points more likely than high school grads to be satisfied with their jobs *after* correcting for income.

27. See, e.g., Ferrante 2009, Fabra and Camisón 2009, and A. Clark and Oswald 1996. Ganzach 2003 finds correcting for intelligence but *not* income, education reduces pay satisfaction but not intrinsic or overall job satisfaction.

28. See, e.g., Argyle 1999, p. 355.

29. See Oreopoulos and Salvanes 2011, pp. 160–61. Di Tella et al. 2001, p. 340, finds a smaller effect.

30. Helliwell 2003. In the General Social Survey, the effect of education on happiness disappears after correcting for income and health but reappears correcting for intelligence. In any case, the effect is miniscule.

31. Yazzie-Mintz 2010, pp. 6–7.

32. Larson and Richards 1991, pp. 427–29.

33. Bridgeland et al. 2006, pp. 3–4; see also Eckstein and Wolpin 1999. For frank interviews with "at-risk" high school students, see Farrell et al. 1988.

34. Mann and Robinson 2009, pp. 249–50.

35. See Romer 1993, pp. 168–70.

36. Simpsons Archive 1997.

37. A. Krueger et al. 2009, p. 47.

38. Csikszentmihalyi and Hunter 2003 report similar results.

39. See, e.g., Cutler and Lleras-Muney 2008, p. 39, and Ross and Mirowsky 1999. Sporadic counterexamples include Liu, Buka, Kubzansky, et al. 2013, Liu, Buka, Linkletter, et al. 2011, and Backlund et al. 1999.

40. See especially Cutler and Lleras-Muney 2008, Deaton and Paxson 2001, Backlund et al. 1999, and Elo and Preston 1996.

41. Mortality studies normally report the effect of education on mortality risk. I then simulate the implications for life expectancy using standard U.S. Census tables for life expectancy. For example, according to Deaton and Paxson 2001, a year of education

reduces mortality by 1.2 percent after correcting for income. To calculate the effect of an extra year of education on life expectancy, I multiply observed mortality statistics by $(1-.012)=.988$, then subtract actual life expectancy from simulated life expectancy.

42. Lantz et al. 1998. Without adjusting for lifestyle, this study gets the usual result that more education leads to longer life. Either way, education has no statistically significant effect on mortality.

43. Lleras-Muney 2005, p. 215. Note these results do not control for income.

44. Backlund et al. 1999.

45. The rule, to repeat, is that poor measurement *conceals* true importance; see Chapter 3, section "Underrating the Benefits of Education?"

46. See, e.g., A. Case et al. 2005, and Smith 1999.

47. See, e.g., Cutler and Lleras-Muney 2010.

48. See, e.g., Cutler and Lleras-Muney 2010, pp. 9–11, and 2008, pp. 47–48. The measured effect of health knowledge is small despite the fact that none of the leading data sets measure both health knowledge and IQ. Since IQ has a strong effect on health behavior, health knowledge likely has *zero* effect on health behavior, correcting for IQ.

49. See, e.g., Quesnel-Vallée 2007, and DeSalvo et al. 2006.

50. Author's calculations, from a regression of GSS variable identifier HEALTH on real family income (log of CONINC), years of education, IQ, age, age squared, year, race, and gender.

51. For the high estimate, see Ross and Wu 1995, p. 732, equation 3. For the low estimate, see Leigh 1983, p. 232, last column. Other leading studies that estimate the effect of education on self-rated health, correcting for income, demographics, and other confounds include Van der Pol 2011, Cutler and Lleras-Muney 2008, and Ross and Mirowsky 1999.

52. See generally Smith 1999.

53. In Ross and Mirowsky 1999, pp. 453–54, the effect of a year of education on a five-step scale falls from .03 to .02 after correcting for smoking, drinking, obesity, and exercise. In Ross and Wu 1995, pp. 731–32, correcting for smoking and exercise cuts the effect of a year of education on a five-step scale from .04 to .03 (for 1990 data) and from .07 to .05 (for 1979 data).

54. See, e.g., Braithwaite et al. 2008, and Murphy and Topel 2006.

55. Researchers also estimate the effect of a year of education on people's Quality-Adjusted Life Years, or "QALYs." A major literature review averaging over all this research finds one year of education yields between .036 and .061 QALYs. See Furnée et al. 2008.

56. Phillips Exeter Academy 2015.

57. Harvard College 2015.

58. In 2011, average official tuition and fees for four-year public colleges were $8,244, plus another $1,168 for books and supplies. In the same year, average financial aid—scholarships, grants, and tax benefits but not student loans—came to $5,750 (S. Baum and Ma 2011, p. 6).

59. S. Baum and Ma 2011, p. 15.

60. Looking at all full-time post-B.A. students, over 85% receive some financial aid, 24% receive fellowships or grants, and a lucky 12% get tuition waivers. Ph.D. funding

is especially ample: at public universities, almost 40% of doctoral students get tuition waivers (T. Snyder and Dillow 2013, p. 562).

61. In addition to Mincer 1974, see Munasinghe et al. 2008, Belzil and Hansen 2002, Goldsmith and Veum 2002, Altonji and Williams 1998, Neumark and Taubman 1995, and Topel 1991. Dickens and Lang 1985 find an unusually low linear return to experience of 1.0–1.3%.

62. For detailed discussions of the nonlinearity of the return to experience, see especially Heckman, Lochner, and Todd 2003 and Murphy and Welch 1990.

63. Replacing a constant 2.5% experience premium with a typical quadratic premium (.08 coefficient on experience, −.01 on experience squared) cuts measured returns by about 1 percentage point for each year of high school and half a percentage point for college graduation and raises measured returns by about .7 percentage points for each year of a master's degree.

64. Because .95*1.1+.05*0=1.045, a return of 4.5%. Arithmetically, inflation makes this effect even more severe. If inflation is 3% and a bank charges 10% interest, a 5% default rate cuts the bank's real return from 7% to 1.5%.

65. While most labor economists ignore this point, there are noteworthy exceptions: the seminal Altonji 1993, and, more recently, Webber 2016, Hendricks and Leukhina 2014, M. Johnson 2013, Athreya and Eberly 2013, 2010, Stange 2012, Chatterjee and Ionescu 2012, and Akyol and Athreya 2005. Hartog and Diaz-Serrano 2015 discuss economists' neglect of educational risk.

66. See the Technical Appendix for references.

67. A constant failure rate is mildly inaccurate for high school, where dropout rates continuously rise. During the 2009–10 school year, 2.6% of ninth-graders, 3% of tenth-graders, 3.3% of eleventh-graders, and 5.1% of twelfth-graders officially dropped out (T. Snyder and Dillow 2013, p. 193). The dropout rate for college students, in contrast, genuinely looks fairly constant. See especially Berkner et al. 2003.

68. The Degree Return is the expected annualized return for full-time students who continuously pursue a degree until they either graduate or *fail* to successfully complete a year of their program.

69. Caplan 2017.

70. See, for example, GSS cognitive test results by educational attainment:

Table E3: Cognitive Ability by Education in the General Social Survey (1972–2012)

Education	Average Score (in Standard Deviations)	Percentile
Dropout	−0.71	24th
H.S. Grad	−0.22	41st
B.A.	0.61	73rd
Advanced Degree	0.91	82nd
Average	0.00	50th
Results for 18-to-39-year-olds.		

71. See, e.g., Greenstone and Looney 2011, 2012, 2013, Carnevale and Rose 2011, and Carnevale, Rose, and Cheah 2011. Card 2002, 2001, 1999 avoid advocacy but repeat-

edly affirm that marginal students gain at least as much from education as high-ability students.

72. This does not mean, however, that traditional high school is the *best* option for Fair or Poor students. Learning a trade may give them a richer return. See Chapter 8, section "Why Vocational Education Rules."

73. For details, see Chapter 3, section "Wheat versus Chaff?"

74. Altonji et al. 2012a separately reports earnings for men and women. Since their estimates for both genders are almost identical, however, my calculations just use their estimates for males. T. Snyder and Dillow 2013, pp. 649–51 show unemployment by major. Fine artists' rates were 54% higher, and electrical engineers' rates 23% lower, than the average college graduate's.

What about completion? Counterintuitively, researchers have *not* found "hard" majors have lower completion probabilities than "easy" ones—even correcting for students' preexisting traits (St. John et al. 2004, Montmarquette et al. 2002, Leppel 2001). Still, college students definitely *think* there's a trade-off. Undergrads with weak math and science grades routinely abandon technical majors; see Stinebrickner and Stinebrickner 2014, Ost 2010, and Arcidiacono 2004.

75. See Hoxby 2009 for a critique of popular misconceptions about college selectivity.

76. James et al. 1989, pp. 251–52. For a summary of subsequent evidence, see Ma and Savas 2014.

77. Dale and Krueger 2002, 2014.

78. Dale and Krueger 2002 applies their method to the range-restricted College and Beyond data as well as the nationally representative NLS-72 data set; Dale and Krueger 2014 further analyzes the College and Beyond data. Dale and Krueger 2014, p. 351, defend the generalizability of their findings.

79. In Dale and Krueger 2014, this result holds whether you measure college quality by average SAT, Barron's rating, or net tuition. In Dale and Krueger 2002, however, schools with higher net tuition seem to cause greater success, correcting for *everything*. Dale and Krueger 2014 reanalyzes their earlier anomalous result, concluding it was probably a fluke.

80. Most researchers lump the six Barron's ratings ("non-competitive," "less competitive," "competitive," "very competitive," "highly competitive," and "most competitive") into three broader categories: bottom schools (non- or less competitive, about 30% of schools), middle schools (competitive or very competitive, about 60% of schools), and top schools (highly or most competitive, about 10% of schools). Zhang 2005, p. 579, finds graduates from top public and private schools earn 19–20% more than comparable graduates from low-quality public schools. Ignoring college application data, Dale and Krueger 2002, p. 1517 (column 4), finds grads from top public and private schools earn 16–24% more than comparables from low-quality publics. Monks 2000, p. 285 (specification 3), reports graduates of top schools earn 19% more than graduates from bottom schools. Brewer et al. 1999, p. 113 (annual earnings columns), finds compared to graduates from bottom public schools, graduates from top public schools earn 28–30% extra, and graduates from top private schools earn 21–48% extra. Brand and Halaby 2006, p. 762 (model 2), lumps bottom and middle schools then compares them to top schools. When graduates of top schools were in their 30s, they out-earned graduates of lower schools by only 3%. By their mid-50s, however, this gap had widened to 20%.

81. Ignoring their application measures, Dale and Krueger 2014, p. 341 (column 6) and p. 345 (column 2), report that graduating from a school with an extra 100 SAT points raises earnings by 5–8%. Dale and Krueger 2002, p. 1507 (column 1), similarly finds an extra 100 SAT points raises earnings by 8%. In M. Long 2008, p. 596 (column 1), 100 SAT points adds 2–3%. Zhang 2005, p. 586, finds top public degrees pay 6% more and top private degrees 11% more than degrees from bottom public schools.

82. In M. Long 2008, p. 597 (column 1), a $3,132 increase in net tuition raises male earnings by 4.7% and female earnings by 0.1%. His data come from 1992, so in 2011 dollars this means a $1,000 increase raises male earnings by 1.1%. Zhang 2005, p. 589, finds a $1,000 increase in tuition raises earnings by 1.8%; her numbers also come from 1992–93, so in 2011 dollars this too means a $1,000 increase raises earnings by 1.1%. Ignoring their application data, Dale and Krueger 2014, p. 343 (column 2), finds a 10% increase in net tuition raises earnings for their 1976 cohort by 0.8–1.4% (with an outlier of 0.1% during 1983–87), but with zero benefit for their 1989 cohort. In Dale and Krueger 2002, p. 1521 (column 1), 10% more tuition raises graduates' earnings by 1.2%.

83. Leading efforts to measure the premium for private schooling anticipate and handle the concern that students at private schools earn more because they come from richer families. See Zhang 2005, pp. 579, 586, Dale and Krueger 2002, p. 1517 (column 4), Monks 2000, and Brewer et al. 1999.

84. See especially Black, Smith, and Daniel 2005, and Black and Smith 2006, 2004.

85. Black, Smith, and Daniel 2005, p. 429 (columns 4 and 8, quartile estimates), and Black and Smith 2004, p. 114, (column 5, results with years of education controls).

86. See, e.g., Horn 2006.

87. For general discussion and detailed references, see Pascarella and Terenzini 2005, pp. 387–89. Alon and Tienda 2005 and Titus 2004 present typical results.

88. Heil et al. 2014 reports that, after correcting for many preexisting student traits and selection bias, college selectivity at least does not *raise* completion probability.

89. My estimates also assume college quality has the same proportional effect on unemployment; i.e., if high quality raises compensation by 10%, it also cuts unemployment by 10%.

90. Master's degree computations continue to assume a master's year costs the same as a bachelor's year.

91. All tuition figures continue to assume students live at home. Returns come out the same way if students live on campus and value the residential experience at cost.

92. United States Department of Education 2017. For details, see Hoxby 2009, pp. 17–20.

93. Unless . . . the One True Measure of undergraduate college quality turns out to be tuition. If an extra $1,000 of annual tuition raises graduates' earnings by 1%, private school with typical financial aid is a good deal, especially for Excellent and Good Students.

94. See Heckman and LaFontaine 2010, p. 254, table 3, latest cohort (born 1976–80), and DeAngelo et al. 2011, p. 8.

95. See Technical Appendix.

96. I owe this adage to Kalmijn and Flap 2001, p. 1289.

97. See, e.g., Schwartz and Mare 2005, p. 630.

98. See, e.g., Gruber-Baldini et al. 1995, pp. 191, 196, Feng and Baker 1994, p. 361, and Buss 1985, p. 47.

99. In the General Social Survey, an extra year of education seems to increase spousal education by .63 extra years. Correcting for respondent's intelligence, age, age squared,

year, sex, race, church attendance, and biblical literalism, the measured effect falls to .51 years.

100. Kalmijn 1998, p. 409, puts it well: "Some status boundaries are harder to cross than others, however. For education, the strongest boundary is between college graduates and lesser-educated persons."

101. Jepsen 2005 does however find the association between women's education and husbands' earnings has fallen over time.

102. To the best of my knowledge, the only piece that measures men's marital return to education is Bruze 2015.

103. See, e.g., Schwartz 2010, Arum et al. 2008, Sweeney and Cancian 2004, Sweeney 2002, Burtless 1999, Pencavel 1998, and Juhn and Murphy 1997.

104. See especially Goldin 1997, p. 398, and Lefgren and McIntyre 2006, pp. 799–802. Ge 2011 and Gould 2008 find marital returns increase college enrollment for both men and women, but neither calculates a dollar payoff.

105. Buhmann et al. 1988 remains an excellent survey. See also Cowell and Jenkins 1992, Van Praag and Van der Sar 1988, Danziger et al. 1984, and Van der Gaag and Smolensky 1982.

106. Buhmann et al. 1988, pp. 119–22, with further commentary at Caplan 2014e.

107. For simplicity, I assign graduate degree holders the earnings for master's degree holders.

108. Black, Smith, and Daniel 2005, p. 431, find the *quality* of a woman's college raises her own earnings and her spouse's earnings by the same percent. Since husbands continue to out-earn wives, women's payoff in the marriage market exceeds their payoff in the labor market.

109. Despite the Great Recession, 2011 rates were fairly normal by recent standards. Breakdowns by education and gender are available from 2008 to 2013 (T. Snyder and Dillow 2012, p. 620, T. Snyder and Dillow 2016, p. 750). Participation in 2011 was only slightly below average for this period.

110. In 2011, the share of age 25+ workforce participants employed part time or seeking part-time work was 9.3% for men and 21.8% for women (Bureau of Labor Statistics 2015c). To the best of my knowledge, the Bureau of Labor Statistics does not publish part-time/full-time breakdowns by education, so I assume a constant ratio.

111. In 2011, the ratio of part-time to full-time earnings for workers 25 years and over was 31% for males and 38% for females (Bureau of Labor Statistics 2015d, 2015e).

112. Revised participation figures are then:

Table E4: Workforce Participation for 25-to-64-Year-Olds, by Education, Adjusting for Part-Time Work (2011)

	Male	Female
Less Than High School	65.6%	43.3%
High School Diploma	74.2%	58.1%
Bachelor's Degree or More	85.3%	70.1%
Overall	77.5%	62.5%
Source: Snyder and Dillow 2012, p. 620, treating part-time workers as fractional full-time workers.		

113. To the best of my knowledge, only Trostel and Walker 2004 tests for (and confirms) sheepskin effects in work hours.

114. See especially Heckman, Humphries, and Kautz 2014a.

115. D. Shapiro et al. 2013, p. 36.

116. As Kane and Rouse 1999, p. 77, observe, "nursing degrees account for much of the importance of associate's degrees for women."

117. Garrison et al. 2007, p. 1. For a pointed polemic on the J.D.'s selfish return, see Campos 2012.

118. My favorite competing piece is Owen and Sawhill 2013, which breaks down education's return by institution type, college major, and occupation and discusses completion rates as a function of school selectivity. But even this outstanding piece reports returns only for graduates and ignores ability bias, including the interaction between ability and completion probability.

119. Carefully adjusting future benefits and costs by the interest rate, of course.

Chapter 6: We Care If It's Signaling

1. See, e.g., Wolf 2002, pp. 24–28, and Psacharopoulos and Patrinos 2004.

2. Signaling aside, education's networking benefits also seem largely zero-sum. Suppose Harvard grads have higher income and lower unemployment because they help each other in the business world. Socially speaking, it is hard to see how their mutual favoritism enriches mankind.

3. As an early piece on signaling explains: "if educational screening were not permitted, firms would have to use additional resources in order to sort people. Hence, any sorting costs saved by using education as a screen are a benefit to society and must be taken into account when comparing the social and private rates of return" (Taubman and Wales 1973, p. 44).

4. Spence 1973, pp. 364–68. Stiglitz 1975 and Weiss 1995 emphasize special conditions under which individuals *under*signal, but under the normal assumption that "abilities that are correlated with schooling positively affect productivity on all jobs" (Weiss 1995, p. 136), the standard overinvestment result holds.

5. Previous sheepskin calculations assume that, in percentage terms, the last year of high school is worth 3.4 ordinary years, and the last year of bachelor's and master's is worth 6.7 years, so signaling's share is 2.4/6.4 for high school, 5.7/9.7 for the bachelor's, and 5.7/7.7 for the master's.

6. What about employer-side taxes? They are already counted in the CBO's measure of the value of employee benefits (Falk 2012, p. 16).

7. Chapter 5, section "The Selfish Return to Education: The Case of the Good Student."

8. See, e.g., Beeghley 2016.

9. The General Social Survey, for example, has two good measures of status, CLASS and RANK. CLASS (asked regularly from 1972 to 2012) asks: "If you were asked to use one of four names for your social class, which would you say you belong in: the lower class, the working class, the middle class, or the upper class?" RANK (asked sporadically from 1983 to 2012) asks: "In our society there are groups which tend to be towards the top and those that are towards the bottom. Here we have a scale that runs from top (1) to bottom (10). Where would you put yourself on this scale?" Both measures confirm *average* status is very stable over time. When average income

and education rise, status attainment requires more income and education (Caplan 2014b).

10. Comparisons first regress job satisfaction (SATJOB) and happiness (HAPPY) on a constant, demographics, year, real personal income (log of CONRINC), and education. An extra year of education raises job satisfaction by .007 steps on a 4-point scale, and happiness by .015 steps on a 3-point scale. After adding CLASS to the explanatory variables, however, an extra year of education has .000 effect on job satisfaction, and raises happiness by only .005.

11. See, e.g., Sapolsky 2005, Tamashiro et al. 2005, and Blanchard et al. 1993, and broader discussions in Adler, Boyce, et al. 1994, pp. 20–21, and Smith 1999, pp. 163–65.

12. For overviews, see Euteneuer 2014, and Marmot 2006.

13. See, e.g., Wolff et al. 2010, Singh-Manoux, Marmot, and Adler 2005, Singh-Manoux, Adler, and Marmot 2003, and Adler, Epel, et al. 2000.

14. Demakakos 2008 et al., p. 338, reports that, correcting for social status, education's health benefits fall by 20% for women and 25% for men. Operario et al. 2004, p. 243, reports the health effect of education falls by 60% after correcting for status and income.

15. The .04/year estimate comes from regressing GSS variable identifier HEALTH on real family income, years of education, IQ, age, age squared, year, race, and gender. The .02/year estimate comes after adding GSS variable identifiers CLASS and RANK to the explanatory variables.

16. Chapter 5, section "The Selfish Return to Education: The Case of the Good Student."

17. T. Snyder and Dillow 2013, p. 300. Since the *Digest of Education Statistics* lumps primary and secondary education together, I assume the cost of education does not vary by grade.

18. This would *not* ordinarily count implicit land rent—the money schools could have earned by renting the land they own to paying tenants. But even in high-rent areas, this expense is fairly trivial. A high school with 1,000 students typically has about twenty acres of land (Schrader 1963). Average rents are around 5% of sale price (Lincoln Institute of Land Policy 2015). So even when land costs $100,000 per acre, the extra cost per student is only $100 per year. This sum is so small I ignore it. For further discussion, see Caplan 2014d.

19. T. Snyder and Dillow 2013, p. 89, states 13% of students enrolled in public school were officially disabled in 2010–11, the latest available year. Apling 2004 documents existing legislation is based on the "twice-as-expensive" rule of thumb and presents evidence that this rule is roughly accurate. Chambers et al. 1998, pp. 4–5, estimates a ratio between 1.90 and 2.08.

20. If 13% of students are disabled, and special education costs double, then by basic algebra ($.87x + 2*.13x=1$), spending on regular students equals 88% of average spending.

21. See, e.g., Greene and Forster 2002.

22. T. Snyder and Dillow 2013, p. 89, reports 4.8% of students enrolled in public school had "specific learning disabilities" in 2010–11, the latest available year.

23. If 8.2% of students are disabled, and special education costs double, then basic algebra ($.918x + 2*.082x=1$) implies spending on regular students equals 92% of average spending.

24. T. Snyder and Dillow 2013, pp. 298–99. Inflation adjustment is necessary because the original financial figures come from 2009.

25. See, e.g., Winston 1999.

26. To get this number, I averaged the 2011–12 institutional grants for each of the four quartiles of public four-year schools in S. Baum and Payea 2012, p. 30.

27. List price from Figure 5.10.

28. Chapter 7, section "Raising Completion Rates?"

29. See C. Jones 2005 and Simon 1996 for a review of the evidence, and Caplan 2011b, pp. 126–29, for general discussion.

30. Consider two income streams, one that starts at 100 and grows at 1% annually, another that starts at 90 and grows at 2% annually. The discount rate that equalizes these income streams is approximately 11%.

31. Chapter 4, section "The Education Premium: Personal versus National."

32. See A. Krueger and Lindahl 2001, pp. 1124–29, Pritchett 2001, pp. 379–81, C. Jones 1995, and Pack 1994, esp. p. 60.

33. As of 2008–9 (T. Snyder and Dillow 2011, p. 412).

34. On the disconnect between academic science and technological innovation, see, e.g., Niskanen 1997.

35. Chapter 5, section "The Selfish Return to Education: The Case of Everyone Else."

36. To be precise, the social benefit is "all the taxes they start paying and all the transfers they stop collecting" as a share of *productivity*, not compensation. Imagine an extreme case where your pay is $50,000 per year, but your productivity is *$0*. Regardless of the tax rate, your entry into the labor force provides no benefit to society. With a 50% tax rate, for example, society captures half of the nothing you produce.

For simplicity, my calculations continue to treat part-time workers as fractional full-time workers.

37. School attendance obviously depresses workforce participation while students are in school. But since we already subtract students' lost productivity, their depressed participation imposes no *additional* social cost.

38. Sebelius 2012, p. 15. The ACA's Medicaid expansion remained incomplete in 2011, but for simplicity I use long-run eligibility rules.

39. In 2014, maximum SNAP payments for single, childless adults were $194 per month (United States Department of Agriculture 2014). Correcting for inflation between 2011 and 2014, this comes to $2,192 in 2011 dollars.

40. See United States Census Bureau 2015 for historical high school completion rates, and Bureau of Labor Statistics 2011, 2015f for historical labor force participation rates.

41. Harlow 2003, p. 1, reports 41.3% of inmates had "some high school or less" and another 23.4% had GEDs.

42. Sum et al. 2009, pp. 10–11, reports 9.4% of male dropouts are institutionalized, 93% of them in adult correctional or juvenile detention facilities.

43. Western and Wildeman 2009, p. 231.

44. See, e.g., Sweeten et al. 2009, and Hjalmarsson 2008.

45. Agan 2011, Arum and Beattie 1999, Fischer et al. 1996, pp. 236–37, all find education matters less after correcting for IQ. Lochner and Moretti 2004, pp. 177–80, report mixed results.

46. See, e.g., Webbink et al. 2012, Natsuaki et al. 2008, Arum and Beattie 1999, Cullen et al. 1997, Jarjoura 1996, 1993, and White et al. 1994.

47. See, e.g., Lochner 2004, Grogger 1998, and Tauchen et al. 1994.

48. Webbink et al. 2012, pp. 116–17, 119, and Arum and Beattie 1999, pp. 528–32. Students' *reason* for dropping out may also be important. In particular, dropping out of school for financial reasons does *not* seem to increase crime (Sweeten et al. 2009, Jarjoura 1993). Apel, Bushway, et al. 2008 finds child labor laws actually increase youth crime along with high school completion.

49. Crime-and-education researchers chiefly rely on the National Longitudinal Survey of Youth. Since no prior researcher estimated precisely what I was looking for, I extended their work. My naive estimates regress (a) years of incarceration, and (b) ever being incarcerated, on years of education. My revised estimates regress (a) and (b) on years of education, race, sex, age, AFQT, class percentile during last year of school attended, Pearlin Mastery scores, and youthful suspensions, drinking, marijuana use, sexual activity, and running away from home. Estimates pool men and women together; if you focus on men alone, estimated effects roughly double.

50. Schmitt et al. 2010, and Henrichson and Delaney 2012.

51. For a rough breakdown, see Lochner 2004, pp. 836–38.

52. D. Anderson 1999 reports a per capita cost of $4,118 in 1997 dollars. Subtracting his cost of drug trafficking, drug-induced deaths, and drug-related AIDS cases brings the per capita cost down to $2,661. Adjusting for inflation between 1997 and 2011 yields a social cost of $3,729 per capita.

Violent crime rates in 1997 were about 50% higher than in 2011 (Federal Bureau of Investigation 2011). Relative to the last thirty years, however, crime in 1997 was roughly average (United States Census Bureau 2012c). If crime rates permanently remain at their current low level, but enforcement and prevention stay the same, the social cost of crime falls about 16%.

For other efforts to compute the social cost of crime, see, e.g., McCollister et al. 2010, M. Cohen 1998, Lochner and Moretti 2004, pp. 180–83, and Machin et al. 2011, pp. 477–79.

53. Infoplease 2015.

54. Lochner and Moretti 2004, pp. 160–61.

55. To the best of my knowledge, no published paper on education and crime tests for sheepskin effects. I therefore extend previous research using the NLSY, regressing (a) years of incarceration, and (b) ever being incarcerated, on years of education, twelfth-grade completion, and my other controls. Result: twelfth-grade completion still cuts crime, but ordinary school years do not. Lochner and Moretti's 2004 data (generously supplied by the authors) yields almost equally large sheepskin effects even though they ignore juvenile attitudes and behavior: senior year explains 80% of high school's effect on crime.

56. H. Snyder 2012 provides arrests by age. Howden and Meyer 2011, p. 4, provides contemporary age breakdowns for the U.S. population. Crime also drastically varies by gender, but I address this in the section on sex and social returns.

57. See, e.g., the literature review in Lochner 2011, pp. 261–68.

58. See esp. Brennan 2012.

59. Statistics from the General Social Survey. Variable identifiers DEGREE, PADEG, and MADEG.

60. For a long-run, global perspective on intergenerational transmission of status, see G. Clark 2014.

61. For introductions to twin and adoption research, see Caplan 2011b, Segal 2000, Harris 1998, and D. Rowe 1994.

62. See Caplan 2011b, pp. 53–58, for a review of the behavioral genetics of success.

63. Leading studies include Sacerdote 2007, Björklund et al. 2006, Behrman and Taubman 1989, and Miller et al. 2001, 1995.

64. Gill et al. 1985, Olson et al. 2001, and F. Nielsen 2006.

65. See Sacerdote 2007, Björklund et al. 2006, D. Rowe et al. 1998, and Miller et al. 1995.

66. For 2006–10, first-time parents' average age was 23 for women and 25 for men. First-time parents' age sharply rises with education, so no matter how long you stay in school, your children typically wait decades to profit in the labor market (Martinez et al. 2012, pp. 6–7).

67. Monte and Ellis 2014, p. 6. "College grads" means women with a bachelor's degree or higher.

68. See Caplan 2011b, pp. 123–36, for an overview of the neglected social benefits of higher population, and Simon 1996 for a book-length discussion.

69. Chapter 9, section "The Modern Lifestyle."

70. Caplan 2017.

71. Like the Reasonable estimates, these alternate assumptions ignore sheepskin effects. Instead, they assume education raises productivity at a constant rate within each degree program.

72. See, e.g., United States Census Bureau 2014.

73. Another reason to doubt STEM is especially socially valuable: colleges seem to use cheap majors like social science, history, and psychology to cross-subsidize expensive majors like engineering (Stange 2015, Delta Cost Project 2013). For selfish returns, of course, all that matters is what schools charge. For social returns, however, this means expensive majors' social return is overstated—and cheap majors' social return is understated.

74. Results available from the author.

75. Harlow 2003, p. 5.

76. Sagan 1985, p. 5.

77. Sagan 1985, pp. 247–51.

78. F. Shapiro 2006, p. 93. The quip's originator appears to be columnist Ann Landers (Quora 2015).

Chapter 7: The White Elephant in the Room

1. Epigraphs: *Merriam-Webster's Collegiate Dictionary* 2003, p. 1428, *Merriam-Webster Dictionary* 2015.

2. Mulligan et al. 2004, pp. 58–59.

3. Bartels 2008, pp. 12–13.

4. GSS variable identifiers NATEDUCY and PARTYID.

5. Richman 1995, Rothbard 1999, and Leef 2006 are notable exceptions.

6. Wolf 2002, p. 46.

7. Strauss 2011.

8. *The Onion* 2003.

9. See Koch et al. 2015, and Lavecchia et al. 2016.

10. See Lochner and Monge-Naranjo 2011, 2012, and Carneiro and Heckman 2002 for general discussion.

11. See, e.g., Jerrim 2014.

12. See Office of Management and Budget 2014, pp. 50–81, for national defense spending, and T. Snyder and Dillow 2015, p. 58, for education spending and GDP. The 2010–11 results are given by the 2011 column in Office of Management and Budget 2014, but the 2010 row is from T. Snyder and Dillow 2015.

13. T. Snyder and Dillow 2015, p. 61.

14. Congressional Budget Office 2010, p. 10.

15. U.S. Census figures are probably the most transparent and reliable, but international agencies report somewhat lower levels of U.S. government education spending. In their latest publications, the OECD puts it at 4.7% of GDP, the World Bank at 5.4% (OECD 2014, p. 232, World Bank 2015).

16. Figure 7.1, plus T. Snyder and Dillow 2015, p. 61. I say "at least" because T. Snyder and Dillow 2015 does not allocate the $44 billion spent on "other" spending by level.

17. Wikiquote 2016.

18. Quoted in Nye 2014, p. 101. Sections of this article are reprinted with permission from the publisher of *The Independent Review: A Journal of Political Economy* (Summer 2014, vol. 19, no. 1, p. 105). © Copyright 2004, Independent Institute, 100 Swan Way, Oakland, CA 94621-1428 USA; info@independent.org; www.independent.org.

19. Goldin and Katz 2009, pp. 293–308, estimate long-run college and high school wage premiums as functions of relative supply and some controls. Using 2011 census data for 25-to-64-year-olds, I inverted the estimates from their preferred specifications (columns 3 of their tables 8.2 and 8.4) to find the relative supplies consistent with a 100% high school premium and 200% college premiums. Why are the required changes so similar when the target wage premiums are so different? Because Goldin and Katz find college wage premiums are much more sensitive to labor supply than high school wage premiums. Unlike Goldin and Katz, I simplify my calculations by ignoring workers with some college, associates degrees, and advanced degrees.

20. A few papers, most notably Dynarski et al. 2011, and J. Long and Toma 1988, measure the effect of tuition on enrollment in K–12 *private* schools. But since parents retain the option to attend public school for free, this research tells us little about the effect of reduced K–12 subsidies on educational attainment.

21. Dynarski 2000, pp. 632–33, summarizes earlier research. When the paper was published, $1,000 lower net tuition raised graduation rates by 3–5%. Cumulative 1999–2011 inflation was 35%, so $1,000 in 2011 dollars raises graduation rates by 2.2–3.7%. For more recent research, see Hemelt and Marcotte 2011, Dynarski 2008, 2003, Bettinger 2004, and B. Long 2004. Stanley 2003 finds the postwar G.I. bill had a large effect on educational attainment, but funding was so generous and economic conditions so different the results are no longer very relevant.

22. Dynarski 2003, pp. 21–22, finds $1,000 of implicit subsidies via loans has about the same effect as $1,000 of explicit subsidies via grants.

23. Cameron and Heckman 1999, pp. 114–17, review research on the effect of credit constraints on educational attainment, consistently finding little effect.

24. Dynarski 2008 is the most obvious example.

25. Caplan 2011d calculates that child tax credits eventually pay for themselves many times over.

26. Capelli 2015, p. 132.

27. Avery and Turner 2012 critique many popular misconceptions about student loans.

28. See Gillen 2012 for a review of the idea and the evidence.

29. See Pascarella and Terenzini 2005, pp. 398–429, for a detailed review.

30. See, e.g., Astin 2005–6, and Rumberger 2011.

31. Pascarella and Terenzini 2005, p. 409.

32. Dynarski and Scott-Clayton 2013, pp. 24–26.

33. Dynarski 2008 examines Arkansas's and Georgia's merit-based programs, which cover most or all tuition for students who maintain a specific GPA. Scott-Clayton 2010 examines a similar program in West Virginia, which provides free tuition for eligible students.

34. American Presidency Project 2015.

35. See especially Labaree 2012, 1997, Marsh 2011, F. Pryor and Schaffer 2000, and Ware 2015.

36. I owe this example to Jason Brennan.

37. The same holds for private educational charity. Philanthropists who seek to maximize the good their dollars do should consult evidence-based charity evaluator GiveWell, which currently gives top marks to an antimalaria charity, two deworming charities, and Give Directly, a charity that sends cash to impoverished Third World households. None of GiveWell's top-rated charities promote schooling (GiveWell 2015).

38. The full quote is "Whenever you find yourself on the side of the majority, it is time to reform (or pause and reflect)" (Rasmussen 1998, p. 169).

39. Huemer 2013.

40. See generally Richman 1995 and Rothbard 1999.

41. See, e.g., Enlow and Ealy 2006, Friedman 1982, pp. 85–107.

42. O'Roarke 2007, p. xxiv.

43. See, e.g., Tooley and Stanfield 2003, esp. pp. 34–45.

44. Tooley and Stanfield 2003, pp. 37–38, 43.

45. Friedman 2003.

46. See, e.g., Carey 2015a, Craig 2015, Selingo 2013, and Christensen et al. 2011, though as experts their nuance exceeds rank-and-file technophiles'. See also Lacy 2011.

47. Marginal Revolution University is run by my stellar colleagues Tyler Cowen and Alex Tabarrok.

48. Carey 2015b.

49. See Caplan 2007 for detailed discussion.

50. For Social Desirability Bias research reviews, see King and Bruner 2000, and Nederhof 1985.

51. See, e.g., Donald Brown 1991.

Chapter 8: 1 > 0

1. Epigraph: K. Gray 2004, p. 131. Reprinted with permission of Phi Delta Kappa International, www.pdkintl.org. All rights reserved.

2. See especially Chetty, Friedman, and Rockoff 2014 and Hanushek, Peterson, and Woessmann 2013.

3. Chapter 2, section "Measured Learning."

4. See Chetty, Friedman, and Rockoff 2014, pp. 2671–73, and Hanushek 2009.

5. See Hanushek, Peterson, and Woessmann 2013, pp. 69–84, for evidence on U.S. test score gains from 1995 to 2009.

6. For description of German vocational education, see Witte and Kalleberg 1995.

7. See Rosenbaum 1998 for an eloquent defense of these truisms.

8. K. Gray 2004, p. 129. Reprinted with permission of Phi Delta Kappa International, www.pdkintl.org. All rights reserved.

9. Altonji 1995, pp. 421–27, finds that correcting for students' aptitude and achievement (p. 422, columns [7] and [9]), a year of industrial arts does more for wages than a year of science, foreign language, social studies, English, math, commercial arts, or fine arts. Bishop and Mane 2004, pp. 387–92, reports that correcting for student ability, background, and other traits, advanced vocational courses are more remunerative than academic courses (computer courses were initially unrewarding but ultimately the most lucrative). Mane 1999 documents that non-college-bound students profited much more from vocational than academic coursework. Meer 2007 reaches the more moderate conclusion that the technical track is better for students who are currently on it; the average technical student would earn less by switching to academics, even though the average academic student would earn less by switching to technical. According to Hotchkiss 1993, the benefit of vocational education vanishes after correcting for workers' occupation, but the natural interpretation is that vocational ed helps students *enter* higher-earning occupations.

The most contentious issue among researchers is the effectiveness of vocational education in developing countries. Psacharopoulos 1987 argues academic education works better, but Bennell 1996 insists Psacharopoulos misinterprets his own data. Bennell 1996 and Bennell and Segerstrom 1998 both maintain the social return for vocational education is at least as good as normal.

10. In addition to Bishop and Mane 2004 and Mane 1999, see Shavit and Müller 2000, and Arum and Shavit 1995. Hanushek, Woessmann, and Zhang 2011 reports vocational education raises employment probability for workers until they are in their 50s.

11. See especially the summary of research in Kulik 1998, pp. 82–93, as well as Plank 2001, pp. 22–28, Arum 1998, and Rasinski and Pedlow 1998, pp. 187–89.

12. Arum and Beattie 1999.

13. See, e.g., Kang and Bishop 1989.

14. Hanushek, Woessmann, and Zhang 2011.

15. For discussion of the stigma borne by vocational students, see, e.g., K. Gray and Herr 2006, Shavit and Müller 2000, and Arum and Shavit 1995.

16. Bureau of Labor Statistics 2014a, 2014b, 2014c, 2014d, 2014e, 2014g.

17. Bishop 1988 offers an array of promising vocational ed reforms.

18. K. Basu 1999, p. 1089.

19. United States Department of Labor 2013, pp. 3–4.

20. State of California Department of Industrial Relations 2013, pp. 8, 11.

21. Even in the contemporary Third World, however, this dark side is greatly overblown. The largest survey finds only 3% of young children (ages 5–9) and 10% of older children (ages 10–14) work 40 hours or more per week. Average weekly work time is 12 hours for young child workers and 19 hours for older child workers. The vast majority of child workers are employed by their families in agriculture or household chores (Edmonds and Pavcnik 2005, pp. 202–8).

22. Given their immaturity, a more realistic concern is that child workers will bypass low-pay, high-training jobs in favor of jobs with swift cash rewards.

23. United States Department of Labor 2013, p. 3. Federal regulations still apply when parents employ their 16- and 17-year-old children in hazardous occupations, and their under-16-year-old children in manufacturing, mining, and hazardous occupations.

24. Light 1999, p. 308, estimates young men who work 25 hours per week in eleventh and twelfth grades make 6% more 6 years after high school graduation than otherwise identical young men. Ruhm 1997, p. 767, finds that a decade after graduation, seniors who worked 20 hours a week earned 22% more than seniors who didn't work at all. Benefits were smaller for those who worked either 10 or 40 hours in senior year. Carr et al. 1996 confirms high school employment's labor market payoff persists for at least a decade. C. Baum and Ruhm 2014 report the medium-run payoff for high school employment has roughly halved over the last two decades: seniors who worked 20 hours a week in 1979 earned 8.3% extra in 1987–89; seniors with the same record in 1997 earned 4.4% extra in 2009–10. Research on the effect of high school work on adult employment is rare, but according to Carr et al. 1996, pp. 74–76, high school jobs continue to cut unemployment and boost labor force participation a decade after graduation.

Sparse research on Third World child labor finds mixed to negative effects on adult earnings (Edmonds 2007, pp. 29–30). Effects probably vary by age; one study of Brazilian child labor finds males should start working between the ages of 12 and 14 to maximize their adult wages (Emerson and Souza 2011).

25. Ruhm 1997, pp. 737–43 surveys earlier research on the academic effects of high school employment, concluding, "There is currently no consensus on whether student employment improves or worsens school performance, although the data do suggest that any beneficial effects are maximized at low or intermediate hours of work, while harmful effects are most likely for heavy job commitments." He then confirms 10–20 hours a work a week barely depresses educational attainment (pp. 766–68). Carr et al. 1996, pp. 72–74, detect similarly mild effects. D. Rothstein 2007, Warren et al. 2000, Schoenhals et al. 1998, and Mortimer et al. 1996 find employment does little or nothing to depress GPA, though Tyler 2003 detects a modest drag on math scores.

26. Apel, Paternoster, et al. 2006 and Paternoster et al. 2003 review prior research, which generally concludes work aggravates delinquency and substance use. Both papers then negate these pessimistic results by correcting for students' prework traits. Mortimer et al. 1996 similarly find little effect of work on drinking, smoking, or disciplinary problems, though *long* work hours seem to raise alcohol consumption.

27. Apel, Bushway, et al. 2008. The authors note their result coheres neatly with Jarjoura 1993's finding that dropping out of school in order to work does *not* increase criminality.

28. Bureau of Labor Statistics 2015i.

29. Bishop 1996, pp. 14–29, examines research on employer training, wages, and productivity. Unlike economists, industrial psychologists directly verify that on-the-job training raises productivity, not just pay.

30. The only major loophole is, "Employees under 20 years of age may be paid $4.25 per hour during their first consecutive 90 calendar days of employment with an employer" (United States Department of Labor 2013, p. 3).

31. See Bishop 1996, especially pp. 36–38, for discussion of other regulations impeding on-the-job training.

32. United States Department of Labor 2010, p. 1.

33. See P. Ryan 1998, esp. pp. 301–5.

34. Cubberley 1911, p. 463.
35. See Bahrick and Hall 1991, and Chapter 2, section "The Content of the Curriculum."
36. Rosenbaum 1998, pp. 75–76.
37. Technical Appendix.
38. See, e.g., Arum and Shavit 1995.
39. M. Rowe 2012.

Chapter 9: Nourishing Mother

1. Bowen and Bok 1998, p. xxii.
2. For an introduction, see Musgrave 2008.
3. X et al. 1964, pp. 174–76.
4. Confucius 1893, book 14.
5. Pinker 2014.
6. See Chapter 5, section "The Selfish Return to Education: The Case of the Good Student."
7. Internet World Stats 2015.
8. See generally Carey 2015a.
9. As of February 15, 2016, "Kim Kardashian" had roughly 135 million Google hits, versus about 8 million for "Richard Wagner" and 800,000 for "David Hume."
10. Weiss 1995, p. 151.
11. To surmount this "zero-sum" problem, peers must have nonlinear effects in the right direction. As M. Burke and Sass 2013, p. 58, remark, "policy can hope to generate aggregate achievement gains only if peer effects are nonlinear and therefore non-zero-sum in their impact on achievement." See also Lavy and Schlosser 2011, p. 4. Hoxby 2002 discusses the complex empirics of nonlinear peer effects.
12. Bureau of Labor Statistics 2013, pp. 2–3.
13. United States Census Bureau 2011, p. 448.
14. Bureau of Labor Statistics 2013, p. 3.
15. Caplan 2014c.
16. Angel 2011.
17. Wikipedia 2015b.
18. Nielsen 2015.
19. Ovum 2014.
20. Moe 2011, pp. 84–87. Unfortunately, to the best of my knowledge this is the only recent systematic data on K–12 teachers' partisanship.
21. Gross and Simmons 2007, pp. 31–32.
22. Rothman et al. 2005, pp. 5–6.
23. Cardiff and Klein 2005, p. 243. Gross and Simmons 2007 similarly report that the ratio of self-reported liberals to conservatives is lowest at community colleges, and highest at four-year liberal arts and elite Ph.D.-granting colleges.
24. Gross and Simmons 2007, p. 33, Rothman et al. 2005, p. 6. For a good survey of the literature, see Klein and Stern 2009.
25. Gross and Simmons 2007, p. 41.
26. Zipp and Fenwick 2006, Gross and Simmons 2007. Rothman et al. 2005 is a notable exception; their liberal/conservative ratios are about as high as their Democrat/Republican ratios.

27. Results from regressing GSS variable identifier POLVIEWS on a constant and years of education.

28. Chief problem with the simple approach: The well-educated are richer, and the rich are more conservative. As a result, income conceals some of education's effect. If you regress POLVIEWS on a constant, years of education, and log family income, one year of education makes you .028 units more liberal—double the estimate from the simple approach. Further correcting for race, sex, age, and year, one year of education makes you .024 units more liberal.

29. Results from regressing GSS variable identifier PARTYID on a constant and years of education, excluding respondents who support third parties.

30. If you regress PARTYID on a constant, years of education, log family income, race, sex, age, and year, one year of education makes you .029 units more Republican.

31. See, e.g., Coenders and Scheepers 2003, Weakliem 2002, Nie et al. 1996, Golebiowska 1995, and C. Case and Greeley 1990.

32. Nie et al. 1996, and Bobo and Licari 1989.

33. Kingston et al. 2003.

34. Caplan 2007, 2001, Weakliem 2002. Althaus 2003, pp. 97–144, similarly finds better-informed people are more economically conservative, all else equal.

35. Caplan and Miller 2010, plus supplementary calculations from the authors.

36. Measuring effects issue by issue neatly explains education's puzzlingly small impact on ideology and party. Since education simultaneously increases social liberalism *and* economic conservatism, its effect on "liberalism" is ambiguous. And while their social liberalism makes the well-educated more Democratic, their economic conservatism makes them more Republican, leaving partisanship nearly untouched.

37. AzQuotes 2016.

38. Lott 1990 argues dictatorships spend more on education in order to indoctrinate their citizens; Pritchett 2002 argues that this indoctrination motive explains why *all* governments produce schooling. Plausible claims, but they hardly show the indoctrination is very persuasive.

39. See Chapter 2, sections "Measured Learning" and "The Relevance of Relevance."

40. For overviews of research and some basic results, see, e.g., Burden 2009, Nagler 1991, and Powell 1986.

41. The most notable naysayers: Kam and Palmer 2008, p. 612, reports higher education has no effect on turnout after fully accounting for "preadult experiences and influences in place during the senior year of high school." Tenn 2007 finds immediately after gaining an extra year of education, individuals are no more likely to vote than they were in the previous year. Sondheimer and Green 2010 examines three sets of experimental evidence on education and turnout.

42. Burden 2009 reviews the contrast between micro- and macro-level evidence and summarizes the top contending "offsetting factors."

43. The leading defenses of the relative education theory are Tenn 2005, and Nie et al. 1996.

44. Glaeser and Sacerdote 2008, and Iannaccone 1998, pp. 1470–74.

45. In the GSS, I regressed GOD and ATTEND on years of education, the log of real family income, cognitive ability, social class (CLASS), age, age squared, race, gender, and year.

46. Zuckerman et al. 2013, after reviewing a large research literature, concludes intelligence consistently reduces religiosity, especially religious belief. Education, in contrast, has no clear effect on religiosity after correcting for intelligence. Meisenberg et al. 2012, pp. 110–13, finds a large negative effect of intelligence—but no clear effect of education—on religiosity. McCleary and Barro 2006 conclude education seems to increase *both* religious belief and behavior at the global level. Both of the latter studies find former Communist countries are markedly less religious than expected given their other traits.

47. Uecker et al. 2007, p. 1683.

48. See Ono 2009 and Torr 2011.

49. See Schoen and Cheng 2006, pp. 5–6, Isen and Stevenson 2011, pp. 111–24, Lefgren and McIntyre 2006, pp. 793–95, and Torr 2011.

50. See, e.g., Tzeng and Mare 1995.

51. See J. Goldstein and Kenny 2001, pp. 512–16, and Torr 2011, pp. 490–91.

52. See Härkönen and Dronkers 2006, and Kalmijn 2013.

53. Musick et al. 2012, Heaton 2002, Heaton and Blake 1999, Lefgren and McIntyre 2006, Martin 2004, Ono 2009, and Torr 2011 estimate education's effect on diverse measures of marital status in the modern United States, variously controlling for demographics, time trends, age at marriage, marital duration, number of children, family background, and income.

54. In the GSS, I regressed dummy variables for currently married and currently divorced on age, age squared, year, race, sex, an IQ test, and church attendance, limiting the sample to 1994–2012. Running the same regression on GSS data for 1972–92 reveals no effect of education on marriage or divorce.

55. After adding social class to the previous GSS regressions, education's effects on marriage and divorce are approximately zero.

56. See Monte and Ellis 2014, and Isen and Stevenson 2011, pp. 129–32.

57. See Balbo et al. 2013, Meisenberg 2008, and Skirbekk 2008.

58. Skirbekk 2008, p. 161.

59. Lutz and Samir 2011, p. 590.

60. See generally Meisenberg 2008 and Skirbekk 2008.

61. The initial results come from regressing number of children (GSS variable identifier CHILDS) on years of education. The corrected results come from regressing number of children on years of education, IQ, log real family income, age, age squared, race, and sex. Controlling for spousal education cuts the effect of a year of respondents' education from −.10 children to −.06 children.

62. Results from adding spousal education to the preceding regression, then separately analyzing male and female GSS responses.

63. See esp. A. Basu 2002.

64. Results from adding GSS variable identifier CLASS to the preceding regression.

65. United Nations 2016. Germany and Russia have both experienced slight rebounds, but Germany's population peaked in 2003, and Russia's peaked decades ago.

66. See Chapter 7, section "Cutting Education: Why, Where, How," for the response of educational attainment to cost.

67. Bureau of Labor Statistics 2015k, 2015l.

68. Bureau of Labor Statistics 2015m.

69. D. Johnson 1998.
70. Lucretius 1997, p. 5
71. P. Gray 2013, pp. 162–63.
72. Hofferth and Sandberg 2001, p. 206, Hofferth 2009, pp. 17–18.
73. Clements 2004, p. 72.
74. McMurrer 2007, p. 7.
75. Babcock and Marks 2011, 2010.
76. Labaree 2012, pp. 137–38.
77. G. Clark 2014, p. 280.

Chapter 10: Five Chats on Education and Enlightenment

1. I owe this question to William Dickens.
2. This is especially clear when you recall that even with 80% signaling, four years at Harvard studying finance would raise your productivity by about 25%. Poaching Harvard admittees would therefore be profitable only if Goldman Sachs paid them 20% less than Harvard grads. And what kind of Harvard admittee would forego college to join Goldman's "B-team"? Again, a misfit.
3. Bureau of Labor Statistics 2015h.
4. See the references and calculations in Caplan 2011d.

Conclusion

1. Epigraph: Shakespeare 2004, p. 71.
2. IMDB 2015.
3. See Kuran 1997 on preference falsification.
4. For elaboration, see Caplan 2007.
5. Sometimes with the amendment, "And those who can't teach, teach gym" (Allen and Brickman 1977).
6. I thank the invaluable Robin Hanson for suggesting the main themes in this paragraph.

Technical Appendix

1. T. Snyder and Dillow 2013, p. 191, Heckman and LaFontaine 2010, pp. 253–59.
2. See especially Heckman, Humphries, and Kautz 2014a.
3. Heckman and LaFontaine 2010, pp. 253–59.
4. See generally Rumberger 2011. For an encyclopedic literature review, see Rumberger and Lim 2008.
5. Stumbling block: most papers either fail to report their constants, or control for student traits (including academic performance) without reporting their coefficients. These are understandable choices given the authors' research focus, but it renders their research useless for computing completion probabilities.
6. Data sets that lump ordinary high school graduates together with GEDs include the Current Population Survey and the General Social Survey.
7. Herrnstein and Murray 1994, pp. 146–51, 597–98.
8. For example, Belley and Lochner 2007, p. 47, breaks NLSY results down by AFQT quartiles, with very similar results.

9. Herrnstein and Murray's GED results exclude respondents who obtained neither high school diploma nor GED—about 10% of the population. To derive the fraction of the overall population with a GED, I therefore multiply their estimates by .9.

10. More precisely, I plug in the z-scores associated with these percentiles.

11. Heckman and LaFontaine 2010, p. 254, table 3, column for cohort born 1976–80, reports the gender graduation gap for the latest cohort.

12. T. Snyder and Dillow 2013, pp. 527–31.

13. D. Shapiro et al. 2013, p. 12.

14. The problem, again, is that papers either fail to report their constants, or control for student traits (including academic performance) without reporting the controls' coefficients.

15. See especially Bound, Lovenheim, and Turner et al. 2010, and Light and Strayer 2000.

16. DeAngelo et al. 2011.

17. DeAngelo et al. 2011 use combined verbal and math SAT scores. I convert my percentiles to their SAT scores using College Board 2013.

18. DeAngelo et al. 2011, p. 6.

19. In NSC data, the total six-year completion rate of 82% exceeds the "first completion at starting institution" of 72% by 14%.

20. Strayhorn 2010, p. 4, summarizes the evidence. Perna 2004 and Mullen et al. 2003 both confirm strong undergraduates are much more likely to go to graduate school. The 50% graduation rate includes part-time students who almost certainly have below-average completion rates. At the same time, however, an eventual completion rate of 50% implies a much lower *on-time* completion rate. Given these offsetting factors and the sparseness of the evidence, I treat 50% as the on-time rate.

21. See, e.g., J. Rothstein and Yoon 2008, Callahan et al. 2010, and Bair and Haworth 2004.

22. Strayhorn 2010, pp. 8–13, confirms poor undergraduate performance strongly predicts graduate school dropout but does not report constants for his logistic regressions. Luan and Fenske 1996 reports constants but lacks measures of student quality.

References

Acemoglu, Daron. 2003. "Cross-Country Inequality Trends." *Economic Journal* 113 (485): F121–F149.

Acemoglu, Daron, and Joshua Angrist. 2001. "How Large Are Human-Capital Externalities? Evidence from Compulsory Schooling Laws." *NBER Macroeconomics Annual* 15: 9–74.

Adler, Nancy, Thomas Boyce, Margaret Chesney, Sheldon Cohen, Susan Folkman, Robert Kahn, and S. Leonard Syme. 1994. "Socioeconomic Status and Health: The Challenge of the Gradient." *American Psychologist* 49 (1): 15–24.

Adler, Nancy, Elissa Epel, Grace Castellazzo, and Jeannette Ickovics. 2000. "Relationship of Subjective and Objective Social Status with Psychological and Physiological Functioning: Preliminary Data in Healthy, White Women." *Health Psychology* 19 (6): 586–92.

Agan, Amanda. 2011. "Non-cognitive Skills and Crime." *IZA Conference Paper*. http://www.iza.org/conference_files/CoNoCoSk2011/agan_a6558.pdf.

Akerlof, George, William Dickens, George Perry, Robert Gordon, and N. Gregory Mankiw. 1996. "The Macroeconomics of Low Inflation." *Brookings Papers on Economic Activity* 1996 (1): 1–76.

Akerlof, George, and Janet Yellen. 1990. "The Fair Wage-Effort Hypothesis and Unemployment." *Quarterly Journal of Economics* 105 (2): 255–83.

Akyol, Ahmet, and Kartik Athreya. 2005. "Risky Higher Education and Subsidies." *Journal of Economic Dynamics and Control* 29 (6): 979–1023.

Allen, Woody, and Marshall Brickman. 1977. *Annie Hall*. http://www.dailyscript.com/scripts/annie_hall.html.

Alon, Sigal, and Marta Tienda. 2005. "Assessing the 'Mismatch' Hypothesis: Differences in College Graduation Rates by Institutional Selectivity." *Sociology of Education* 78 (4): 294–315.

Althaus, Scott. 2003. *Collective Preferences in Democratic Politics: Opinion Surveys and the Will of the People*. Cambridge, MA: Cambridge University Press.

Altonji, Joseph. 1993. "The Demand for and Return to Education When Education Outcomes Are Uncertain." *Journal of Labor Economics* 11 (6): 48–83.

———. 1995. "The Effects of High School Curriculum on Education and Labor Market Outcomes." *Journal of Human Resources* 30 (3): 409–38.

———. 2005. "Employer Learning, Statistical Discrimination and Occupational Attainment." *American Economic Review* 95 (2): 112–17.

Altonji, Joseph, Erica Blom, and Costas Meghir. 2012a. "Heterogeneity in Human Capital Investments: High School Curriculum, College Major, and Careers." *Annual Review of Economics* 4 (1): 185–223.

———. 2012b. "Supplementary Tables and Figures." http://www.nber.org/data-appendix/w17985/Appendix%20tables%20and%20figures.pdf.

Altonji, Joseph, and Thomas Dunn. 1996. "The Effects of Family Characteristics on the Return to Education." *Review of Economics and Statistics* 78 (4): 692–704.

Altonji, Joseph, and Charles Pierret. 1998. "Employer Learning and the Signaling Value of Education." In *Internal Labour Markets, Incentives, and Employment*, edited by Isao Ohashi, and Toshiaki Tachinanaki, 159–95. New York: St. Martin's.

———. 2001. "Employer Learning and Statistical Discrimination." *Quarterly Journal of Economics* 116 (1): 313–50.

Altonji, Joseph, and Nicolas Williams. 1998. "The Effects of Labor Market Experience, Job Seniority and Mobility on Wage Growth." *Research in Labor Economics* 17: 233–76.

American Presidency Project. 2015. "Lyndon B. Johnson: 'Remarks at Southwest Texas State College upon Signing the Higher Education Act of 1965.'" http://www.presidency.ucsb.edu/ws/?pid=27356.

Anderson, David. 1999. "The Aggregate Burden of Crime." *Journal of Law and Economics* 42 (2): 611–42.

Anderson, Michael. 2003. "Rethinking Interference Theory: Executive Control and the Mechanisms of Forgetting." *Journal of Memory and Language* 49 (4): 415–45.

Angel, Amanda. 2011. "Top Five Classical Record Holders." WQXR. Accessed November 15, 2015. http://www.wqxr.org/#!/story/161365-top-five-classical-record-holders.

Angrist, Joshua, and Jörn-Steffen Pischke. 2015. *Mastering 'Metrics: The Path from Cause to Effect*. Princeton, NJ: Princeton University Press.

———. 2017. "Undergraduate Econometrics Instruction: Through Our Classes, Darkly." NBER Working Paper No. 23144. http://www.nber.org/papers/w23144.

Apel, Robert, Shawn Bushway, Raymond Paternoster, Robert Brame, and Gary Sweeten. 2008. "Using State Child Labor Laws to Identify the Causal Effect of Youth Employment on Deviant Behavior and Academic Achievement." *Journal of Quantitative Criminology* 24 (4): 337–62.

Apel, Robert, Raymond Paternoster, Shawn Bushway, and Robert Brame. 2006. "A Job Isn't Just a Job: The Differential Impact of Formal versus Informal Work on Adolescent Problem Behavior." *Crime and Delinquency* 52 (2): 333–69.

Apling, Richard. 2004. "Individuals with Disabilities Education Act (IDEA): State Grant Formulas." In *Individuals with Disabilities Education Act (IDEA): Background and Issues*, edited by Nancy Jones, Richard Apling, and Bonnie Mangan, 73–96. New York: Nova Science.

Arcidiacono, Peter. 2004. "Ability Sorting and the Returns to College Major." *Journal of Econometrics* 121 (1): 343–75.

Arcidiacono, Peter, Patrick Bayer, and Aurel Hizmo. 2010. "Beyond Signaling and Human Capital: Education and the Revelation of Ability." *American Economic Journal: Applied Economics* 2 (4): 76–104.

Argyle, Michael. 1999. "Causes and Correlates of Happiness." In *Well-Being: The Foundations of Hedonic Psychology*, edited by Daniel Kahneman, Edward Diener, and Nobert Schwarz, 353–73. New York: Russell Sage.

Arkes, Jeremy. 1999. "What Do Educational Credentials Signal and Why Do Employers Value Credentials?" *Economics of Education Review* 18 (1): 133–41.

Arrow, Kenneth. 1973a. "Higher Education as a Filter." *Journal of Public Economics* 2 (3): 193–216.

———. 1973b. "The Theory of Discrimination." In *Discrimination in Labor Markets*, edited by Orley Ashenfelter and Albert Rees, 3–33. Princeton, NJ: Princeton University Press.

———. 1998. "What Has Economics to Say about Racial Discrimination?" *Journal of Economic Perspectives* 12 (2): 91–100.

Arthur, Winfred, Winston Bennett, Pamela Stanush, and Theresa McNelly. 1998. "Factors That Influence Skill Decay and Retention: A Quantitative Review and Analysis." *Human Performance* 11 (1): 57–101.

Arum, Richard. 1998. "Invested Dollars or Diverted Dreams: The Effect of Resources on Vocational Students' Educational Outcomes." *Sociology of Education* 71 (2): 130–51.

Arum, Richard, and Irenee Beattie. 1999. "High School Experience and the Risk of Adult Incarceration." *Criminology* 37 (3): 515–40.

Arum, Richard, and Josipa Roksa. 2011. *Academically Adrift: Limited Learning on College Campuses*. Chicago: University of Chicago Press.

Arum, Richard, Josipa Roksa, and Michelle Budig. 2008. "The Romance of College Attendance: Higher Education Stratification and Mate Selection." *Research in Social Stratification and Mobility* 26 (2): 107–21.

Arum, Richard, and Yossi Shavit. 1995. "Secondary Vocational Education and the Transition from School to Work." *Sociology of Education* 68 (3): 187–204.

Ashenfelter, Orley, Colm Harmon, and Hessel Oosterbeek. 1999. "A Review of Estimates of the Schooling/Earnings Relationship, with Tests for Publication Bias." *Labour Economics* 6 (4): 453–70.

Assaad, Ragui. 1997. "The Effects of Public Sector Hiring and Compensation Policies on the Egyptian Labor Market." *World Bank Economic Review* 11 (1): 85–118.

Astin, Alexander. 2005–6. "Making Sense out of Degree Completion Rates." *Journal of College Student Retention* 7 (1–2): 5–17.

ASVAB. 2015. "Test Score Precision." Accessed November 15. http://official-asvab.com /reliability_res.htm.

Athreya, Kartik, and Janice Eberly. 2010. "The Education Risk Premium." Last updated December 22. http://citeseerx.ist.psu.edu/viewdoc/download?doi=10.1.1.364.5315 &rep=rep1&type=pdf.

———. 2013. "The Supply of College-Educated Workers: The Roles of College Premia, College Costs, and Risk." Federal Reserve Bank of Richmond Working Paper 13-02. http:// www.richmondfed.org/publications/research/working_papers/2013/pdf/wp13-02.pdf.

Attewell, Paul, David Lavin, Thurston Domina, and Tania Levey. 2006. "New Evidence on College Remediation." *Journal of Higher Education* 77 (5): 886–924.

Autor, David. 2010. "Lecture Note 18—Education, Human Capital, and Labor Market Signaling." Accessed November 15, 2015. http://ocw.mit.edu/courses /economics/14-03-microeconomic-theory-and-public-policy-fall-2010/lecture -notes/MIT14_03F10_lec18.pdf.

Avery, Christopher, and Sarah Turner. 2012. "Student Loans: Do College Students Borrow Too Much—or Not Enough?" *Journal of Economic Perspectives* 26 (1): 165–92.

AzQuotes. 2016. "Francis Xavier Quotes." Accessed February 16, 2016. http://www .azquotes.com/author/26122-Francis_Xavier.

Babcock, Phillip, and Mindy Marks. 2010. "Leisure College, USA." *American Enterprise Institute Education Outlook* 8. August. https://www.aei.org/wp-content /uploads/2011/10/07-EduO-Aug-2010-g-new.pdf.

———. 2011. "The Falling Time Cost of College: Evidence from Half a Century of Time Use Data." *Review of Economics and Statistics* 93 (2): 468–78.

Backlund, Eric, Paul Sorlie, and Norman Johnson. 1999. "A Comparison of the Relationships of Education and Income with Mortality: The National Longitudinal Mortality Study." *Social Science and Medicine* 49 (10): 1373–84.

Bahrick, Harry, and Lynda Hall. 1991. "Lifetime Maintenance of High School Mathematics Content." *Journal of Experimental Psychology: General* 120 (1): 20–33.

Bair, Carolyn, and Jennifer Haworth. 2004. "Doctoral Student Attrition and Persistence: A Meta-synthesis of Research." In *Higher Education: Handbook of Theory and Research*, edited by John Smart, 481–534. Dordrecht: Springer.

Baker, George, Michael Jensen, and Kevin Murphy. 1988. "Compensation and Incentives: Practice vs. Theory." *Journal of Finance* 43 (3): 593–616.

Balbo, Nicoletta, Francesco Billari, and Melinda Mills. 2013. "Fertility in Advanced Societies: A Review of Research." *European Journal of Population* 29 (1): 1–38.

Baldwin, Timothy, and J. Ford. 1988. "Transfer of Training: A Review and Directions for Future Research." *Personnel Psychology* 41 (1): 63–105.

Bangerter, Adrian, Nicolas Roulin, and Cornelius König. 2012. "Personnel Selection as a Signaling Game." *Journal of Applied Psychology* 97 (4): 719–38.

Bar, Talia, Vrinda Kadiyali, and Asaf Zussman. 2009. "Grade Information and Grade Inflation: The Cornell Experiment." *Journal of Economic Perspectives* 23 (3): 93–108.

Barnett, Steven. 2011. "Effectiveness of Early Educational Intervention." *Science* 333 (6045): 975–78

Barnett, Susan, and Stephen Ceci. 2002. "When and Where Do We Apply What We Learn? A Taxonomy for Far Transfer." *Psychological Bulletin* 128 (4): 612–37.

Barrick, Murray, and Michael Mount. 1991. "The Big Five Personality Dimensions and Job Performance: A Meta-analysis." *Personality Psychology* 44 (1): 1–26.

Barro, Robert, and John-Wha Lee. 2001. "International Data on Educational Attainment: Updates and Implications." *Oxford Economic Papers* 53 (3): 541–63.

———. 2013. "A New Data Set of Educational Attainment in the World, 1950–2010." *Journal of Development Economics* 104: 184–98.

Bartels, Larry. 2008. "The Opinion-Policy Disconnect: Cross-National Spending Preferences and Democratic Representation." Accessed November 15, 2015. http://www .researchgate.net/publication/237653519_The_Opinion-Policy_Disconnect_Cross -National_Spending_Preferences_and_Democratic_Representation.

Bassok, Miriam, and Keith Holyoak. 1989. "Interdomain Transfer between Isomorphic Topics in Algebra and Physics." *Journal of Experimental Psychology: Learning, Memory, and Cognition* 15 (1): 153–66.

Basu, Alaka. 2002. "Why Does Education Lead to Lower Fertility? A Critical Review of Some of the Possibilities." *World Development* 30 (10): 1779–90.

Basu, Kaushik. 1999. "Child Labor: Cause, Consequence, and Cure, with Remarks on International Labor Standards." *Journal of Economic Literature* 37 (3): 1083–119.

Bauer, Thomas, and John Haisken-DeNew. 2001. "Employer Learning and the Returns to Schooling." *Labour Economics* 8 (2): 161–80.

Baum, Charles, and Christopher Ruhm. 2014. "The Changing Benefits of Early Work Experience." NBER Working Paper No. 20413. http://www.nber.org/papers/w20413.

Baum, Sandy, and Jennifer Ma. 2011. *Trends in College Pricing, 2011*. New York: College Board and Advocacy Center. http://trends.collegeboard.org/sites/default/files/College _Pricing_2011.pdf.

Baum, Sandy, and Kathleen Payea. 2012. *Trends in Student Aid, 2012*. New York: College Board Advocacy and Policy Center. http://trends.collegeboard.org/sites/default/files /student-aid-2012-full-report.pdf.

Beck, Glen, and Kyle Olson. 2014. *Conform: Exposing the Truth about Common Core and Public Education*. New York: Threshold Editions.

Becker, Gary. 2006. "On For-Profit Colleges Again." *Becker-Posner Blog*. Last modified January 29. http://www.becker-posner-blog.com/2006/01/on-for-profit-colleges -again-becker.html.

Beeghley, Leonard. 2016. *The Structure of Social Stratification in the United States*. New York: Routledge.

Behrman, Jere, and Paul Taubman. 1989. "Is Schooling 'Mostly in the Genes'? Nature-Nurture Decomposition Using Data on Relatives." *Journal of Political Economy* 97 (6): 1425–46.

Belley, Philippe, and Lance Lochner. 2007. "The Changing Role of Family Income and Ability in Determining Educational Achievement." *Journal of Human Capital* 1 (1): 37–89.

Belman, Dale, and John Heywood. 1997. "Sheepskin Effects by Cohort: Implications of Job Matching in a Signaling Model." *Oxford Economic Papers* 49 (4): 623–37.

Belzil, Christian, and Jörgen Hansen. 2002. "Unobserved Ability and the Return to Schooling." *Econometrica* 70 (5): 2075–91.

Bender, Keith. 1998. "The Central Government Private Sector Wage Differential." *Journal of Economic Surveys* 12 (2): 177–220.

———. 2003. "Examining Equality between Public- and Private-Sector Wage Distributions." *Economic Inquiry* 41 (1): 62–79.

Benhabib, Jess, and Mark Spiegel. 1994. "The Role of Human Capital in Economic Development: Evidence from Aggregate Cross-Country Data." *Journal of Monetary Economics* 34 (2): 143–73.

Bennell, Paul. 1996. "Using and Abusing Rates of Return: A Critique of the World Bank's 1995 Education Sector Review." *International Journal of Educational Development* 16 (3): 235–48.

Bennell, Paul, and Jan Segerstrom. 1998. "Vocational Education and Training in Developing Countries: Has the World Bank Got It Right?" *International Journal of Educational Development* 18 (4): 271–87.

Berg, Ivar. 1970. *Education and Jobs: The Great Training Robbery*. New York: Praeger.

Berkner, Lutz, Shirley He, and Emily Cataldi. 2003. "Descriptive Summary of 1995–96 Beginning Postsecondary Students: Six Years Later." *Education Statistics Quarterly* 5 (1): 62–67.

Berry, Mindy, ZeeAnn Mason, Scott Stephenson, and Annie Hsiao. 2009. *The American Revolution: Who Cares?* Philadelphia: American Revolution Center.

Bettinger, Eric. 2004. "How Financial Aid Affects Persistence." In *College Choices: The Economics of Where to Go, When to Go, and How to Pay for It*, edited by Caroline Hoxby, 207–33. Chicago: University of Chicago Press.

Bewley, Truman. 1999. *Why Wages Don't Fall during a Recession*. Cambridge, MA: Harvard University Press.

Bills, David. 1988. "Educational Credentials and Promotions: Does Schooling Do More Than Get You in the Door?" *Sociology of Education* 61 (1): 52–60.

———. 2003. "Credentials, Signals, and Screens: Explaining the Relationship between Schooling and Job Assignment." *Review of Educational Research* 73 (4): 441–69.

———. 2004. *The Sociology of Education and Work*. Malden, MA: Blackwell.

Bils, Mark, and Peter Klenow. 2000. "Does Schooling Cause Growth?" *American Economic Review* 90 (5): 1160–83.

Bishop, John. 1988. "Vocational Education for At-Risk Youth: How Can It Be Made More Effective?" CAHRS Working Paper No. 88–11. http://digitalcommons.ilr.cornell.edu /cgi/viewcontent.cgi?article=1431&context=cahrswp.

———. 1989. "Is the Test Score Decline Responsible for the Productivity Growth Decline?" *America Economic Review* 79 (1): 178–97.

———. 1992. "The Impact of Academic Competencies on Wages, Unemployment, and Job Performance." *Carnegie-Rochester Conference Series on Public Policy* 37 (1): 127–94.

———. 1996. "What We Know about Employer-Provided Training: A Review of the Literature." CAHRS Working Paper No. 96-09. http://digitalcommons.ilr.cornell.edu /cgi/viewcontent.cgi?article=1179&context=cahrswp.

Bishop, John, and Ferran Mane. 2004. "The Impacts of Career-Technical Education on High School Labor Market Success." *Economics of Education Review* 23 (4): 381–402.

Bitzan, John. 2009. "Do Sheepskin Effects Help Explain Racial Earnings Differences?" *Economics of Education Review* 28 (6): 759–66.

Björklund, Anders, Mikael Lindahl, and Erik Plug. 2006. "The Origins of Intergenerational Associations: Lessons from Swedish Adoption Data." *Quarterly Journal of Economics* 121 (3): 999–1028.

Black, Dan, Seth Sanders, and Lowell Taylor. 2003. "The Economic Reward for Studying Economics." *Economic Inquiry* 41 (3): 365–77.

Black, Dan, and Jeffrey Smith. 2004. "How Robust Is the Evidence on the Effects of College Quality? Evidence from Matching." *Journal of Econometrics* 121 (1): 99–124.

———. 2006. "Estimating the Returns to College Quality with Multiple Proxies for Quality." *Journal of Labor Economics* 24 (3): 701–28.

Black, Dan, Jeffrey Smith, and Kermit Daniel. 2005. "College Quality and Wages in the United States." *German Economic Review* 6 (3): 415–43.

Blackburn, McKinley, and David Neumark. 1995. "Are OLS Estimates of the Return to Schooling Biased Downward? Another Look." *Review of Economics and Statistics* 77 (2): 217–30.

Blanchard, Caroline, Randall Sakai, Bruce McEwen, Scott Weiss, and Robert Blanchard. 1993. "Subordination Stress: Behavioral, Brain, and Neuroendocrine Correlates." *Behavioural Brain Research* 58 (1): 113–21.

Bobo, Lawrence, and Frederick Licari. 1989. "Education and Political Tolerance: Testing the Effects of Cognitive Sophistication and Target Group Affect." *Public Opinion Quarterly* 53 (3): 285–308.

Borjas, George. 2002. "The Wage Structure and the Sorting of Workers into the Public Sector." NBER Working Paper No. 9313. http://www.nber.org/papers/w9313.

Bosworth, Barry, and Susan Collins. 2003. "The Empirics of Growth: An Update." *Brookings Papers on Economic Activity* 2003 (2): 113–206.

Bound, John, Charles Brown, and Nancy Mathiowetz. 2001. "Measurement Error in Survey Data." In *Handbook of Econometrics*, vol. 5, edited by James Heckman and Edward Leamer, 3705–843. Amsterdam: Elsevier.

Bound, John, David Jaeger, and Regina Baker. 1995. "Problems with Instrumental Variables Estimation When the Correlation between the Instruments and the Endogenous Explanatory Variable Is Weak." *Journal of the American Statistical Association* 90 (430): 443–50.

Bound, John, Michael Lovenheim, and Sarah Turner. 2010. "Why Have College Completion Rates Declined? An Analysis of Changing Student Preparation and Collegiate Resources." *American Economic Journal: Applied Economics* 2 (3): 129–57.

Bound, John, and Gary Solon. 1999. "Double Trouble: On the Value of Twins-Based Estimation of the Return to Schooling." *Economics of Education Review* 18 (2): 169–82.

Bowen, William, and Derek Bok. 1998. *The Shape of the River: Long-Term Consequences of Considering Race in College and University Admissions*. Princeton, NJ: Princeton University Press.

Bowles, Samuel, Herbert Gintis, and Melissa Osborne. 2001. "The Determinants of Earnings: A Behavioral Approach." *Journal of Economic Literature* 39 (4): 1137–76.

Braithwaite, Scott, David Meltzer, Joseph King, Douglas Leslie, and Mark Roberts. 2008. "What Does the Value of Modern Medicine Say about the $50,000 per Quality-Adjusted Life-Year Decision Rule?" *Medical Care* 46 (4): 349–56.

Brand, Jennie, and Charles Halaby. 2006. "Regression and Matching Estimates of the Effects of Elite College Attendance on Educational and Career Achievement." *Social Science Research* 35 (3): 749–70.

Brennan, Jason. 2012. *The Ethics of Voting*. Princeton, NJ: Princeton University Press.

Brewer, Dominic, Eric Eide, and Ronald Ehrenberg. 1999. "Does It Pay to Attend an Elite Private College? Cross-Cohort Evidence on the Effects of College Type on Earnings." *Journal of Human Resources* 34 (1): 104–23.

Bridgeland, John, John DiIulio Jr., and Karen Morison. 2006. *The Silent Epidemic: Perspectives of High School Dropouts*. Washington, DC: Civic Enterprises. http://files.eric.ed.gov/fulltext/ED513444.pdf.

Bronars, Stephen, and Gerald Oettinger. 2006. "Estimates of the Return to Schooling and Ability: Evidence from Sibling Data." *Labour Economics* 13 (1): 19–34.

Brown, David. 1995. *Degrees of Control: A Sociology of Educational Expansion and Occupational Credentialism*. New York: Teachers College Press.

———. 2001. "The Social Sources of Educational Credentialism: Status Cultures, Labor Markets, and Organizations." *Sociology of Education* 74 (extra issue): 19–34.

Brown, Donald. 1991. *Human Universals*. New York: McGraw-Hill.

Bruze, Gustaf. 2015. "Male and Female Marriage Returns to Schooling." *International Economic Review* 56 (1): 207–34.

Buhmann, Brigitte, Lee Rainwater, Guenther Schmaus, and Timothy Smeeding. 1988. "Equivalence Scales, Well-Being, Inequality, and Poverty: Sensitivity Estimates across Ten Countries Using the Luxembourg Income Study (LIS) Database." *Review of Income and Wealth* 34 (2): 115–42.

Burden, Barry. 2009. "The Dynamic Effects of Education on Voter Turnout." *Electoral Studies* 28 (4): 540–49.

Bureau of Labor Statistics 2011. "Household Data Annual Averages." http://www.bls.gov/cps/cpsa2011.pdf.

———. 2012. "Employer Costs for Employee Compensation—December 2011." Last modified March 14. http://www.bls.gov/news.release/archives/ecec_03142012.pdf.

———. 2013. "Consumer Expenditures in 2011." Accessed November 15, 2015. http://www.bls.gov/opub/reports/cex/consumer_expenditures2011.pdf.

———. 2014a. "Occupational Outlook Handbook: Automotive Service Technicians and Mechanics." Accessed November 15, 2015. http://www.bls.gov/ooh/installation-maintenance-and-repair/automotive-service-technicians-and-mechanics.htm.

———. 2014b. "Occupational Outlook Handbook: Carpenters." Accessed November 15, 2015. http://www.bls.gov/ooh/construction-and-extraction/carpenters.htm.

———. 2014c. "Occupational Outlook Handbook: Historians." Accessed November 15, 2015. http://www.bls.gov/ooh/life-physical-and-social-science/historians.htm.

———. 2014d. "Occupational Outlook Handbook: Interpreters and Translators." Accessed November 15, 2015. http://www.bls.gov/ooh/media-and-communication/interpreters-and-translators.htm.

———. 2014e. "Occupational Outlook Handbook: Plumbers, Pipefitters, and Steamfitters." Accessed November 15, 2015. http://www.bls.gov/ooh/construction-and-extraction/plumbers-pipefitters-and-steamfitters.htm.

———. 2014f. "Occupational Outlook Handbook: Psychologists." Accessed November 15, 2015. http://www.bls.gov/ooh/Life-Physical-and-Social-Science/Psychologists.htm.

———. 2014g. "Occupational Outlook Handbook: Writers and Authors." Accessed November 15, 2015. http://www.bls.gov/ooh/media-and-communication/writers-and-authors.htm.

———. 2015a. "Economic News Release—Table 1: Union Affiliation of Employed Wage and Salary Workers by Selected Characteristics." Last modified January 23. http://www.bls.gov/news.release/union2.t01.htm.

———. 2015b. "Employer Costs for Employee Compensation—September 2015." Last modified December 9. http://www.bls.gov/news.release/archives/ecec_12092015.pdf.

———. 2015c. "Household Data Annual Averages—Employed and Unemployed Full and Part Time Workers by Age, Sex, Race, and Hispanic or Latino Ethnicity." Accessed November 15, 2015. http://www.bls.gov/cps/aa2011/cpsaat08.pdf.

———. 2015d. "Household Data Annual Averages—Median Weekly Earnings of Full-Time Wage and Salary Workers by Selected Characteristics." Accessed November 15, 2015. http://www.bls.gov/cps/aa2011/cpsaat37.pdf.

———. 2015e. "Household Data Annual Averages—Median Weekly Earnings of Part-Time Wage and Salary Workers by Selected Characteristics." Accessed November 15, 2015. http://www.bls.gov/cps/aa2011/cpsaat38.pdf.

———. 2015f. "Labor Force Statistics from the Current Population Survey." Accessed November 15, 2015. http://data.bls.gov/timeseries/LFS600001.

———. 2015g. "Occupational Outlook Handbook: Reporters, Correspondents, and Broadcast News Analysts." Accessed November 15, 2015. http://www.bls.gov/ooh/media-and-communication/reporters-correspondents-and-broadcast-news-analysts.htm.

———. 2015h. "Occupational Employment and Wages: Refuse and Recyclable Material Collectors." Last modified March 25. http://www.bls.gov/oes/current/oes537081.htm.

———. 2015i. "Table A-1. Employment Status of the Civilian Population by Sex and Age." Accessed November 15, 2015. http://www.bls.gov/news.release/empsit.t01.htm.

———. 2015j. "Work Experience of the Population—2014." Accessed February 8, 2016. http://www.bls.gov/news.release/pdf/work.pdf.

———. 2015k. "Employment by Major Occupational Group." Last modified December 8. http://www.bls.gov/emp/ep_table_101.htm.

———. 2015l. "Occupations with the Most Job Growth." Last modified December 8. http://www.bls.gov/emp/ep_table_104.htm.

———. 2015m. *Occupational Outlook Handbook.* Last modified December 17. http://www.bls.gov/ooh.

Burke, Lisa, and Holly Hutchins. 2007. "Training Transfer: An Integrative Literature Review." *Human Resource Development Review* 6 (3): 263–96.

Burke, Mary, and Tim Sass. 2013. "Classroom Peer Effects and Student Achievement." *Journal of Labor Economics* 31 (1): 51–82.

Burtless, Gary. 1999. "Effects of Growing Wage Disparities and Changing Family Composition on the US Income Distribution." *European Economic Review* 43 (4): 853–65.

Buss, David. 1985. "Human Mate Selection: Opposites Are Sometimes Said to Attract, but in Fact We Are Likely to Marry Someone Who Is Similar to Us in Almost Every Variable." *American Scientist* 73 (1): 47–51.

Callahan, Clara, Mohammadreza Hojat, Jon Veloski, James Erdmann, and Joseph Gonnella. 2010. "The Predictive Validity of Three Versions of the MCAT in Relation to Performance in Medical School, Residency, and Licensing Examinations: A Longitudinal Study of 36 Classes of Jefferson Medical College." *Academic Medicine* 85 (6): 980–87.

Cameron, Stephen, and James Heckman. 1999. "Can Tuition Policy Combat Rising Inequality?" In *Financing College Tuition: Government Policies and Educational Priorities,* edited by Marvin Kosters, 76–124. Washington, DC: AEI.

Campos, Paul. 2012. *Don't Go to Law School (Unless): A Law Professor's Inside Guide to Maximizing Opportunity and Minimizing Risk.* Seattle: Amazon Digital Services.

Capelli, Peter. 2015. *Will College Pay Off? A Guide to the Most Important Financial Decision You'll Ever Make.* New York: Public Affairs.

Caplan, Bryan. 2001. "What Makes People Think Like Economists? Evidence on Economic Cognition from the 'Survey of Americans and Economists on the Economy.'" *Journal of Law and Economics* 44 (2): 395–426.

———. 2007. *The Myth of the Rational Voter: Why Democracies Choose Bad Policies.* Princeton, NJ: Princeton University Press.

———. 2011a. "Martorell and Clark's 'The Signaling Value of a High School Diploma.'" *EconLog.* July 20. http://econlog.econlib.org/archives/2011/07/martorell_and_c .html.

———. 2011b. *Selfish Reasons to Have More Kids: Why Being a Great Parent Is Less Work and More Fun Than You Think.* New York: Basic Books.

———. 2011c. "I Am Not Alone: Kauffman Econ Bloggers on Educational Signaling." *EconLog.* November 2. http://econlog.econlib.org/archives/2011/11/kauffman_econ_b.html.

———. 2011d. "Population, Fertility, and Liberty." *Cato Unbound.* May 2. http://www .cato-unbound.org/2011/05/02/bryan-caplan/population-fertility-liberty.

———. 2011e. "Teachers and Income: What Did the Kindergarten Study Really Find?" *EconLog.* October 14. http://econlog.econlib.org/archives/2011/10/teachers_and_in .html.

———. 2011f. "Proving You're Qualified; or Not." *EconLog*. December 22. http://econlog .econlib.org/archives/2011/12/proving_youre_q.html.

———. 2012a. "Why Don't Applicants Volunteer Their Test Scores?" *EconLog*. May 10. http://econlog.econlib.org/archives/2012/05/why_dont_applic.html.

———. 2012b. "Why Applicants Don't Volunteer Their Test Scores." *EconLog*. May 14. http://econlog.econlib.org/archives/2012/05/why_applicants.html.

———. 2012c. "The Degree and Origin of Foreign Language Competence." *EconLog*. August 11. http://econlog.econlib.org/archives/2012/08/the_degree_and.html.

———. 2013. "Dehiring: Win-Win-Lose." *EconLog*. August 20. http://econlog.econlib .org/archives/2013/08/dehiring_win-wi.html.

———. 2014a. "Employment and the Return to Education: The Right Way to Count." *EconLog*. January 2. http://econlog.econlib.org/archives/2014/01/employment_and .html.

———. 2014b. "40 Years on the Status Treadmill." *EconLog*. March 7. http://econlog .econlib.org/archives/2014/03/40_years_on_the.html.

———. 2014c. "What to Learn from *The Catcher in the Rye*." *EconLog*. July 23. http:// econlog.econlib.org/archives/2014/07/what_to_learn_f_1.html.

———. 2014d. "How High Is Schools' Implicit Land Rent?" *EconLog*. September 19. http://econlog.econlib.org/archives/2014/09/how_high_is_sch.html.

———. 2014e. "How Rival Marriage Is." *EconLog*. February 7. http://econlog.econlib.org /archives/2014/02/how_rival_marri.html.

———. 2017. "Education's Selfish and Social Returns." http://www.bcaplan.com/returns .htm.

Caplan, Bryan, and Stephen Miller. 2010. "Intelligence Makes People Think Like Economists: Evidence from the General Social Survey." *Intelligence* 38 (6): 636–47.

Card, David. 1999. "The Causal Effect of Education on Earnings." In *Handbook of Labor Economics*, vol. 3A, edited by Orley Ashenfelter and David Card, 1801–63. Amsterdam: Elsevier.

———. 2001. "Estimating the Return to Schooling: Progress on Some Persistence Econometric Problems." *Econometrica* 69 (5): 1127–60.

———. 2002. "Education Matters." *Milken Institute Review* 4th quarter: 73–77.

Cardiff, Christopher, and Daniel Klein. 2005. "Faculty Partisan Affiliations in All Disciplines: A Voter-Registration Study." *Critical Review* 17 (3–4): 237–55.

Carey, Kevin. 2015a. *The End of College: Creating the Future of Learning and the University of Everywhere*. London: Penguin.

———. 2015b. "Here's What Will Truly Change Higher Education: Online Degrees That Are Seen as Official." *New York Times*. March 5. http://www.nytimes.com/2015/03/08/ upshot/true-reform-in-higher-education-when-online-degrees-are-seen-as-official .html.

Carlsson, Magnus, Gordon Dahl, Björn Öckert, and Dan-Olof Rooth. 2015. "The Effect of Schooling on Cognitive Skills." *Review of Economics and Statistics* 97 (3): 533–47.

Carneiro, Pedro, and James Heckman. 2002. "The Evidence on Credit Constraints in Post-secondary Education." *Economic Journal* 112 (482): 705–34.

Carnevale, Anthony, and Stephen Rose. 2011. *The Undereducated American*. Washington, DC: Georgetown University Center on Education and the Workforce. http://files .eric.ed.gov/fulltext/ED524302.pdf.

Carnevale, Anthony, Stephen Rose, and Ban Cheah. 2011. *The College Payoff: Education, Occupations, Lifetime Earnings*. Washington, DC: Georgetown University Center on Education and the Workforce. https://www2.ed.gov/policy/highered/reg/hearule making/2011/collegepayoff.pdf.

Carnevale, Anthony, Nicole Smith, and Jeff Strohl. 2010a. *Help Wanted: Projections of Job and Education Requirements through 2018*. Washington, DC: Georgetown University Center on Education and the Workforce. http://files.eric.ed.gov/fulltext /ED524310.pdf.

———. 2010b. "The Real Education Crisis: Are 35% of All College Degrees in New England Unnecessary?" *New England Journal of Higher Education*. http://www.nebhe .org/thejournal/the-real-education-crisis-are-35-of-all-college-degrees-in new -england-unnecessary.

Carr, Rhoda, James Wright, and Charles Brody. 1996. "Effects of High School Work Experience a Decade Later: Evidence from the National Longitudinal Survey." *Sociology of Education* 69 (1): 66–81.

Cascio, Elizabeth, and Douglas Staiger. 2012. "Knowledge, Tests, and Fadeout in Educational Interventions." NBER Working Paper No. 18038. http://www.nber.org/papers /w18038.

Cascio, W., Rick Jacobs, and Jay Silva. 2009. "Validity, Utility, and Adverse Impact: Practical Implications from 30 Years of Data." In *Adverse Impact: Implications for Organizational Staffing and High Stakes Selection*, edited by James Outtz, 271–88. London: Routledge.

Case, Anne, Angela Fertig, and Christina Paxson. 2005. "The Lasting Impact of Childhood Health and Circumstance." *Journal of Health Economics* 24 (2): 365–89.

Case, Charles, and Andrew Greeley. 1990. "Attitudes toward Racial Equality." *Humboldt Journal of Social Relations* 16 (1): 67–94.

Cebi, Merve. 2007. "Locus of Control and Human Capital Investment Revisited." *Journal of Human Resources* 42 (4): 919–32.

Ceci, Stephen. 1991. "How Much Does Schooling Influence General Intelligence and Its Cognitive Components? A Reassessment of the Evidence." *Developmental Psychology* 27 (5): 703–22.

———. 2009. *On Intelligence . . . More or Less: A Biological Treatise on Intellectual Development*. Cambridge, MA: Harvard University Press.

Chambers, Jay, Thomas Parrish, Joanne Lieberman, and Jean Wolman. 1998. "What Are We Spending on Special Education in the US?" Center for Special Education Finance Brief No. 8. http://www.csef-air.org/publications/csef/briefs/brief8.pdf.

Chatterjee, Satyajit, and Felicia Ionescu. 2012. "Insuring Student Loans against the Financial Risk of Failing to Complete College." *Quantitative Economics* 3 (3): 393–420.

Chetty, Raj, John Friedman, Nathaniel Hilger, Emmanuel Saez, and Diane Schanzenbach. 2011. "How Does Your Kindergarten Classroom Affect Your Earnings? Evidence from Project STAR." *Quarterly Journal of Economics* 126 (4): 1593–660.

Chetty, Raj, John Friedman, and Jonah Rockoff. 2014. "Measuring the Impacts of Teachers II: Teacher Value-Added and Student Outcomes in Adulthood." *American Economic Review* 104 (9): 2633–79.

Chevalier, Arnaud. 2003. "Measuring Over-education." *Economica* 70 (279): 509–31.

Chevalier, Arnaud, Colm Harmon, Ian Walker, and Yu Zhu. 2004. "Does Education Raise Productivity, or Just Reflect It?" *Economic Journal* 114 (499): F499–F517.

Chi, Michelene, and Kurt VanLehn. 2012. "Seeing Deep Structure from the Interactions of Surface Features." *Educational Psychologist* 47 (3): 177–88.

Christensen, Clayton, Michael Horn, Louis Caldera, and Louis Soares. 2011. *Disrupting College: How Disruptive Innovation Can Deliver Quality and Affordability to Postsecondary Education*. Washington DC: Center for American Progress. https://cdn.american progress.org/wp-content/uploads/issues/2011/02/pdf/disrupting_college.pdf.

Chua, Amy. 2011. *Battle Hymn of the Tiger Mother*. London: Bloomsbury.

Ciccone, Antonio, and Giovanni Peri. 2006. "Identifying Human-Capital Externalities: Theory with Applications." *Review of Economic Studies* 73 (2): 381–412.

Clark, Andrew, and Andrew Oswald. 1996. "Satisfaction and Comparison Income." *Journal of Public Economics* 61 (3): 359–81.

Clark, Damon, and Paco Martorell. 2014. "The Signaling Value of a High School Diploma." *Journal of Political Economy* 122 (2): 282–318.

Clark, Gregory. 2014. *The Son Also Rises: Surnames and the History of Social Mobility*. Princeton, NJ: Princeton University Press.

Clement, John. 1982. "Students' Preconceptions in Introductory Mechanics." *American Journal of Physics* 50 (1): 66–71.

Clements, Rhonda. 2004. "An Investigation of the Status of Outdoor Play." *Contemporary Issues in Early Childhood* 5 (1): 68–80.

Coenders, Marcel, and Peer Scheepers. 2003. "The Effect of Education on Nationalism and Ethnic Exclusionism: An International Comparison." *Political Psychology* 24 (2): 313–43.

Cohen, Daniel, and Marcelo Soto. 2007. "Growth and Human Capital: Good Data, Good Results." *Journal of Economic Growth* 12 (1): 51–76.

Cohen, Mark. 1998. "The Monetary Value of Saving a High-Risk Youth." *Journal of Quantitative Criminology* 14 (1): 5–33.

College Board. 2013. "Interpreting and Using SAT Scores." Accessed November 15, 2015. http://www.collegeboard.com/prod_downloads/counselors/hs/sat/resources /handbook/4_InterpretingScores.pdf.

Collins, Brian, ed. 1997. *When In Doubt, Tell the Truth, and Other Quotations from Mark Twain*. New York: Columbia University Press.

Collins, Randall. 1979. *The Credential Society: An Historical Sociology of Education and Stratification*. New York: Academic Press.

Committee on Ability Testing. 1982. "Historical and Legal Context of Ability Testing." In *Ability Testing: Uses, Consequences, and Controversies, Part 1; Report of the Committee*, edited by Alexandra Wigdor, and Wendell Garner, 81–118. Washington DC: National Academy Press.

Confucius. 1893. *The Analects*. Translated by James Legge. https://en.wikisource.org /wiki/The_Analects.

Congressional Budget Office. 2010. "Costs and Policy Options for Federal Student Loan Programs." https://www.cbo.gov/sites/default/files/111th-congress-2009-2010 /reports/03-25-studentloans.pdf.

———. 2013. "The Distribution of Household Income and Federal Taxes, 2010." https:// www.cbo.gov/sites/default/files/113th-congress-2013-2014/reports/44604-Average TaxRates.pdf.

Cooper, Harris, Barbara Nye, Kelly Charlton, James Lindsay, and Scott Greathouse. 1996. "The Effects of Summer Vacation on Achievement Test Scores: A Narrative and Meta-Analytic Review." *Review of Educational Research* 66 (3): 227–68.

Cormier, Stephen, and Joseph Hagman, eds. 1987. *Transfer of Learning: Contemporary Research and Applications.* San Diego, CA: Academic Press.

Cowell, Frank, and Stephen Jenkins. 1992. "Equivalence Scale Relativities and the Extent of Inequality and Poverty." *Economic Journal* 102 (414): 1067–82.

Cowen, Tyler. 2008. *Discover Your Inner Economist: Use Incentives to Fall in Love, Survive Your Next Meeting, and Motivate Your Dentist.* London: Penguin.

———. 2010. "My Debate with Bryan Caplan on Education." *Marginal Revolution.* September 9. http://marginalrevolution.com/marginalrevolution/2010/09/my-debate -with-bryan-caplan-on-education.html.

———. 2011a. "More on the Returns to Education." *Marginal Revolution.* June 28. http:// marginalrevolution.com/marginalrevolution/2011/06/more-on-the-returns-to -education.html.

———. 2011b. "When Are Signaling and Human Capital Theories of Education Observationally Equivalent?" *Marginal Revolution.* July 5. http://marginalrevolution.com /marginalrevolution/2011/07/when-are-signaling-and-human-capital-theories-of -education-observationally-equivalent.html.

———. 2013. "How Much of Education and Earnings Variation Is Signalling? (Bryan Caplan Asks)?" *Marginal Revolution.* July 12. http://marginalrevolution.com/marginal revolution/2013/07/how-much-of-education-is-signalling-bryan-caplan-asks.html.

Cox, Stephen, and Michael Kramer. 1995. "Communication during Employee Dismissals: Social Exchange Principles and Group Influences on Employee Exit." *Management Communication Quarterly* 9 (2): 156–90.

Craig, Ryan. 2015. *College Disrupted: The Great Unbundling of Higher Education.* New York: Palgrave Macmillan.

Cribb, Kenneth. 2008. *Our Fading Heritage: Americans Fail a Basic Test on Their History and Institutions.* Wilmington: Intercollegiate Studies Institute.

Csikszentmihalyi, Mihaly, and Jeremy Hunter. 2003. "Happiness in Everyday Life: The Uses of Experience Sampling." *Journal of Happiness Studies* 4 (2): 185–99.

Cubberley, Ellwood. 1911. "Does the Present Trend toward Vocational Education Threaten Liberal Culture?" *School Review* 19 (7): 455–65.

Cullen, Francis, Paul Gendreau, G. Jarjoura, and John Wright. 1997. "Crime and the Bell Curve: Lessons from Intelligent Criminology." *Crime and Delinquency* 43 (4): 387–411.

Cutler, David, and Adriana Lleras-Muney. 2008. "Education and Health: Evaluating Theories and Evidence." In *Making Americans Healthier: Social and Economic Policy as Health Policy*, edited by James House, Robert Schoeni, George Kaplan, and Harold Pollack, 29–60. New York: Russell Sage.

———. 2010. "Understanding Differences in Health Behaviors by Education." *Journal of Health Economics* 29 (1): 1–28.

Dale, Stacy, and Alan Krueger. 2002. "Estimating the Payoff to Attending a More Selective College: An Application of Selection on Observables and Unobservables." *Quarterly Journal of Economics* 117 (4): 1491–527.

———. 2014. "Estimating the Effects of College Characteristics over the Career Using Administrative Earnings Data." *Journal of Human Resources* 49 (2): 323–58.

Danziger, Sheldon, Jacques Van der Gaag, Michael Taussig, and Eugene Smolensky. 1984. "The Direct Measurement of Welfare Levels: How Much Does It Cost to Make Ends Meet?" *Review of Economics and Statistics* 66 (3): 500–505.

DeAngelo, Linda, Ray Frank, Sylvia Hurtado, John Pryor, and Serge Tran. 2011. *Completing College: Assessing Graduation Rates at Four-Year Institutions*. Los Angeles: Higher Education Research Institute. http://heri.ucla.edu/DARCU/Completing College2011.pdf.

Deary, Ian. 2001. *Intelligence: A Very Short Introduction*. Oxford: Oxford University Press.

Deaton, Angus, and Christina Paxson. 2001. "Mortality, Education, Income, and Inequality among American Cohorts." In *Themes in the Economics of Aging*, edited by David Wise, 129–70. Chicago: University of Chicago Press.

de la Fuente, Angel, and Rafael Doménech. 2000. "Human Capital in Growth Regressions: How Much Difference Does Data Quality Make?" OECD Economics Department Working Paper No. 262. http://www.oecd.org/innovation/research/1825500.pdf.

———. 2006a. "Human Capital in Growth Regressions: How Much Difference Does Data Quality Make?" *Journal of the European Economic Association* 4: 1–36.

———. 2006b. "Human Capital in Growth Regressions: How Much Difference Does Data Quality Make? Appendix." Unpublished manuscript.

Delli Carpini, Michael, and Scott Keeter. 1996. *What Americans Know about Politics and Why It Matters*. New Haven, CT: Yale University Press.

Delta Cost Project. 2013. "How Much Does It Cost Institutions to Produce STEM Degrees?" *American Institutes for Research*. September. http://www.deltacostproject.org/sites/default/files/products/Cost%20to%20Institutions%20of%20STEM%20Degrees.pdf.

Demakakos, Panayotes, James Nazroo, Elizabeth Breeze, and Michael Marmot. 2008. "Socioeconomic Status and Health: The Role of Subjective Social Status." *Social Science and Medicine* 67 (2): 330–40.

DeSalvo, Karen, Nicole Bloser, Kristi Reynolds, Jiang He, and Paul Muntner. 2006. "Mortality Prediction with a Single General Self-Rated Health Question." *Journal of General Internal Medicine* 21 (3): 267–75.

Detterman, Douglas. 1993. "The Case for the Prosecution: Transfer as an Epiphenomenon." In *Transfer on Trial: Intelligence, Cognition, and Instruction*, edited by Douglas Detterman and Robert Sternberg, 1–24. New York: Ablex.

Detterman, Douglas, and Robert Sternberg, eds. 1993. *Transfer on Trial: Intelligence, Cognition, and Instruction*. New York: Ablex.

Dickens, William. 2010. "Bill Dickens versus the Signaling Model of Education." *EconLog*. August 25. http://econlog.econlib.org/archives/2010/08/bill_dickens_ve.html.

Dickens, William, and James Flynn. 2001. "Heritability Estimates versus Large Environmental Effects: The IQ Paradox Resolved." *Psychological Review* 108 (2): 346–69.

Dickens, William, and Kevin Lang. 1985. "A Test of Dual Labor Market Theory." *American Economic Review* 75 (4): 792–805.

Disney, Richard, and Amanda Gosling. 1998. "Does It Pay to Work in the Public Sector?" *Fiscal Studies* 19 (4): 347–74.

Di Tella, Rafael, Robert MacCulloch, and Andrew Oswald. 2001. "Preferences over Inflation and Unemployment: Evidence from Surveys of Happiness." *America Economic Review* 91 (1): 335–41.

Dolton, Peter, and Anna Vignoles. 2002. "Is a Broader Curriculum Better?" *Economics of Education Review* 21 (5): 415–29.

Donnellan, Brent, Frederick Oswald, Brendan Baird, and Richard Lucas. 2006. "The Mini-IPIP Scales: Tiny-Yet-Effective Measures of the Big Five Factors of Personality." *Psychological Assessment* 18 (2): 192–203.

Donohue, John, and Peter Siegelman. 1991. "The Changing Nature of Employment Discrimination Litigation." *Stanford Law Review* 43 (5): 983–1033.

Drago, Francesco. 2011. "Self-Esteem and Earnings." *Journal of Economic Psychology* 32 (3): 480–88.

Draper, Jamie, and June Hicks. 2002. "Foreign Language Enrollments in Public Secondary Schools, Fall 2000." American Council on the Teaching of Foreign Languages. http://aappl.actfl.org/sites/default/files/pdfs/public/Enroll2000.pdf.

D'Souza, Dinesh. 1991. *Illiberal Education: The Politics of Race and Sex on Campus.* New York: Free Press.

Duncan, Greg, and Rachel Dunifon. 1998. "'Soft Skills' and Long-Run Labor Market Success." *Research in Labor Economics* 17: 123–49.

Dynarski, Susan. 2000. "Hope for Whom? Financial Aid for the Middle Class and Its Impact on College Attendance." *National Tax Journal* 53 (3): 629–61.

———. 2003. "Loans, Liquidity, and Schooling Decisions." Kennedy School of Government Working Paper. http://users.nber.org/~dynarski/Dynarski_loans.pdf.

———. 2008. "Building the Stock of College-Educated Labor." *Journal of Human Resources* 43 (3): 576–610.

Dynarski, Susan, Jonathan Gruber, and Danielle Li. 2011. "Cheaper by the Dozen: Using Sibling Discounts to Estimate the Price Elasticity of Private School Attendance." *Center for Economic Studies Discussion Paper* 11-34. Accessed November 15, 2015. http://www2.census.gov/ces/wp/2011/CES-WP-11-34.pdf.

Dynarski, Susan, and Judith Scott-Clayton. 2013. "Financial Aid Policy: Lessons from Research." NBER Working Paper No. 18710. http://www.nber.org/papers/w18710.

Eckstein, Zvi, and Kenneth Wolpin. 1999. "Why Youths Drop Out of High School: The Impact of Preferences, Opportunities, and Abilities." *Econometrica* 67 (6): 1295–339.

Edmonds, Eric. 2007. "Child Labor." NBER Working Paper No. 12926. http://www.nber.org/papers/w12926.

Edmonds, Eric, and Nina Pavcnik. 2005. "Child Labor in the Global Economy." *Journal of Economic Perspectives* 19 (1): 199–220.

Ehrenberg, Ronald. 2012. "American Higher Education in Transition." *Journal of Economic Perspectives* 26 (1): 193–216.

Elo, Irma, and Samuel Preston. 1996. "Educational Differentials in Mortality: United States, 1979–1985." *Social Science and Medicine* 42 (1): 47–57.

Emerson, Patrick, and André Souza. 2011. "Is Child Labor Harmful? The Impact of Starting to Work as a Child on Adult Earnings." *Economic Development and Cultural Change* 59 (2): 345–85.

Enlow, Robert, and Lenore Ealy, eds. 2006. *Liberty and Learning: Milton Friedman's Voucher Idea at Fifty.* Washington, DC: Cato Institute.

Epstein, David. 2006. "'Hotness' and Quality." *Inside Higher Education.* May 8. https://www.insidehighered.com/news/2006/05/08/rateprof.

Ericsson, K. 2008. "Deliberate Practice and Acquisition of Expert Performance: A General Overview." *Academic Emergency Medicine* 15 (11): 988–94.

Ericsson, K., Ralf Krampe, and Clemens Tesch-Romer. 1993. "The Role of Deliberate Practice in the Acquisition of Expert Performance." *Psychological Review* 100 (3): 363–406.

Ericsson, K., Michael Prietula, and Edward Cokely. 2007. "The Making of an Expert." *Harvard Business Review* 85 (7–8): 114–21.

Euteneuer, Frank. 2014. "Subjective Social Status and Health." *Current Opinion in Psychiatry* 27 (5): 337–43.

Fabra, Eugenia, and Cesar Camisón. 2009. "Direct and Indirect Effects of Education on Job Satisfaction: A Structural Equation Model for the Spanish Case." *Economics of Education Review* 28 (5): 600–610.

Falk, Justin. 2012. "Comparing the Compensation of Federal and Private-Sector Employees." Congressional Budget Office. January. http://www.cbo.gov/sites/default/files/cbofiles/attachments/01-30-FedPay.pdf.

Fang, Hanming. 2006. "Disentangling the College Wage Premium: Estimating a Model with Endogenous Education Choices." *International Economic Review* 47 (4): 1151–85.

Fang, Hanming, and Andrea Moro. 2011. "Theories of Statistical Discrimination and Affirmative Action: A Survey." In *Handbook of Social Economics*, vol. 1A, edited by Jess Benhabib, Matthew Jackson, and Alberto Bisin, 133–200. Amsterdam: Elsevier.

Farber, Henry, and Robert Gibbons. 1996. "Learning and Wage Dynamics." *Quarterly Journal of Economics* 111 (4): 1007–47.

Farrell, Edwin, George Peguero, Rasheed Lindsey, and Ronald White. 1988. "Giving Voice to High School Students: Pressure and Boredom, Ya Know What I'm Sayin'?" *American Educational Research Journal* 25 (4): 489–502.

Federal Bureau of Investigation. 2011. "Crime in the United States 2011—Table 1." Accessed November 15, 2015. http://www.fbi.gov/about-us/cjis/ucr/crime-in-the-u.s/2011/crime-in-the-u.s.-2011/tables/table-1.

Federal Reserve Bank of St. Louis. 2015. "Federal Reserve Economic Data." Accessed November 15, 2015. http://research.stlouisfed.org/fred2.

Fehr, Ernst, and Simon Gächter. 1998. "Reciprocity and Economics: The Economic Implications of Homo Reciprocans." *European Economic Review* 42 (3): 845–59.

Feng, Du, and Laura Baker. 1994. "Spouse Similarity in Attitudes, Personality, and Psychological Well-Being." *Behavior Genetics* 24 (4): 357–64.

Ferrante, Francesco. 2009. "Education, Aspirations and Life Satisfaction." *Kyklos* 62 (4): 542–62.

Ferrer, Ana, and W. Riddell. 2002. "The Role of Credentials in the Canadian Labour Market." *Canadian Journal of Economics/Revue Canadienne D'économique* 35 (4): 879–905.

Fischer, Claude, Michael Hout, Martin Sanchez Jankowski, Samuel Lucas, Ann Swidler, Kim Voss, and Lawrence Bobo. 1996. *Inequality by Design: Cracking the Bell Curve Myth*. Princeton, NJ: Princeton University Press.

Flores-Lagunes, Alfonso, and Audrey Light. 2010. "Interpreting Degree Effects in the Returns to Education." *Journal of Human Resources* 45 (2): 439–67.

Foer, Joshua. 2006. "Kaavya Syndrome: The Accused Harvard Plagiarist Doesn't Have a Photographic Memory. No One Does." *Slate*. April 27. http://www.slate.com/articles/health_and_science/science/2006/04/kaavya_syndrome.single.html.

Fogg, Neeta, and Paul Harrington. 2011. "Rising Mal-Employment and the Great Recession: The Growing Disconnection between Recent College Graduates and the College Labor Market." *Continuing Higher Education Review* 75: 51–65.

Folger, Robert, and Daniel Skarlicki. 1998. "When Tough Times Make Tough Bosses: Managerial Distancing as a Function of Layoff Blame." *Academy of Management Journal* 41 (1): 79–87.

Fong, Geoffrey, David Krantz, and Richard Nisbett. 1986. "The Effects of Statistical Training on Thinking about Everyday Problems." *Cognitive Psychology* 18 (3): 253–92.

Frank, Robert. 1999. *Luxury Fever: Money and Happiness in An Age of Excess*. Princeton, NJ: Princeton University Press.

Frazis, Harley. 1993. "Selection Bias and the Degree Effect." *Journal of Human Resources* 28 (3): 538–54.

———. 2002. "Human Capital, Signaling, and the Pattern of Returns to Education." *Oxford Economic Papers* 54 (2): 298–320.

Freund, Philipp, and Heinz Holling. 2011. "How to Get Really Smart: Modeling Retest and Training Effects in Ability Testing Using Computer-Generated Figural Matrix Items." *Intelligence* 39 (4): 233–43.

Friedman, Milton. 1982. *Capitalism and Freedom*. Chicago: University of Chicago Press.

———. 2003. "Letter to Richard Vedder." September 12. Unpublished.

Furnée, Carin, Wim Groot, and Henriëtte Maassen van Den Brink. 2008. "The Health Effects of Education: A Meta-analysis." *European Journal of Public Health* 18 (4): 417–21.

Ganzach, Yoav. 2003. "Intelligence, Education, and Facets of Job Satisfaction." *Work and Occupations* 30 (1): 97–122.

Garber, Steven, and Steven Klepper. 1980. "Extending the Classical Normal Errors-in-Variables Model." *Econometrica* 48 (6): 1541–46.

Gardner, Howard. 1991. *The Unschooled Mind: How Children Learn and How Schools Should Teach*. New York: Basic Books.

Garrison, G., C. Mikesell, and D. Matthew. 2007. "Medical School Graduation and Attrition Rates." *AAMC Analysis in Brief* 7 (2): 1–2.

Ge, Suqin. 2011. "Women's College Decisions: How Much Does Marriage Matter?" *Journal of Labor Economics* 29 (4): 773–818.

Gensowski, Miriam. 2014. "Personality, IQ, and Lifetime Earnings." IZA Discussion Paper Series No. 8235. http://ftp. iza.org/dp8235.pdf.

Georghiades, Petros. 2000. "Beyond Conceptual Change in Science Education: Focusing on Transfer, Durability, and Metacognition." *Educational Research* 42 (2): 119–39.

Gick, Mary, and Keith Holyoak. 1983. "Schema Induction and Analogical Transfer." *Cognitive Psychology* 15 (1): 1–38.

Gill, C., R. Jardine, and N. Martin. 1985. "Further Evidence for Genetic Influences on Educational Achievement." *British Journal of Educational Psychology* 55 (3): 240–50.

Gillen, Andrew. 2012. *Introducing Bennett Hypothesis 2.0*. Washington, DC: Center for College Affordability and Productivity. http://files.eric.ed.gov/fulltext/ED536151.pdf.

GiveWell. 2015. "GiveWell: Top Charities." Accessed November 15. http://www.givewell.org/charities/top-charities.

Gladwell, Malcolm. 2008. *Outliers: The Story of Success*. Hachette: Back Bay Books.

Glaeser, Edward, and Bruce Sacerdote. 2008. "Education and Religion." *Journal of Human Capital* 2 (2): 188–215.

Glewwe, Paul, Eric Hanushek, Sarah Humpage, and Renato Ravina. 2014. "School Resources and Educational Outcomes in Developing Countries: A Review of the Literature from 1990 to 2010." In *Education Policy in Developing Countries*, edited by Paul Glewwe, 13–64. Chicago: University of Chicago Press.

Goldin, Claudia. 1997. "Exploring the 'Present through the Past': Career and Family across the Last Century." *American Economic Review* 87 (2): 396–99.

Goldin, Claudia, and Lawrence Katz. 2009. *The Race between Education and Technology*. Cambridge, MA: Harvard University Press.

Goldsmith, Arthur, and Jonathan Veum. 2002. "Wages and the Composition of Experience." *Southern Economic Journal* 69 (2): 429–43.

Goldstein, Dana. 2014. *The Teacher Wars: A History of America's Most Embattled Profession*. New York: Doubleday.

Goldstein, Joshua, and Catherine Kenney. 2001. "Marriage Delayed or Marriage Forgone? New Cohort Forecasts of First Marriage for US Women." *American Sociological Review* 66 (4): 506–19.

Golebiowska, Ewa. 1995. "Individual Value Priorities, Education, and Political Tolerance." *Political Behavior* 17 (1): 23–48.

Gottfredson, Linda. 1997. "Why g Matters: The Complexity of Everyday Life." *Intelligence* 24 (1): 79–132.

Gould, Eric. 2005. "Inequality and Ability." *Labour Economics* 12 (2): 169–89.

———. 2008. "Marriage and Career: The Dynamic Decisions of Young Men." *Journal of Human Capital* 2 (4): 337–78.

Granada Hills Charter High School. 2015. "Graduation Requirements." Accessed December 1, 2015. http://www.ghchs.com/offices/counseling/graduation_requirements.

Granholm, Axel. 1991. *Handbook of Employee Termination*. New York: Wiley.

Gray, Kenneth. 2004. "Is High School Career and Technical Education Obsolete?" *Phi Delta Kappan* 86 (2): 129–34.

Gray, Kenneth, and Edwin Herr. 2006. *Other Ways to Win: Creating Alternatives for High School Students*. Thousand Oaks, CA: Corwin.

Gray, Peter. 2013. *Free to Learn: Why Unleashing the Instinct to Play Will Make Our Children Happier, More Self-Reliant, and Better Students for Life*. New York: Basic Books.

Greene, Jay, and Greg Forster. 2002. *Effects of Funding Incentives on Special Education Enrollment*. New York: Manhattan Institute for Policy Research. http://www.manhattan-institute.org/pdf/cr_32.pdf.

Greenstone, Michael, and Adam Looney. 2011. "Where Is the Best Place to Invest $102,000—in Stocks, Bonds, or a College Degree?" *Hamilton Project*. June 25. http://www.hamiltonproject.org/blog/where_is_the_best_place_to_invest_102000_in_stocks_bonds_or_a_college_.

———. 2012. "Regardless of the Cost, College Still Matters." *Hamilton Project*. October 5. http://www.hamiltonproject.org/papers/regardless_of_the_cost_college_still_matters.

———. 2013. "Is Starting College and Not Finishing Really That Bad?" *Hamilton Project*. June 7. http://www.hamiltonproject.org/assets/legacy/files/downloads_and_links/May_Jobs_Blog_20130607_FINAL_2.pdf.

Gregory, Robert, and Jeff Borland. 1999. "Recent Developments in Public Sector Labor Markets." In *Handbook of Labor Economics*, vol. 3C, edited by Orley Ashenfelter and David Card, 3573–630. Amsterdam: Elsevier.

Grogger, Jeff. 1998. "Market Wages and Youth Crime." *Journal of Labor Economics* 16 (4): 756–91.

Groot, Wim, and Henriètte Van den Brink. 2000. "Overeducation in the Labor Market: A Meta-analysis." *Economics of Education Review* 19 (2): 149–58.

Gross, Neil, and Solon Simmons. 2007. "The Social and Political Views of American Professors." Working Paper, Harvard University. Accessed November 15, 2015. http://citeseerx.ist.psu.edu/viewdoc/download?doi=10.1.1.147.6141&rep=rep1&type=pdf.

Groves, Melissa. 2005. "How Important Is Your Personality? Labor Market Returns to Personality for Women in the US and UK." *Journal of Economic Psychology* 26 (6): 827–41.

Gruber-Baldini, Ann, K. Warner, and Sherry Willis. 1995. "Similarity in Married Couples: A Longitudinal Study of Mental Abilities and Rigidity-Flexibility." *Journal of Personality and Social Psychology* 69 (1): 191–203.

Gyourko, Joseph, and Joseph Tracy. 1988. "An Analysis of Public and Private Sector Wages Allowing for Endogenous Choices of Both Government and Union Status." *Journal of Labor Economics* 6 (2): 229–53.

Hambrick, David, Frederick Oswald, Erik Altmann, Elizabeth Meinz, Fernand Gobet, and Guillermo Campitelli. 2014. "Deliberate Practice: Is That All It Takes to Become an Expert?" *Intelligence* 45: 34–45.

Hamermesh, Daniel, and Stephen Donald. 2008. "The Effect of College Curriculum on Earnings: An Affinity Identifier for Non-ignorable Non-response Bias." *Journal of Econometrics* 144 (2): 479–91.

Hanushek, Eric. 2003. "The Failure of Input-Based Schooling Policies." *Economic Journal* 113 (485): F64–F98.

———. 2009. "Deselecting Teachers." In *Creating a New Teaching Profession*, edited by Dan Goldhaber and Jane Hannaway, 165–80. Washington DC: Urban Institute Press.

Hanushek, Eric, and Dennis Kimko. 2000. "Schooling, Labor-Force Quality, and the Growth of Nations." *American Economic Review* 90 (5): 1184–208.

Hanushek, Eric, Paul Peterson, and Ludger Woessmann. 2013. *Endangering Prosperity: A Global View of the American School*. Washington, DC: Brookings Institution.

Hanushek, Eric, Guido Schwerdt, Simon Wiederhold, and Ludger Woessmann. 2015. "Returns to Skill around the World: Evidence from PIAAC." *European Economic Review* 73: 103–30.

Hanushek, Eric, and Ludger Woessmann. 2008. "The Role of Cognitive Skills in Economic Development." *Journal of Economic Literature* 46 (3): 607–68.

———. 2011. "Economics of International Differences in Educational Achievement." In *Handbook of the Economics of Education*, vol. 3, edited by Eric Hanushek, Stephen Machin, and Ludger Woessmann, 89–200. Amsterdam: Elsevier.

———. 2012. "Do Better Schools Lead to More Growth? Cognitive Skills, Economic Outcomes, and Causation." *Journal of Economic Growth* 17 (4): 266–321.

Hanushek, Eric, Ludger Woessmann, and Lei Zhang. 2011. "General Education, Vocational Education, and Labor-Market Outcomes over the Life-Cycle." NBER Working Paper No. 17504. http://www.nber.org/papers/w17504.

Hanushek, Eric, and Lei Zhang. 2006. "Quality-Consistent Estimates of International Returns to Skill." NBER Working Paper No. 12664. http://www.nber.org/papers/w12664.

———. 2009. "Quality-Consistent Estimates of International Schooling and Skill Gradients." *Journal of Human Capital* 3 (2): 107–43.

Härkönen, Juho, and Jaap Dronkers. 2006. "Stability and Change in the Educational Gradient of Divorce. A Comparison of Seventeen Countries." *European Sociological Review* 22 (5): 501–17.

Harlow, Caroline. 2003. "Education and Correctional Populations." Bureau of Justice Statistics. Accessed November 15, 2015. http://www.bjs.gov/content/pub/pdf/ecp.pdf.

Harrington, Paul, and Andrew Sum. 2010a. "College Labor Shortages in 2018?" *New England Journal of Higher Education*. http://www.nebhe.org/thejournal/college-labor-shortages-in-2018.

———. 2010b. "College Labor Shortages in 2018? Part Deux." *New England Journal of Higher Education*. http://www.nebhe.org/thejournal/college-labor-shortages-in-2018-part-two.

Harris, Judith. 1998. *The Nurture Assumption: Why Children Turn Out the Way They Do*. New York: Simon and Schuster.

Hartog, Joop. 2000. "Over-education and Earnings: Where Are We, Where Should We Go?" *Economics of Education Review* 19 (2): 131–47.

Hartog, Joop, and Luis Diaz-Serrano. 2015. "Why Do We Ignore the Risk in Schooling Decisions?" *De Economist* 163 (2): 125–53.

Harvard College. 2015. "Cost of Attendance." Accessed November 15, 2015. https://college.harvard.edu/financial-aid/how-aid-works/cost-attendance.

Haskell, Robert. 2001. *Transfer of Learning: Cognition, Instruction, and Reasoning*. San Diego, CA: Academic Press.

Hausknecht, John, Jane Halpert, Nicole Di Paolo, and Meghan Gerrard. 2007. "Retesting in Selection: A Meta-analysis of Coaching and Practice Effects for Tests of Cognitive Ability." *Journal of Applied Psychology* 92 (2): 373–85.

Hayes, Charles. 1995. *Proving You're Qualified: Strategies for Competent People without College Degrees*. Wasilla, AK: Autodidact Press.

Heaton, Tim. 2002. "Factors Contributing to Increasing Marital Stability in the United States." *Journal of Family Issues* 23 (3): 392–409.

Heaton, Tim, and Ashley Blake. 1999. "Gender Differences in Determinants of Marital Disruption." *Journal of Family Issues* 20 (1): 25–45.

Heckman, James. 1995. "Lessons from the Bell Curve." *Journal of Political Economy* 103 (5): 1091–120.

Heckman, James, John Humphries, and Tim Kautz, eds. 2014a. *The Myth of Achievement Tests: The GED and the Role of Character in American Life*. Chicago: University of Chicago Press.

———. 2014b. "The Economic and Social Benefits of GED Certification." In *The Myth of Achievement Tests: The GED and the Role of Character in American Life*, edited by James Heckman, John Humphries, and Tim Kautz, 171–267. Chicago: University of Chicago Press.

Heckman, James, and Paul LaFontaine. 2010. "The American High School Graduation Rate: Trends and Levels." *Review of Economics and Statistics* 92 (2): 244–62.

Heckman, James, Lance Lochner, and Petra Todd. 2003. "Fifty Years of Mincer Earnings Regressions." NBER Working Paper No. 9732. http://www.nber.org/papers/w9732.

———. 2008. "Earnings Functions and Rates of Return." *Journal of Human Capital* 2 (1): 1–31.

Heckman, James, Jora Stixrud, and Sergio Urzua. 2006. "The Effects of Cognitive and Noncognitive Abilities on Labor Market Outcomes and Social Behavior." NBER Working Paper No. 12006. http://www.nber.org/papers/w12006.

Heil, Scott, Liza Reisel, and Paul Attewell. 2014. "College Selectivity and Degree Completion." *American Educational Research Journal* 51 (5): 913–35.

Heisz, Andrew, and Philip Oreopoulos. 2006. "The Importance of Signalling in Job Placement and Promotion." Statistics Canada, Analytical Studies Branch Research Paper Series No. 236. http://www.statcan.gc.ca/pub/11f0019m/11f0019m2006236-eng.pdf.

Helliwell, John. 2003. "How's Life? Combining Individual and National Variables to Explain Subjective Well-Being." *Economic Modelling* 20 (2): 331–60.

Hemelt, Steven, and Dave Marcotte. 2011. "The Impact of Tuition Increases on Enrollment at Public Colleges and Universities." *Educational Evaluation and Policy Analysis* 33 (4): 435–57.

Hendricks, Lutz, and Oksana Leukhina. 2014. "The Return to College: Selection Bias and Dropout Risk." CESifo Working Paper Series 4733. Last modified April 5. http://ssrn.com/abstract=2432905.

Henrichson, Christian, and Ruth Delaney. 2012. "The Price of Prisons: What Incarceration Costs Taxpayers." *Federal Sentencing Reporter* 25 (1): 68–80.

Hérault, Nicolas, and Rezida Zakirova. 2015. "Returns to Education: Accounting for Enrolment and Completion Effects." *Education Economics* 23 (1): 84–100.

Herrnstein, Richard, and Charles Murray. 1994. *The Bell Curve: Intelligence and Class Structure in American Life*. New York: Free Press.

Hersch, Joni. 1991. "Equal Employment Opportunity Law and Firm Profitability." *Journal of Human Resources* 26 (1): 139–53.

Hjalmarsson, Randi. 2008. "Criminal Justice Involvement and High School Completion." *Journal of Urban Economics* 63 (2): 613–30.

Hocutt, Anne. 1996. "Effectiveness of Special Education: Is Placement the Critical Factor?" *Future of Children* 6 (1): 77–102.

Hofferth, Sandra. 2009. "Changes in American Children's Time—1997 to 2003." *Electronic International Journal of Time Use Research* 6 (1): 26–47.

Hofferth, Sandra, and John Sandberg. 2001. "Changes in American Children's Time, 1981–1997." In *Children at the Millennium: Where Have We Come From, Where Are We Going?*, vol. 6, edited by Timothy Owens and Sandra Hofferth, 193–229. Amsterdam: Elsevier.

Hope, Yen. 2012. "In Weak Job Market, One in Two College Graduates Are Jobless or Underemployed." *Huffington Post*. April 22. http://www.huffingtonpost.com/2012/04/22/job-market-college-graduates_n_1443738.html.

Horn, Laura. 2006. *Placing College Graduation Rates in Context: How 4-Year College Graduation Rates Vary with Selectivity and the Size of Low-Income Enrollment*. Washington, DC: National Center for Education Statistics. http://nces.ed.gov/pubs2007/2007161.pdf.

Hornby, Nick. 2009. "An Education." Internet Movie Script Database. Accessed December 3, 2015. http://www.imsdb.com/scripts/An-Education.html.

Horowitz, David. 2007. *Indoctrination U: The Left's War against Academic Freedom*. New York: Encounter Books.

Hotchkiss, Lawrence. 1993. "Effects of Training, Occupation, and Training-Occupation Match on Wage." *Journal of Human Resources* 28 (3): 482–96.

Howden, Lindsay, and Julie Meyer. 2011. "Age and Sex Composition: 2010." United States Census Bureau. http://www.census.gov/prod/cen2010/briefs/c2010br-03.pdf.

HowStuffWorks. 2015. "The 21 Best-Selling Books of All Time." Accessed March 25, 2015. http://entertainment.howstuffworks.com/arts/literature/21-best-sellers.htm.

Hoxby, Caroline. 2002. "The Power of Peers." *Education Next* 2 (2): 57–63.

———. 2009. "The Changing Selectivity of American Colleges." *Journal of Economic Perspectives* 23 (4): 95–118.

Huber, Christopher, and Nathan Kuncel. 2016. "Does College Teach Critical Thinking? A Meta-analysis." *Review of Educational Research* 86 (2): 431–68.

Huemer, Michael. 2013. *The Problem of Political Authority: An Examination of the Right to Coerce and the Duty to Obey*. New York: Palgrave Macmillan.

Hungerford, Thomas, and Gary Solon. 1987. "Sheepskin Effects in the Returns to Education." *Review of Economics and Statistics* 69 (1): 175–77.

Iannaccone, Laurence. 1998. "Introduction to the Economics of Religion." *Journal of Economic Literature* 36 (3): 1465–96.

IMDB. 2015. "Quotes for Eomer from *The Lord of the Rings: The Two Towers*." Accessed November 30. http://www.imdb.com/character/ch0000144/quotes.

Infoplease. 2015. "Homicide Rate (per 100,000), 1950–2013." Accessed November 15, 2015. http://www.infoplease.com/ipa/A0873729.html.

Internal Revenue Service. 2011. *Tax Guide 2011*. Washington, DC: Internal Revenue Service. http://www.irs.gov/pub/irs-prior/p17-2011.pdf.

———. 2015. "2011 Tax Year EITC Income Limits, Maximum Credit Amounts and Tax Law Updates." Last modified November 6. http://www.irs.gov/Individuals/2011-Tax-Year-EITC-Income-Limits,-Maximum-Credit-Amounts-and-Tax-Law-Updates.

———. 2016. "EITC, Earned Income Tax Credit, Questions and Answers." Last modified February 4. https://www.irs.gov/Credits-&-Deductions/Individuals/Earned-Income-Tax-Credit/EITC,-Earned-Income-Tax-Credit,-Questions-and-Answers.

International Lyrics Playground. 2016. "There Lived a King." Accessed August 29, 2016. http://lyricsplayground.com/alpha/songs/t/therelivedaking.shtml.

Internet World Stats. 2015. "Internet Usage Statistics—World Internet Users and 2014 Population Stats." Last modified March 19, 2015. http://www.internetworldstats.com/stats.htm.

Ioannides, Yannis, and Linda Loury. 2004. "Job Information Networks, Neighborhood Effects, and Inequality." *Journal of Economic Literature* 42 (4): 1056–93.

Isen, Adam, and Betsey Stevenson. 2011. "Women's Education and Family Behavior." In *Demography and the Economy*, edited by John Shoven, 107–40. Chicago: University of Chicago Press.

Islam, Nazrul. 1995. "Growth Empirics: A Panel Data Approach." *Quarterly Journal of Economics* 110 (4): 1127–70.

Jacob, Brian, Lars Lefgren, and David Sims. 2010. "The Persistence of Teacher-Induced Learning." *Journal of Human Resources* 45 (4): 915–43.

Jaeger, David, and Marianne Page. 1996. "Degrees Matter: New Evidence on Sheep-skin Effects in the Returns to Education." *Review of Economics and Statistics* 78 (4): 733–40.

James, Estelle, Nabeel Alsalam, Joseph Conaty, and Duc-Le To. 1989. "College Quality and Future Earnings. Where Should You Send Your Child to College?" *American Economic Review* 79 (2): 247–52.

Jarjoura, Roger. 1993. "Does Dropping Out of School Enhance Delinquent Involvement? Results from a Large-Scale National Probability Sample." *Criminology* 31 (2): 149–72.

———. 1996. "The Conditional Effect of Social Class on the Dropout-Delinquency Relationship." *Journal of Research in Crime and Delinquency* 33 (2): 232–55.

Jencks, Christopher, and Meredith Phillips. 1999. "Aptitude or Achievement: Why Do Test Scores Predict Educational Attainment and Earnings?" In *Earning and Learning: How Schools Matter*, edited by Susan Mayer and Paul Peterson, 15–47. Washington, DC: Brookings Institution; New York: Russell Sage.

Jensen, Arthur. 1998. *The g Factor: The Science of Mental Ability*. Westport: Praeger.

Jepsen, Lisa. 2005. "The Relationship between Wife's Education and Husband's Earnings: Evidence from 1960 to 2000." *Review of Economics of the Household* 3 (2): 197–214.

Jerrim, John. 2014. "The Unrealistic Educational Expectations of High School Pupils: Is America Exceptional?" *Sociological Quarterly* 55 (1): 196–231.

Joensen, Juanna, and Helena Nielsen. 2009. "Is There a Causal Effect of High School Math on Labor Market Outcomes?" *Journal of Human Resources* 44 (1): 171–98.

Johnson, Dirk. 1998. "Many Schools Putting an End to Child's Play." *New York Times*. April 7. http://www.nytimes.com/1998/04/07/us/many-schools-putting-an-end-to-child-s-play.html.

Johnson, Matthew. 2013. "Borrowing Constraints, College Enrollment, and Delayed Entry." *Journal of Labor Economics* 31 (4): 669–725.

Jones, Charles. 1995. "Time Series Tests of Endogenous Growth Models." *Quarterly Journal of Economics* 110 (2): 495–525.

———. 2005. "Growth and Ideas." In *Handbook of Economic Growth*, vol. 1, edited by Philippe Aghion and Steven Durlauf, 1063–111. Amsterdam: Elsevier.

Jones, Garett. 2016. *Hive Mind: How Your Nation's IQ Matters So Much More Than Your Own*. Stanford, CA: Stanford University Press.

Jones, Garett, and W. Schneider. 2010. "IQ in the Production Function: Evidence from Immigrant Earnings." *Economic Inquiry* 48 (3): 743–55.

Juhn, Chinhui, and Kevin Murphy. 1997. "Wage Inequality and Family Labor Supply." *Journal of Labor Economics* 15 (1): 72–97.

Julian, Tiffany, and Robert Kominski. 2011. "Education and Synthetic Work-Life Earnings Estimates: American Community Survey Reports; ACS-14." United States Census Bureau. September. http://files.eric.ed.gov/fulltext/ED523770.pdf.

———. 2012. "Work-Life Earnings by Field of Degree and Occupation for People with a Bachelor's Degree: 2011. American Community Survey Reports." United States Census Bureau. October. http://files.eric.ed.gov/fulltext/ED537269.pdf.

Kahneman, Daniel. 2011. *Thinking, Fast and Slow*. London: Macmillan.

Kaiser Family Foundation. 2013. "Medicaid Eligibility for Adults as of January 1, 2014." October 1. http://kff.org/medicaid/fact-sheet/medicaid-eligibility-for-adults-as-of-january-1-2014.

Kalmijn, Matthijs. 1998. "Intermarriage and Homogamy: Causes, Patterns, Trends." *Annual Review of Sociology* 24: 395–421.

———. 2013. "The Educational Gradient in Marriage: A Comparison of 25 European Countries." *Demography* 50 (4): 1499–520.

Kalmijn, Matthijs, and Henk Flap. 2001. "Assortative Meeting and Mating: Unintended Consequences of Organized Settings for Partner Choices." *Social Forces* 79 (4): 1289–312.

Kam, Cindy, and Carl Palmer. 2008. "Reconsidering the Effects of Education on Political Participation." *Journal of Politics* 70 (3): 612–31.

Kambourov, Gueorgui, and Iourii Manovskii. 2009. "Occupational Specificity of Human Capital." *International Economic Review* 50 (1): 63–115.

Kane, Thomas, and Cecilia Rouse. 1995. "Labor-Market Returns to Two- and Four-Year College." *America Economic Review* 85 (3): 600–614.

———. 1999. "The Community College: Educating Students at the Margin between College and Work." *Journal of Economic Perspectives* 13 (1): 63–84.

Kane, Thomas, Cecilia Rouse, and Douglas Staiger. 1999. "Estimating Returns to Schooling When Schooling Is Misreported." NBER Working Paper No. 7235. http://www.nber.org/papers/w7235.

Kang, Suk, and John Bishop. 1989. "Vocational and Academic Education in High School: Complements or Substitutes." *Economics of Education Review* 8 (2): 133–48.

Katz, Lawrence, and Alan Krueger. 1991. "Changes in the Structure of Wages in the Public and Private Sectors." NBER Working Paper No. 3667. http://www.nber.org/papers/w3667.

Kerckhoff, Alan. 2000. "Transition from School to Work in Comparative Perspective." In *Handbook of the Sociology of Education*, edited by Maureen Hallinan, 453–74. New York: Kluwer.

Keyes, Daniel. 2005. *Flowers for Algernon*. Orlando, FL: Harcourt Books.

King, Maryon, and Gordon Bruner. 2000. "Social Desirability Bias: A Neglected Aspect of Validity Testing." *Psychology and Marketing* 17 (2): 79–103.

Kingston, Paul, Ryan Hubbard, Brent Lapp, Paul Schroeder, and Julia Wilson. 2003. "Why Education Matters." *Sociology of Education* 76 (1): 53–70.

Kirkland, Edward. 1964. *Dream and Thought in the Business Community, 1860–1900*. Chicago: Quadrangle Books.

Kirsch, Irwin. 1993. *Adult Literacy in America: A First Look at the Results of the National Adult Literacy Survey*. Washington, DC: National Center for Education Statistics. http://nces.ed.gov/pubs93/93275.pdf.

Klaas, Brian, and Gregory Dell'Omo. 1997. "Managerial Use of Dismissal: Organizational-Level Determinants." *Personnel Psychology* 50 (4): 927–53.

Klein, Daniel, and Charlotta Stern. 2009. "By the Numbers: The Ideological Profile of Professors." In *The Politically Correct University: Problems, Scope, and Reforms*, edited by Robert Maranto, Richard Redding, and Frederick Hess, 15–37. Washington, DC: American Enterprise Institute Press.

Kleiner, Morris. 2006. *Licensing Occupations: Ensuring Quality or Restricting Competition?* Kalamazoo, MI: W. E. Upjohn Institute. http://research.upjohn.org/up_press/18.

Kleiner, Morris, and Alan Krueger. 2010. "The Prevalence and Effects of Occupational Licensing." *British Journal of Industrial Relations* 48 (4): 676–87.

Kling, Arnold. 2006. "College Customers vs. Suppliers." *EconLog*. August 16. http://econlog.econlib.org/archives/2006/08/college_custome.html.

Koch, Alexander, Julia Nafziger, and Helena Nielsen. 2015. "Behavioral Economics of Education." *Journal of Economic Behavior and Organization* 115: 3–17.

Koppel, Nathan. 2009. "Job Discrimination Cases Tend to Fare Poorly in Court." *Wall Street Journal*. February 19. http://www.wsj.com/articles/SB123500883048618747.

Kotkin, Minna. 2007. "Outing Outcomes: An Empirical Study of Confidential Employment Discrimination Settlements." *Washington and Lee Law Review* 64 (1): 111–63.

Krueger, Alan, Daniel Kahneman, David Schkade, Norbert Schwarz, and Arthur Stone. 2009. "National Time Accounting: The Currency of Life." In *Measuring the Subjective Well-Being of Nations: National Accounts of Time Use and Well-Being*, edited by Alan Krueger, 9–86. Chicago: University of Chicago Press.

Krueger, Alan, and Mikael Lindahl. 2001. "Education for Growth: Why and for Whom?" *Journal of Economic Literature* 39 (4): 1101–36.

Krueger, Dirk, Fabrizio Perri, Luigi Pistaferri, and Giovanni Violante. 2010. "Cross-Sectional Facts for Macroeconomists." *Review of Economic Dynamics* 13 (1): 1–14.

Krugman, Paul. 2000. "And Now for Something Completely Different: An Alternative Model of Trade, Education, and Inequality." In *The Impact of International Trade on Wages*, edited by Robert Feenstra, 15–36. Chicago: University of Chicago Press.

Krumpal, Ivar. 2013. "Determinants of Social Desirability Bias in Sensitive Surveys: A Literature Review." *Quality and Quantity* 47 (4): 2025–47.

Kulik, James. 1998. "Curricular Tracks and High School Vocational Education." In *The Quality of Vocational Education: Background Papers from the 1994 National Assessment of Vocational Education*, edited by Adam Gamoran, 65–131. Washington, DC: U.S. Department of Education.

Kuran, Timur. 1997. *Private Truths, Public Lies: The Social Consequences of Preference Falsification*. Cambridge, MA: Harvard University Press.

Kutner, Mark, Elizabeth Greenberg, Ying Jin, Bridget Boyle, Yung-chen Hsu, and Eric Dunleavy. 2007. "Literacy in Everyday Life: Results From the 2003 National Assessment of Adult Literacy." Washington, DC: National Center for Education Statistics. http://nces.ed.gov/pubs2007/2007480.pdf.

Labaree, David. 1997. *How to Succeed in School without Really Learning*. New Haven, CT: Yale University Press.

———. 2012. *Someone Has to Fail: The Zero-Sum Game of Public Schooling*. Cambridge, MA: Harvard University Press.

Lacy, Sarah. 2011. "Peter Thiel: We're in a Bubble and It's Not the Internet. It's Higher Education." *TechCrunch*. April 10. http://techcrunch.com/2011/04/10/peter-thiel-were-in-a-bubble-and-its-not-the-internet-its-higher-education.

Lahelma, Elina. 2002. "School Is for Meeting Friends: Secondary School as Lived and Remembered." *British Journal of Sociology of Education* 23 (3): 367–81.

Lang, Kevin, and Erez Siniver. 2011. "Why Is an Elite Undergraduate Education Valuable? Evidence from Israel." *Labour Economics* 18 (6): 767–77.

Lange, Fabian. 2007. "The Speed of Employer Learning." *Journal of Labor Economics* 25 (1): 1–35.

Lange, Fabian, and Robert Topel. 2006. "The Social Value of Education and Human Capital." In *Handbook of the Economics of Education*, vol. 1, edited by Eric Hanushek and Finis Welch, 459–509. Amsterdam: Elsevier.

Lantz, P., J. House, J. Lepkowski, D. Williams, R. Mero, and J. Chen. 1998. "Socioeconomic Factors, Health Behaviors, and Mortality: Results from a Nationally Representative Prospective Study of US Adults." *JAMA* 279 (21): 1703–8.

Larson, Reed, and Maryse Richards. 1991. "Boredom in the Middle School Years: Blaming Schools versus Blaming Students." *American Journal of Education* 99 (4): 418–43.

Last, Jonathan. 2013. *What to Expect When No One's Expecting: America's Coming Demographic Disaster*. New York: Encounter Books.

Latzer, Barry. 2004. "The Hollow Core: Failure of the General Education Curriculum." Washington, DC: American Council of Trustees and Alumni.

Lavecchia, Adam, Heidi Liu, and Philip Oreopoulos. 2016. "Behavioral Economics of Education: Progress and Possibilities." In *Handbook of the Economics of Education*, vol. 5, edited by Eric Hanushek, Stephen Machin, and Ludger Woessmann, 1–74. Amsterdam: Elsevier.

Layard, Richard, and George Psacharopoulos. 1974. "The Screening Hypothesis and the Returns to Education." *Journal of Political Economy* 82 (5): 985–98.

Lavy, Victor, and Analia Schlosser. 2011. "Mechanisms and Impacts of Gender Peer Effects at School." *American Economic Journal: Applied Economics* (2): 1–33.

Lederman, Doug. 2013. "Less Academically Adrift?" *Inside Higher Ed*. May 20. https://www.insidehighered.com/news/2013/05/20/studies-challenge-findings -academically-adrift.

Leef, George. 2006. "The Overselling of Higher Education." *Academic Questions* 19 (2): 17–34.

Lefgren, Lars, and Frank McIntyre. 2006. "The Relationship between Women's Education and Marriage Outcomes." *Journal of Labor Economics* 24 (4): 787–830.

Lehman, Darrin, Richard Lempert, and Richard Nisbett. 1988. "The Effects of Graduate Training on Reasoning: Formal Discipline and Thinking about Everyday-Life Events." *American Psychologist* 43 (6): 431–42.

Lehman, Darrin, and Richard Nisbett. 1990. "A Longitudinal Study of the Effects of Undergraduate Training on Reasoning." *Developmental Psychology* 26 (6): 952–60.

Leigh, Paul. 1983. "Direct and Indirect Effects of Education on Health." *Social Science and Medicine* 17 (4): 227–34.

Leonhardt, David. 2011. "Even for Cashiers, College Pays Off." *New York Times*. June 25. http://www.nytimes.com/2011/06/26/sunday-review/26leonhardt.html?_r=0.

Leping, Kristjan-Olari. 2007. "Racial Differences in Availability of Fringe Benefits as an Explanation for the Unexplained Black-White Wage Gap for Males in the U.S." University of Tartu—Faculty of Economics and Business Administration Working Paper Series 57: 3–39.

Leppel, Karen. 2001. "The Impact of Major on College Persistence among Freshmen." *Higher Education* 41 (3): 327–42.

Leshowitz, Barry. 1989. "It Is Time We Did Something about Scientific Illiteracy." *American Psychologist* 44 (8): 1159–60.

Levine, Phillip, and David Zimmerman. 1995. "The Benefit of Additional High-School Math and Science Classes for Young Men and Women." *Journal of Business and Economic Statistics* 13 (2): 137–49.

Light, Audrey. 1999. "High School Employment, High School Curriculum, and Post-school Wages." *Economics of Education Review* 18 (3): 291–309.

———. 2001. "In-School Work Experience and the Returns to Schooling." *Journal of Labor Economics* 19 (1): 65–93.

Light, Audrey, and Wayne Strayer. 2000. "Determinants of College Completion: School Quality or Student Ability?" *Journal of Human Resources* 35 (2): 299–332.

———. 2004. "Who Receives the College Wage Premium? Assessing the Labor Market Returns to Degrees and College Transfer Patterns." *Journal of Human Resources* 39 (3): 746–73.

Lincoln Institute of Land Policy. 2015. "Gross Rent-Price Ratio, U.S. Stock of Owner-Occupied Housing 1960–2014." Accessed November 15. https://www.lincolninst.edu/subcenters/land-values/data/dlm-rents-prices-2014q1.xls.

Lind, Allan, Jerald Greenberg, Kimberly Scott, and Thomas Welchans. 2000. "The Winding Road from Employee to Complainant: Situational and Psychological Determinants of Wrongful-Termination Claims." *Administrative Science Quarterly* 45 (3): 557–90.

Liu, Sze, Stephen Buka, Crystal Linkletter, Ichiro Kawachi, Laura Kubzansky, and Eric Loucks. 2011. "The Association between Blood Pressure and Years of Schooling versus Educational Credentials: Test of the Sheepskin Effect." *Annals of Epidemiology* 21 (2): 128–38.

Liu, Sze, Stephen Buka, Laura Kubzansky, Ichiro Kawachi, Stephen Gilman, and Eric Loucks. 2013. "Sheepskin Effects of Education in the 10-Year Framingham Risk of Coronary Heart Disease." *Social Science and Medicine* 80: 31–36.

Livingstone, David. 1998. *The Education-Jobs Gap: Underemployment or Economic Democracy*. New York: Westview.

Lleras-Muney, Adriana. 2005. "The Relationship between Education and Adult Mortality in the United States." *Review of Economic Studies* 72 (1): 189–221.

Lochner, Lance. 2004. "Education, Work, and Crime: A Human Capital Approach." *International Economic Review* 45 (3): 811–43.

———. 2011. "Nonproduction Benefits of Education: Crime, Health, and Good Citizenship." In *Handbook of the Economics of Education*, vol. 4, edited by Eric Hanushek, Stephen Machin, and Ludger Woessmann, 183–282.

Lochner, Lance, and Alexander Monge-Naranjo. 2011. "The Nature of Credit Constraints and Human Capital." *American Economic Review* 101 (6): 2487–529.

———. 2012. "Credit Constraints in Education." *Annual Review of Economics* 4: 225–56.

Lochner, Lance, and Enrico Moretti. 2004. "The Effect of Education on Crime: Evidence from Prison Inmates, Arrests, and Self-Reports." *America Economic Review* 94 (1): 155–89.

Long, Bridget. 2004. "How Have College Decisions Changed over Time? An Application of the Conditional Logistic Choice Model." *Journal of Econometrics* 121 (1–2): 271–96.

Long, James, and Eugenia Toma. 1988. "The Determinants of Private School Attendance, 1970–1980." *Review of Economics and Statistics* 70 (2): 351–57.

Long, Mark. 2008. "College Quality and Early Adult Outcomes." *Economics of Education Review* 27 (5): 588–602.

Los Angeles Times. 2016. "Los Angeles Teacher Ratings: FAQ and About." Accessed September 14, 2016. http://projects.latimes.com/value-added/faq.

Lott, John. 1990. "An Explanation for the Public Provision of Schooling: The Importance of Indoctrination." *Journal of Law and Economics* 33 (1): 199–231.

Loury, Linda. 2006. "Some Contacts Are More Equal Than Others: Informal Networks, Job Tenure, and Wages." *Journal of Labor Economics* 24 (2): 299–318.

Luan, Jing, and Robert Fenske. 1996. "Financial Aid, Persistence, and Degree Completion in Masters Degree Programs." *Journal of Student Financial Aid* 26 (1): 17–31.

Lucretius. 1997. *On the Nature of the Universe.* Oxford: Oxford University Press.

Lutz, Wolfgang, and K. Samir. 2011. "Global Human Capital: Integrating Education and Population." *Science* 333 (6042): 587–92.

Ma, Yingyi, and Gokhan Savas. 2014. "Which Is More Consequential: Fields of Study or Institutional Selectivity?" *Review of Higher Education* 37 (2): 221–47.

Machin, Stephen, Olivier Marie, and Sunčica Vujić. 2011. "The Crime Reducing Effect of Education." *Economic Journal* 121 (552): 463–84.

Macnamara, Brooke, David Hambrick, and Frederick Oswald. 2014. "Deliberate Practice and Performance in Music, Games, Sports, Education, and Professions: A Meta-analysis." *Psychological Science* 25 (8): 1608–18.

Mane, Ferran. 1999. "Trends in the Payoff to Academic and Occupation-Specific Skills: The Short and Medium Run Returns to Academic and Vocational High School Courses for Non–College Bound Students." *Economics of Education Review* 18 (4): 417–37.

Mann, Sandi, and Andrew Robinson. 2009. "Boredom in the Lecture Theatre: An Investigation into the Contributors, Moderators and Outcomes of Boredom amongst University Students." *British Educational Research Journal* 35 (2): 243–58.

Marmaros, David, and Bruce Sacerdote. 2002. "Peer and Social Networks in Job Search." *European Economic Review* 46 (4): 870–79.

Marmot, Michael. 2006. "Status Syndrome: A Challenge to Medicine." *Journal of the American Medical Association* 295 (11): 1304–7.

Marsh, John. 2011. *Class Dismissed: Why We Cannot Teach or Learn Our Way Out of Inequality.* New York: Monthly Review Press.

Martin, Steven. 2004. "Growing Evidence for a 'Divorce Divide'? Education and Marital Dissolution Rates in the U.S. since the 1970's." Working Paper, University of Maryland. Accessed November 15, 2015. https://www.russellsage.org/sites/all/files/u4/Martin_0.pdf.

Martinez, Gladys, Kimberly Daniels, and Anjani Chandra. 2012. "Fertility of Men and Women Aged 15–44 Years in the United States: National Survey of Family Growth, 2006–2010." *National Health Statistics Reports* 51: 1–28.

Mayer, Gerald. 2004. *Union Membership Trends in the United States.* Washington, DC: Congressional Research Service. http://digitalcommons.ilr.cornell.edu/cgi/viewcontent.cgi?article=1176&context=key_workplace.

———. 2011. *Selected Characteristics of Private and Public Sector Workers.* Washington, DC: Congressional Research Service. July 1. http://www.govexec.com/pdfs/071911kl1.pdf.

McArdle, Megan. 2013. "Why a BA Is Now a Ticket to a Job in a Coffee Shop." *Daily Beast.* March 27. http://www.thedailybeast.com/articles/2013/03/27/why-a-ba-is-now-a-ticket-to-a-job-in-a-coffee-shop.html.

McCleary, Rachel, and Robert Barro. 2006. "Religion and Political Economy in an International Panel." *Journal for the Scientific Study of Religion* 45 (2): 149–75.

McCollister, Kathryn, Michael French, and Hai Fang. 2010. "The Cost of Crime to Society: New Crime-Specific Estimates for Policy and Program Evaluation." *Drug and Alcohol Dependence* 108 (1): 98–109.

McCord, Linnea. 1999. "Defamation vs. Negligent Referral: A Policy of Giving Only Basic Employee References May Lead to Liability." *Graziadio Business Review* 2 (2). https://gbr.pepperdine.edu/2010/08/defamation-vs-negligent-referral.

McDaniel, Michael, Frank Schmidt, and John Hunter. 1988. "Job Experience Correlates of Job Performance." *Journal of Applied Psychology* 73 (2): 327–30.

McKeough, Anne, Judy Lupart, and Anthony Marini, eds. 1995. *Teaching for Transfer: Fostering Generalization in Learning.* Mahwah, NJ: Lawrence Erlbaum Associates.

McMahon, Walter. 1998. "Conceptual Framework for the Analysis of the Social Benefits of Lifelong Learnings." *Education Economics* 6 (3): 309–46.

McMurrer, Jennifer. 2007. *Choices, Changes, and Challenges: Curriculum and Instruction in the NCLB Era.* Washington, DC: Center on Education Policy. http://www.cep-dc .org/cfcontent_file.cfm?Attachment=McMurrer%5FFullReport%5FCurricAndInstr uction%5F072407%2Epdf.

Meer, Jonathan. 2007. "Evidence on the Returns to Secondary Vocational Education." *Economics of Education Review* 26 (5): 559–73.

Meisenberg, Gerhard. 2008. "How Universal Is the Negative Correlation between Education and Fertility?" *Journal of Social Political and Economic Studies* 33 (2): 205–29.

Meisenberg, Gerhard, Heiner Rindermann, Hardik Patel, and M. Woodley. 2012. "Is It Smart to Believe in God? The Relationship of Religiosity with Education and Intelligence." *Temas em Psicologia* 20 (1): 101–20.

Melly, Blaise. 2005. "Public-Private Sector Wage Differentials in Germany: Evidence from Quantile Regression." *Empirical Economics* 30 (2): 505–20.

Merriam-Webster Dictionary. 2015. Accessed November 15, 2015. http://www.merriam-webster.com/dictionary.

Merriam-Webster's Collegiate Dictionary. 2003. 11th ed. Springfield, MA: Merriam-Webster.

Miller, Paul, Charles Mulvey, and Nick Martin. 1995. "What Do Twins Studies Reveal about the Economic Returns to Education? A Comparison of Australian and US Findings." *America Economic Review* 85 (3): 586–99.

———. 2001. "Genetic and Environmental Contributions to Educational Attainment in Australia." *Economics of Education Review* 20 (3): 211–24.

Mincer, Jacob. 1974. *Schooling, Experience, and Earnings.* New York: Columbia University Press.

Moe, Terry. 2011. *Special Interest: Teachers Unions and America's Public Schools.* Washington, DC: Brookings Institution.

Mok, Wallace, and Zahra Siddique. 2011. "Racial and Ethnic Inequality in Employer-Provided Fringe Benefits." IZA Discussion Paper Series No. 6255. http://ftp. iza.org /dp6255.pdf.

Monks, James. 2000. "The Returns to Individual and College Characteristics: Evidence from the National Longitudinal Survey of Youth." *Economics of Education Review* 19 (3): 279–89.

Monte, Lindsay, and Renee Ellis. 2014. *Fertility of Women in the United States: 2012.* Washington, DC: United States Census Bureau. https://www.census.gov/content /dam/Census/library/publications/2014/demo/p20-575.pdf.

Montgomery, James. 1991. "Social Networks and Labor-Market Outcomes: Toward an Economic Analysis." *America Economic Review* 81 (5): 1408–18.

Montmarquette, Claude, Kathy Cannings, and Sophie Mahseredjian. 2002. "How Do Young People Choose College Majors?" *Economics of Education Review* 21 (6): 543–56.

Moretti, Enrico. 2004. "Estimating the Social Return to Higher Education: Evidence from Longitudinal and Repeated Cross-Sectional Data." *Journal of Econometrics* 121 (1): 175–212.

Mortimer, Jeylan, Michael Finch, Seongryeol Ryu, Michael Shanahan, and Kathleen Call. 1996. "The Effect of Work Intensity on Adolescent Mental Health, Achievement, and Behavioral Adjustments." *Child Development* 67 (3): 1243–61.

Mouw, Ted. 2003. "Social Capital and Finding a Job: Do Contacts Matter?" *American Sociological Review* 68 (6): 868–98.

Mujika, Iñigo, and Sabino Padilla. 2000a. "Detraining: Loss of Training-Induced Physiological and Performance Adaptations: Part I; Short Term Insufficient Training Stimulus." *Sports Medicine* 30 (2): 79–87.

———. 2000b. "Detraining: Loss of Training-Induced Physiological and Performance Adaptations: Part II; Long Term Insufficient Training Stimulus." *Sports Medicine* 30 (3): 145–54.

Mullen, Ann, Kimberly Goyette, and Joseph Soares. 2003. "Who Goes to Graduate School? Social and Academic Correlates of Educational Continuation after College." *Sociology of Education* 76 (2): 143–69.

Mulligan, Casey, Ricard Gil, and Xavier Sala-i-Martin. 2004. "Do Democracies Have Different Public Policies than Nondemocracies?" *Journal of Economic Perspectives* 18 (1): 51–74.

Munasinghe, Lalith, Tania Reif, and Alice Henriques. 2008. "Gender Gap in Wage Returns to Job Tenure and Experience." *Labour Economics* 15 (6): 1296–316.

Murnane, Richard, John Willett, Yves Duhaldeborde, and John Tyler. 2000. "How Important Are the Cognitive Skills of Teenagers in Predicting Subsequent Earnings?" *Journal of Policy Analysis and Management* 19 (4): 547–68.

Murnane, Richard, John Willett, and Frank Levy. 1995. "The Growing Importance of Cognitive Skills in Wage Determination." *Review of Economics and Statistics* 77 (2): 251–66.

Murphy, Kevin. 2002. "Can Conflicting Perspectives on the Role of g in Personnel Selection Be Resolved?" *Human Performance* 15 (1–2): 173–86.

Murphy, Kevin, and Robert Topel. 2006. "The Value of Health and Longevity." *Journal of Political Economy* 114 (5): 871–904.

Murphy, Kevin, and Finis Welch. 1990. "Empirical Age-Earnings Profiles." *Journal of Labor Economics* 8 (2): 202–29.

Murray, Charles. 2008. *Real Education: Four Simple Truths for Bringing America's Schools Back to Reality*. New York: Crown Forum.

Musgrave, Richard. 2008. "Merit Goods." In *The New Palgrave: A Dictionary of Economics*, edited by Steven Durlauf and Lawrence Blume. New York: Palgrave Macmillan. http://www.palgraveconnect.com/pc/doifinder/view/10.1057/9781137336583.1168.

Musick, Kelly, Jennie Brand, and Dwight Davis. 2012. "Variation in the Relationship Between Education and Marriage: Marriage Market Mismatch?" *Journal of Marriage and Family* 74 (1): 53–69.

Nagler, Jonathan. 1991. "The Effect of Registration Laws and Education on US Voter Turnout." *American Political Science Review* 85 (4): 1393–405.

National Science Board. 2012. "Science and Engineering Indicators 2012." http://www .nsf.gov/statistics/seind12/pdf/seind12.pdf.

Natsuaki, Misaki, Xiaojia Ge, and Ernst Wenk. 2008. "Continuity and Changes in the Developmental Trajectories of Criminal Career: Examining the Roles of Timing of First Arrest and High School Graduation." *Journal of Youth and Adolescence* 37 (4): 431–44.

Neal, Derek, and William Johnson. 1996. "The Role of Premarket Factors in Black-White Wage Differences." *Journal of Political Economy* 104 (5): 869–95.

Nederhof, Anton. 1985. "Methods of Coping with Social Desirability Bias: A Review." *European Journal of Social Psychology* 15 (3): 263–80.

Neumark, David. 1999. "Biases in Twin Estimates of the Return to Schooling." *Economics of Education Review* 18 (2): 143–48.

Neumark, David, and Paul Taubman. 1995. "Why Do Wage Profiles Slope Upward? Tests of the General Human Capital Model." *Journal of Labor Economics* 13 (4): 736–61.

Nie, Norman, Jane Junn, and Kenneth Stehlik-Barry. 1996. *Education and Democratic Citizenship in America*. Chicago: University of Chicago Press.

Nielsen. 2015. "2014 Nielsen Music U.S. Report." Accessed November 15. http:// www.nielsen.com/content/dam/corporate/us/en/public%20factsheets/Soundscan /nielsen-2014-year-end-music-report-us.pdf.

Nielsen, François. 2006. "Achievement and Ascription in Educational Attainment: Genetic and Environmental Influences on Adolescent Schooling." *Social Forces* 85 (1): 193–216.

Nielsen, Laura, and Aaron Beim. 2004. "Media Misrepresentation: Title VII, Print Media, and Public Perceptions of Discrimination Litigation." *Stanford Law and Policy Review* 15 (1): 237–65.

Nielsen, Laura, Robert Nelson, and Ryon Lancaster. 2010. "Individual Justice or Collective Legal Mobilization? Employment Discrimination Litigation in the Post Civil Rights United States." *Journal of Empirical Legal Studies* 7 (2): 175–201.

Nielsen, Laura, Robert Nelson, Ryon Lancaster, and Nicholas Pedriana. 2008. *Contesting Workplace Discrimination in Court: Characteristics and Outcomes of Federal Employment Discrimination Litigation 1987–2003*. Chicago: American Bar Foundation. http://www.americanbarfoundation.org/uploads/cms/documents/nielsen_abf_edl _report_08_final.pdf.

Niskanen, William. 1997. "R&D and Economic Growth—Cautionary Thoughts." In *Science for the Twenty-First Century: The Bush Report Revisited*, edited by Claude Barfield, 81–94. Washington, DC: American Enterprise Institute.

Nobel Prize. 2015. "A. Michael Spence—Facts." Accessed November 15. http://www .nobelprize.org/nobel_prizes/economic-sciences/laureates/2001/spence-facts.html.

Nye, John. 2014. "Ronald Coase: An Appreciation." *Independent Review* 19 (1): 101–8.

Obukhova, Elena. 2012. "Motivation vs. Relevance: Using Strong Ties to Find a Job in Urban China." *Social Science Research* 41 (3): 570–80.

Obukhova, Elena, and George Lan. 2013. "Do Job Seekers Benefit from Contacts? A Direct Test with Contemporaneous Searches." *Management Science* 59 (10): 2204–16.

OECD. 2014. *Education at a Glance 2014: OECD Indicators*. Paris: OECD. http://www .oecd.org/edu/Education-at-a-Glance-2014.pdf.

Office of Management and Budget. 2014. *The Budget for Fiscal Year 2015, Historical Tables*. Washington, DC: U.S. Government Printing Office. https://www.whitehouse .gov/sites/default/files/omb/budget/fy2015/assets/hist.pdf.

O'Keefe, Bryan, and Richard Vedder. 2008. *Griggs v. Duke Power: Implications for College Credentialing*. Raleigh, NC: John William Pope Center for Higher Education Policy. http://www.popecenter.org/acrobat/Griggs_vs_Duke_Power.pdf.

Olson, James, Philip Vernon, Julie Harris, and Kerry Jang. 2001. "The Heritability of Attitudes: A Study of Twins." *Journal of Personality and Social Psychology* 80 (6): 845–60.

The Onion. 2003. "U.S. Government to Discontinue Long-Term, Low-Yield Investment in Nation's Youth." Last modified September 24. http://www.theonion.com/article /us-government-to-discontinue-long-term-low-yield-i-751.

Ono, Hiromi. 2009. "Husbands' and Wives' Education and Divorce in the United States and Japan, 1946–2000." *Journal of Family History* 34 (3): 292–322.

Operario, Don, Nancy Adler, and David Williams. 2004. "Subjective Social Status: Reliability and Predictive Utility for Global Health." *Psychology and Health* 19 (2): 237–46.

Oreopoulos, Philip, and Uros Petronijevic. 2013. "Making College Worth It: A Review of the Returns to Higher Education." *Future of Children* 23 (1): 41–65.

Oreopoulos, Philip, and Kjell Salvanes. 2011. "Priceless: The Nonpecuniary Benefits of Schooling." *Journal of Economic Perspectives* 25 (1): 159–84.

O'Roarke, P. J. 2007. *A Parliament of Whores: A Lone Humorist Attempts to Explain the Entire U.S. Government*. New York: Grove/Atlantic.

Ost, Ben. 2010. "The Role of Peers and Grades in Determining Major Persistence in the Sciences." *Economics of Education Review* 29 (6): 923–34.

Ovum. 2014. "Pop Still the Biggest Music Genre, but Retail Sales Slide 7.6% in 2013." *Music and Copyright*. July 15. https://musicandcopyright.wordpress.com/2014/07/15 /pop-still-the-biggest-music-genre-but-retail-sales-slide-7-6-in-2013.

Owen, Stephanie, and Isabel Sawhill. 2013. *Should Everyone Go to College?* Washington, DC: Brookings Institute. http://www.brookings.edu/~/media/research/files /papers/2013/05/07-should-everyone-go-to-college-owen-sawhill/08-should-every one-go-to-college-owen-sawhill.pdf.

Pack, Howard. 1994. "Endogenous Growth Theory: Intellectual Appeal and Empirical Shortcomings." *Journal of Economic Perspectives* 8 (1): 55–72.

Park, Jin. 1994. "Estimation of Sheepskin Effects and Returns to Schooling Using the Old and the New CPS Measures of Educational Attainment." Industrial Relations Section, Princeton University Working Paper No. 338. http://harris.princeton.edu /pubs/pdfs/338.pdf.

———. 1999. "Estimation of Sheepskin Effects Using the Old and the New Measures of Educational Attainment in the Current Population Survey." *Economics Letters* 62 (2): 237–40.

Pascarella, Ernest, and Patrick Terenzini. 2005. *How College Affects Students*. Vol. 2, *A Third Decade of Research*. San Francisco: Jossey-Bass Wiley.

Pasche, Cyril. 2009. "A Multiple Ability Approach to Employer Learning." University of Geneva, Economics of Education Project. http://www.educationeconomics.unige.ch /Projets/Competences/Pasche_09.pdf.

Paternoster, Raymond, Shawn Bushway, Robert Brame, and Robert Apel. 2003. "The Effect of Teenage Employment on Delinquency and Problem Behaviors." *Social Forces* 82 (1): 297–335.

Pellizzari, Michele. 2010. "Do Friends and Relatives Really Help in Getting a Good Job?" *Industrial and Labor Relations Review* 63 (3): 494–510.

Pencavel, John. 1998. "Assortative Mating by Schooling and the Work Behavior of Wives and Husbands." *American Economic Review* 88 (2): 326–29.

Pérez, Ruth, and Gerardo Loera. 2015. "Los Angeles Unified School District Reference Guide REF-4236.11." Last modified June 22. http://notebook.lausd.net/pls/ptl/docs /page/ca_lausd/fldr_organizations/fldr_instructional_svcs/ref-4236.11.pdf.

Perkins, David. 1985. "Postprimary Education Has Little Impact on Informal Reasoning." *Journal of Educational Psychology* 77 (5): 562–71.

Perkins, David, and Gavriel Salomon. 2012. "Knowledge to Go: A Motivational and Dispositional View of Transfer." *Educational Psychologist* 47 (3): 248–58.

Perna, Laura. 2004. "Understanding the Decision to Enroll in Graduate School: Sex and Racial/Ethnic Group Differences." *Journal of Higher Education* 75 (5): 487–527.

Phelps, Edmund. 1972. "The Statistical Theory of Racism and Sexism." *American Economic Review* 62 (4): 659–61.

Phillips Exeter Academy. 2015. "Tuition and Fees." Accessed March 17, 2015. http:// www.exeter.edu/admissions/109_1370.aspx.

Pinker, Steven. 2014. "The Trouble with Harvard: The Ivy League Is Broken and Only Standardized Tests Can Fix It." *New Republic*. September 4. http://www.newrepublic .com/article/119321/harvard-ivy-league-should-judge-students-standardized-tests.

Pithers, Robert, and Rebecca Soden. 2000. "Critical Thinking in Education: A Review." *Educational Research* 42 (3): 237–49.

Plank, Stephen. 2001. *Career and Technical Education in the Balance: An Analysis of High School Persistence, Academic Achievement, and Postsecondary Destinations*. St. Paul, MN: National Research Center for Career and Technical Education.

Popowych, Krista. 2004. "De-hiring a Problem Employee." *IDEA Health and Fitness Association*. Last modified January 1. http://www.ideafit.com/fitness-library /de-hiring-a-problem-employee.

Posner, Richard. 2008. "The New Gender Gap in Education—Posner's Comment." *Becker-Posner Blog*. March 2. http://www.becker-posner-blog.com/2008/03 /the-new-gender-gap-in-education-posners-comment/comments/page/2.

Powell, G. 1986. "American Voter Turnout in Comparative Perspective." *American Political Science Review* 80 (1): 17–43.

Powers, Donald, and Donald Rock. 1999. "Effects of Coaching on SAT I: Reasoning Test Scores." *Journal of Educational Measurement* 36 (2): 93–118.

Princeton University. 2015. "Undergraduate Admission: Fees and Payment Options." Accessed December 9, 2015. https://admission.princeton.edu/financialaid /fees-payment-options.

Pritchett, Lant. 2001. "Where Has All the Education Gone?" *World Bank Economic Review* 15 (3): 367–91.

———. 2002. " 'When Will They Ever Learn?' Why *All* Governments Produce Schooling." Unpublished manuscript. http://www.ksg.harvard.edu/fs/lpritch/Education%20-%20 docs/ED%20-%20Gov%20action/whenlearn_v1.pdf.

———. 2006. "Does Learning to Add Up Add Up? The Returns to Schooling in Aggregate Data." *Handbook of the Economics of Education* 1: 635–95.

———. 2013. *The Rebirth of Education: Schooling Ain't Learning.* Washington, DC: Center for Global Development.

Pryor, John, Kevin Eagan, Laura Blake, Sylvia Hurtado, Jennifer Berdan, and Matthew Case. 2012. *The American Freshman: National Norms Fall 2012.* Los Angeles: Higher Education Research Institute. https://www.heri.ucla.edu/monographs/TheAmerican Freshman2012.pdf.

Pryor, Frederic, and David Schaffer. 2000. *Who's Not Working and Why: Employment, Cognitive Skills, Wages, and the Changing US Labor Market.* Cambridge: Cambridge University Press.

Psacharopoulos, George. 1987. "To Vocationalize or Not to Vocationalize: That Is the Curriculum Question." *International Review of Education* 33 (2): 187–211.

Psacharopoulos, George, and Harry Patrinos. 2004. "Returns to Investment in Education: A Further Update." *Education Economics* 12 (2): 111–34.

Quesnel-Vallée, Amélie. 2007. "Self-Rated Health: Caught in the Crossfire of the Quest for 'True' Health?" *International Journal of Epidemiology* 36 (6): 1161–64.

Quiñones, Miguel, J. Ford, and Mark Teachout. 1995. "The Relationship between Work Experience and Job Performance: A Conceptual and Meta-analytic Review." *Personnel Psychology* 48 (4): 887–910.

Quora. 2015. "Who Said 'If You Think Education Is Expensive, Try Ignorance?'" Accessed March 25, 2015. http://www.quora.com/Who-said-If-you-think -education-is-expensive-try-ignorance.

Rampell, Catherine. 2011. "Many with New College Degree Find the Job Market Humbling." *New York Times.* May 18. http://www.nytimes.com/2011/05/19/business /economy/19grads.html.

Randall, Donna, and Maria Fernandes. 1991. "The Social Desirability Response Bias in Ethics Research." *Journal of Business Ethics* 10 (11): 805–17.

Ranker. 2015. "The Best-Selling Books of All Time." Accessed March 25, 2015. http://www.ranker.com/list/best-selling-books-of-all-time/jeff419?var=4&utm _expid=16418821-179.vk2gM_coRrOMcxn9T2riGQ.3.

Rasinski, Kenneth, and Steven Pedlow. 1998. "The Effect of High School Vocational Education on Academic Achievement Gain and High School Persistence: Evidence from NELS:88." In *The Quality of Vocational Education: Background Papers from the 1994 National Assessment of Vocational Education,* edited by Adam Gamoran, 177–207. Washington, DC: U.S. Department of Education.

Rasmussen, R. 1998. *The Quotable Mark Twain: His Essential Aphorisms, Witticisms and Concise Opinions.* New York: McGraw-Hill.

Raudenbush, Stephen, and Rafa Kasim. 1998. "Cognitive Skill and Economic Inequality: Findings from the National Adult Literacy Survey." *Harvard Educational Review* 68 (1): 33–80.

Ravitch, Diane. 2011. *The Death and Life of the Great American School System: How Testing and Choice Are Undermining Education.* New York: Basic Books.

Reed, Stephen. 1993. "A Schema-Based Theory of Transfer." In *Transfer on Trial: Intelligence, Cognition, and Instruction,* edited by Douglas Detterman and Robert Sternberg, 39–67. New York: Ablex.

Rees, Albert. 1993. "The Role of Fairness in Wage Determination." *Journal of Labor Economics* 11 (1): 243–52.

Richards, Lynne. 1988. "The Appearance of Youthful Subculture: A Theoretical Perspective on Deviance." *Clothing and Textiles Research Journal* 6 (3): 56–64.

Richman, Sheldon. 1995. *Separating School and State: How to Liberate America's Families*. Fairfax, VA: Future of Freedom Foundation.

Riddell, W. 2008. "Understanding 'Sheepskin Effects' in the Return to Education: The Role of Changing Cognitive Skills." Paper presented at the CLSRN Workshop, University of Toronto, November 18–19. Accessed November 18, 2015. http://www.clsrn .econ.ubc.ca/hrsdc/papers/Paper%20no.%202%20-%20Craig%20Riddell%20-%20 Sheepskin%20Effects.pdf.

Riddell, W., and Xueda Song. 2011. "The Impact of Education on Unemployment Incidence and Re-employment Success: Evidence from the US Labour Market." *Labour Economics* 18 (4): 453–63.

Riley, John. 2001. "Silver Signals: Twenty-Five Years of Screening and Signaling." *Journal of Economic Literature* 39 (2): 432–78.

Ritter, Joseph, and Lowell Taylor. 2011. "Racial Disparity in Unemployment." *Review of Economics and Statistics* 93 (1): 30–42.

Robinson, Ken, and Lou Aronica. 2015. *Creative Schools: The Grassroots Revolution That's Transforming Education*. New York: Viking.

Robst, John. 1995. "College Quality and Overeducation." *Economics of Education Review* 14 (3): 221–28.

———. 2007. "Education and Job Match: The Relatedness of College Major and Work." *Economics of Education Review* 26 (4): 397–407.

Rodriguez, Orlando. 1978. "Occupational Shifts and Educational Upgrading in the American Labor Force between 1950 and 1970." *Sociology of Education* 51 (1): 55–67.

Roehling, Mark. 2002. "The 'Good Cause Norm' in Employment Relations: Empirical Evidence and Policy Implications." *Employee Responsibilities and Rights Journal* 14 (2–3): 91–104.

Rochling, Mark, and Wendy Boswell. 2004. " 'Good Cause Beliefs' in an 'At-Will World'? A Focused Investigation of Psychological versus Legal Contracts." *Employee Responsibilities and Rights Journal* 16 (4): 211–31.

Rogers, Jenny. 2010. "Getting the Ax from George Clooney: Do Firing Consultants Really Exist?" *Slate*. Last modified January 7. http://www.slate.com/articles/news_and _politics/explainer/2010/01/getting_the_ax_from_george_clooney.html.

Romano, Andrew. 2011. "How Dumb Are We?" *Newsweek*. March 28/April 4. http:// www.nscsd.org/webpages/jleach/files/how%20dumb.pdf.

Romer, David. 1993. "Do Students Go to Class? Should They?" *Journal of Economic Perspectives* 7 (3): 167–74.

Rose, Heather, and Julian Betts. 2004. "The Effect of High School Courses on Earnings." *Review of Economics and Statistics* 86 (2): 497–513.

Rosenbaum, James. 1998. "College-for-All: Do Students Understand What College Demands?" *Social Psychology of Education* 2 (1): 55–80.

Rosenbaum, James, and Stephanie Jones. 2000. "Interactions between High Schools and Labor Markets." In *Handbook of the Sociology of Education*, edited by Maureen Hallinan, 411–36. New York: Kluwer.

Ross, Catherine, and John Mirowsky. 1999. "Refining the Association between Education and Health: The Effects of Quantity, Credential, and Selectivity." *Demography* 36 (4): 445–60.

Ross, Catherine, and Chia-ling Wu. 1995. "The Links between Education and Health." *American Sociological Review* 60 (5): 719–45.

Roth, Philip, Craig BeVier, Fred Switzer, and Jeffery Schippmann. 1996. "Meta-analyzing the Relationship between Grades and Job Performance." *Journal of Applied Psychology* 81 (5): 548–56.

Roth, Philip, and Richard Clarke. 1998. "Meta-analyzing the Relation between Grades and Salary." *Journal of Vocational Behavior* 53 (3): 386–400.

Rothbard, Murray. 1999. *Schooling: Free and Compulsory*. Auburn, AL: Ludwig von Mises Institute.

Rothman, Stanley, Robert Lichter, and Neil Nevitte. 2005. "Politics and Professional Advancement among College Faculty." *Forum* 3 (1). http://www.cwu.edu/~manwellerm/academic%20bias.pdf.

Rothstein, Donna. 2007. "High School Employment and Youths' Academic Achievement." *Journal of Human Resources* 42 (1): 194–213.

Rothstein, Jesse. 2015. "Revisiting the Impacts of Teachers." UC Berkeley Working Paper. http://eml.berkeley.edu/~jrothst/workingpapers/rothstein_cfr.pdf.

Rothstein, Jesse, and Albert Yoon. 2008. "Mismatch in Law School." NBER Working Paper No. 14275. http://www.nber.org/papers/w14275.

Rowe, David. 1994. *The Limits of Family Influence: Genes, Experience, and Behavior*. New York: Guilford.

Rowe, David, Wendy Vesterdal, and Joseph Rodgers. 1998. "Herrnstein's Syllogism: Genetic and Shared Environmental Influences on IQ, Education, and Income." *Intelligence* 26 (4): 405–23.

Rowe, Mike. 2012. "The First Four Years Are the Hardest . . ." *Mike Rowe*. September 3. http://mikerowe.com/2012/09/the-first-four-years-are-the-hardest.

Rubb, Stephen. 2003. "Overeducation: A Short or Long Run Phenomenon for Individuals?" *Economics of Education Review* 22 (4): 389–94.

Ruhm, Christopher. 1997. "Is High School Employment Consumption or Investment?" *Journal of Labor Economics* 15 (4): 735–76.

Rumberger, Russell. 2011. *Dropping Out: Why Students Drop Out of High School and What Can Be Done about It*. Cambridge, MA: Harvard University Press.

Rumberger, Russell, and Sun Lim. 2008. "Why Students Drop Out of School: A Review of 25 Years of Research." *California Dropout Research Project, Policy Brief 15*. http://www.slocounty.ca.gov/Assets/CSN/PDF/Flyer+-+Why+students+drop+out.pdf.

Ryan, Ann, Lynn McFarland, Helen Baron, and Ron Page. 1999. "An International Look at Selection Practices: Nation and Culture as Explanations for Variability in Practice." *Personnel Psychology* 52 (2): 359–92.

Ryan, Paul. 1998. "Is Apprenticeship Better? A Review of the Economic Evidence." *Journal of Vocational Education and Training* 50 (2): 289–329.

Sabot, Richard, and John Wakeman-Linn. 1991. "Grade Inflation and Course Choice." *Journal of Economic Perspectives* 5 (1): 159–70.

Sacerdote, Bruce. 2007. "How Large Are the Effects from Changes in Family Environment? A Study of Korean American Adoptees." *Quarterly Journal of Economics* 122 (1): 119–57.

Sackett, Paul, Matthew Borneman, and Brian Connelly. 2008. "High Stakes Testing in Higher Education and Employment: Appraising the Evidence for Validity and Fairness." *American Psychologist* 63 (4): 215–27.

Sagan, Carl. 1985. *Cosmos*. New York: Random House.

Salomon, Gavriel, and David Perkins. 1989. "Rocky Roads to Transfer: Rethinking Mechanism of a Neglected Phenomenon." *Educational Psychologist* 24 (2): 113–42.

Sandewall, Örjan, David Cesarini, and Magnus Johannesson. 2014. "The Co-twin Methodology and Returns to Schooling—Testing a Critical Assumption." *Labour Economics* 26: 1–10.

Sapolsky, Robert. 2005. "The Influence of Social Hierarchy on Primate Health." *Science* 308 (5722): 648–52.

Schelling, Thomas. 1980. *The Strategy of Conflict*. Cambridge, MA: Harvard University Press.

Schmidt, Frank. 2009. "Select on Intelligence." In *Handbook of Principles of Organizational Behavior*, edited by Edwin Locke, 3–17. Hoboken, NJ: Wiley.

Schmidt, Frank, and John Hunter. 2004. "General Mental Ability in the World of Work: Occupational Attainment and Job Performance." *Journal of Personality and Social Psychology* 86 (1): 162–73.

Schmitt, John, Kris Warner, and Sarika Gupta. 2010. *The High Budgetary Cost of Incarceration*. Washington, DC: Center for Economic and Policy Research. http://www.cepr.net/documents/publications/incarceration-2010-06.pdf.

Schneider, James. 1993. "Flight into L.A." Unpublished manuscript.

Schoen, Robert, and Yen-hsin Cheng. 2006. "Partner Choice and the Differential Retreat from Marriage." *Journal of Marriage and Family* 68 (1): 1–10.

Schoenhals, Mark, Marta Tienda, and Barbara Schneider. 1998. "The Educational and Personal Consequences of Adolescent Employment." *Social Forces* 77 (2): 723–61.

Schrader, James. 1963. "School Site Selection." American Planning Association, Information Report No. 175. https://www.planning.org/pas/at60/report175.htm.

Schwartz, Christine. 2010. "Earnings Inequality and the Changing Association between Spouses' Earnings." *American Journal of Sociology* 115 (5): 1524–57.

Schwartz, Christine, and Robert Mare. 2005. "Trends in Educational Assortative Marriage from 1940 to 2003." *Demography* 42 (4): 621–46.

Scott-Clayton, Judith. 2010. "On Money and Motivation: A Quasi-Experimental Analysis of Financial Incentives for College Achievement." *Journal of Human Resources* 46 (3): 614–46.

Sebelius, Kathleen. 2012. *2012 Actuarial Report on the Financial Outlook for Medicaid*. Washington, DC: Department of Health and Human Services.

Segal, Nancy. 2000. *Entwined Lives*. London: Penguin.

Segalla, Michael, Gabriele Jacobs-Belschak, and Christiane Müller. 2001. "Cultural Influences on Employee Termination Decisions: Firing the Good, Average or the Old?" *European Management Journal* 19 (1): 58–72.

Selingo, Jeffrey. 2013. *College (Un)Bound*. Las Vegas: Amazon.

Shakespeare, William. 2004. *Julius Caesar*. New York: Simon and Schuster.

Shapiro, Ben. 2004. *Brainwashed: How Universities Indoctrinate America's Youth*. Nashville: Thomas Nelson.

Shapiro, Doug, Afet Dundar, Jin Chen, Mary Ziskin, Eunkyoung Park, Vasti Torres, and Yi-Chen Chiang. 2013. *Completing College: A State-Level View of Student Attainment*

Rates. Herndon, VA: National Student Clearinghouse Research Center. https://nsc researchcenter.org/wp-content/uploads/NSC_Signature_Report_6_StateSupp.pdf.

Shapiro, Fred, ed. 2006. *The Yale Book of Quotations.* New Haven, CT: Yale University Press.

Shavell, Steven. 1987. "The Optimal Use of Nonmonetary Sanctions as a Deterrent." *American Economic Review* 77 (4): 584–92.

Shavit, Yossi, and Walter Müller. 2000. "Vocational Secondary Education: Where Diversion and Where Safety Net?" *European Societies* 2 (1): 29–50.

Sianesi, Barbara, and John Van Reenen. 2003. "The Returns to Education: Macroeconomics." *Journal of Economic Surveys* 17 (2): 157–200.

Simon, Julian. 1996. *The Ultimate Resource 2.* Princeton, NJ: Princeton University Press.

Simpsons Archive. 1997. "Two Bad Neighbors." Last modified February 22. http://www .simpsonsarchive.com/episodes/3F09.html.

Singh-Manoux, Archana, Nancy Adler, and Michael Marmot. 2003. "Subjective Social Status: Its Determinants and Its Association with Measures of Ill-Health in the Whitehall II Study." *Social Science and Medicine* 56 (6): 1321–33.

Singh-Manoux, Archana, Michael Marmot, and Nancy Adler. 2005. "Does Subjective Social Status Predict Health and Change in Health Status Better Than Objective Status?" *Psychosomatic Medicine* 67 (6): 855–61.

Singley, Mark, and John Anderson. 1989. *The Transfer of Cognitive Skill.* Cambridge, MA: Harvard University Press.

Skirbekk, Vegard. 2008. "Fertility Trends by Social Status." *Demographic Research* 18 (5): 145–80.

Smith, James. 1999. "Healthy Bodies and Thick Wallets." *Journal of Economic Perspectives* 13 (2): 145–66.

Snyder, Howard. 2012. *Arrest in the United States, 1990–2010.* Washington, DC: Bureau of Justice Statistics. http://www.bjs.gov/content/pub/pdf/aus9010.pdf.

Snyder, Thomas, and Sally Dillow. 2011. *Digest of Education Statistics 2010.* Washington, DC: National Center for Education Statistics. https://nces.ed.gov/pubs2011/2011015 .pdf.

———. 2012. *Digest of Education Statistics 2011.* Washington, DC: National Center for Education Statistics. http://nces.ed.gov/pubs2012/2012001.pdf.

———. 2013. *Digest of Education Statistics 2012.* Washington, DC: National Center for Education Statistics. http://nces.ed.gov/pubs2014/2014015.pdf.

———. 2015. *Digest of Education Statistics 2013.* Washington, DC: National Center for Education Statistics. http://nces.ed.gov/pubs2015/2015011.pdf.

———. 2016. *Digest of Education Statistics 2014.* Washington, DC: National Center for Education Statistics. http://nces.ed.gov/pubs2016/2016006.pdf.

Somin, Ilya. 2013. *Democracy and Political Ignorance: Why Smaller Government Is Smarter.* Stanford, CA: Stanford University Press.

Sondheimer, Rachel, and Donald Green. 2010. "Using Experiments to Estimate the Effects of Education on Voter Turnout." *American Journal of Political Science* 54 (1): 174–89.

Spence, Michael. 1973. "Job Market Signaling." *Quarterly Journal of Economics* 87 (3): 355–74.

———. 1974. *Market Signaling: Informational Transfer in Hiring and Related Screening Processes.* Cambridge, MA: Harvard University Press.

———. 2002. "Signaling in Retrospect and the Informational Structure of Markets." *American Economic Review* 92 (3): 434–59.

Spencer, Mason, and Robert Weisberg. 1986. "Context-Dependent Effects on Analogical Transfer." *Memory and Cognition* 14 (5): 442–49.

Spilerman, Seymour, and Tormod Lunde. 1991. "Features of Educational Attainment and Job Promotion Prospects." *American Journal of Sociology* 97 (3): 689–720.

Stange, Kevin. 2012. "An Empirical Investigation of the Option Value of College Enrollment." *American Economic Journal: Applied Economics* 4 (1): 49–84.

———. 2015. "Differential Pricing in Undergraduate Education: Effects on Degree Production by Field." *Journal of Policy Analysis and Management* 34 (1): 107–35.

Stanley, Marcus. 2003. "College Education and the Midcentury GI Bills." *Quarterly Journal of Economics* 118 (2): 671–708.

State of California Department of Industrial Relations. 2013. "Child Labor Laws." Accessed November 18, 2015. http://www.dir.ca.gov/DLSE/ChildLaborLawPamphlet.pdf.

Stelzl, Ingeborg, Ferdinand Merz, Theodor Ehlers, and Herbert Remer. 1995. "The Effect of Schooling on the Development of Fluid and Cristallized Intelligence: A Quasi-experimental Study." *Intelligence* 21 (3): 279–96.

Stephens, Melvin, and Dou-Yan Yang. 2014. "Compulsory Education and the Benefits of Schooling." *American Economic Review* 104 (6): 1777–92.

Sternberg, Robert, Elena Grigorenko, and Donald Bundy. 2001. "The Predictive Value of IQ." *Merrill-Palmer Quarterly* 47 (1): 1–41.

Stiglitz, Joseph. 1975. "The Theory of 'Screening,' Education, and the Distribution of Income." *American Economic Review* 65 (3): 283–300.

Stiglitz, Joseph, and Andrew Weiss. 1990. "Sorting Out the Differences between Signalling and Screening Models." In *Mathematical Models in Economics*, edited by M. Bacharach, M. Dempster, and J. Enos, 1–34. Oxford: Oxford University Press.

Stinebrickner, Ralph, and Todd Stinebrickner. 2012. "Learning about Academic Ability and the College Dropout Decision." *Journal of Labor Economics* 30 (4): 707–48.

———. 2014. "A Major in Science? Initial Beliefs and Final Outcomes for College Major and Dropout." *Review of Economic Studies* 81 (1): 426–72.

St. John, Edward, Shouping Hu, Ada Simmons, Deborah Carter, and Jeff Weber. 2004. "What Difference Does a Major Make? The Influence of College Major Field on Persistence by African American and White Students." *Research in Higher Education* 45 (3): 209–32.

Stone, Chad, and William Chen. 2014. *Introduction to Unemployment Insurance*. Washington, DC: Center on Budget and Policy Priorities. http://www.cbpp. org/files/12 -19-02ui.pdf.

Strauss, Valerie. 2011. "Who Was the 'Best' Education President?" *Washington Post.* November 21. https://www.washingtonpost.com/blogs/answer-sheet/post/who was -the-best-education-president/2011/11/20/gIQAL3kggN_blog.html.

Strayhorn, Terrell. 2010. "Money Matters: The Influence of Financial Factors on Graduate Student Persistence." *Journal of Student Financial Aid* 40 (3): 4–25.

Sum, Andrew, Ishwar Khatiwada, Joseph McLaughlin, and Sheila Palma. 2009. *The Consequences of Dropping Out of High School: Joblessness and Jailing for High School Dropouts and the High Cost for Taxpayers*. Boston: Center for Labor Market Studies Publications. http://www.northeastern.edu/clms/wp-content/uploads/The_Conse quences_of_Dropping_Out_of_High_School.pdf.

Sweeney, Megan. 2002. "Two Decades of Family Change: The Shifting Economic Foundations of Marriage." *American Sociological Review* 67 (1): 132–47.

Sweeney, Megan, and Maria Cancian. 2004. "The Changing Importance of White Women's Economic Prospects for Assortative Mating." *Journal of Marriage and Family* 66 (4): 1015–28.

Sweet, Donald. 1989. *A Manager's Guide to Conducting Terminations: Minimizing Emotional Stress and Legal Risks.* New York: Lexington Books.

Sweeten, Gary, Shawn Bushway, and Raymond Paternoster. 2009. "Does Dropping Out of School Mean Dropping into Delinquency?" *Criminology* 47 (1): 47–91.

Tabarrok, Alex. 2012. "Cheating and Signaling." *Marginal Revolution.* June 5. http://marginalrevolution.com/marginalrevolution/2012/06/cheating-and-signaling.html.

Taber, Christopher. 2001. "The Rising College Premium in the Eighties: Return to College or Return to Unobserved Ability?" *Review of Economic Studies* 68 (3): 665–91.

Tamashiro, Kellie, Mary Nguyen, and Randall Sakai. 2005. "Social Stress: From Rodents to Primates." *Frontiers in Neuroendocrinology* 26 (1): 27–40.

Taubman, Paul, and Terence Wales. 1973. "Higher Education, Mental Ability, and Screening." *Journal of Political Economy* 81 (1): 28–55.

Tauchen, Helen, Ann Dryden Witte, and Harriet Griesinger. 1994. "Criminal Deterrence: Revisiting the Issue with a Birth Cohort." *Review of Economics and Statistics* 76 (3): 399–412.

Te Nijenhuis, Jan, Olga Voskuijl, and Natasja Schijve. 2001. "Practice and Coaching on IQ Tests: Quite a Lot of g." *International Journal of Selection and Assessment* 9 (4): 302–8.

Tenn, Steven. 2005. "An Alternative Measure of Relative Education to Explain Voter Turnout." *Journal of Politics* 67 (1): 271–82.

———. 2007. "The Effect of Education on Voter Turnout." *Political Analysis* 15 (4): 446–64.

Terpstra, David, and Elizabeth Rozell. 1997. "Why Some Potentially Effective Staffing Practices Are Seldom Used." *Public Personnel Management* 26 (4): 483–95.

Tess-Mattner, Marna. 2004. "Employer-Employee Issues: Eight Danger Areas." *GP Solo Magazine.* Last modified April/May. http://www.americanbar.org/newsletter/publications/gp_solo_magazine_home/gp_solo_magazine_index/employeremployeeissues.html.

Thurow, Lester. 1972. "Education and Economic Equality." *Public Interest* 28: 66–81.

Titus, Marvin. 2004. "An Examination of the Influence of Institutional Context on Student Persistence at 4-Year Colleges and Universities: A Multilevel Approach." *Research in Higher Education* 45 (7): 673–99.

Toole, John Kennedy. 1980. *A Confederacy of Dunces.* Baton Rouge, LA: Louisiana State University Press.

Tooley, James, and James Stanfield, eds. 2003. *Government Failure: E. G. West on Education.* London: Institute for Economic Affairs.

Topel, Robert. 1991. "Specific Capital, Mobility, and Wages: Wages Rise with Job Seniority." *Journal of Political Economy* 99 (1): 145–76.

Torr, Berna. 2011. "The Changing Relationship between Education and Marriage in the United States, 1940–2000." *Journal of Family History* 36 (4): 483–503.

Trostel, Philip, and Ian Walker. 2004. "Sheepskin Effects in Work Behavior." *Applied Economics* 36 (17): 1959–66.

Trostel, Philip, Ian Walker, and Paul Woolley. 2002. "Estimates of the Economic Return to Schooling for 28 Countries." *Labour Economics* 9 (1): 1 16.

Tyler, John. 2003. "Using State Child Labor Laws to Identify the Effect of School-Year Work on High School Achievement." *Journal of Labor Economics* 21 (2): 381–408.

Tzeng, Jessie, and Robert Mare. 1995. "Labor Market and Socioeconomic Effects on Marital Stability." *Social Science Research* 24 (4): 329–51.

Uecker, Jeremy, Mark Regnerus, and Margaret Vaaler. 2007. "Losing My Religion: The Social Sources of Religious Decline in Early Adulthood." *Social Forces* 85 (4): 1667–92.

United Nations. 2016. "Data: Population, Total." Accessed February 16, 2016. http://data.worldbank.org/indicator/SP. POP. TOTL.

United States Census Bureau. 2011. *Statistical Abstract of the United States: 2012.* Washington, DC: U.S. Department of Commerce. http://www2.census.gov/library/publications/2011/compendia/statab/131ed/2012-statab.pdf.

———. 2012a. "PINC-04. Educational Attainment—People 18 Years Old and over, by Total Money Earnings in 2011, Work Experience in 2011, Age, Race, Hispanic Origin, and Sex." Accessed November 30, 2015. https://www.census.gov/hhes/www/cpstables/032012/perinc/pinc04_001.xls.

———. 2012b. "Educational Attainment in the United States: 2009." Accessed November 15, 2015. http://www.census.gov/prod/2012pubs/p20-566.pdf.

———. 2012c. "Law Enforcement, Courts, and Prisons—Table 306." Accessed November 15, 2015. http://www.census.gov/prod/2011pubs/12statab/law.pdf.

———. 2012d. "PINC-04. Educational Attainment—People 18 Years Old and over, by Total Money Earnings in 2011, Work Experience in 2011, Age, Race, Hispanic Origin, and Sex: Male." Accessed November 30, 2015. https://www.census.gov/hhes/www/cpstables/032012/perinc/pinc04_010.xls.

———. 2012e. "PINC-04. Educational Attainment—People 18 Years Old and over, by Total Money Earnings in 2011, Work Experience in 2011, Age, Race, Hispanic Origin, and Sex: Female." Accessed November 30, 2015. https://www.census.gov/hhes/www/cpstables/032012/perinc/pinc04_019.xls.

———. 2014. "Census Bureau Reports Majority of STEM College Graduates Do Not Work in STEM Occupations." Accessed November 15, 2015. http://www.census.gov/newsroom/press-releases/2014/cb14-130.html.

———. 2015. "Percent of People 25 Years and over Who Have Completed High School or College, by Race, Hispanic Origin and Sex: Selected Years 1940 to 2014." Accessed March 27, 2015. http://www.census.gov/hhes/socdemo/education/data/cps/historical/tabA-2.xlsx.

United States Department of Agriculture. 2014. "Supplemental Nutrition Assistance Program—Fact Sheet on Resources, Income, and Benefits." Last modified October 3. http://www.fns.usda.gov/snap/fact-sheet-resources-income-and-benefits.

United States Department of Education. 2017. "College Scorecard: Harvard University." Accessed January 26, 2017. https://collegescorecard.ed.gov/school/?166027-Harvard-University.

United States Department of Labor. 2010. "Fact Sheet #71: Internship Programs under the Fair Labor Standards Act." Accessed August 19, 2015. http://www.dol.gov/whd/regs/compliance/whdfs71.pdf.

———. 2013. "Child Labor Bulletin 101: Child Labor Provisions for Nonagricultural Occupations." Accessed August 18, 2015. http://www.dol.gov/whd/regs/compliance/childlabor101.pdf.

———. 2014. "State Unemployment Insurance Benefits." Last modified June 3. http://workforcesecurity.doleta.gov/unemploy/uifactsheet.asp.

United States Department of the Treasury. 2016. "Resource Center: Daily Treasury Yield Curve Rates." Accessed March 30, 2016. https://www.treasury.gov/resource-center/data-chart-center/interest-rates/Pages/TextView.aspx?data=yield.

United States Equal Opportunity Commission. 2015. "Prohibited Employment Policies /Practices." Accessed February 28, 2015. http://www.eeoc.gov/laws/practices/index.cfm.

University of California Berkeley. 2015a. "Berkeley Economics: Major Requirements." Accessed December 2, 2015. https://www.econ.berkeley.edu/undergrad/current/major-requirements.

———. 2015b. "Summary of Degree Requirements." Last modified November 15. http://ls-advise.berkeley.edu/requirement/summary.html.

Vaisey, Stephen. 2006. "Education and Its Discontents: Overqualification in America, 1972–2002." *Social Forces* 85 (2): 835–64.

Van der Gaag, Jacques, and Eugene Smolensky. 1982. "True Household Equivalence Scales and Characteristics of the Poor in the United States." *Review of Income and Wealth* 28 (1): 17–28.

Van der Pol, Marjon. 2011. "Health, Education and Time Preference." *Health Economics* 20 (8): 917–29.

Van de Werfhorst, Herman, and Robert Andersen. 2005. "Social Background, Credential Inflation and Educational Strategies." *Acta Sociologica* 48 (4): 321–40.

Van Praag, Bernard, and Nico Van der Sar. 1988. "Household Cost Functions and Equivalence Scales." *Journal of Human Resources* 23 (8): 193–210.

Vedder, Richard, Christopher Denhart, and Jonathan Robe. 2013. *Why Are Recent College Graduates Underemployed? University Enrollments and Labor-Market Realities.* Washington, DC: Center for College Affordability and Productivity. http://centerforcollegeaffordability.org/uploads/Underemployed%20Report%202.pdf.

Villain Instructional. 2016. "A Little Late for Could've's Marge—Homer Simpson." Accessed January 28, 2016. https://villainplaybook.wordpress.com/2003/10/02/a-little-late-for-couldves-marge-homer-simpson.

Voss, James, Jeffrey Blais, Mary Means, Terry Greene, and Ellen Ahwesh. 1986. "Informal Reasoning and Subject Matter Knowledge in the Solving of Economics Problems by Naive and Novice Individuals." *Cognition and Instruction* 3 (3): 269–302.

Wang, Xuan, and George Yancey. 2012. "The Benefit of a Degree in IO Psychology or Human Resources." *TIP: The Industrial-Organizational Psychologist* 50 (1): 45–50.

Ware, Alan. 2015. "The Great British Education 'Fraud' of the Twentieth and Twenty-First Centuries." *Political Quarterly* 86 (4): 475–84.

Warren, John, Paul LePore, and Robert Mare. 2000. "Employment during High School: Consequences for Students' Grades in Academic Courses." *American Educational Research Journal* 37 (4): 943–69.

Wax, Amy. 2011. "Disparate Impact Realism." *William and Mary Law Review* 53 (2): 621–712.

Weakliem, David. 2002. "The Effects of Education on Political Opinions: An International Study." *International Journal of Public Opinion Research* 14 (2): 141–57.

Webber, Douglas. 2016. "Are College Costs Worth It? How Ability, Major, and Debt Affect the Return to Schooling." *Economics of Education Review* 53: 296–310.

Webbink, Dinand, Pierre Koning, Sunčica Vujić, and Nicholas Martin. 2012. "Why Are Criminals Less Educated Than Non-criminals? Evidence from a Cohort of Young Australian Twins." *Journal of Law, Economics, and Organization* 29 (1): 115–44.

Weiss, Andrew. 1983. "A Sorting-cum-Learning Model of Education." *Journal of Political Economy* 91 (3): 420–42.

———. 1995. "Human Capital vs. Signalling Explanations of Wages." *Journal of Economic Perspectives* 9 (4): 133–54.

Wendy's Wizard of Oz. 2015. "*The Wizard of Oz*: Movie Script." Accessed December 1, 2015. http://www.wendyswizardofoz.com/printablescript.htm.

Western, Bruce, and Christopher Wildeman. 2009. "The Black Family and Mass Incarceration." *Annals of the American Academy of Political and Social Science* 621 (1): 221–42.

White, Jennifer, Terrie Moffitt, Avshalom Caspi, Dawn Bartusch, Douglas Needles, and Magda Stouthamer-Loeber. 1994. "Measuring Impulsivity and Examining Its Relationship to Delinquency." *Journal of Abnormal Psychology* 103 (2): 192–205.

Wigdor, Alexandra. 1982. "Psychological Testing and the Law of Employment Discrimination." In *Ability Testing: Uses, Consequences, and Controversies, Part 2; Uses, Consequences, and Controversies*, edited by Alexandra Wigdor and Wendell Garner, 39–69. Washington DC: National Academy Press.

Wikipedia. 2015a. "Bill Gates, Early Life." Accessed November 15, 2015. http://en.wikipedia.org/wiki/Bill_Gates.

———. 2015b. "List of Best-Selling Albums." Accessed November 15, 2015. http://en.wikipedia.org/wiki/List_of_best-selling_albums.

———. 2015c. "List of Best-Selling Books." Accessed November 15, 2015. https://en.wikipedia.org/wiki/List_of_best-selling_books.

Wikiquote. 2016. "Walt Kelly." Accessed February 15, 2016. https://en.wikiquote.org/wiki/Walt_Kelly.

Wiles, Peter. 1974. "The Correlation between Education and Earnings: The External-Test-Not-Content Hypothesis (ETNC)." *Higher Education* 3 (1): 43–58.

Williams, Robert. 2013. "Overview of the Flynn Effect." *Intelligence* 41 (6): 753–64.

Winship, Christopher, and Sanders Korenman. 1997. "Does Staying in School Make You Smarter? The Effect of Education on IQ in *The Bell Curve*." In *Intelligence, Genes, and Success*, edited Bernie Devlin, Stephen Fienberg, Daniel Resnick, and Kathryn Roeder, 215–34. New York: Springer.

Winston, Gordon. 1999. "Subsidies, Hierarchy and Peers: The Awkward Economics of Higher Education." *Journal of Economic Perspectives* 13 (1): 13–36.

Witte, James, and Arne Kalleberg. 1995. "Matching Training and Jobs: The Fit between Vocational Education and Employment in the German Labour Market." *European Sociological Review* 11 (3): 293–317.

Wolf, Alison. 2002. *Does Education Matter? Myths about Education and Economic Growth*. London: Penguin Books.

Wolff, Lisa, S. Subramanian, Dolores Acevedo-Garcia, Deanne Weber, and Ichiro Kawachi. 2010. "Compared to Whom? Subjective Social Status, Self-Rated Health, and

Referent Group Sensitivity in a Diverse US Sample." *Social Science and Medicine* 70 (12): 2019–28.

Wood, Tom. 2009. "The Sheepskin Effect." *National Association of Scholars.* Last modified July 30. http://www.nas.org/articles/The_Sheepskin_Effect.

World Bank. 2015. "Government Expenditure on Education, Total (% of GDP)." Accessed June 1, 2015. http://data.worldbank.org/indicator/SE.XPD.TOTL.GD.ZS.

X, Malcolm, Alex Haley, and Attallah Shabazz. 1964. *The Autobiography of Malcolm X.* New York: Ballantine Books.

Yazzie-Mintz, Ethan. 2010. *Charting the Path from Engagement to Achievement: A Report on the 2009 High School Survey of Student Engagement.* Bloomington, IN: Center for Evaluation and Education Policy. http://ceep. indiana.edu/hssse/images /HSSSE_2010_Report.pdf.

Zagorsky, Jay. 2007. "Do You Have to Be Smart to Be Rich? The Impact of IQ on Wealth, Income and Financial Distress." *Intelligence* 35 (5): 489–501.

Zhang, Liang. 2005. "Do Measures of College Quality Matter? The Effect of College Quality on Graduates' Earnings." *Review of Higher Education* 28 (4): 571–96.

Zipp, John, and Rudy Fenwick. 2006. "Is the Academy a Liberal Hegemony? The Political Orientations and Educational Values of Professors." *Public Opinion Quarterly* 70 (3): 304–26.

Zuckerman, Miron, Jordan Silberman, and Judith Hall. 2013. "The Relation between Intelligence and Religiosity: A Meta-analysis and Some Proposed Explanations." *Personality and Social Psychology Review* 17 (4): 325–54.

Index